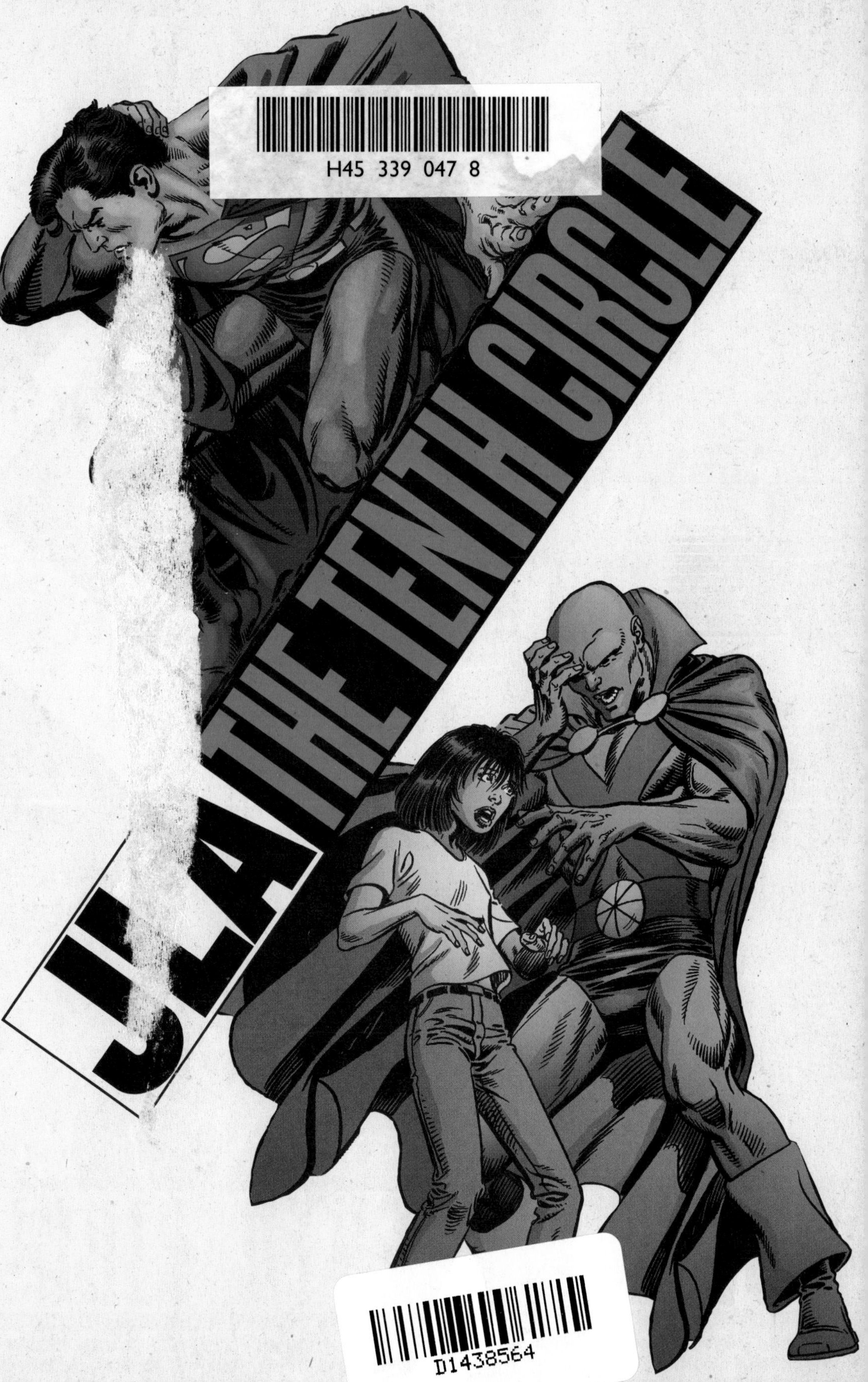
JLA
THE TENTH CIRCLE

JLA THE TENTH CIRCLE

Dan DiDio VP-Editorial Mike Carlin Editor-original series Valerie D'Orazio Assistant Editor-original series Robert Greenberger Senior Editor-collected edition Robbin Brosterman Senior Art Director Paul Levitz President & Publisher Georg Brewer VP-Design & Retail Product Development Richard Bruning Senior VP-Creative Director Patrick Caldon Senior VP-Finance & Operations Chris Caramalis VP-Finance Terri Cunningham VP-Managing Editor Alison Gill VP-Manufacturing Rich Johnson VP-Book Trade Sales Hank Kanalz VP-General Manager, WildStorm Lillian Laserson Senior VP & General Counsel Jim Lee Editorial Director WildStorm David McKillips VP-Advertising & Custom Publishing John Nee VP-Business Development Gregory Noveck Senior VP-Creative Affairs Cheryl Rubin Senior VP-Brand Management Bob Wayne VP-Sales

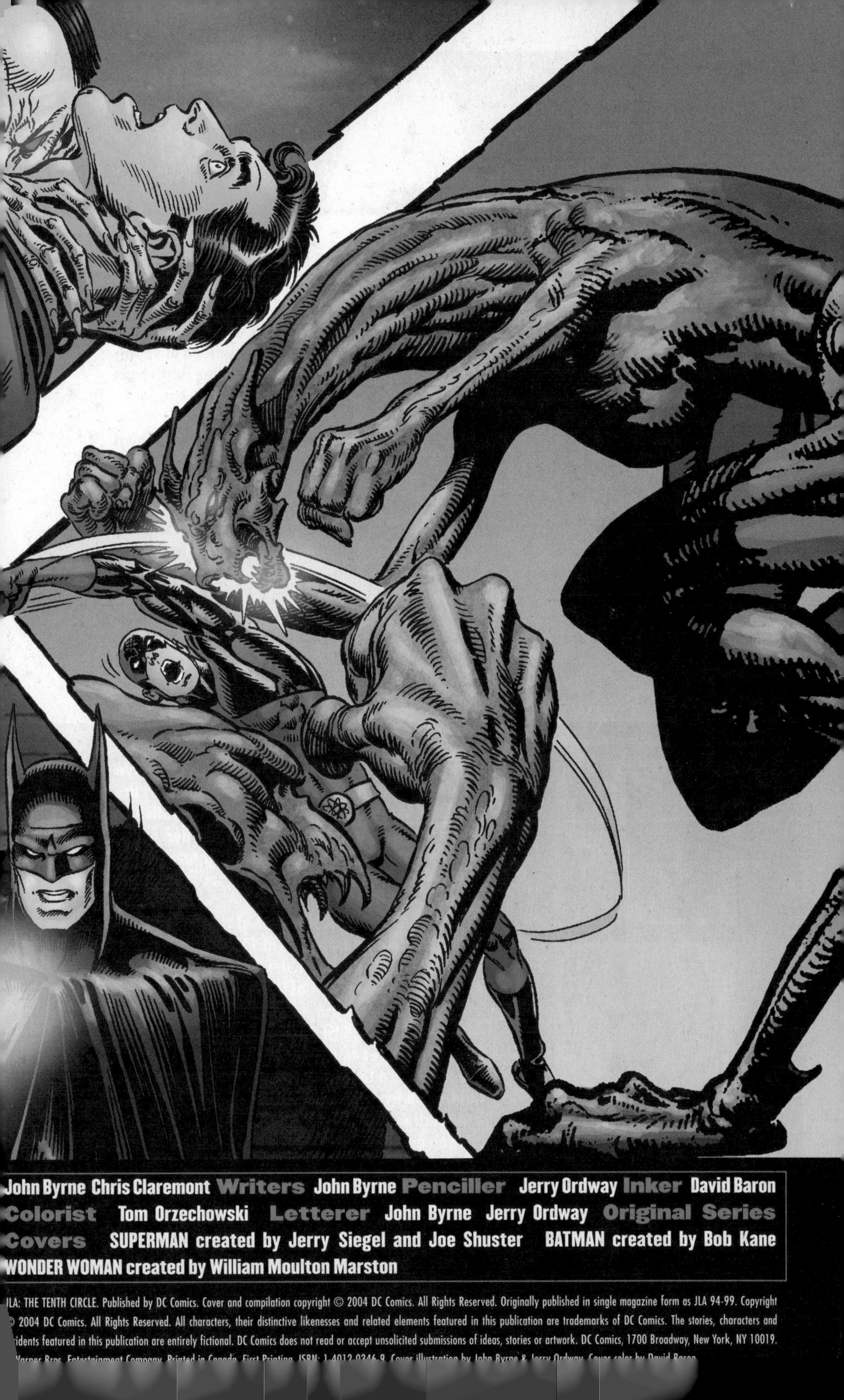

John Byrne Chris Claremont **Writers** John Byrne **Penciller** Jerry Ordway **Inker** David Baron **Colorist** Tom Orzechowski **Letterer** John Byrne Jerry Ordway **Original Series Covers** SUPERMAN created by Jerry Siegel and Joe Shuster BATMAN created by Bob Kane WONDER WOMAN created by William Moulton Marston

Warner Bros. Entertainment Company. Printed in Canada. First Printing. ISBN: 1-4012-0346-9. Cover illustration by John Byrne & Jerry Ordway. Cover color by David Baron.

JLA

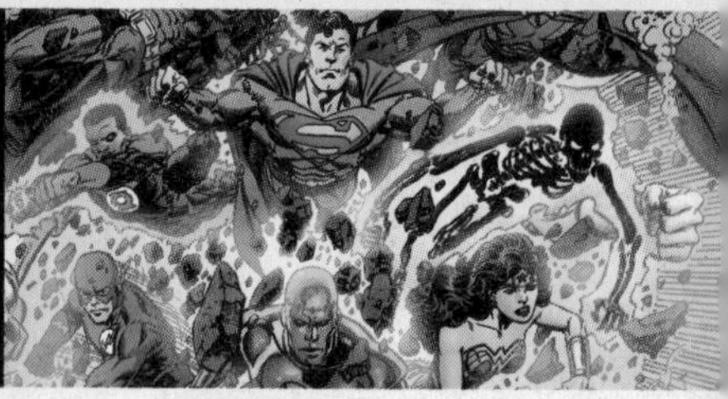

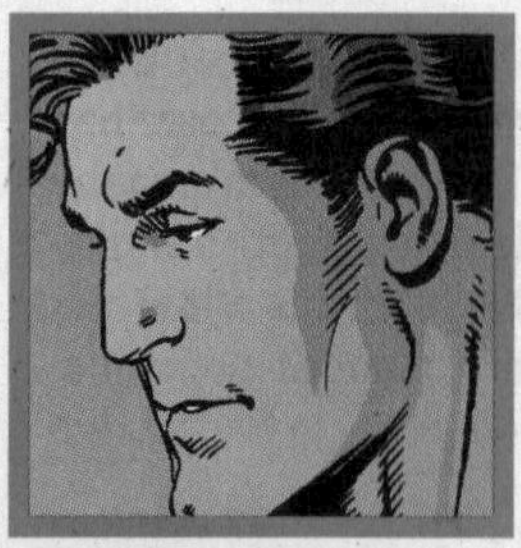

JLA: The Justice League of America is Earth's first and last line of defense, a pantheon of super-powered protectors watching over the Earth from a fortress on the Moon.

Superman: The last son of the doomed planet Krypton, Kal-El uses his incredible powers of flight, super-strength, and invulnerability to fight for truth and justice on his adopted planet, Earth. When not protecting the planet, he is Daily Planet reporter Clark Kent, married to fellow journalist Lois Lane.

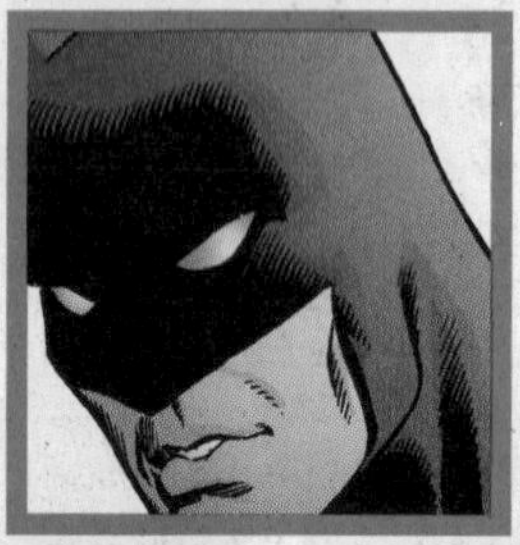

Batman: Dedicated to ridding the world of crime since the brutal murder of his parents, billionaire Bruce Wayne dons the cape and cowl of the Dark Knight to battle evil from the shadows of Gotham City.

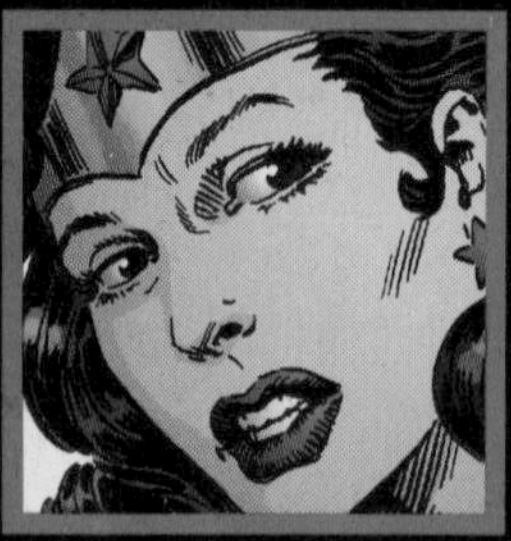

Wonder Woman: Born an Amazonian princess, Diana was chosen to serve as her people's ambassador of peace in the World of Man. Armed with the Lasso of Truth and indestructible bracelets, she directs her gods-given abilities of strength and speed toward the betterment of mankind.

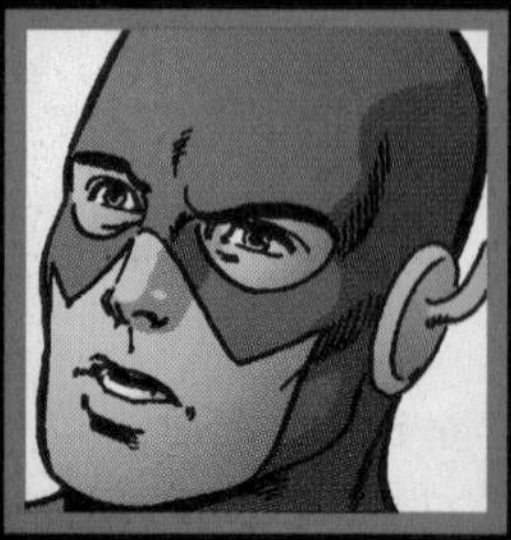

The Flash: A member of the Teen Titans when he was known as Kid Flash, Wally West now takes the place of the fallen Flash, Barry Allen, as the speedster of the Justice League.

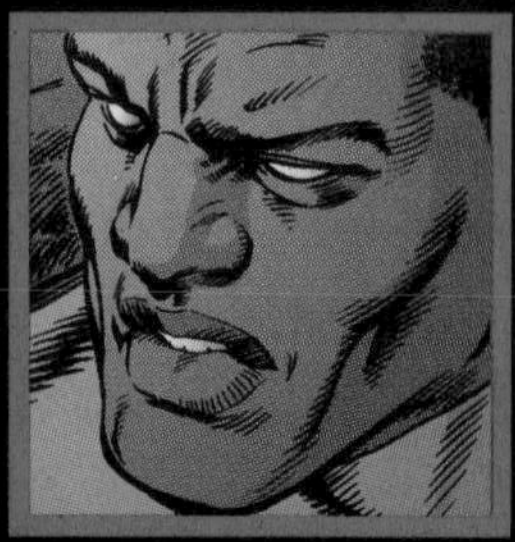

Green Lantern: John Stewart has worn the power ring, symbol of the intergalactic Green Lantern Corps, during several tours of duty. Controlled by his will power, the ring makes his imagination manifest, and being an architect, he conceives some pretty cool objects. But the life of a hero has not been an easy one, filled as it is with defeat and despair, and the challenge of overcoming physical and mental obstacles. But when called, he never shirks his obligation to protect the helpless.

Martian Manhunter: The most dedicated member of the Justice League, J'onn J'onzz has been present for every one of the team's many incarnations. His strength rivals that of Earth's mightiest heroes, and his shape-shifting abilities allow him to pass anonymously among our planet's populace. Also, his awesome mental powers serve to link the entire JLA in thought.

The Atom: One of the first heroes to join after the League's founding, Ray Palmer is a scientist who harnessed the properties of a white dwarf star. This led to the creation of unique size and weight controls that enable him to reduce his physical form to that of an atom, or even smaller. Forgoing the world of heroics for research and teaching, the Atom remains available as a reserve member. He has been working closely with Firestorm to help him master his powers.

Manitou Raven: An Apache American from 3000 years ago with uncanny magical powers, he is one of the newest members of the JLA. With his wife Dawn, he is adjusting to his new century, his role as earthly champion, and is still learning about his teammates.

Faith: No one is sure who Faith is, or the extent of her abilities; however, Batman recommended her to the JLA, and the others have accepted her on his word. Faith's powers include an aura that makes people trust her completely, flight, and some incredible energy. The Tenth Circle case may prove to be her final adventure as a member of the team.

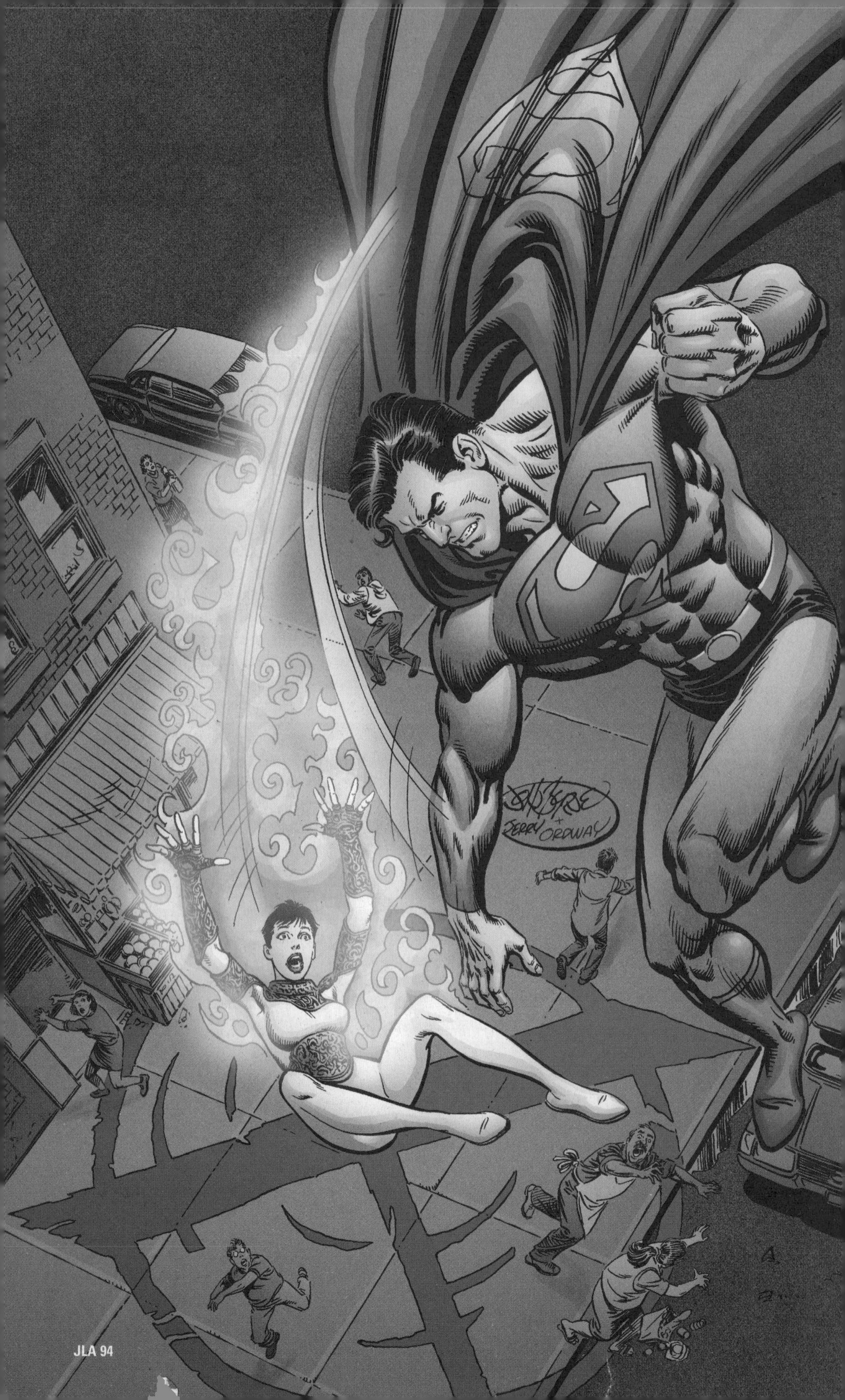

JLA 94

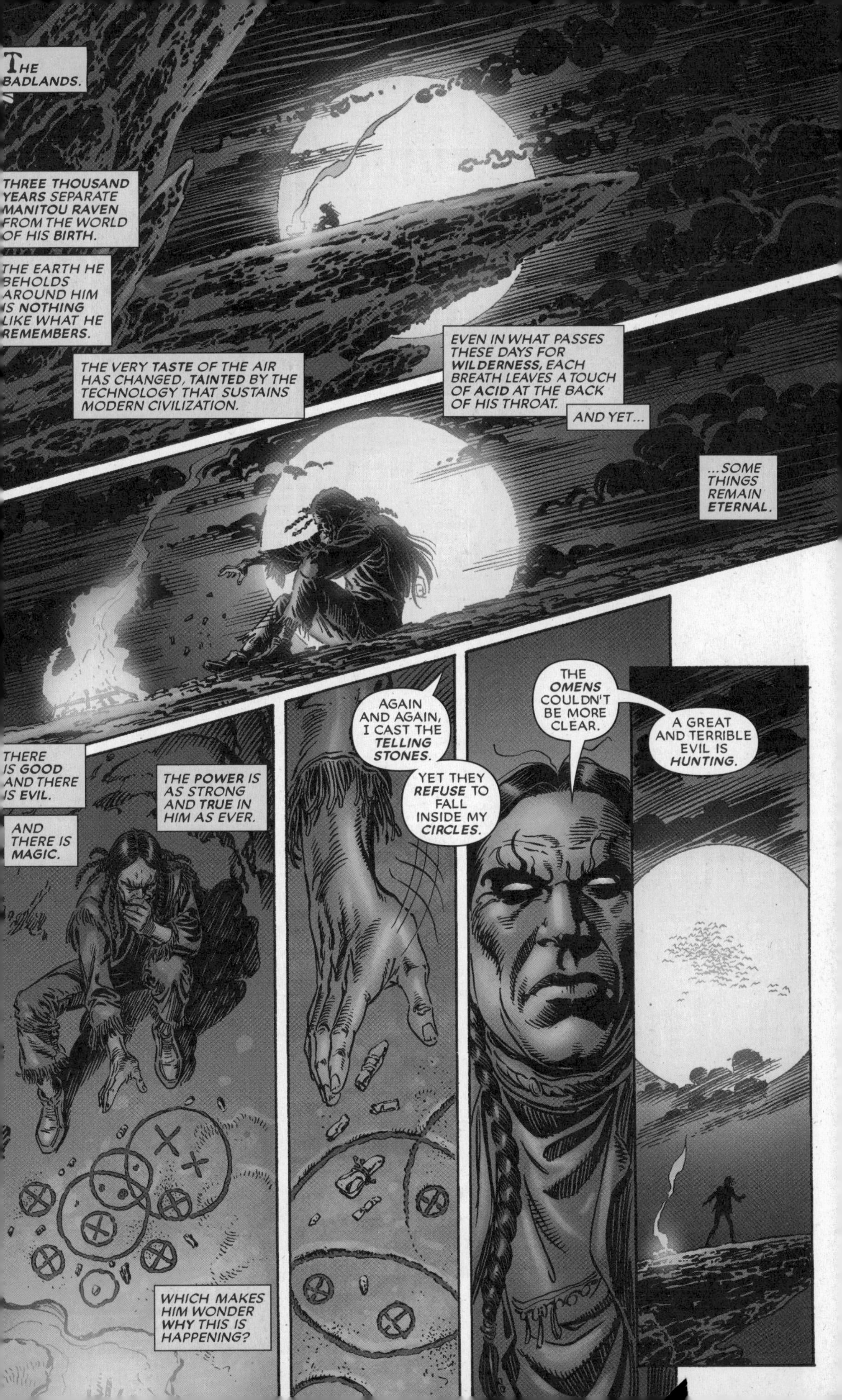
THE BADLANDS.
THREE THOUSAND YEARS SEPARATE MANITOU RAVEN FROM THE WORLD OF HIS BIRTH.
THE EARTH HE BEHOLDS AROUND HIM IS NOTHING LIKE WHAT HE REMEMBERS.
THE VERY TASTE OF THE AIR HAS CHANGED, TAINTED BY THE TECHNOLOGY THAT SUSTAINS MODERN CIVILIZATION.
EVEN IN WHAT PASSES THESE DAYS FOR WILDERNESS, EACH BREATH LEAVES A TOUCH OF ACID AT THE BACK OF HIS THROAT.
AND YET...
...SOME THINGS REMAIN ETERNAL.
THERE IS GOOD AND THERE IS EVIL.
AND THERE IS MAGIC.
THE POWER IS AS STRONG AND TRUE IN HIM AS EVER.
WHICH MAKES HIM WONDER WHY THIS IS HAPPENING?
AGAIN AND AGAIN, I CAST THE TELLING STONES.
YET THEY REFUSE TO FALL INSIDE MY CIRCLES.
THE OMENS COULDN'T BE MORE CLEAR.
A GREAT AND TERRIBLE EVIL IS HUNTING.

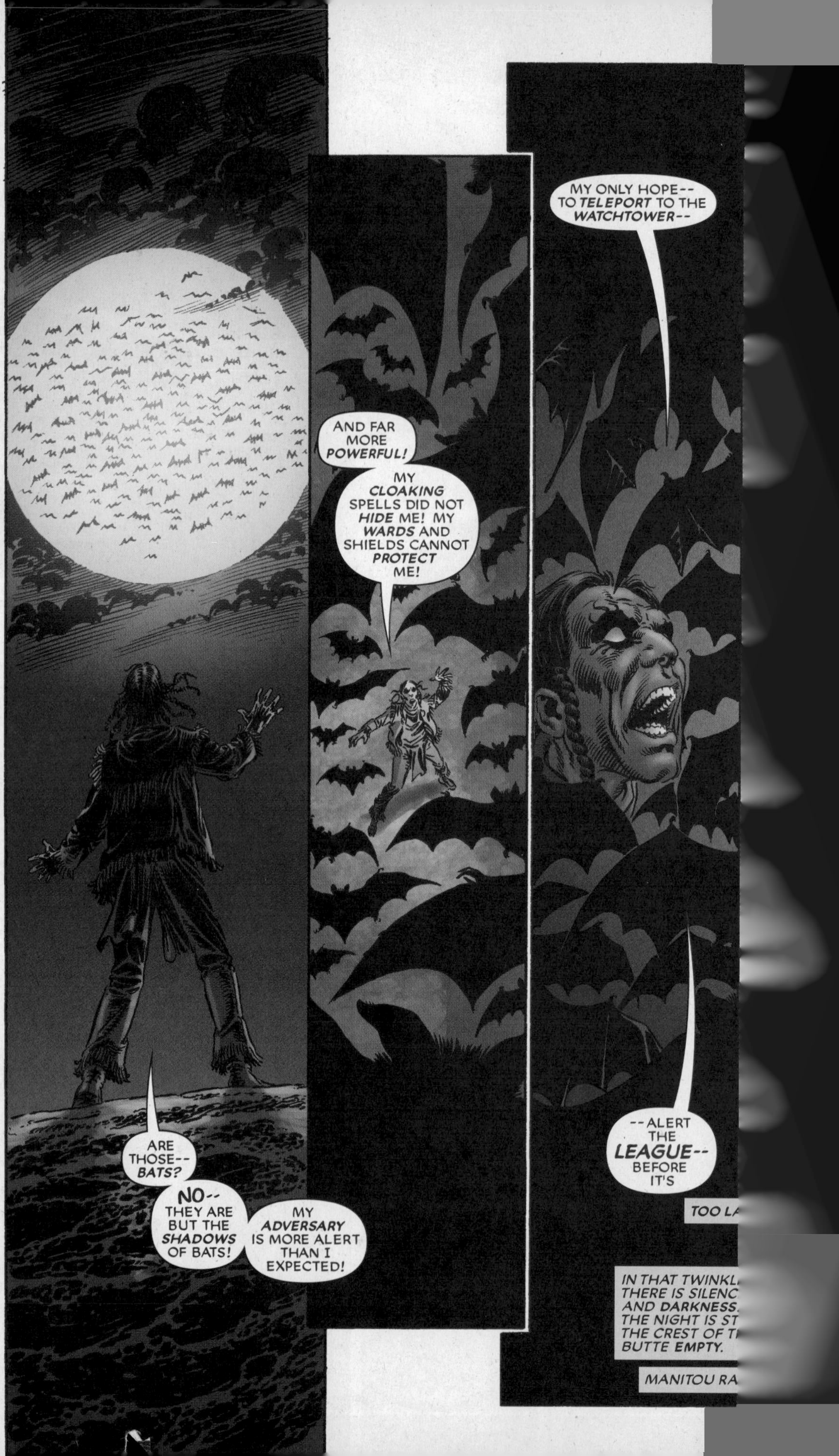

ARE THOSE-- BATS?
NO-- THEY ARE BUT THE SHADOWS OF BATS!
MY ADVERSARY IS MORE ALERT THAN I EXPECTED!
AND FAR MORE POWERFUL!
MY CLOAKING SPELLS DID NOT HIDE ME! MY WARDS AND SHIELDS CANNOT PROTECT ME!
MY ONLY HOPE-- TO TELEPORT TO THE WATCHTOWER--
--ALERT THE LEAGUE-- BEFORE IT'S

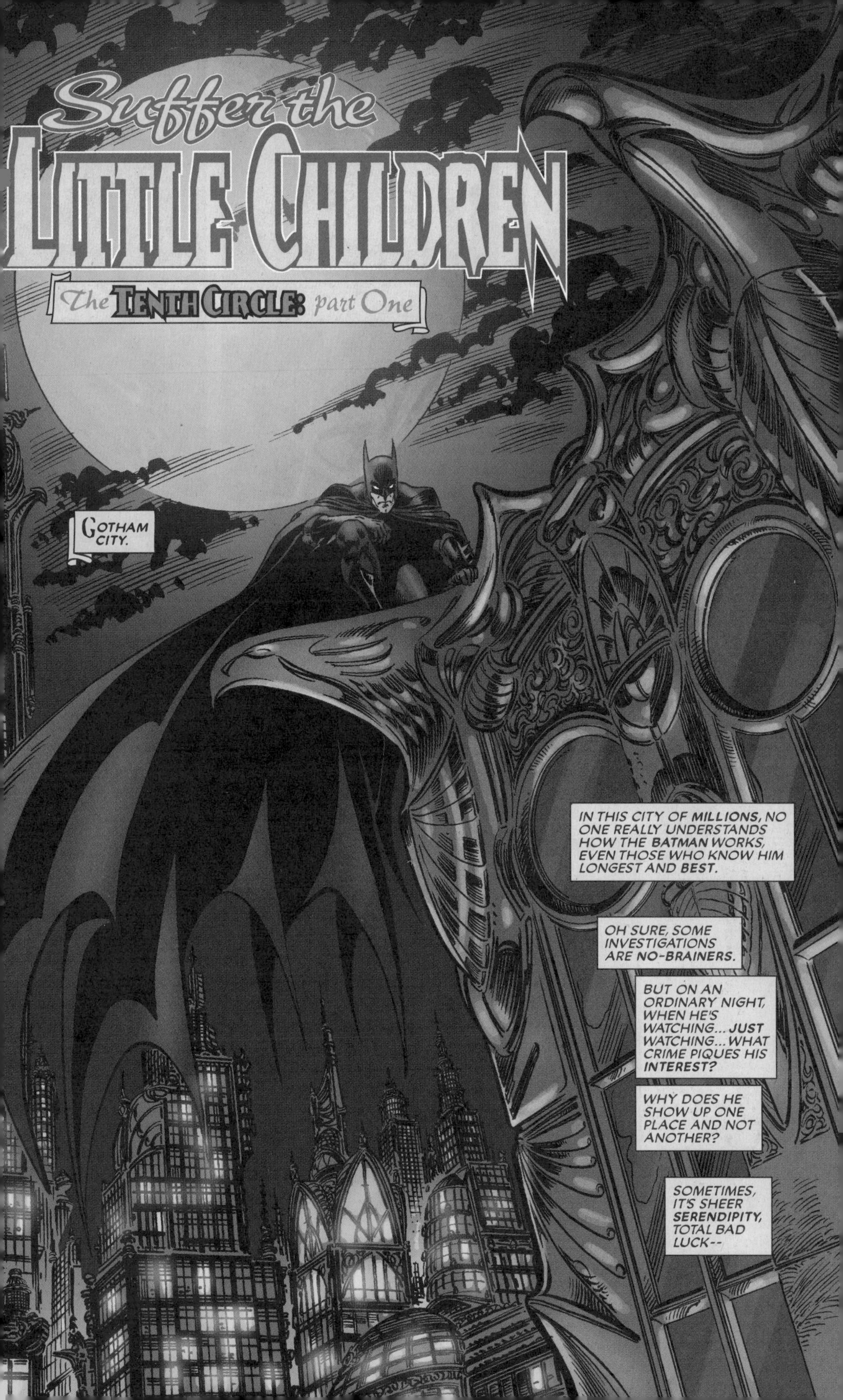
Suffer the
LITTLE CHILDREN
The TENTH CIRCLE: part One
GOTHAM CITY.
IN THIS CITY OF MILLIONS, NO ONE REALLY UNDERSTANDS HOW THE BATMAN WORKS, EVEN THOSE WHO KNOW HIM LONGEST AND BEST.
OH SURE, SOME INVESTIGATIONS ARE NO-BRAINERS.
BUT ON AN ORDINARY NIGHT, WHEN HE'S WATCHING... JUST WATCHING... WHAT CRIME PIQUES HIS INTEREST?
WHY DOES HE SHOW UP ONE PLACE AND NOT ANOTHER?
SOMETIMES, IT'S SHEER SERENDIPITY, TOTAL BAD LUCK--

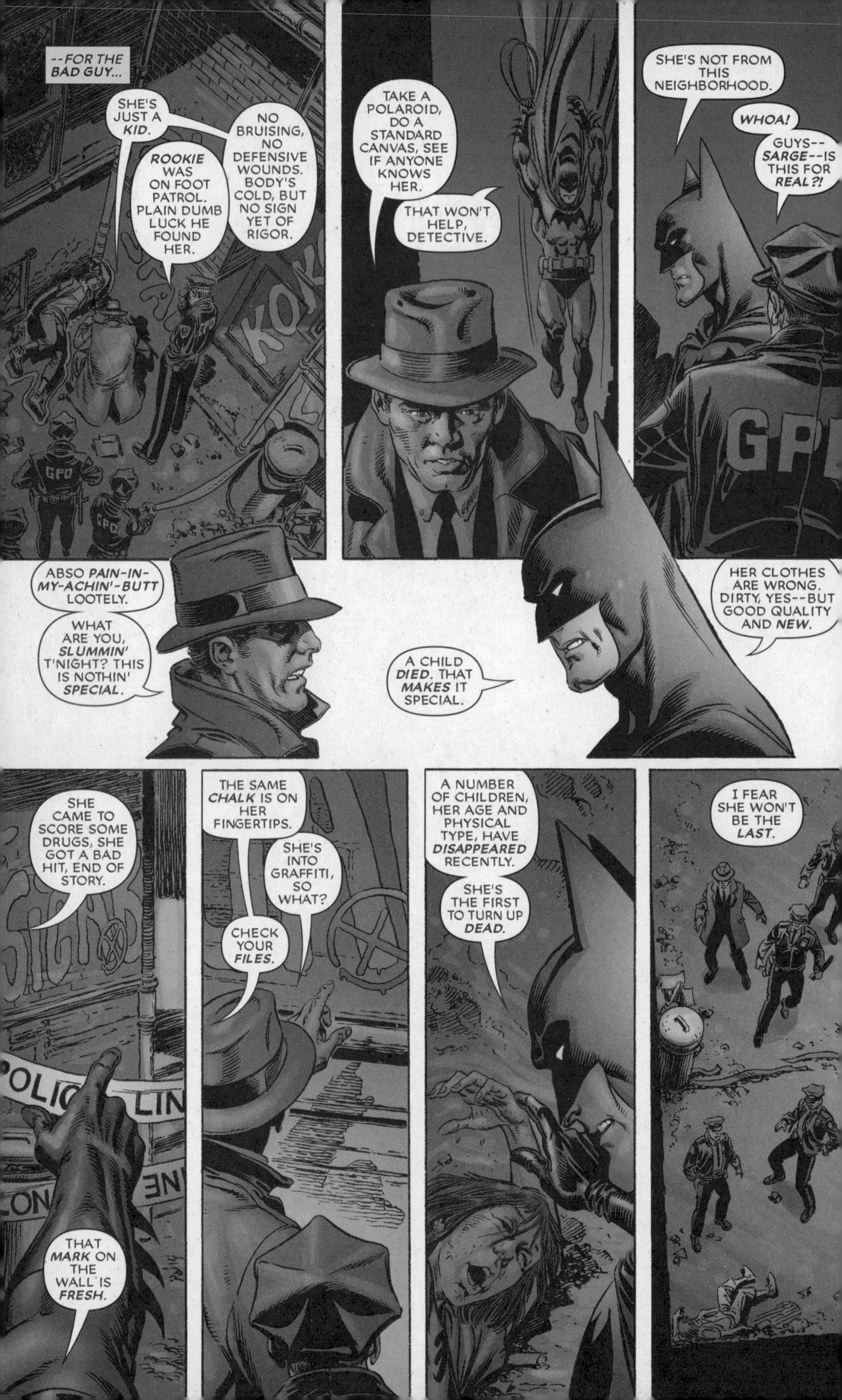

--FOR THE BAD GUY...
SHE'S JUST A KID.
ROOKIE WAS ON FOOT PATROL. PLAIN DUMB LUCK HE FOUND HER.
NO BRUISING, NO DEFENSIVE WOUNDS. BODY'S COLD, BUT NO SIGN YET OF RIGOR.
TAKE A POLAROID, DO A STANDARD CANVAS, SEE IF ANYONE KNOWS HER.
THAT WON'T HELP, DETECTIVE.
SHE'S NOT FROM THIS NEIGHBORHOOD.
WHOA!
GUYS--SARGE--IS THIS FOR REAL?!
GPD
ABSO PAIN-IN-MY-ACHIN'-BUTT LOOTELY.
WHAT ARE YOU, SLUMMIN' T'NIGHT? THIS IS NOTHIN' SPECIAL.
A CHILD DIED. THAT MAKES IT SPECIAL.
HER CLOTHES ARE WRONG. DIRTY, YES--BUT GOOD QUALITY AND NEW.
SHE CAME TO SCORE SOME DRUGS, SHE GOT A BAD HIT, END OF STORY.
THAT MARK ON THE WALL IS FRESH.
THE SAME CHALK IS ON HER FINGERTIPS.
SHE'S INTO GRAFFITI, SO WHAT?
CHECK YOUR FILES.
A NUMBER OF CHILDREN, HER AGE AND PHYSICAL TYPE, HAVE DISAPPEARED RECENTLY.
SHE'S THE FIRST TO TURN UP DEAD.
I FEAR SHE WON'T BE THE LAST.

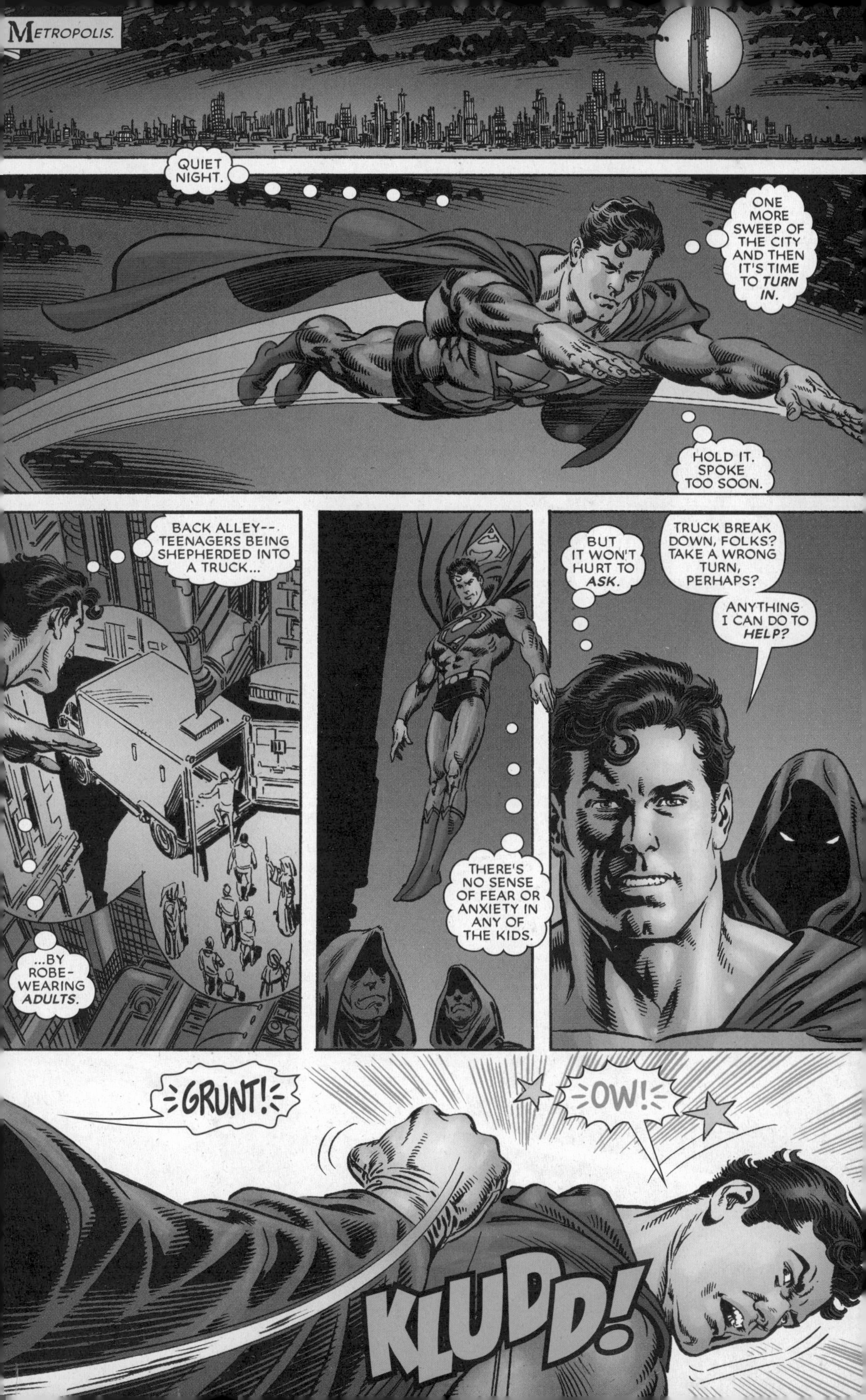
METROPOLIS.
QUIET NIGHT.
ONE MORE SWEEP OF THE CITY AND THEN IT'S TIME TO TURN IN.
HOLD IT. SPOKE TOO SOON.
BACK ALLEY-- TEENAGERS BEING SHEPHERDED INTO A TRUCK...
...BY ROBE-WEARING ADULTS.
THERE'S NO SENSE OF FEAR OR ANXIETY IN ANY OF THE KIDS.
BUT IT WON'T HURT TO ASK.
TRUCK BREAK DOWN, FOLKS? TAKE A WRONG TURN, PERHAPS?
ANYTHING I CAN DO TO HELP?
GRUNT!
OW!
KLUDD!

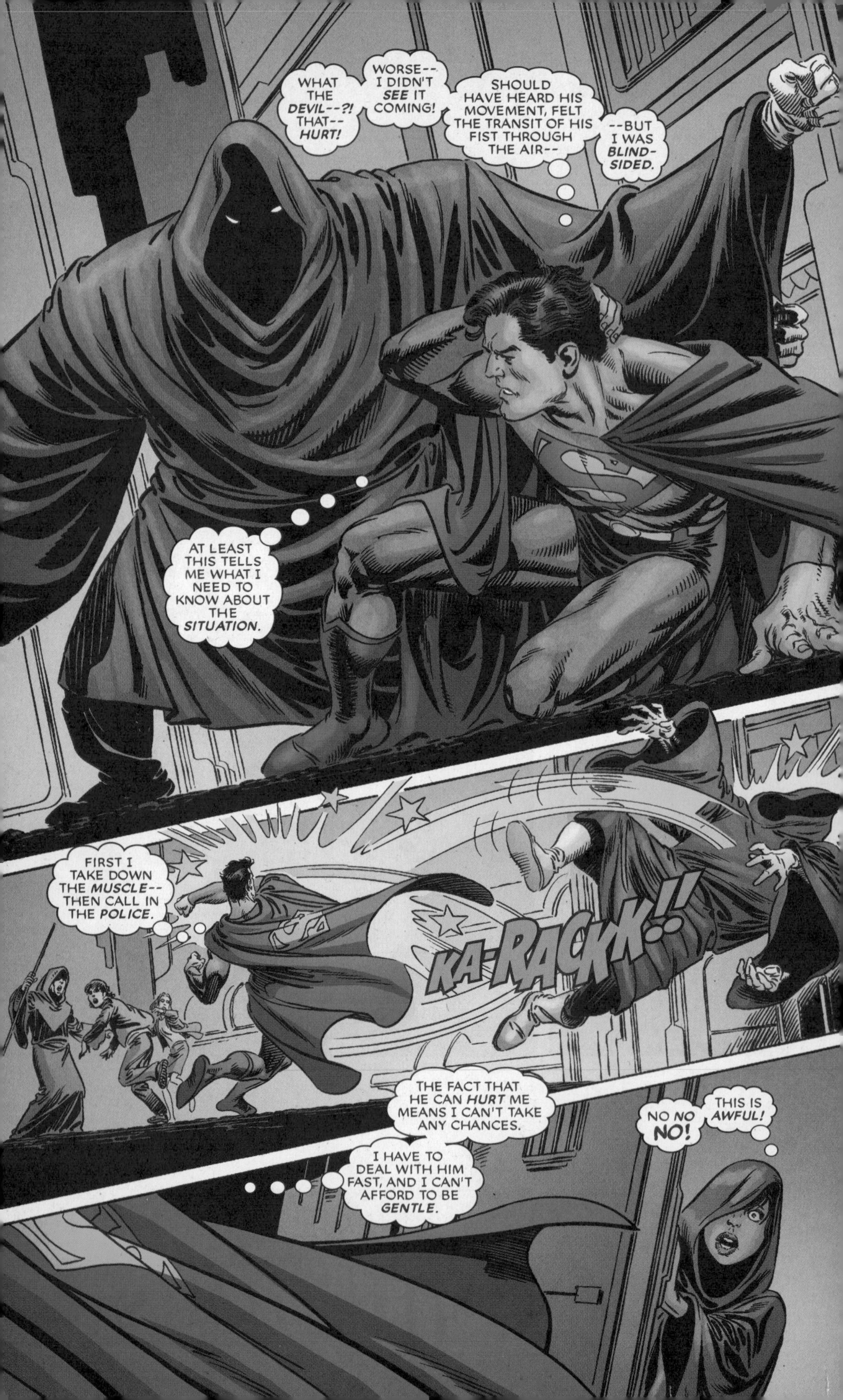
WHAT THE DEVIL--?! THAT-- HURT!
WORSE-- I DIDN'T SEE IT COMING!
SHOULD HAVE HEARD HIS MOVEMENT, FELT THE TRANSIT OF HIS FIST THROUGH THE AIR--
--BUT I WAS BLIND-SIDED.
AT LEAST THIS TELLS ME WHAT I NEED TO KNOW ABOUT THE SITUATION.
FIRST I TAKE DOWN THE MUSCLE-- THEN CALL IN THE POLICE.
KA-RACKK!!
THE FACT THAT HE CAN HURT ME MEANS I CAN'T TAKE ANY CHANCES.
I HAVE TO DEAL WITH HIM FAST, AND I CAN'T AFFORD TO BE GENTLE.
NO NO NO!
THIS IS AWFUL!

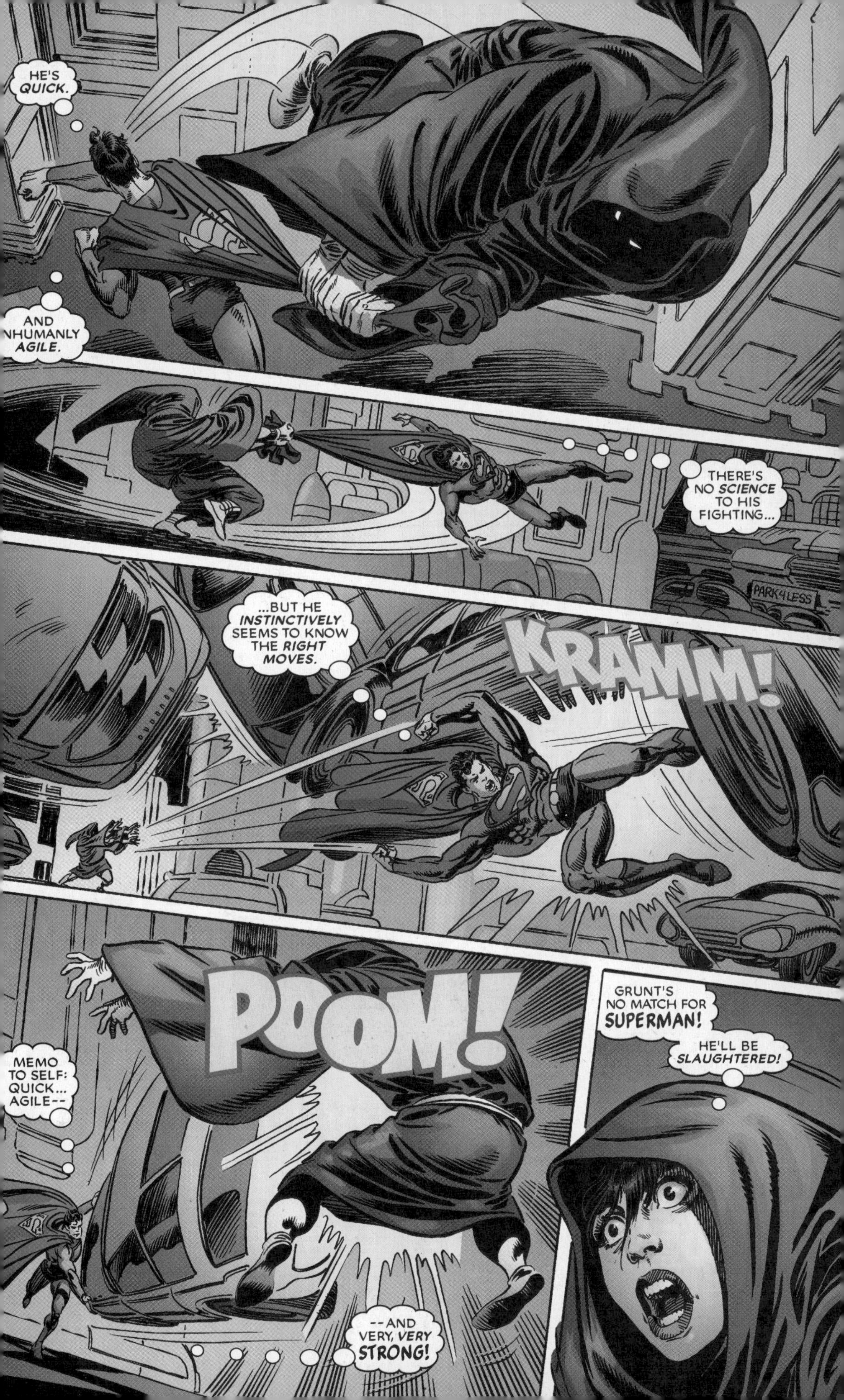

HE'S QUICK.
AND INHUMANLY AGILE.
THERE'S NO SCIENCE TO HIS FIGHTING...
...BUT HE INSTINCTIVELY SEEMS TO KNOW THE RIGHT MOVES.
PARK 4 LESS
KRAMM!
POOM!
MEMO TO SELF: QUICK... AGILE--
--AND VERY, VERY STRONG!
GRUNT'S NO MATCH FOR SUPERMAN!
HE'LL BE SLAUGHTERED!

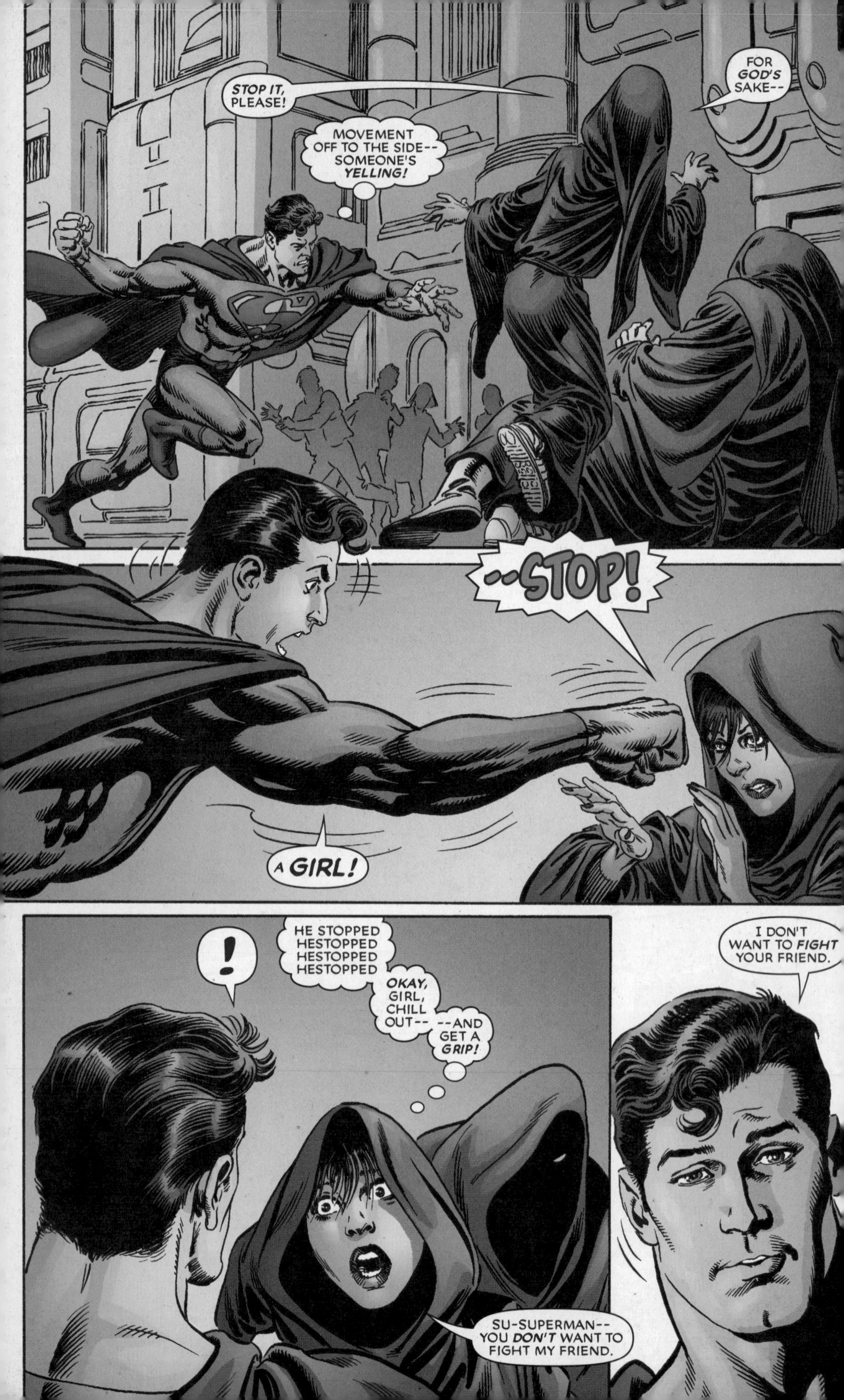
STOP IT, PLEASE!
FOR GOD'S SAKE--
MOVEMENT OFF TO THE SIDE-- SOMEONE'S YELLING!
--STOP!
A GIRL!
!
HE STOPPED HESTOPPED HESTOPPED HESTOPPED
OKAY, GIRL, CHILL OUT--
--AND GET A GRIP!
I DON'T WANT TO FIGHT YOUR FRIEND.
SU-SUPERMAN-- YOU DON'T WANT TO FIGHT MY FRIEND.

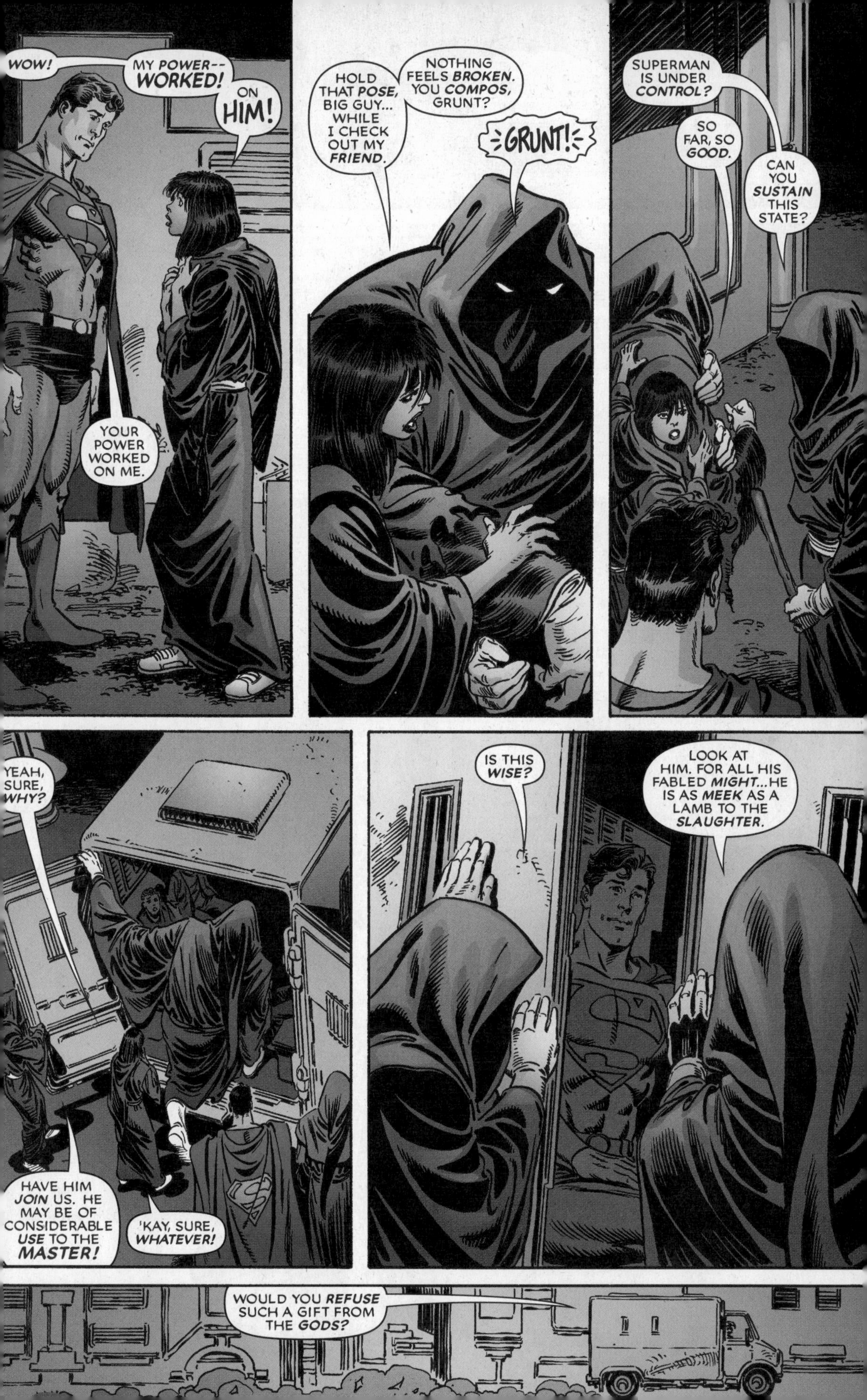
WOW!
MY POWER-- WORKED!
ON HIM!
YOUR POWER WORKED ON ME.
HOLD THAT POSE, BIG GUY... WHILE I CHECK OUT MY FRIEND.
NOTHING FEELS BROKEN. YOU COMPOS, GRUNT?
GRUNT!
SUPERMAN IS UNDER CONTROL?
SO FAR, SO GOOD.
CAN YOU SUSTAIN THIS STATE?
YEAH, SURE, WHY?
HAVE HIM JOIN US. HE MAY BE OF CONSIDERABLE USE TO THE MASTER!
'KAY, SURE, WHATEVER!
IS THIS WISE?
LOOK AT HIM. FOR ALL HIS FABLED MIGHT...HE IS AS MEEK AS A LAMB TO THE SLAUGHTER.
WOULD YOU REFUSE SUCH A GIFT FROM THE GODS?

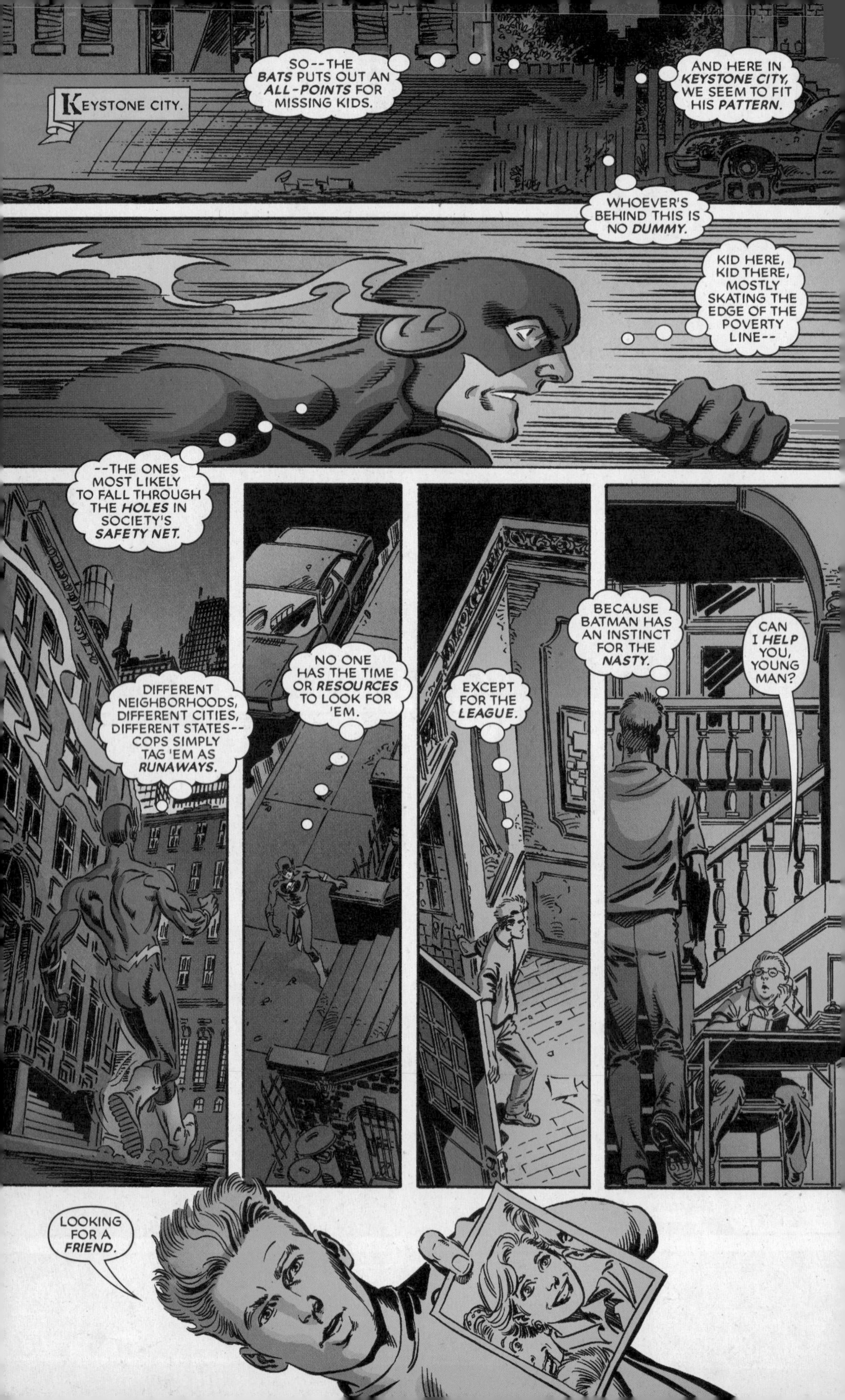
KEYSTONE CITY.
SO--THE BATS PUTS OUT AN ALL-POINTS FOR MISSING KIDS.
AND HERE IN KEYSTONE CITY, WE SEEM TO FIT HIS PATTERN.
WHOEVER'S BEHIND THIS IS NO DUMMY.
KID HERE, KID THERE, MOSTLY SKATING THE EDGE OF THE POVERTY LINE--
--THE ONES MOST LIKELY TO FALL THROUGH THE HOLES IN SOCIETY'S SAFETY NET.
DIFFERENT NEIGHBORHOODS, DIFFERENT CITIES, DIFFERENT STATES--COPS SIMPLY TAG 'EM AS RUNAWAYS.
NO ONE HAS THE TIME OR RESOURCES TO LOOK FOR 'EM.
EXCEPT FOR THE LEAGUE.
BECAUSE BATMAN HAS AN INSTINCT FOR THE NASTY.
CAN I HELP YOU, YOUNG MAN?
LOOKING FOR A FRIEND.

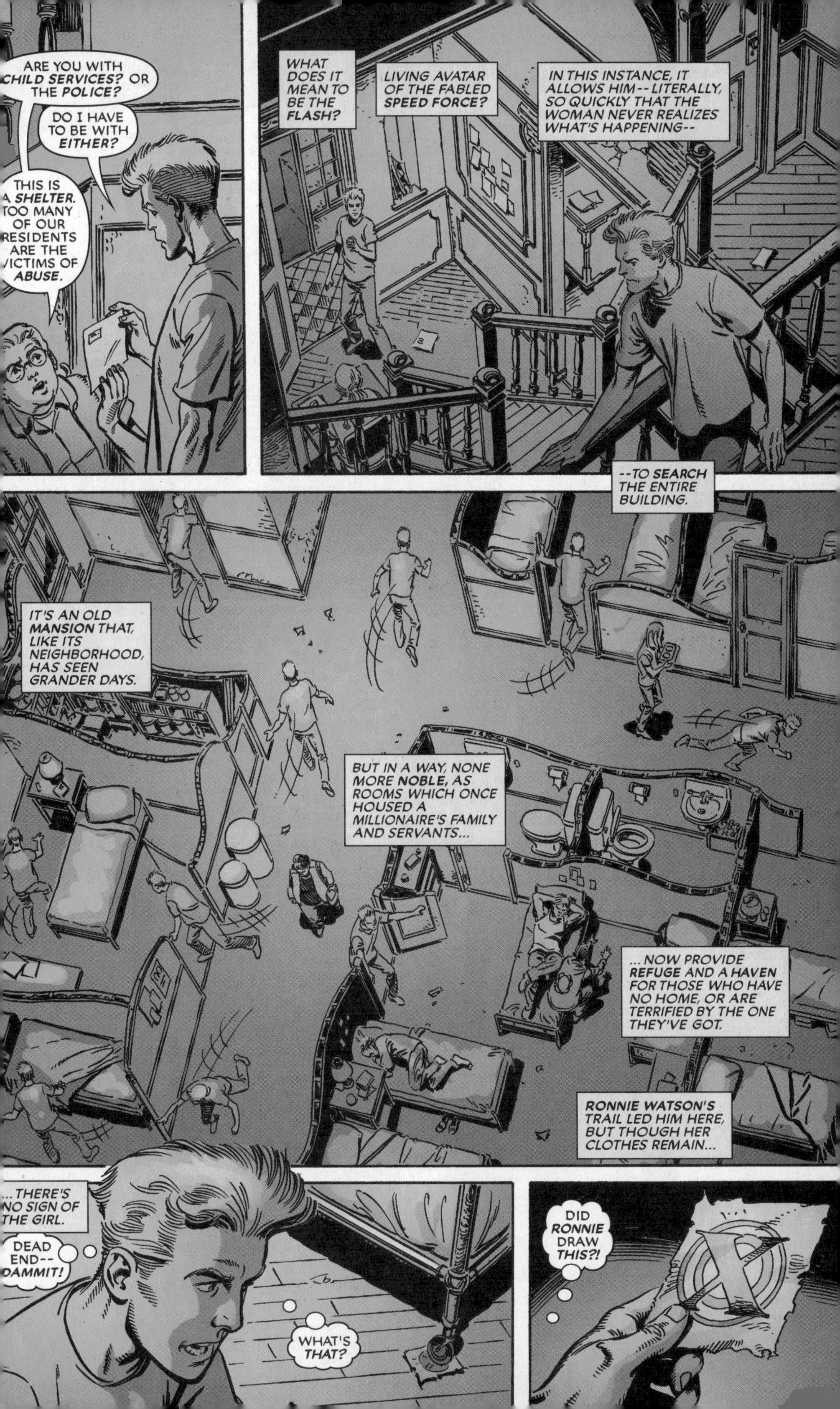
ARE YOU WITH CHILD SERVICES? OR THE POLICE?
DO I HAVE TO BE WITH EITHER?
THIS IS A SHELTER. TOO MANY OF OUR RESIDENTS ARE THE VICTIMS OF ABUSE.
WHAT DOES IT MEAN TO BE THE FLASH?
LIVING AVATAR OF THE FABLED SPEED FORCE?
IN THIS INSTANCE, IT ALLOWS HIM--LITERALLY, SO QUICKLY THAT THE WOMAN NEVER REALIZES WHAT'S HAPPENING--
--TO SEARCH THE ENTIRE BUILDING.
IT'S AN OLD MANSION THAT, LIKE ITS NEIGHBORHOOD, HAS SEEN GRANDER DAYS.
BUT IN A WAY, NONE MORE NOBLE, AS ROOMS WHICH ONCE HOUSED A MILLIONAIRE'S FAMILY AND SERVANTS...
...NOW PROVIDE REFUGE AND A HAVEN FOR THOSE WHO HAVE NO HOME, OR ARE TERRIFIED BY THE ONE THEY'VE GOT.
RONNIE WATSON'S TRAIL LED HIM HERE, BUT THOUGH HER CLOTHES REMAIN...
...THERE'S NO SIGN OF THE GIRL.
DEAD END--DAMMIT!
WHAT'S THAT?
DID RONNIE DRAW THIS?!

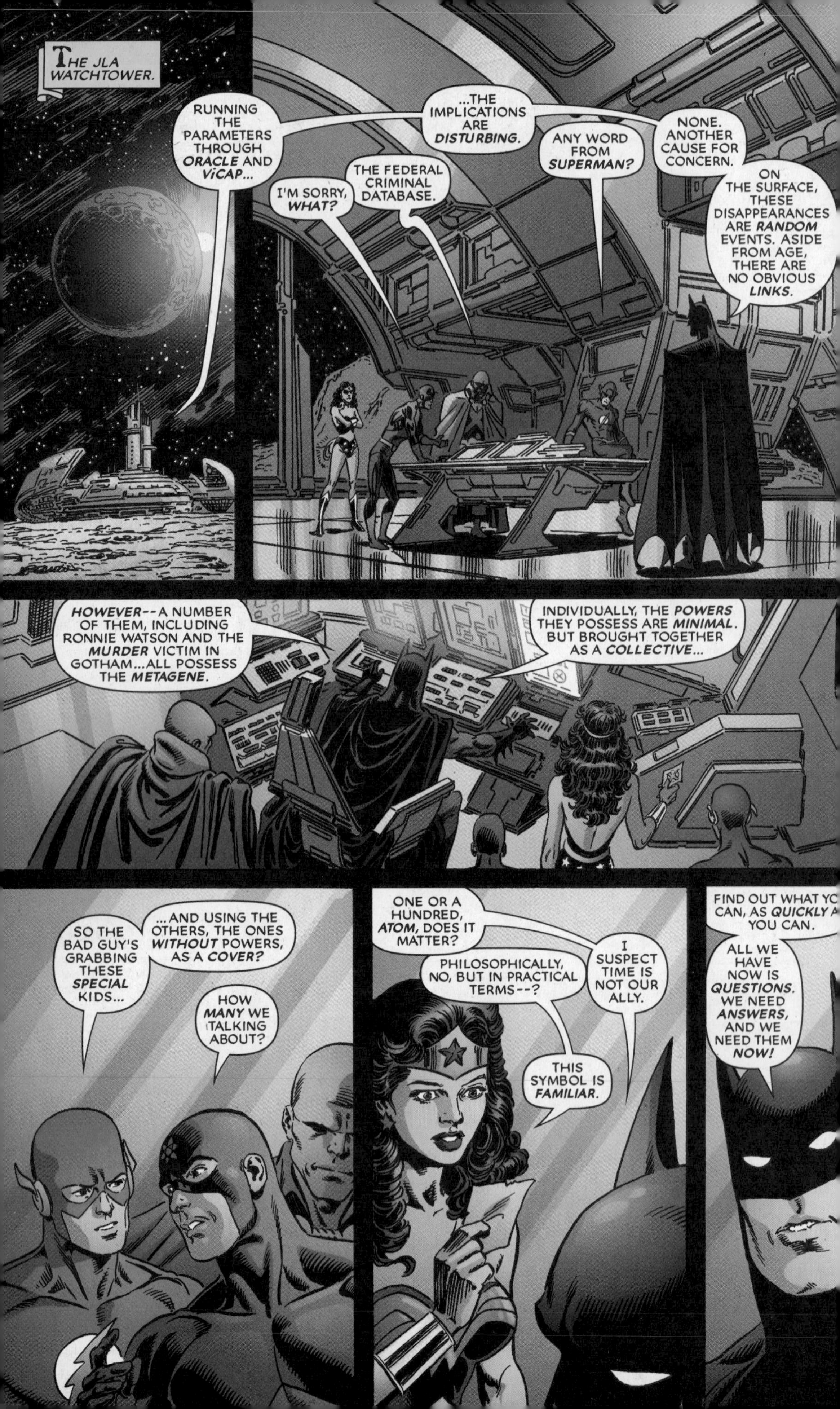
THE JLA WATCHTOWER.
RUNNING THE PARAMETERS THROUGH ORACLE AND ViCAP...
I'M SORRY, WHAT?
THE FEDERAL CRIMINAL DATABASE.
...THE IMPLICATIONS ARE DISTURBING.
ANY WORD FROM SUPERMAN?
NONE. ANOTHER CAUSE FOR CONCERN.
ON THE SURFACE, THESE DISAPPEARANCES ARE RANDOM EVENTS. ASIDE FROM AGE, THERE ARE NO OBVIOUS LINKS.
HOWEVER--A NUMBER OF THEM, INCLUDING RONNIE WATSON AND THE MURDER VICTIM IN GOTHAM...ALL POSSESS THE METAGENE.
INDIVIDUALLY, THE POWERS THEY POSSESS ARE MINIMAL. BUT BROUGHT TOGETHER AS A COLLECTIVE...
SO THE BAD GUY'S GRABBING THESE SPECIAL KIDS...
...AND USING THE OTHERS, THE ONES WITHOUT POWERS, AS A COVER?
HOW MANY WE TALKING ABOUT?
ONE OR A HUNDRED, ATOM, DOES IT MATTER?
PHILOSOPHICALLY, NO, BUT IN PRACTICAL TERMS--?
I SUSPECT TIME IS NOT OUR ALLY.
THIS SYMBOL IS FAMILIAR.
FIND OUT WHAT YO CAN, AS QUICKLY A YOU CAN.
ALL WE HAVE NOW IS QUESTIONS. WE NEED ANSWERS, AND WE NEED THEM NOW!

KEY MORDAZ.

ONE OF THE MOST REMOTE OF THE FLORIDA KEYS...

...AND NAMED FOR THE CORROSIVE EFFECTS OF SALT SPRAY.

IT WAS BUILT IN 1861 AS A CONFEDERATE PRISON.

TAKEN OVER BY THE UNION AFTER APPOMATOX, IT WAS A MAINSTAY OF THE FEDERAL PRISON SYSTEM UNTIL DECOMMISSIONED A CENTURY LATER.

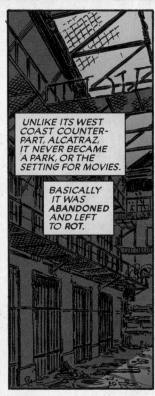

UNLIKE ITS WEST COAST COUNTER-PART, ALCATRAZ, IT NEVER BECAME A PARK, OR THE SETTING FOR MOVIES.

BASICALLY IT WAS ABANDONED AND LEFT TO ROT.

AROUND THE MILLENNIUM IT WAS SOLD TO THE PRIVATE SECTOR.

SINCE THEN, VISITORS HAVE BEEN ACTIVELY, ALBEIT POLITELY, DISCOURAGED.

WHAT GOES ON HERE PRETTY MUCH STAYS HERE.

AT LEAST, THAT WAS THE IDEA.

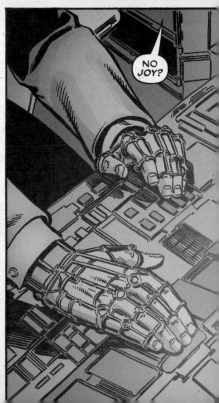

NO JOY?

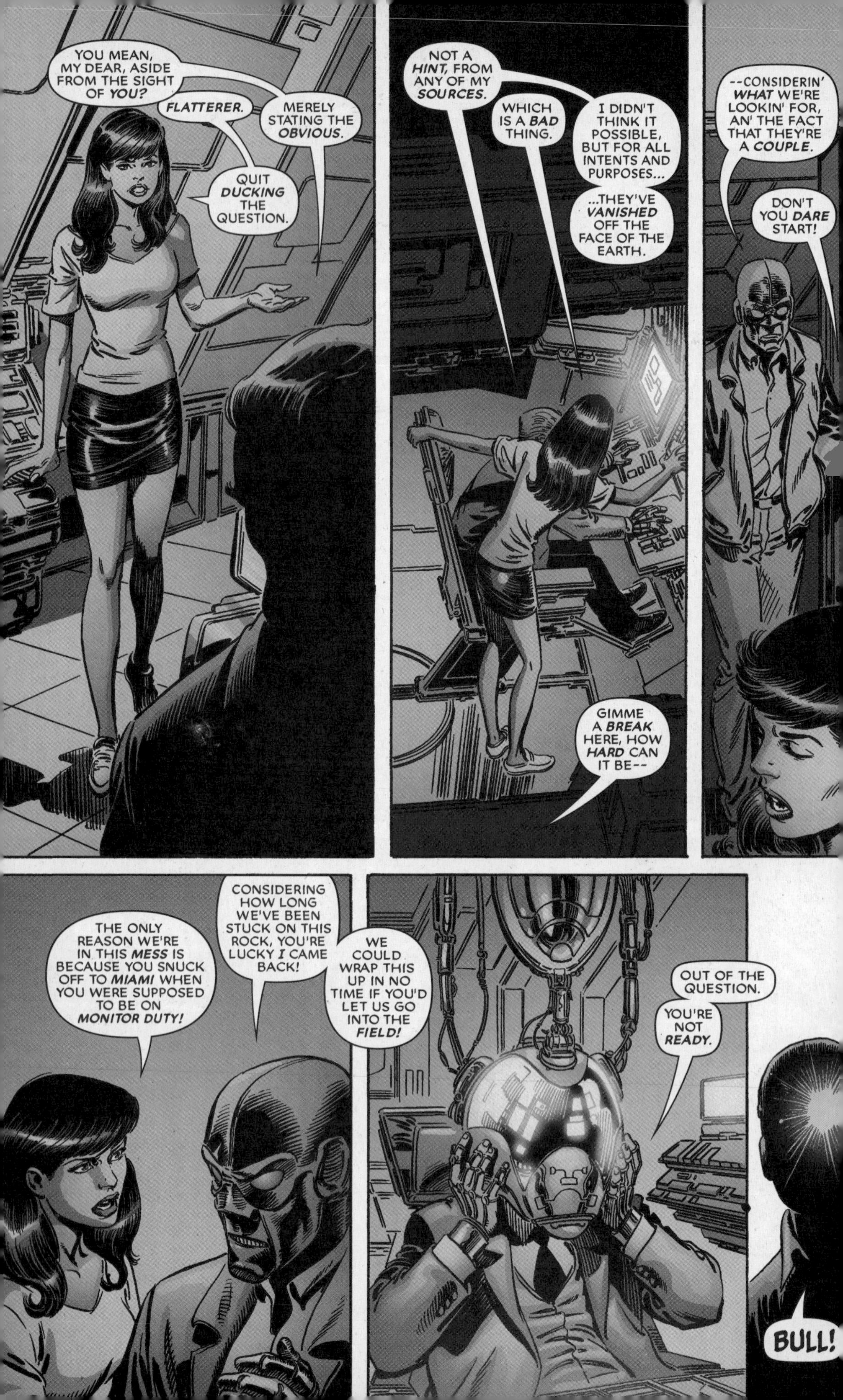
YOU MEAN, MY DEAR, ASIDE FROM THE SIGHT OF *YOU?*
FLATTERER.
MERELY STATING THE *OBVIOUS*.
QUIT *DUCKING* THE QUESTION.
NOT A *HINT,* FROM ANY OF MY *SOURCES*.
WHICH IS A *BAD* THING.
I DIDN'T THINK IT POSSIBLE, BUT FOR ALL INTENTS AND PURPOSES...
...THEY'VE *VANISHED* OFF THE FACE OF THE EARTH.
GIMME A *BREAK* HERE, HOW *HARD* CAN IT BE--
--CONSIDERIN' *WHAT* WE'RE LOOKIN' FOR, AN' THE FACT THAT THEY'RE A *COUPLE*.
DON'T YOU *DARE* START!
THE ONLY REASON WE'RE IN THIS *MESS* IS BECAUSE YOU SNUCK OFF TO *MIAMI* WHEN YOU WERE SUPPOSED TO BE ON *MONITOR DUTY!*
CONSIDERING HOW LONG WE'VE BEEN STUCK ON THIS ROCK, YOU'RE LUCKY *I* CAME BACK!
WE COULD WRAP THIS UP IN NO TIME IF YOU'D LET US GO INTO THE *FIELD!*
OUT OF THE QUESTION.
YOU'RE NOT *READY*.
BULL!

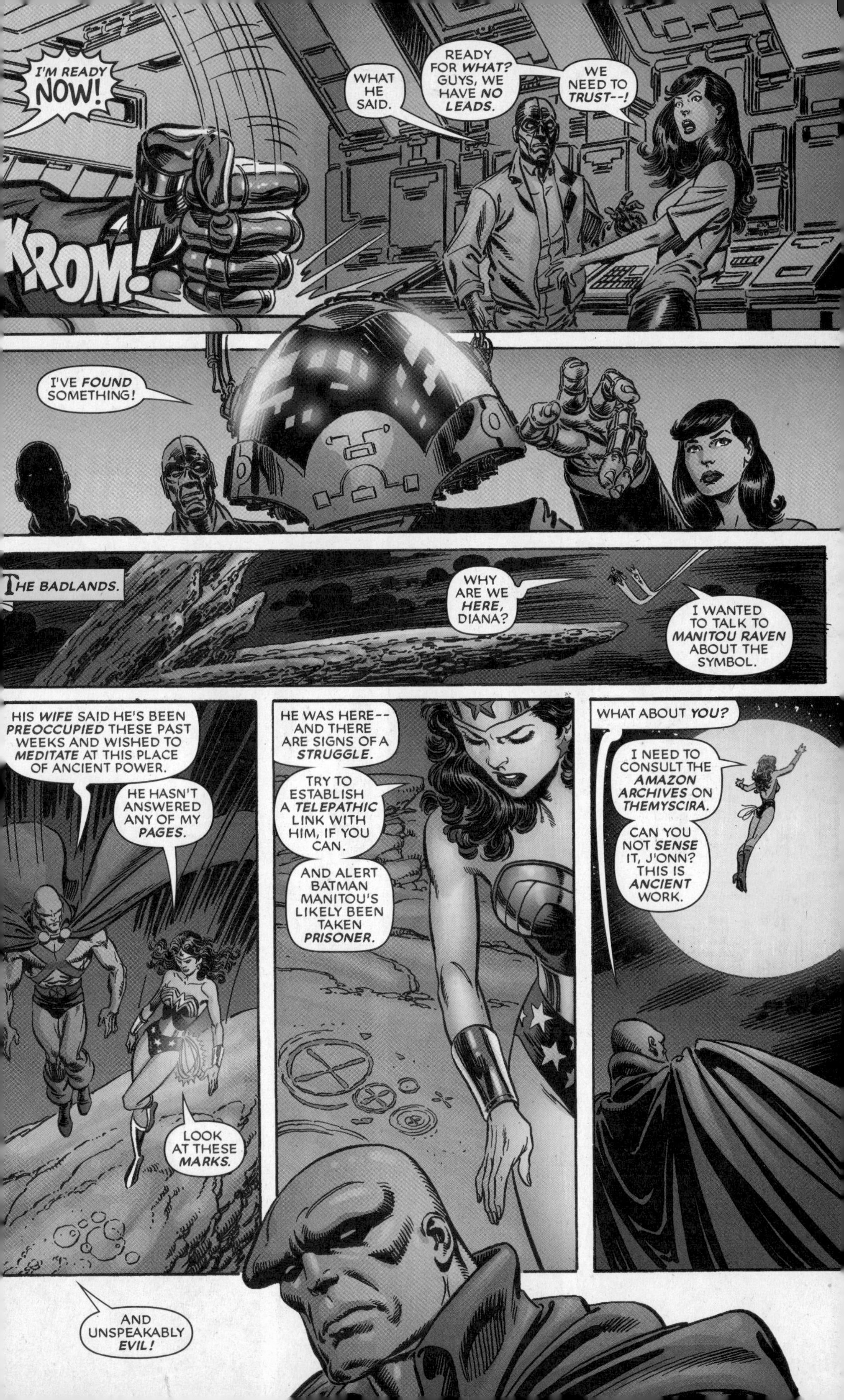
I'M READY NOW!
WHAT HE SAID.
READY FOR WHAT? GUYS, WE HAVE NO LEADS.
WE NEED TO TRUST--!
KROM!
I'VE FOUND SOMETHING!
THE BADLANDS.
WHY ARE WE HERE, DIANA?
I WANTED TO TALK TO MANITOU RAVEN ABOUT THE SYMBOL.
HIS WIFE SAID HE'S BEEN PREOCCUPIED THESE PAST WEEKS AND WISHED TO MEDITATE AT THIS PLACE OF ANCIENT POWER.
HE HASN'T ANSWERED ANY OF MY PAGES.
LOOK AT THESE MARKS.
HE WAS HERE--AND THERE ARE SIGNS OF A STRUGGLE.
TRY TO ESTABLISH A TELEPATHIC LINK WITH HIM, IF YOU CAN.
AND ALERT BATMAN MANITOU'S LIKELY BEEN TAKEN PRISONER.
WHAT ABOUT YOU?
I NEED TO CONSULT THE AMAZON ARCHIVES ON THEMYSCIRA.
CAN YOU NOT SENSE IT, J'ONN? THIS IS ANCIENT WORK.
AND UNSPEAKABLY EVIL!

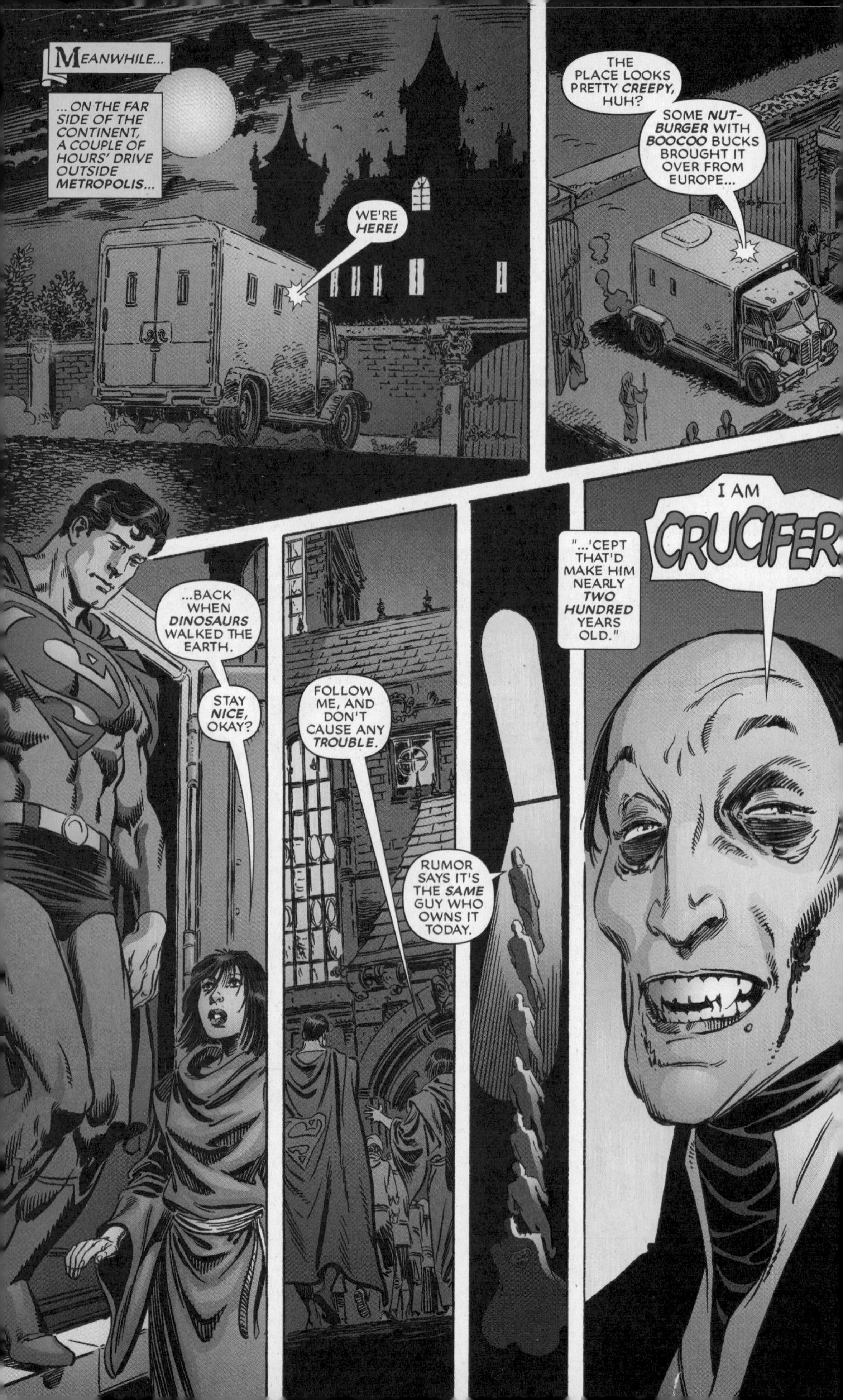
MEANWHILE...
...ON THE FAR SIDE OF THE CONTINENT, A COUPLE OF HOURS' DRIVE OUTSIDE METROPOLIS...
WE'RE HERE!
THE PLACE LOOKS PRETTY CREEPY, HUH?
SOME NUT-BURGER WITH BOOCOO BUCKS BROUGHT IT OVER FROM EUROPE...
...BACK WHEN DINOSAURS WALKED THE EARTH.
STAY NICE, OKAY?
FOLLOW ME, AND DON'T CAUSE ANY TROUBLE.
RUMOR SAYS IT'S THE SAME GUY WHO OWNS IT TODAY.
"...'CEPT THAT'D MAKE HIM NEARLY TWO HUNDRED YEARS OLD."
I AM
CRUCIFER.

I BID YOU ALL *WELCOME.*

ENTER *FREELY* AND OF YOUR OWN WILL.

DON'T BE *FRIGHTENED.*

I WILL TAKE *SPLENDID* CARE OF YOU.

BY THE *ABYSS--!?!*

WHO BROUGHT *HIM* HERE?!?

IT'S *OKAY,* HE'S *COOL!*

HE'S ON MY *LEASH.*

YOU HAVE *SURPRISED* ME, CHILD. AND THAT IS A *RARE* COMPLIMENT.

YOU HAVE *PLEASED* ME. WHICH IS *RARER* STILL.

NEVER IN MY *WILDEST* EXPECTATIONS DID I ANTICIPATE SUCH AN EXTRAORDINARY *OPPORTUNITY.*

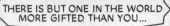
THERE IS BUT ONE IN THE WORLD MORE GIFTED THAN YOU...

...AND YOU HAVE PROVIDED ME THE *IDEAL* MEANS TO *ACQUIRE* HER.

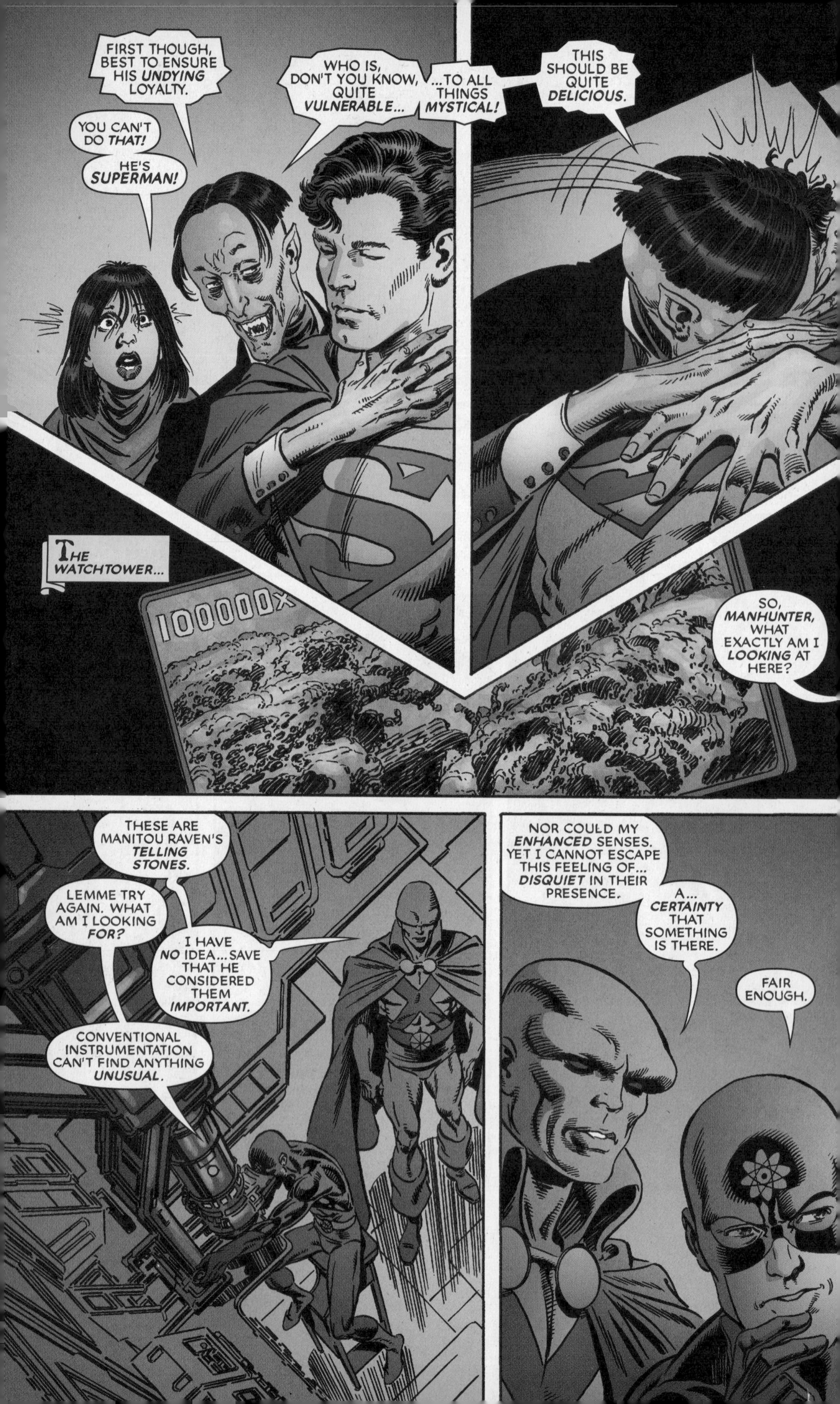

FIRST THOUGH, BEST TO ENSURE HIS UNDYING LOYALTY.
YOU CAN'T DO THAT!
HE'S SUPERMAN!
WHO IS, DON'T YOU KNOW, QUITE VULNERABLE...
...TO ALL THINGS MYSTICAL!
THIS SHOULD BE QUITE DELICIOUS.
THE WATCHTOWER...
100000X
SO, MANHUNTER, WHAT EXACTLY AM I LOOKING AT HERE?
THESE ARE MANITOU RAVEN'S TELLING STONES.
LEMME TRY AGAIN. WHAT AM I LOOKING FOR?
I HAVE NO IDEA... SAVE THAT HE CONSIDERED THEM IMPORTANT.
CONVENTIONAL INSTRUMENTATION CAN'T FIND ANYTHING UNUSUAL.
NOR COULD MY ENHANCED SENSES. YET I CANNOT ESCAPE THIS FEELING OF... DISQUIET IN THEIR PRESENCE.
A... CERTAINTY THAT SOMETHING IS THERE.
FAIR ENOUGH.

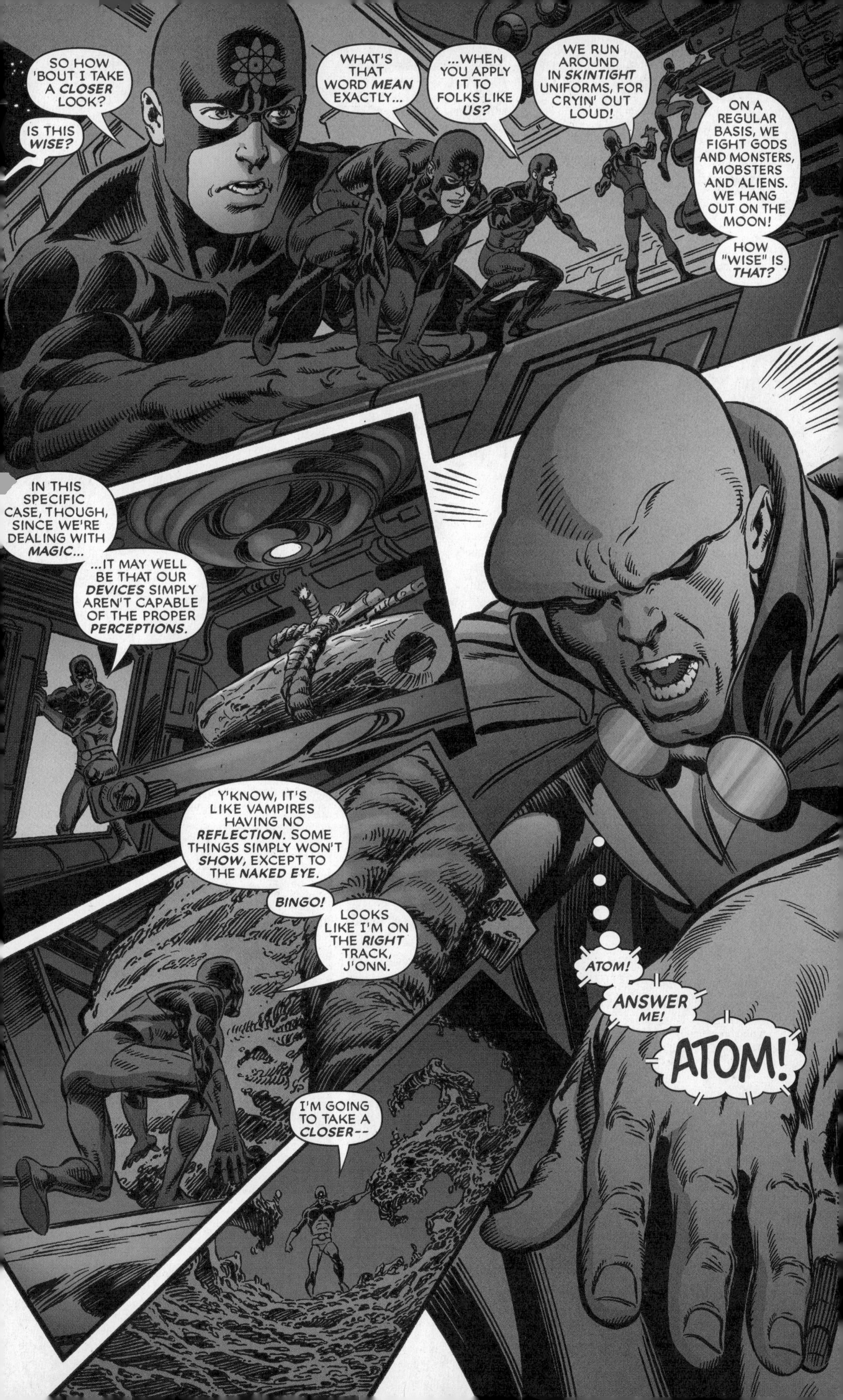
SO HOW 'BOUT I TAKE A CLOSER LOOK?
IS THIS WISE?
WHAT'S THAT WORD MEAN EXACTLY...
...WHEN YOU APPLY IT TO FOLKS LIKE US?
WE RUN AROUND IN SKINTIGHT UNIFORMS, FOR CRYIN' OUT LOUD!
ON A REGULAR BASIS, WE FIGHT GODS AND MONSTERS, MOBSTERS AND ALIENS. WE HANG OUT ON THE MOON!
HOW "WISE" IS THAT?
IN THIS SPECIFIC CASE, THOUGH, SINCE WE'RE DEALING WITH MAGIC...
...IT MAY WELL BE THAT OUR DEVICES SIMPLY AREN'T CAPABLE OF THE PROPER PERCEPTIONS.
Y'KNOW, IT'S LIKE VAMPIRES HAVING NO REFLECTION. SOME THINGS SIMPLY WON'T SHOW, EXCEPT TO THE NAKED EYE.
BINGO!
LOOKS LIKE I'M ON THE RIGHT TRACK, J'ONN.
I'M GOING TO TAKE A CLOSER--
ATOM!
ANSWER ME!
ATOM!

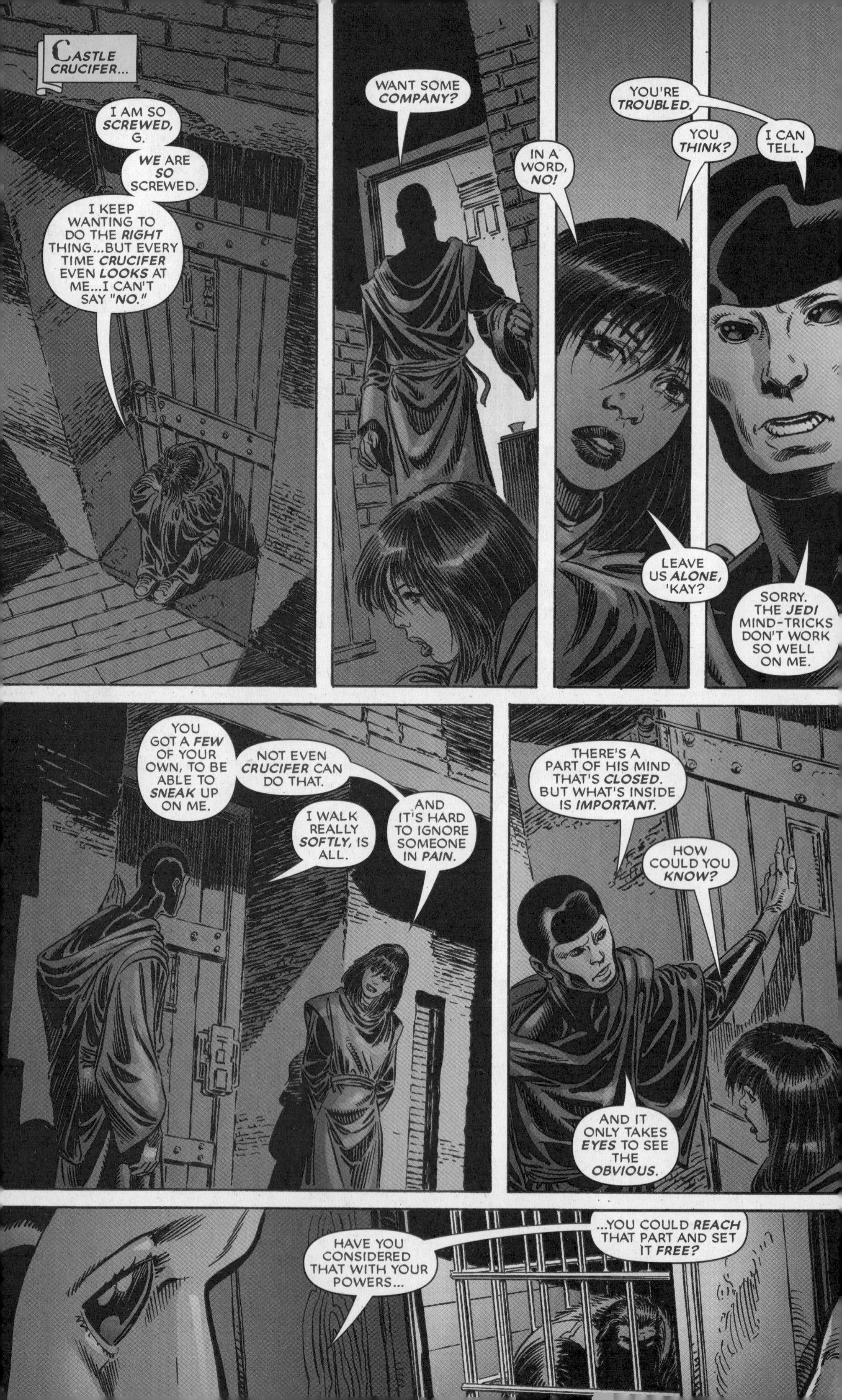
CASTLE CRUCIFER...
I AM SO SCREWED, G.
WE ARE SO SCREWED.
I KEEP WANTING TO DO THE RIGHT THING...BUT EVERY TIME CRUCIFER EVEN LOOKS AT ME...I CAN'T SAY "NO."
WANT SOME COMPANY?
IN A WORD, NO!
YOU'RE TROUBLED.
YOU THINK?
I CAN TELL.
LEAVE US ALONE, 'KAY?
SORRY. THE JEDI MIND-TRICKS DON'T WORK SO WELL ON ME.
YOU GOT A FEW OF YOUR OWN, TO BE ABLE TO SNEAK UP ON ME.
NOT EVEN CRUCIFER CAN DO THAT.
I WALK REALLY SOFTLY, IS ALL.
AND IT'S HARD TO IGNORE SOMEONE IN PAIN.
THERE'S A PART OF HIS MIND THAT'S CLOSED. BUT WHAT'S INSIDE IS IMPORTANT.
HOW COULD YOU KNOW?
AND IT ONLY TAKES EYES TO SEE THE OBVIOUS.
HAVE YOU CONSIDERED THAT WITH YOUR POWERS...
...YOU COULD REACH THAT PART AND SET IT FREE?

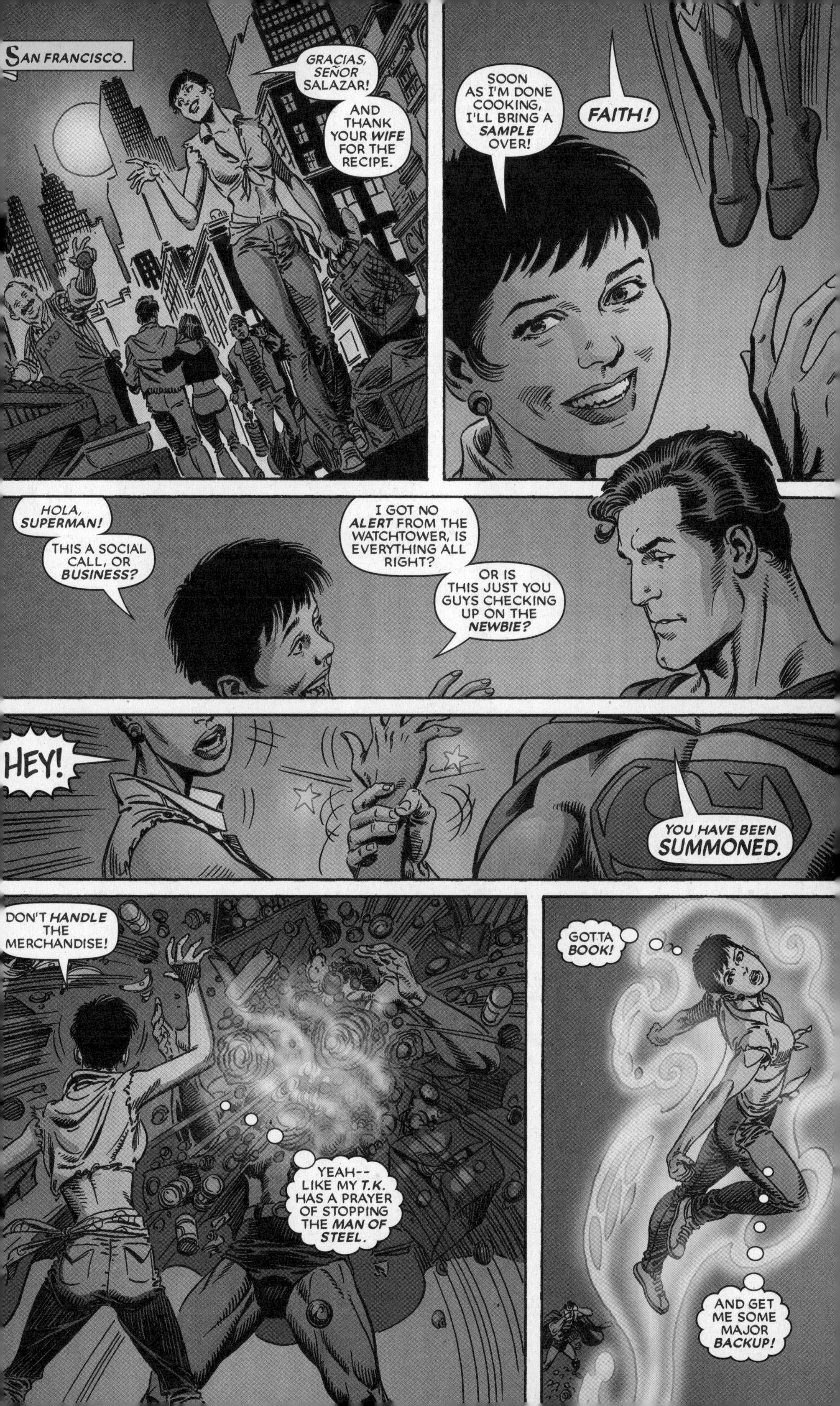
SAN FRANCISCO.
GRACIAS, SEÑOR SALAZAR!
AND THANK YOUR WIFE FOR THE RECIPE.
SOON AS I'M DONE COOKING, I'LL BRING A SAMPLE OVER!
FAITH!
HOLA, SUPERMAN!
THIS A SOCIAL CALL, OR BUSINESS?
I GOT NO ALERT FROM THE WATCHTOWER, IS EVERYTHING ALL RIGHT?
OR IS THIS JUST YOU GUYS CHECKING UP ON THE NEWBIE?
HEY!
YOU HAVE BEEN SUMMONED.
DON'T HANDLE THE MERCHANDISE!
YEAH-- LIKE MY T.K. HAS A PRAYER OF STOPPING THE MAN OF STEEL.
GOTTA BOOK!
AND GET ME SOME MAJOR BACKUP!

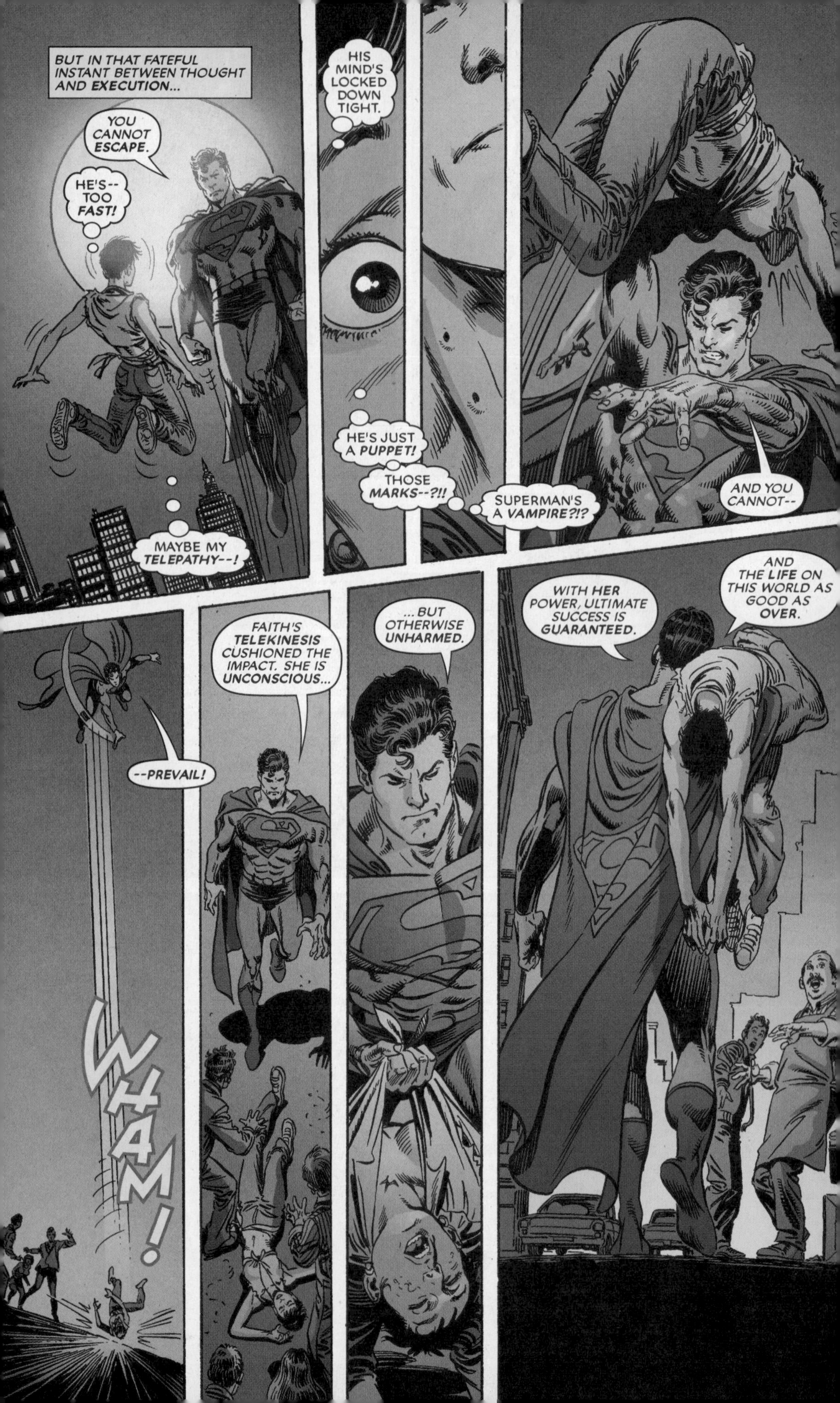
BUT IN THAT FATEFUL INSTANT BETWEEN THOUGHT AND EXECUTION...
YOU CANNOT ESCAPE.
HE'S-- TOO FAST!
MAYBE MY TELEPATHY--!
HIS MIND'S LOCKED DOWN TIGHT.
HE'S JUST A PUPPET!
THOSE MARKS--?!!
SUPERMAN'S A VAMPIRE?!?
AND YOU CANNOT--
--PREVAIL!
WHAM!
FAITH'S TELEKINESIS CUSHIONED THE IMPACT. SHE IS UNCONSCIOUS...
...BUT OTHERWISE UNHARMED.
WITH HER POWER, ULTIMATE SUCCESS IS GUARANTEED.
AND THE LIFE ON THIS WORLD AS GOOD AS OVER.

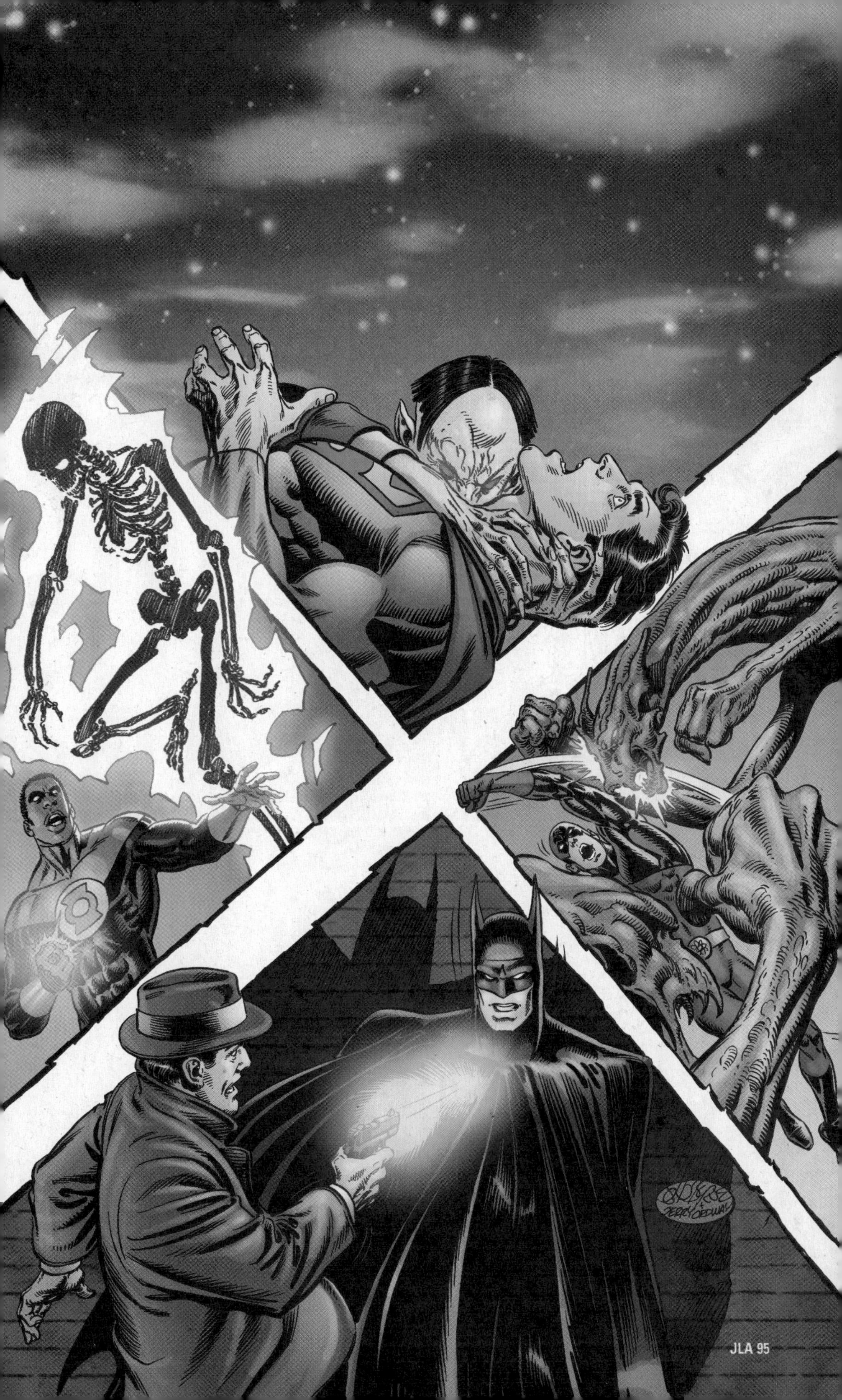

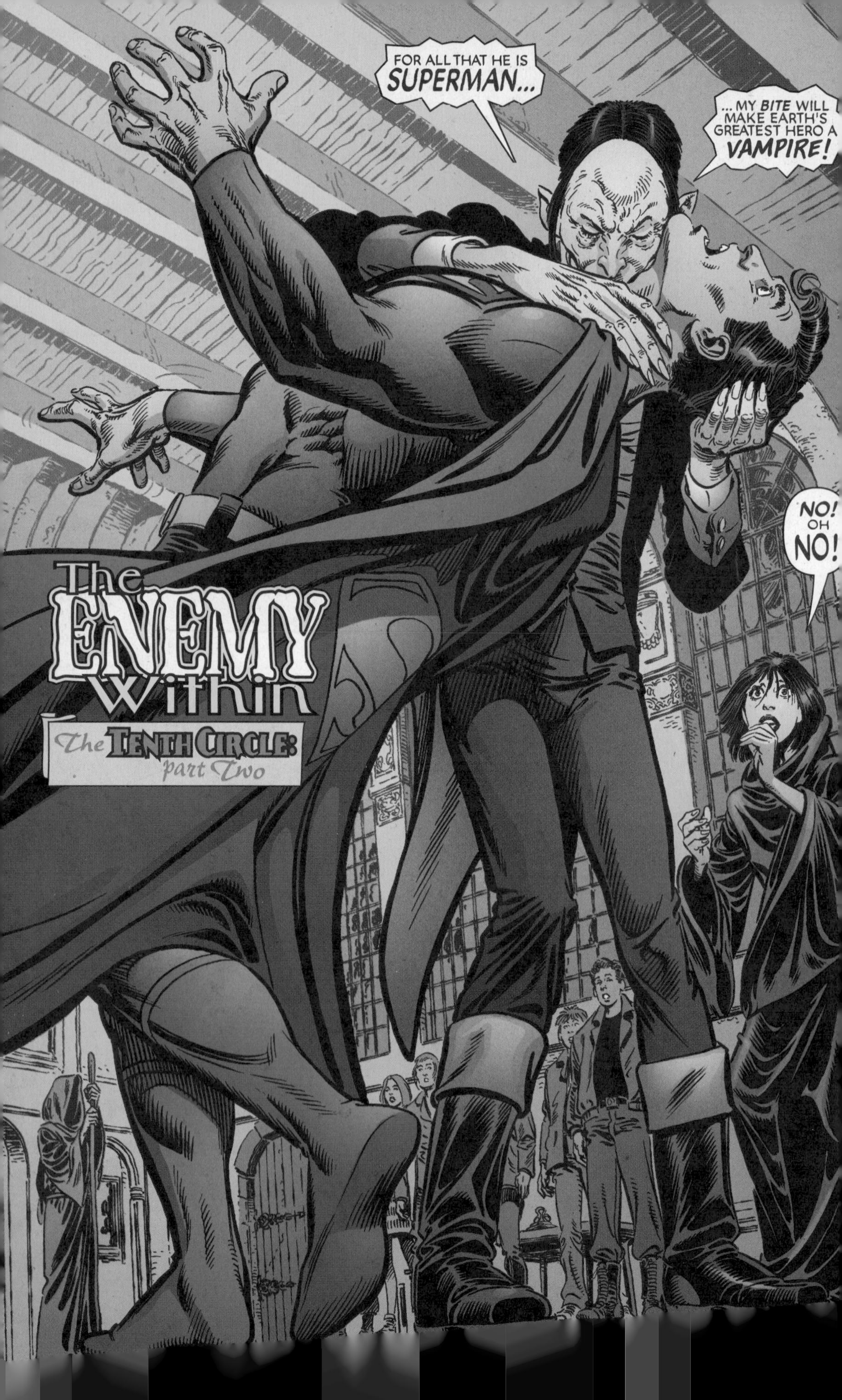
FOR ALL THAT HE IS SUPERMAN...
... MY BITE WILL MAKE EARTH'S GREATEST HERO A VAMPIRE!
NO! OH NO!
The ENEMY Within
The TENTH CIRCLE: part Two

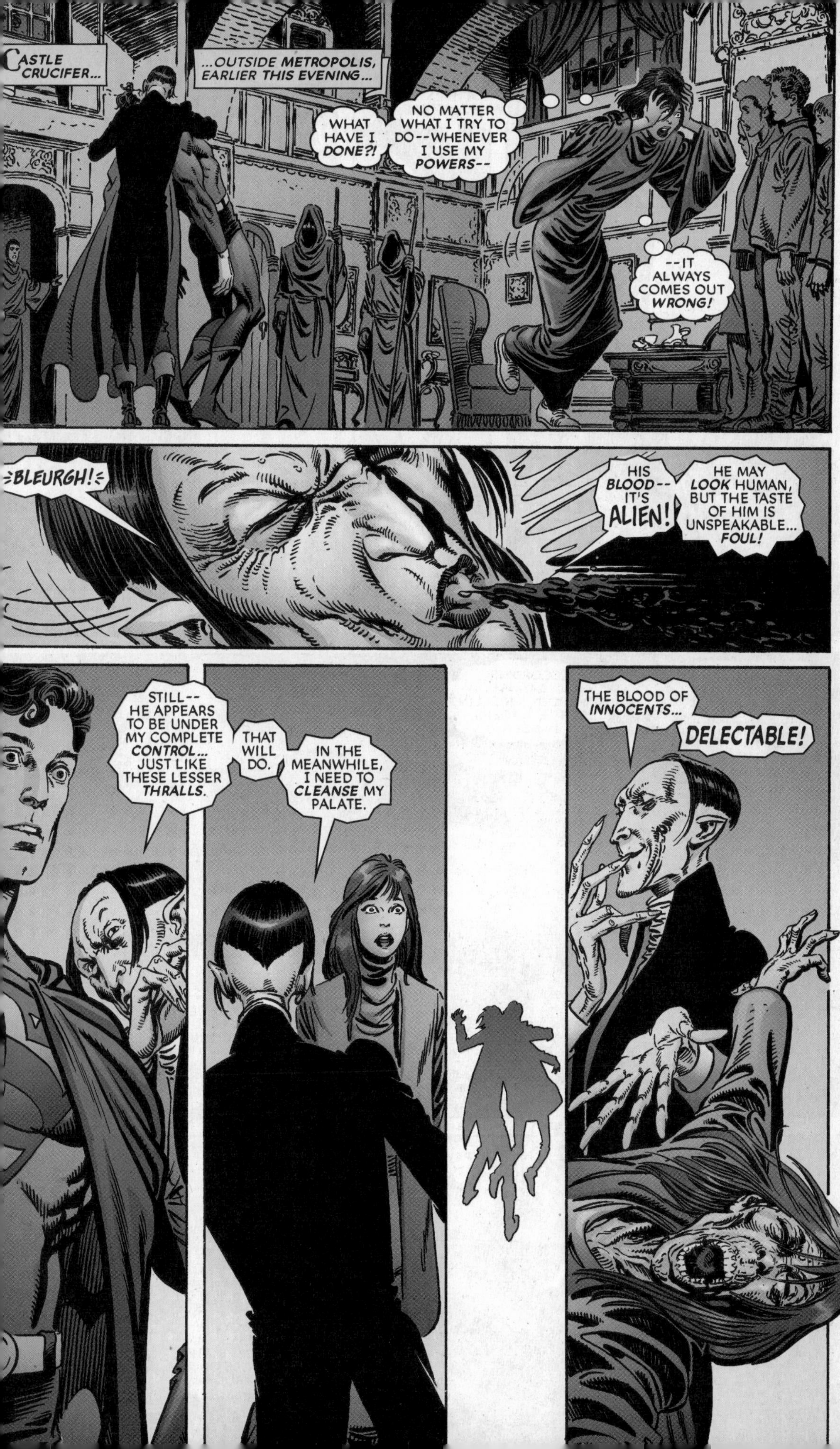
CASTLE CRUCIFER...
...OUTSIDE METROPOLIS, EARLIER THIS EVENING...
WHAT HAVE I DONE?!
NO MATTER WHAT I TRY TO DO--WHENEVER I USE MY POWERS--
--IT ALWAYS COMES OUT WRONG!
BLEURGH!
HIS BLOOD--IT'S ALIEN!
HE MAY LOOK HUMAN, BUT THE TASTE OF HIM IS UNSPEAKABLE... FOUL!
STILL--HE APPEARS TO BE UNDER MY COMPLETE CONTROL... JUST LIKE THESE LESSER THRALLS.
THAT WILL DO.
IN THE MEANWHILE, I NEED TO CLEANSE MY PALATE.
THE BLOOD OF INNOCENTS...
DELECTABLE!

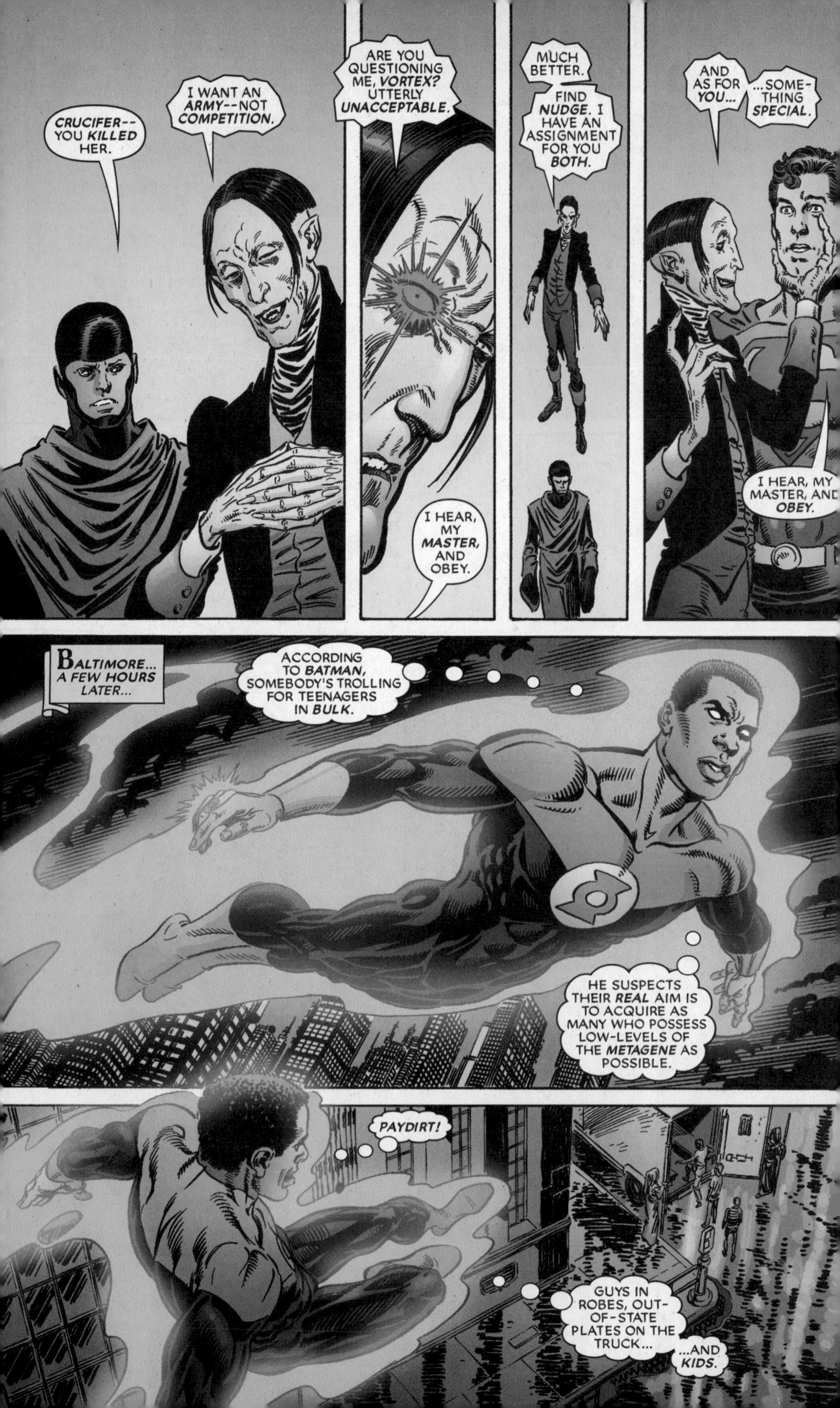
CRUCIFER-- YOU KILLED HER.
I WANT AN ARMY--NOT COMPETITION.
ARE YOU QUESTIONING ME, VORTEX? UTTERLY UNACCEPTABLE.
I HEAR, MY MASTER, AND OBEY.
MUCH BETTER.
FIND NUDGE. I HAVE AN ASSIGNMENT FOR YOU BOTH.
AND AS FOR YOU...
...SOMETHING SPECIAL.
I HEAR, MY MASTER, AND OBEY.
BALTIMORE... A FEW HOURS LATER...
ACCORDING TO BATMAN, SOMEBODY'S TROLLING FOR TEENAGERS IN BULK.
HE SUSPECTS THEIR REAL AIM IS TO ACQUIRE AS MANY WHO POSSESS LOW-LEVELS OF THE METAGENE AS POSSIBLE.
PAYDIRT!
GUYS IN ROBES, OUT-OF-STATE PLATES ON THE TRUCK...
...AND KIDS.

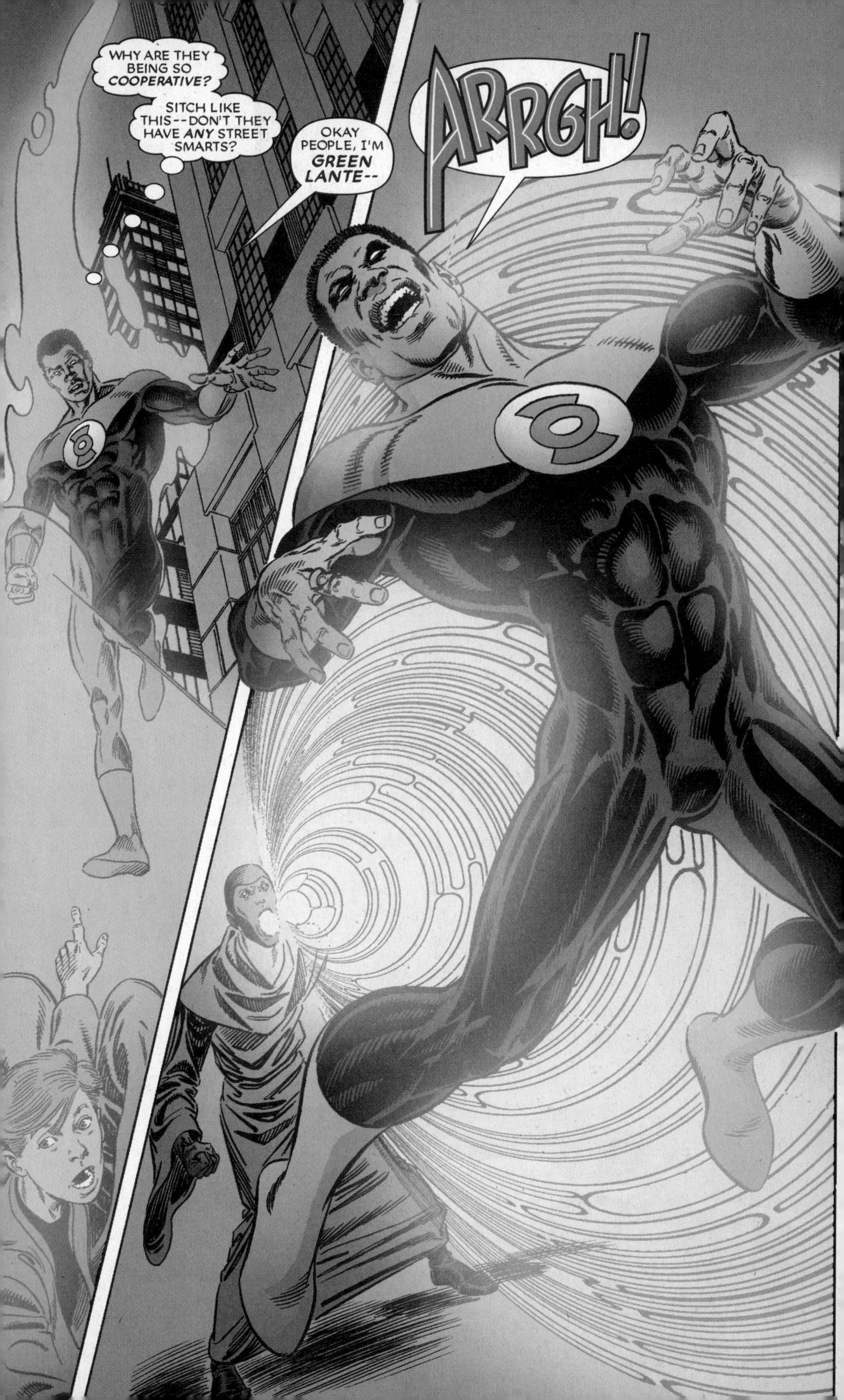
WHY ARE THEY BEING SO COOPERATIVE?
SITCH LIKE THIS--DON'T THEY HAVE ANY STREET SMARTS?
OKAY PEOPLE, I'M GREEN LANTE--
ARRGH!

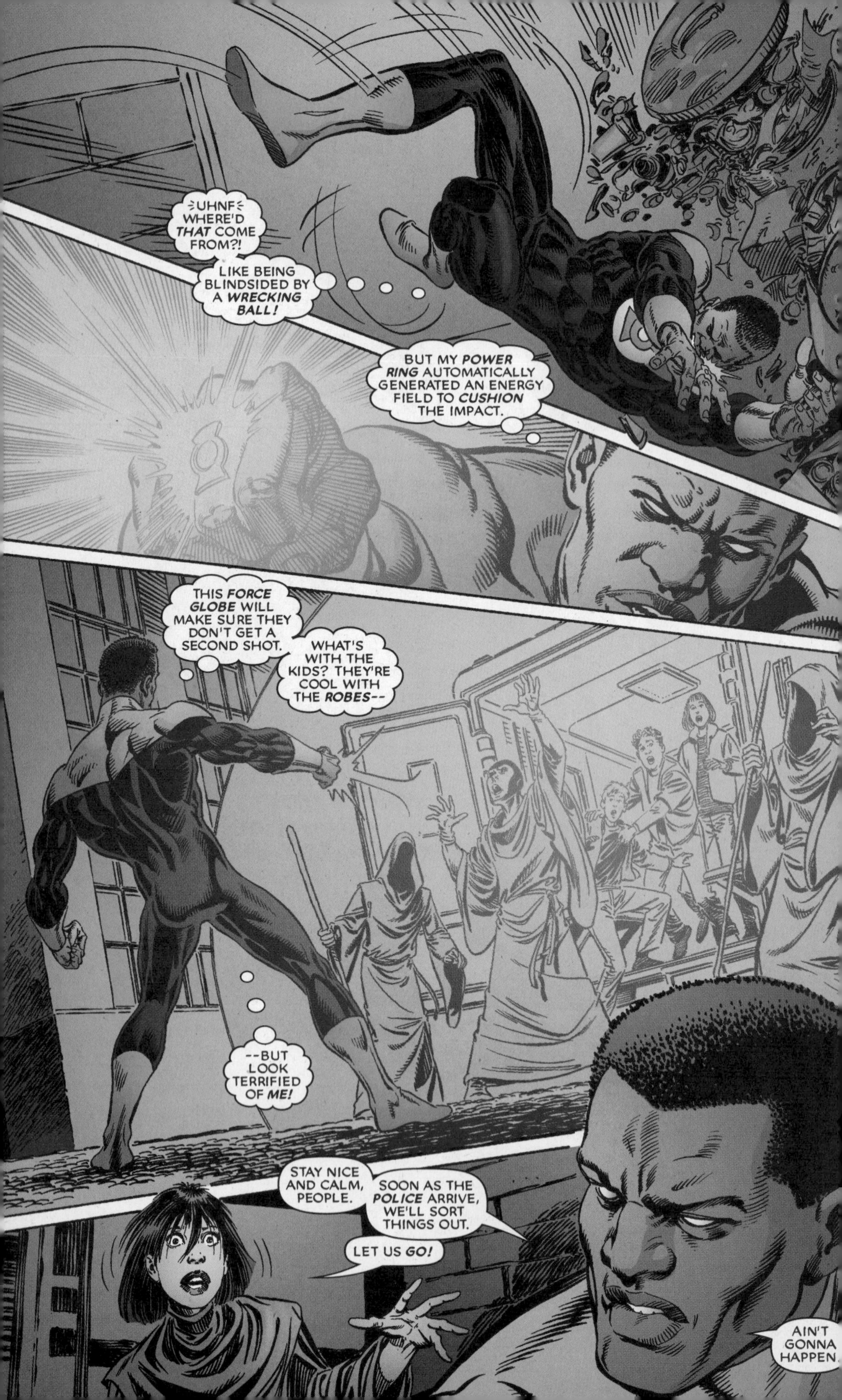
UHNF WHERE'D THAT COME FROM?!
LIKE BEING BLINDSIDED BY A WRECKING BALL!
BUT MY POWER RING AUTOMATICALLY GENERATED AN ENERGY FIELD TO CUSHION THE IMPACT.
THIS FORCE GLOBE WILL MAKE SURE THEY DON'T GET A SECOND SHOT.
WHAT'S WITH THE KIDS? THEY'RE COOL WITH THE ROBES--
--BUT LOOK TERRIFIED OF ME!
STAY NICE AND CALM, PEOPLE.
SOON AS THE POLICE ARRIVE, WE'LL SORT THINGS OUT.
LET US GO!
AIN'T GONNA HAPPEN.

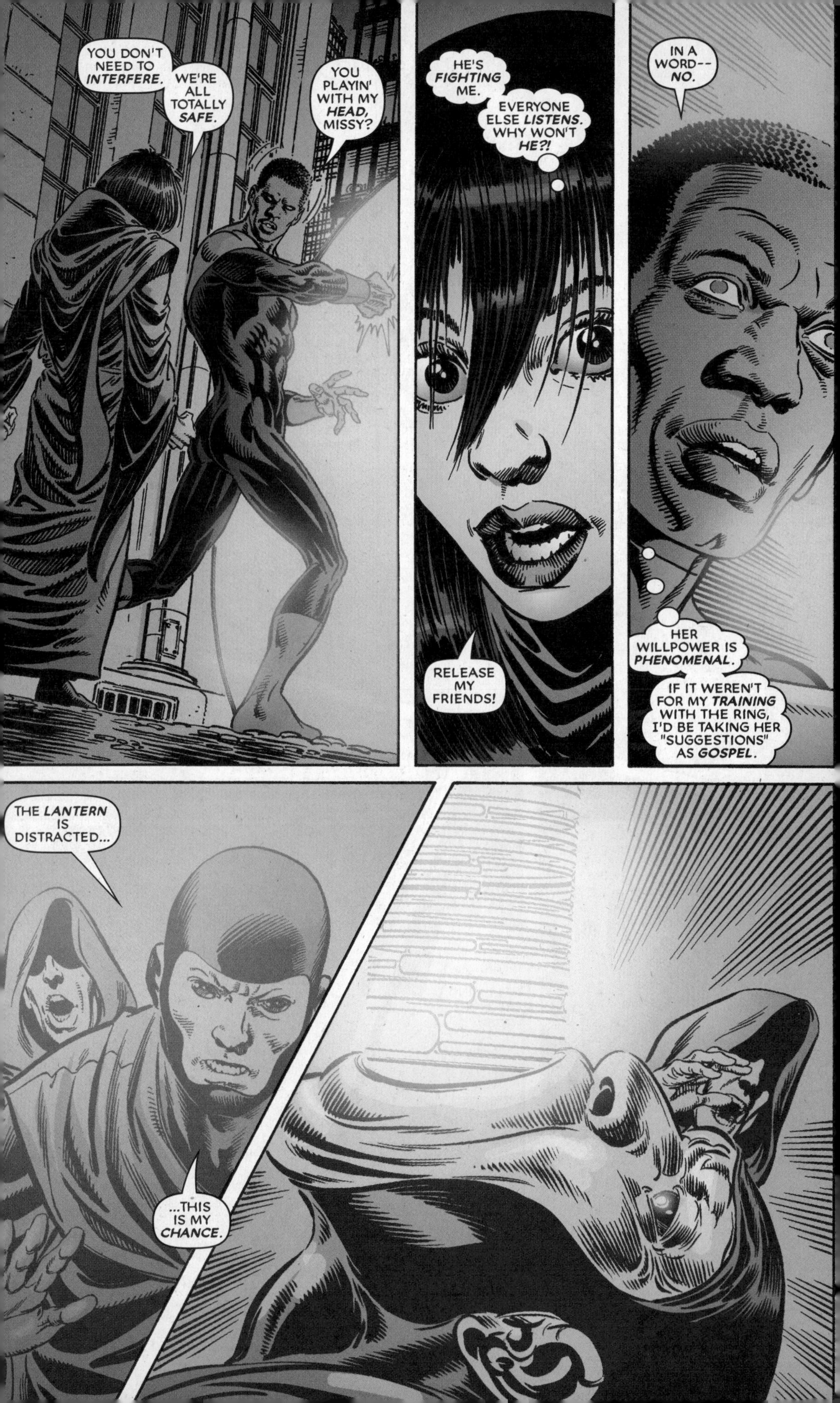

YOU DON'T NEED TO INTERFERE.
WE'RE ALL TOTALLY SAFE.
YOU PLAYIN' WITH MY HEAD, MISSY?
HE'S FIGHTING ME.
EVERYONE ELSE LISTENS. WHY WON'T HE?!
RELEASE MY FRIENDS!
IN A WORD-- NO.
HER WILLPOWER IS PHENOMENAL.
IF IT WEREN'T FOR MY TRAINING WITH THE RING, I'D BE TAKING HER "SUGGESTIONS" AS GOSPEL.
THE LANTERN IS DISTRACTED...
...THIS IS MY CHANCE.

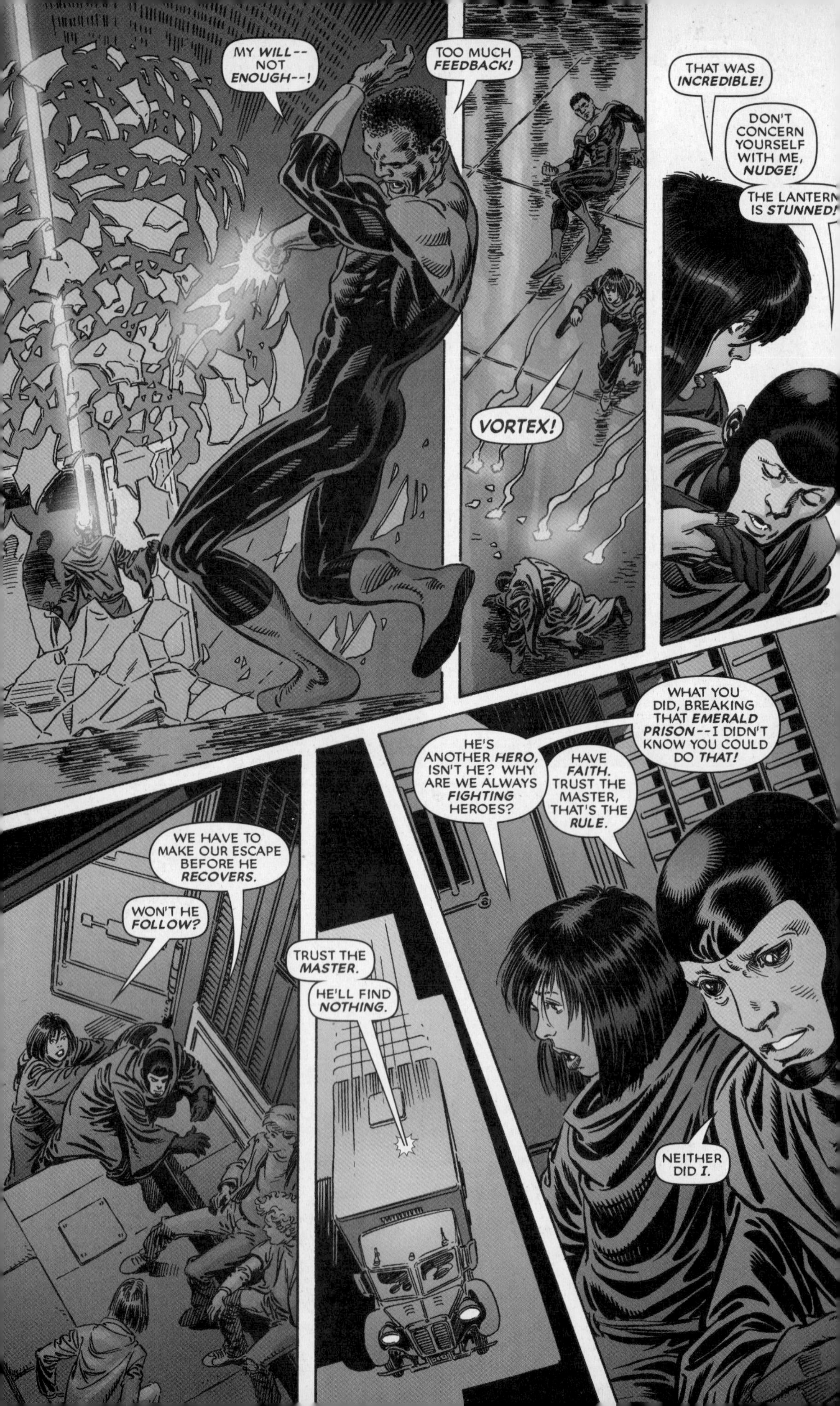

MY WILL-- NOT ENOUGH--!
TOO MUCH FEEDBACK!
VORTEX!
THAT WAS INCREDIBLE!
DON'T CONCERN YOURSELF WITH ME, NUDGE!
THE LANTERN IS STUNNED!
WE HAVE TO MAKE OUR ESCAPE BEFORE HE RECOVERS.
WON'T HE FOLLOW?
TRUST THE MASTER.
HE'LL FIND NOTHING.
WHAT YOU DID, BREAKING THAT EMERALD PRISON--I DIDN'T KNOW YOU COULD DO THAT!
HE'S ANOTHER HERO, ISN'T HE? WHY ARE WE ALWAYS FIGHTING HEROES?
HAVE FAITH. TRUST THE MASTER, THAT'S THE RULE.
NEITHER DID I.

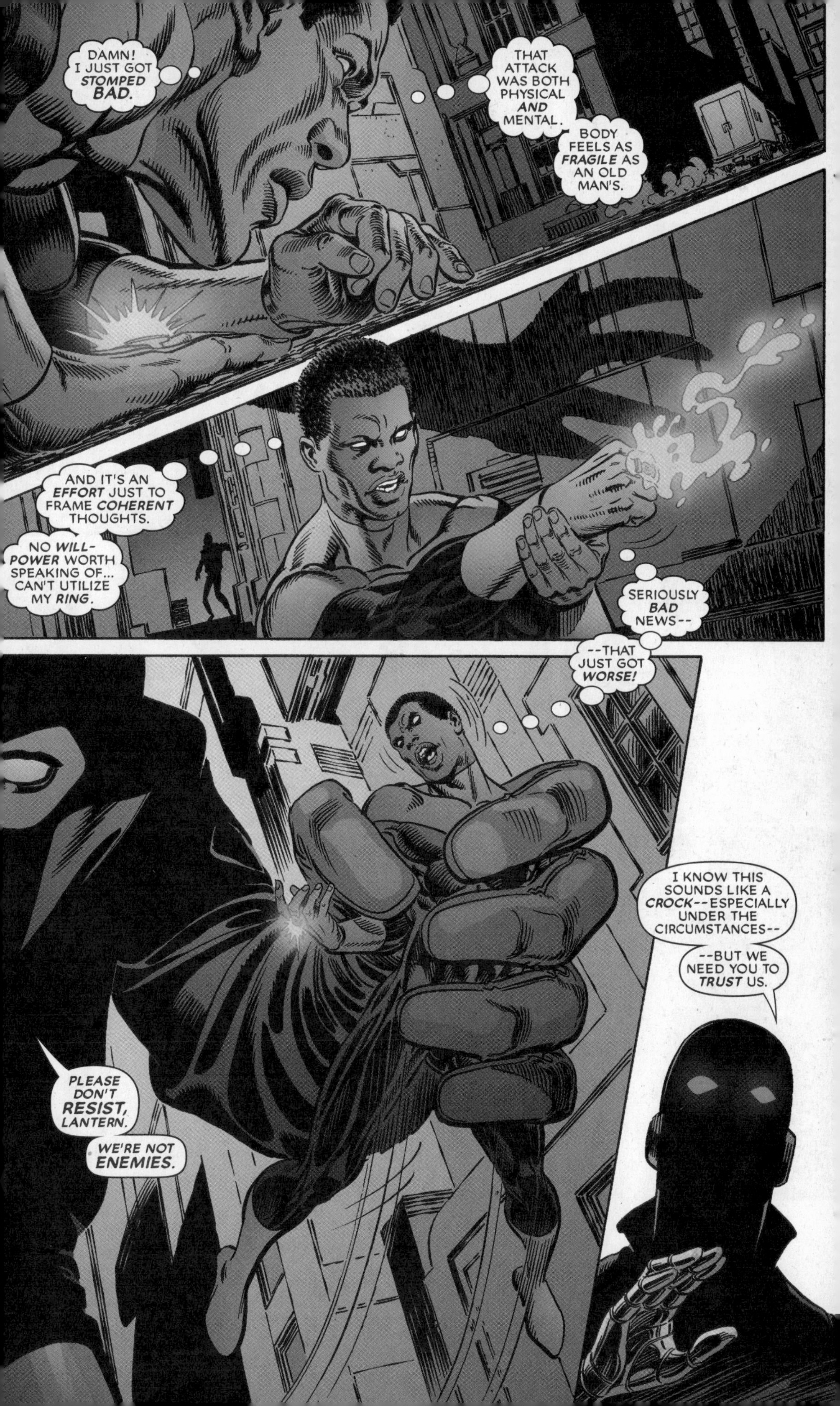
DAMN! I JUST GOT STOMPED BAD.
THAT ATTACK WAS BOTH PHYSICAL AND MENTAL.
BODY FEELS AS FRAGILE AS AN OLD MAN'S.
AND IT'S AN EFFORT JUST TO FRAME COHERENT THOUGHTS.
NO WILL-POWER WORTH SPEAKING OF... CAN'T UTILIZE MY RING.
SERIOUSLY BAD NEWS--
--THAT JUST GOT WORSE!
I KNOW THIS SOUNDS LIKE A CROCK--ESPECIALLY UNDER THE CIRCUMSTANCES--
--BUT WE NEED YOU TO TRUST US.
PLEASE DON'T RESIST, LANTERN.
WE'RE NOT ENEMIES.

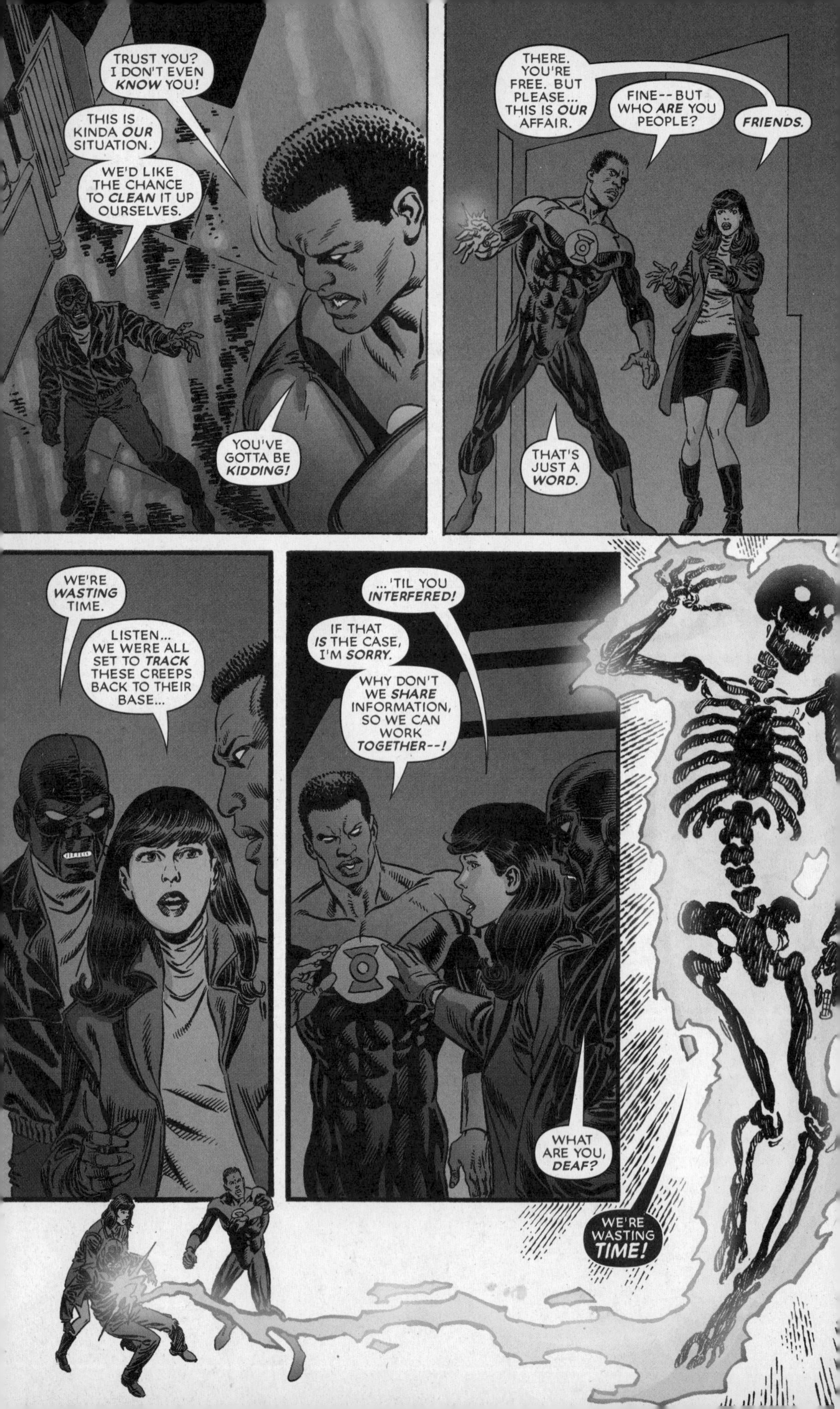
TRUST YOU? I DON'T EVEN *KNOW* YOU!
THIS IS KINDA *OUR* SITUATION.
WE'D LIKE THE CHANCE TO *CLEAN* IT UP OURSELVES.
YOU'VE GOTTA BE *KIDDING!*
THERE. YOU'RE FREE. BUT PLEASE... THIS IS *OUR* AFFAIR.
FINE--BUT WHO *ARE* YOU PEOPLE?
FRIENDS.
THAT'S JUST A *WORD.*
WE'RE *WASTING* TIME.
LISTEN... WE WERE ALL SET TO *TRACK* THESE CREEPS BACK TO THEIR BASE...
...'TIL YOU *INTERFERED!*
IF THAT *IS* THE CASE, I'M *SORRY.*
WHY DON'T WE *SHARE* INFORMATION, SO WE CAN WORK *TOGETHER--!*
WHAT ARE YOU, *DEAF?*
WE'RE WASTING *TIME!*

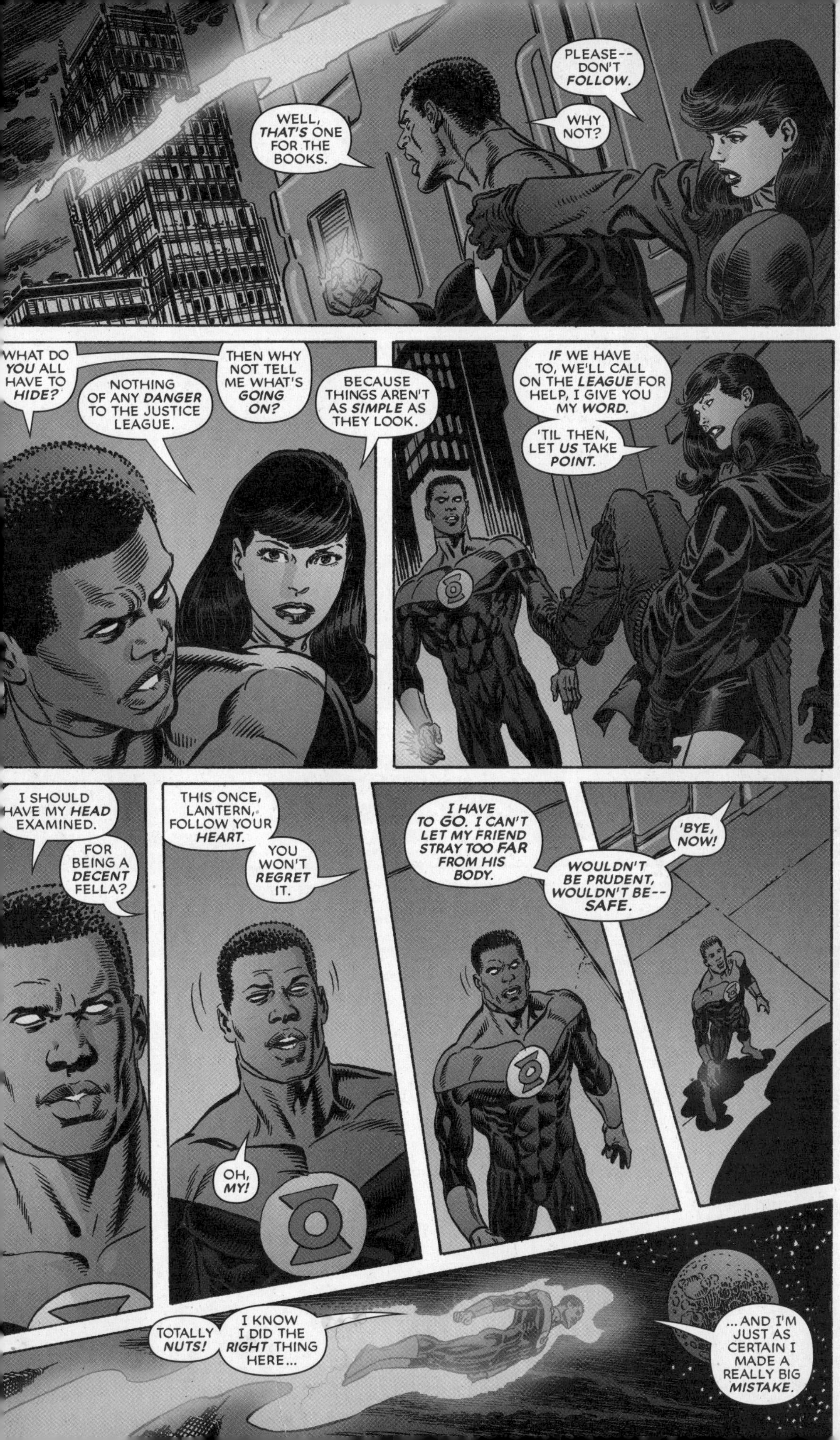
WELL, THAT'S ONE FOR THE BOOKS.
PLEASE-- DON'T FOLLOW.
WHY NOT?
WHAT DO YOU ALL HAVE TO HIDE?
NOTHING OF ANY DANGER TO THE JUSTICE LEAGUE.
THEN WHY NOT TELL ME WHAT'S GOING ON?
BECAUSE THINGS AREN'T AS SIMPLE AS THEY LOOK.
IF WE HAVE TO, WE'LL CALL ON THE LEAGUE FOR HELP, I GIVE YOU MY WORD.
'TIL THEN, LET US TAKE POINT.
I SHOULD HAVE MY HEAD EXAMINED.
FOR BEING A DECENT FELLA?
THIS ONCE, LANTERN, FOLLOW YOUR HEART.
YOU WON'T REGRET IT.
OH, MY!
I HAVE TO GO. I CAN'T LET MY FRIEND STRAY TOO FAR FROM HIS BODY.
WOULDN'T BE PRUDENT, WOULDN'T BE-- SAFE.
'BYE, NOW!
TOTALLY NUTS!
I KNOW I DID THE RIGHT THING HERE...
...AND I'M JUST AS CERTAIN I MADE A REALLY BIG MISTAKE.

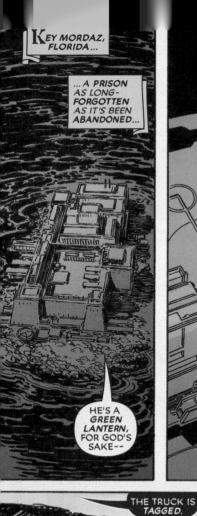

KEY MORDAZ, FLORIDA...

...A PRISON AS LONG-FORGOTTEN AS IT'S BEEN ABANDONED...

HE'S A GREEN LANTERN, FOR GOD'S SAKE--

--HE'S ONE OF THE JUSTICE LEAGUE!

CAN WE SAY "NO-BRAINER" HERE, ON WHETHER WE HOOK UP WITH HIM OR KEEP GOIN' SOLO--

--OR JUST NO "BRAINS" BECAUSE WE'RE BETTIN' THE FARM ON "MR. DAY-GLO"?

I HEARD THAT.

NEXT TIME, SAY IT TO MY FACE, WE'LL SEE WHO'S STILL STANDIN' WHEN WE'RE DONE.

PROMISES, PROMISES.

THE TRUCK IS TAGGED.

I'M IMPRESSED. HE DIDN'T SCREW UP.

WE'RE NONE OF US PERFECT.

THAT'S WHY WE'RE... HERE.

YOU GOT A DECENT SIGNAL?

I COULD TRACK IT THROUGH A MOUN--!

STOPPING IN MID-SENTENCE, NOT A GOOD SIGN.

THE TRUCK HAS VANISHED.

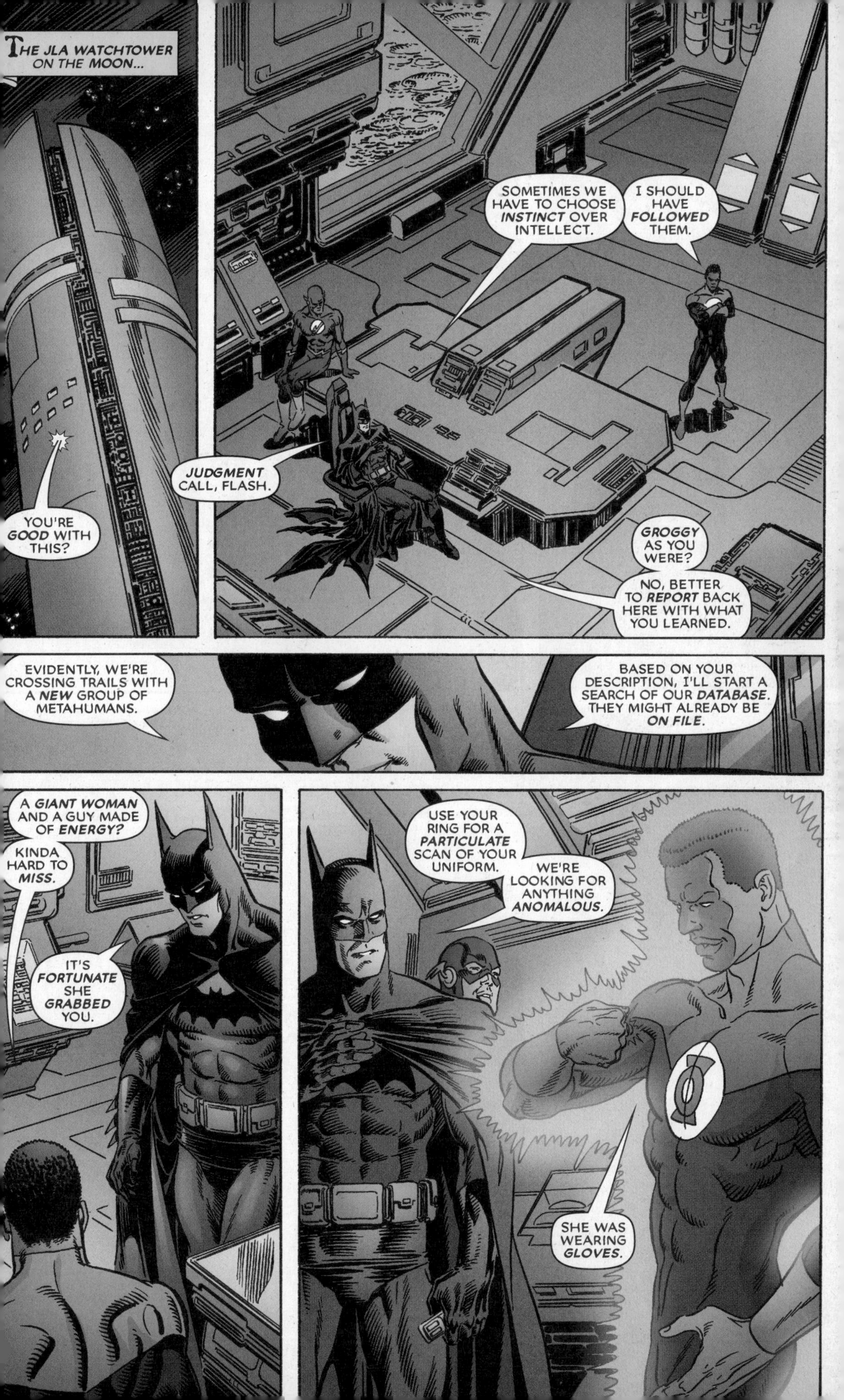
THE JLA WATCHTOWER ON THE MOON...
YOU'RE GOOD WITH THIS?
SOMETIMES WE HAVE TO CHOOSE INSTINCT OVER INTELLECT.
I SHOULD HAVE FOLLOWED THEM.
JUDGMENT CALL, FLASH.
GROGGY AS YOU WERE?
NO, BETTER TO REPORT BACK HERE WITH WHAT YOU LEARNED.
EVIDENTLY, WE'RE CROSSING TRAILS WITH A NEW GROUP OF METAHUMANS.
BASED ON YOUR DESCRIPTION, I'LL START A SEARCH OF OUR DATABASE. THEY MIGHT ALREADY BE ON FILE.
A GIANT WOMAN AND A GUY MADE OF ENERGY?
KINDA HARD TO MISS.
IT'S FORTUNATE SHE GRABBED YOU.
USE YOUR RING FOR A PARTICULATE SCAN OF YOUR UNIFORM.
WE'RE LOOKING FOR ANYTHING ANOMALOUS.
SHE WAS WEARING GLOVES.

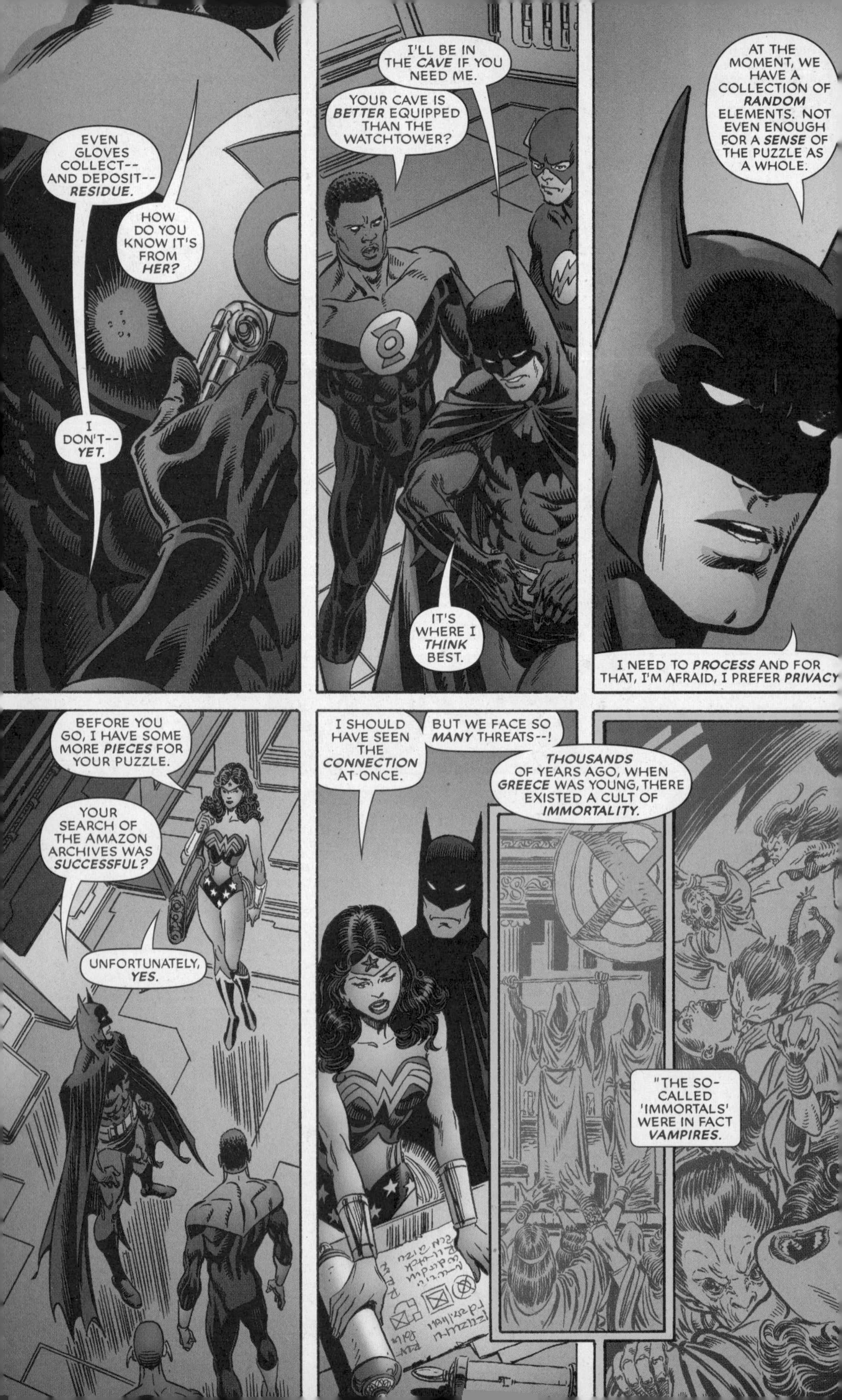

EVEN GLOVES COLLECT-- AND DEPOSIT-- RESIDUE.
HOW DO YOU KNOW IT'S FROM HER?
I DON'T-- YET.
I'LL BE IN THE CAVE IF YOU NEED ME.
YOUR CAVE IS BETTER EQUIPPED THAN THE WATCHTOWER?
IT'S WHERE I THINK BEST.
AT THE MOMENT, WE HAVE A COLLECTION OF RANDOM ELEMENTS. NOT EVEN ENOUGH FOR A SENSE OF THE PUZZLE AS A WHOLE.
I NEED TO PROCESS AND FOR THAT, I'M AFRAID, I PREFER PRIVACY.
BEFORE YOU GO, I HAVE SOME MORE PIECES FOR YOUR PUZZLE.
YOUR SEARCH OF THE AMAZON ARCHIVES WAS SUCCESSFUL?
UNFORTUNATELY, YES.
I SHOULD HAVE SEEN THE CONNECTION AT ONCE.
BUT WE FACE SO MANY THREATS--!
THOUSANDS OF YEARS AGO, WHEN GREECE WAS YOUNG, THERE EXISTED A CULT OF IMMORTALITY.
"THE SO-CALLED 'IMMORTALS' WERE IN FACT VAMPIRES.

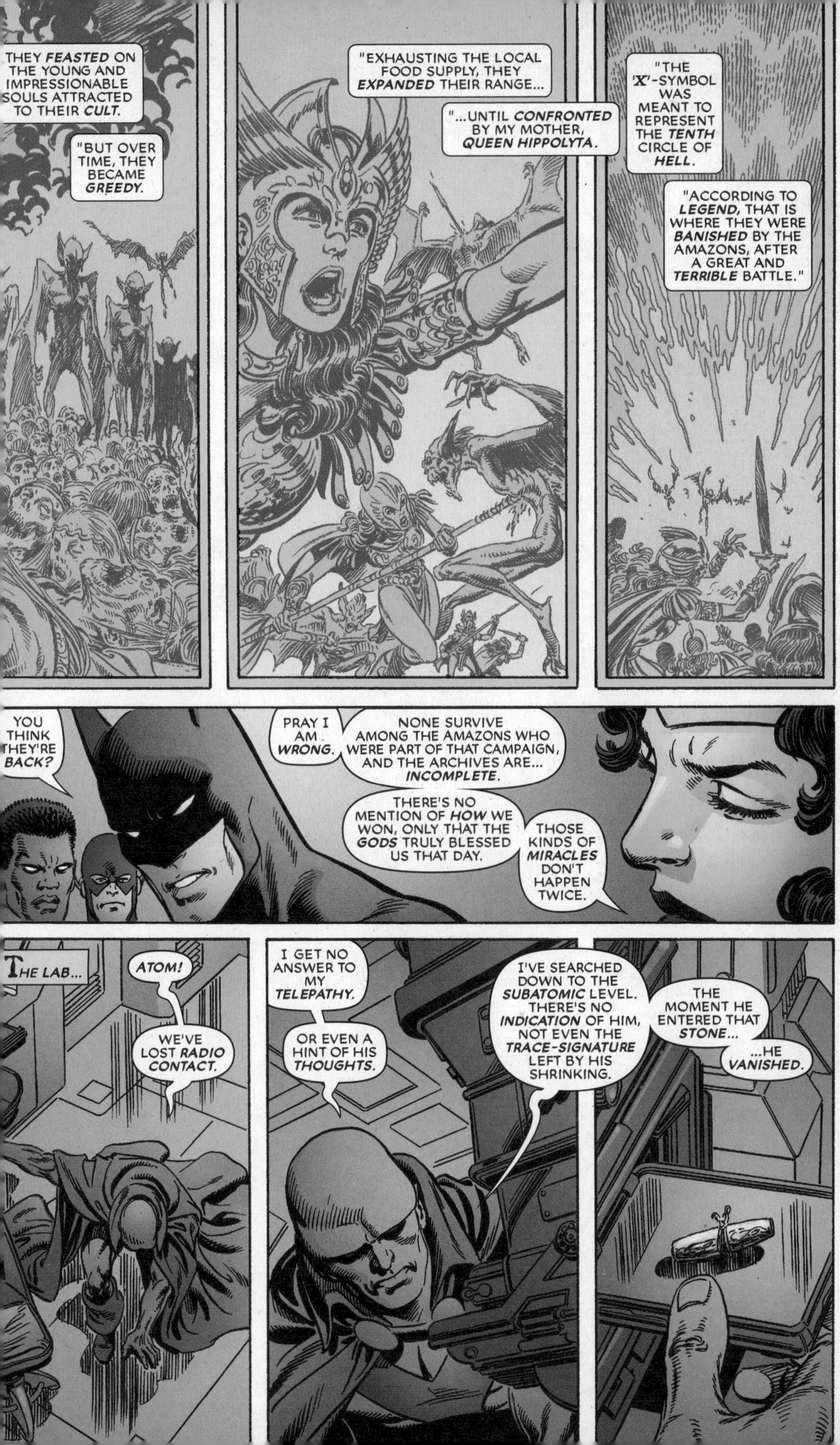

THEY FEASTED ON THE YOUNG AND IMPRESSIONABLE SOULS ATTRACTED TO THEIR CULT.
"BUT OVER TIME, THEY BECAME GREEDY.
"EXHAUSTING THE LOCAL FOOD SUPPLY, THEY EXPANDED THEIR RANGE...
"...UNTIL CONFRONTED BY MY MOTHER, QUEEN HIPPOLYTA.
"THE 'X'-SYMBOL WAS MEANT TO REPRESENT THE TENTH CIRCLE OF HELL.
"ACCORDING TO LEGEND, THAT IS WHERE THEY WERE BANISHED BY THE AMAZONS, AFTER A GREAT AND TERRIBLE BATTLE."
YOU THINK THEY'RE BACK?
PRAY I AM WRONG.
NONE SURVIVE AMONG THE AMAZONS WHO WERE PART OF THAT CAMPAIGN, AND THE ARCHIVES ARE... INCOMPLETE.
THERE'S NO MENTION OF HOW WE WON, ONLY THAT THE GODS TRULY BLESSED US THAT DAY.
THOSE KINDS OF MIRACLES DON'T HAPPEN TWICE.
THE LAB...
ATOM!
WE'VE LOST RADIO CONTACT.
I GET NO ANSWER TO MY TELEPATHY.
OR EVEN A HINT OF HIS THOUGHTS.
I'VE SEARCHED DOWN TO THE SUBATOMIC LEVEL. THERE'S NO INDICATION OF HIM, NOT EVEN THE TRACE-SIGNATURE LEFT BY HIS SHRINKING.
THE MOMENT HE ENTERED THAT STONE...
...HE VANISHED.

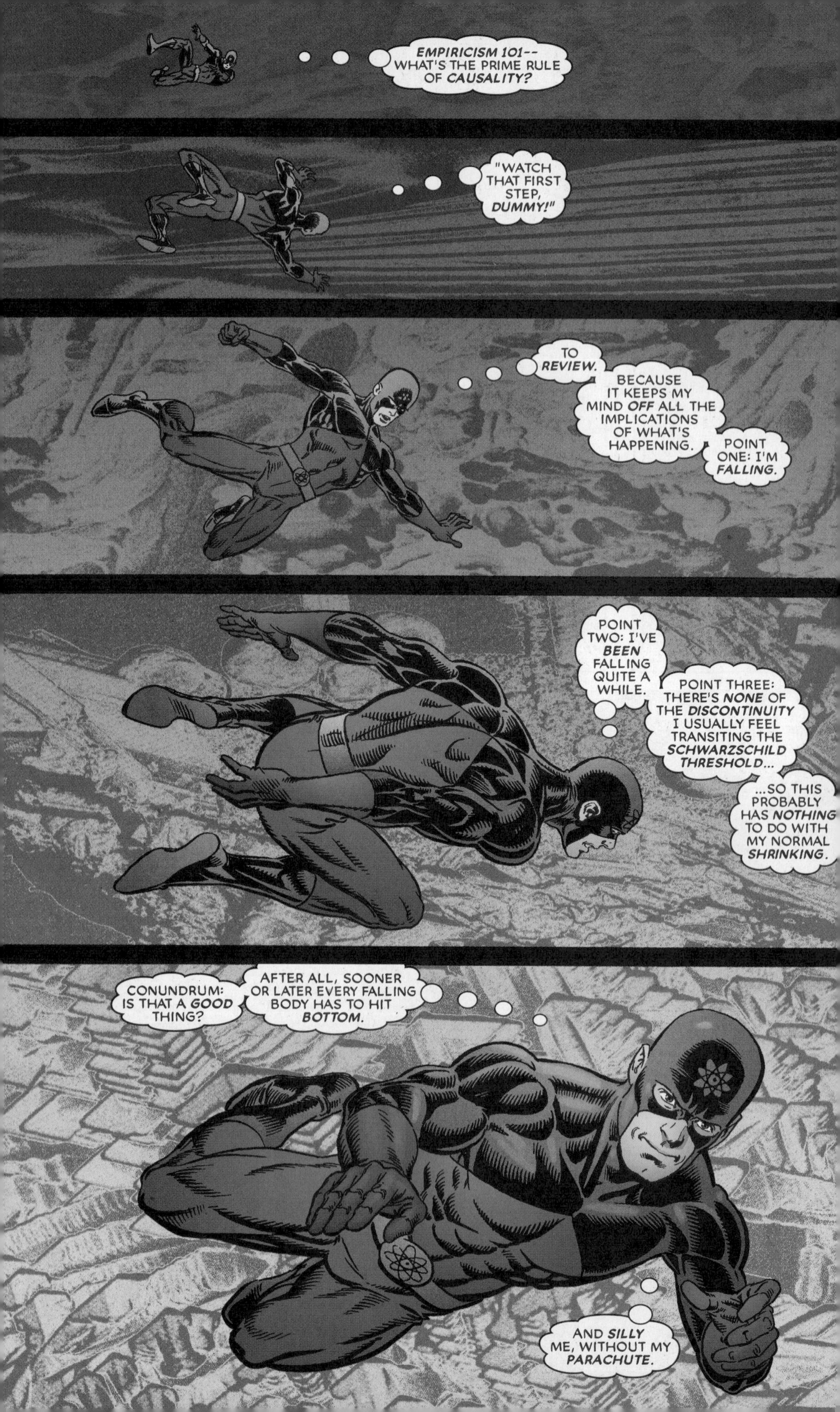
EMPIRICISM 101-- WHAT'S THE PRIME RULE OF CAUSALITY?
"WATCH THAT FIRST STEP, DUMMY!"
TO REVIEW.
BECAUSE IT KEEPS MY MIND OFF ALL THE IMPLICATIONS OF WHAT'S HAPPENING.
POINT ONE: I'M FALLING.
POINT TWO: I'VE BEEN FALLING QUITE A WHILE.
POINT THREE: THERE'S NONE OF THE DISCONTINUITY I USUALLY FEEL TRANSITING THE SCHWARZSCHILD THRESHOLD...
...SO THIS PROBABLY HAS NOTHING TO DO WITH MY NORMAL SHRINKING.
CONUNDRUM: IS THAT A GOOD THING?
AFTER ALL, SOONER OR LATER EVERY FALLING BODY HAS TO HIT BOTTOM.
AND SILLY ME, WITHOUT MY PARACHUTE.

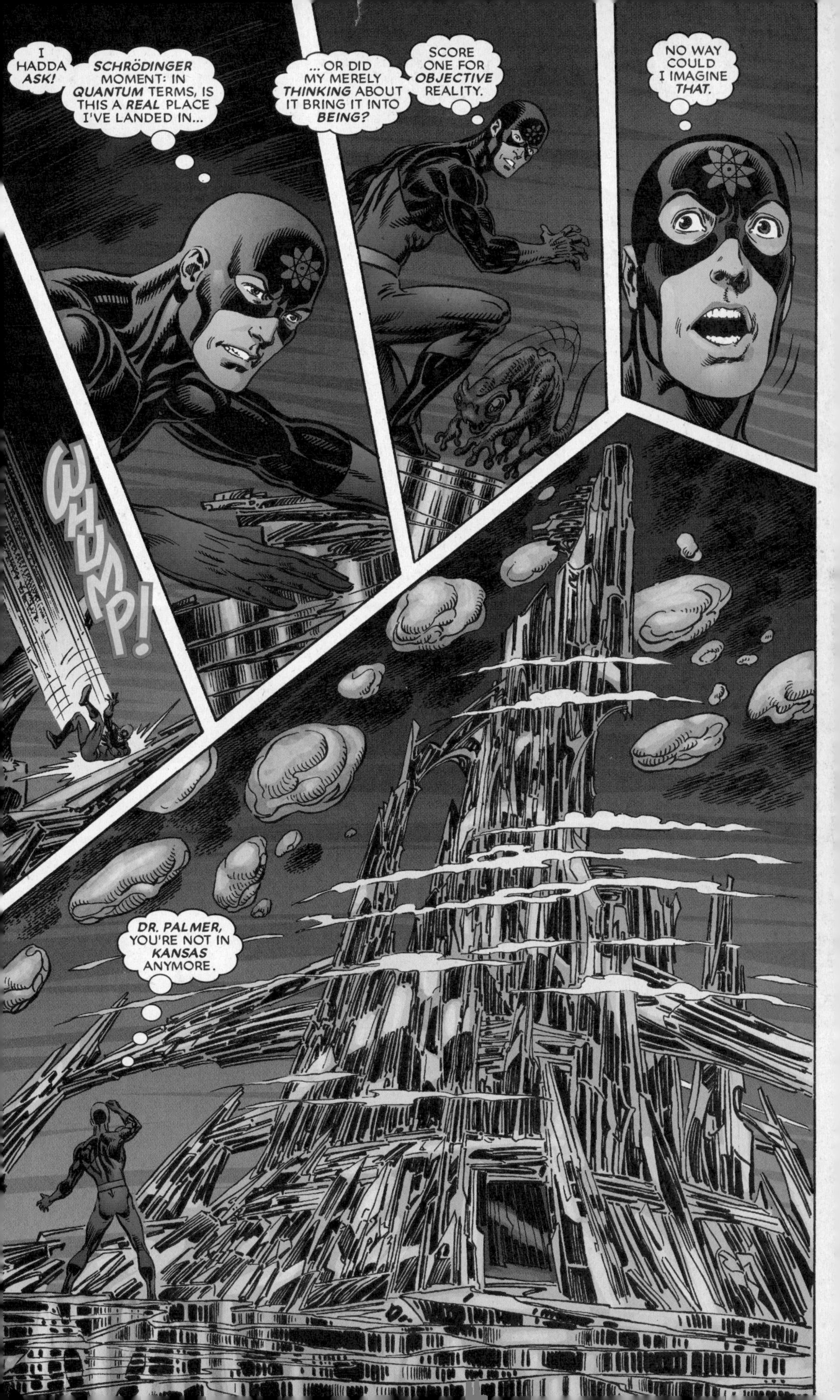
I HADDA ASK!
SCHRÖDINGER MOMENT: IN QUANTUM TERMS, IS THIS A REAL PLACE I'VE LANDED IN...
...OR DID MY MERELY THINKING ABOUT IT BRING IT INTO BEING?
SCORE ONE FOR OBJECTIVE REALITY.
NO WAY COULD I IMAGINE THAT.
WHUMP!
DR. PALMER, YOU'RE NOT IN KANSAS ANYMORE.

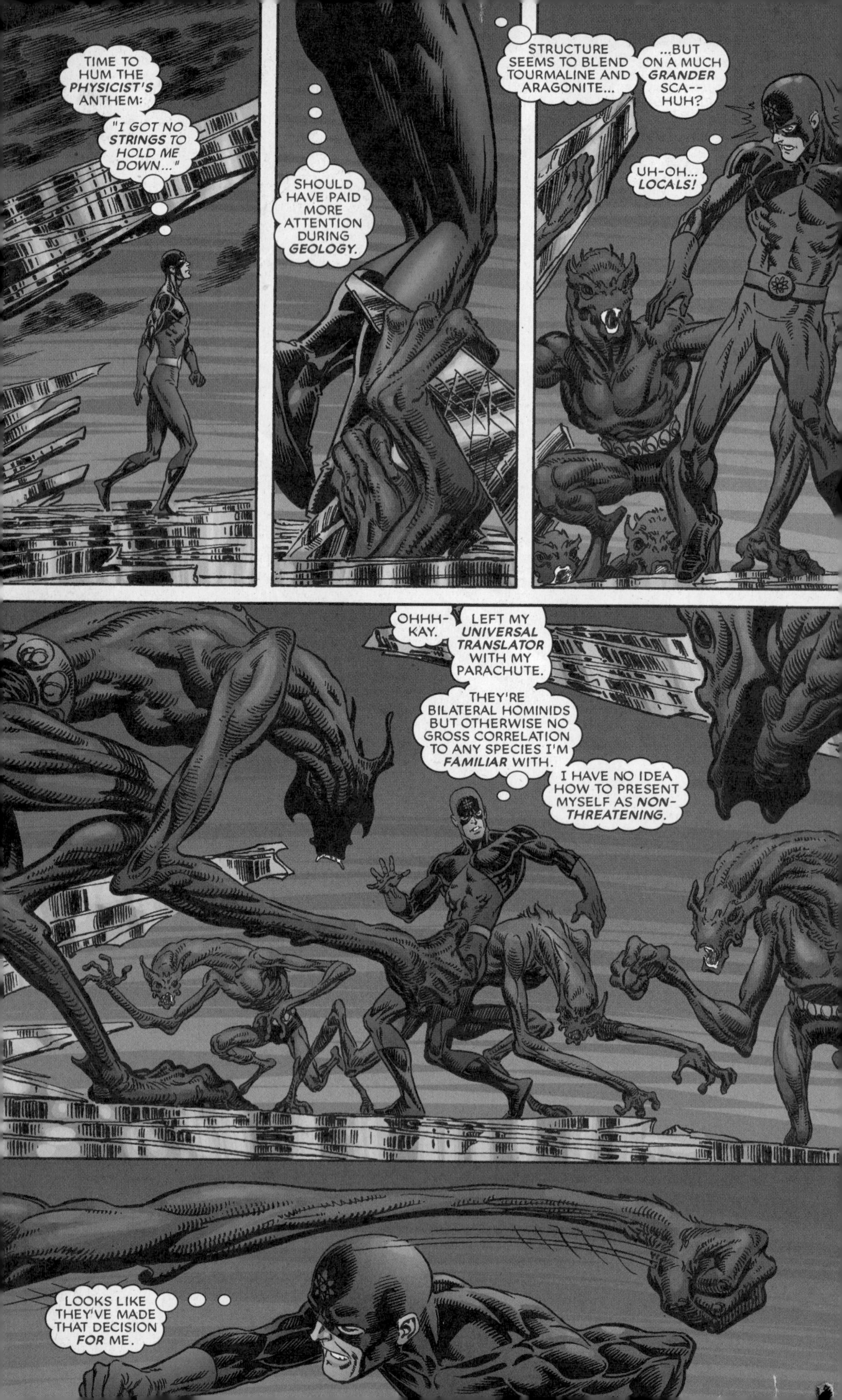
TIME TO HUM THE PHYSICIST'S ANTHEM:
"I GOT NO STRINGS TO HOLD ME DOWN..."
SHOULD HAVE PAID MORE ATTENTION DURING GEOLOGY.
STRUCTURE SEEMS TO BLEND TOURMALINE AND ARAGONITE...
...BUT ON A MUCH GRANDER SCA-- HUH?
UH-OH... LOCALS!
OHHH-KAY.
LEFT MY UNIVERSAL TRANSLATOR WITH MY PARACHUTE.
THEY'RE BILATERAL HOMINIDS BUT OTHERWISE NO GROSS CORRELATION TO ANY SPECIES I'M FAMILIAR WITH.
I HAVE NO IDEA HOW TO PRESENT MYSELF AS NON-THREATENING.
LOOKS LIKE THEY'VE MADE THAT DECISION FOR ME.

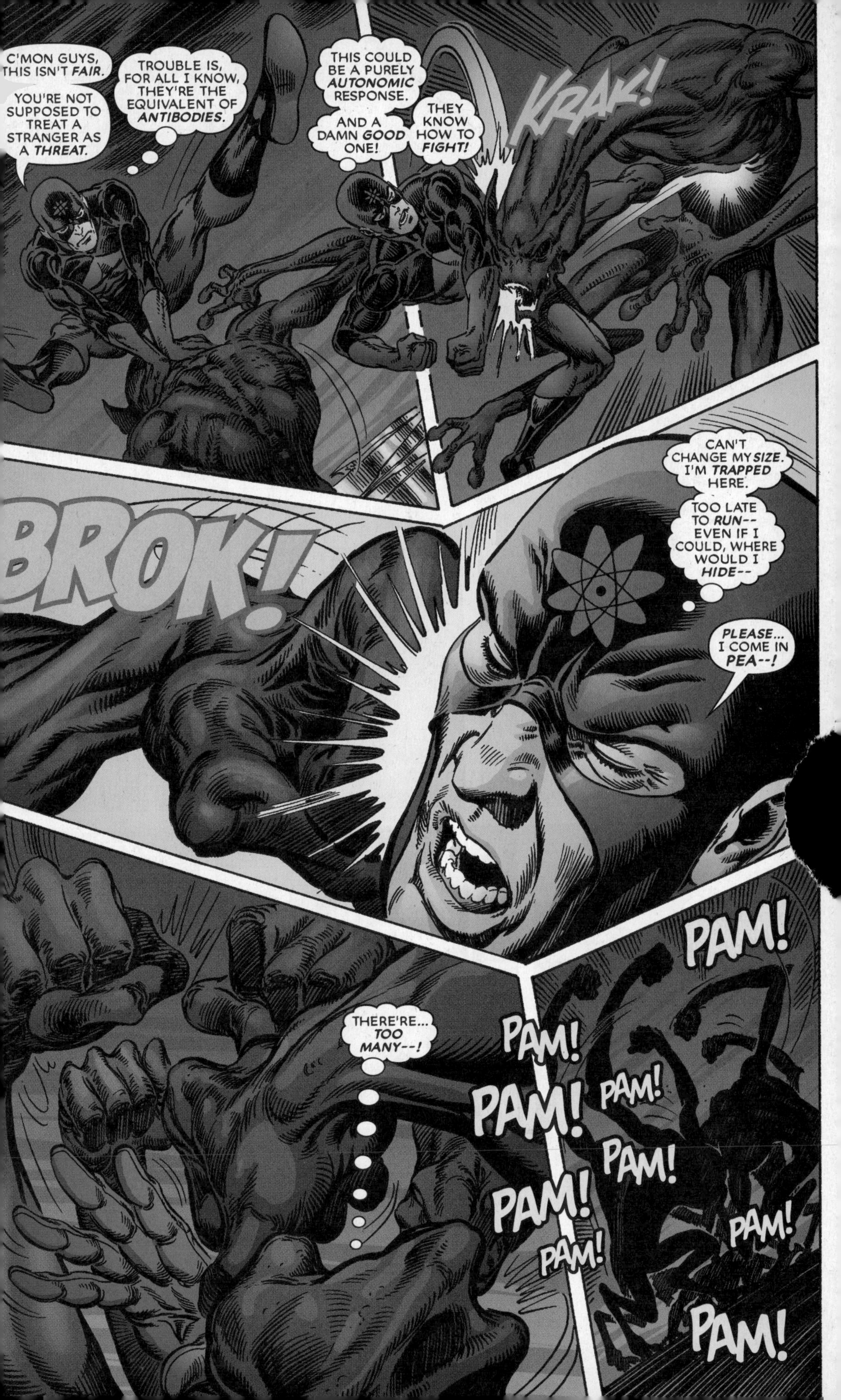
C'MON GUYS, THIS ISN'T FAIR.
YOU'RE NOT SUPPOSED TO TREAT A STRANGER AS A THREAT.
TROUBLE IS, FOR ALL I KNOW, THEY'RE THE EQUIVALENT OF ANTIBODIES.
THIS COULD BE A PURELY AUTONOMIC RESPONSE.
AND A DAMN GOOD ONE!
THEY KNOW HOW TO FIGHT!
KRAK!
CAN'T CHANGE MY SIZE. I'M TRAPPED HERE.
TOO LATE TO RUN-- EVEN IF I COULD, WHERE WOULD I HIDE--
BROK!
PLEASE... I COME IN PEA--!
PAM!
THERE'RE... TOO MANY--!
PAM!
PAM!
PAM!
PAM!
PAM!
PAM!
PAM!
PAM!

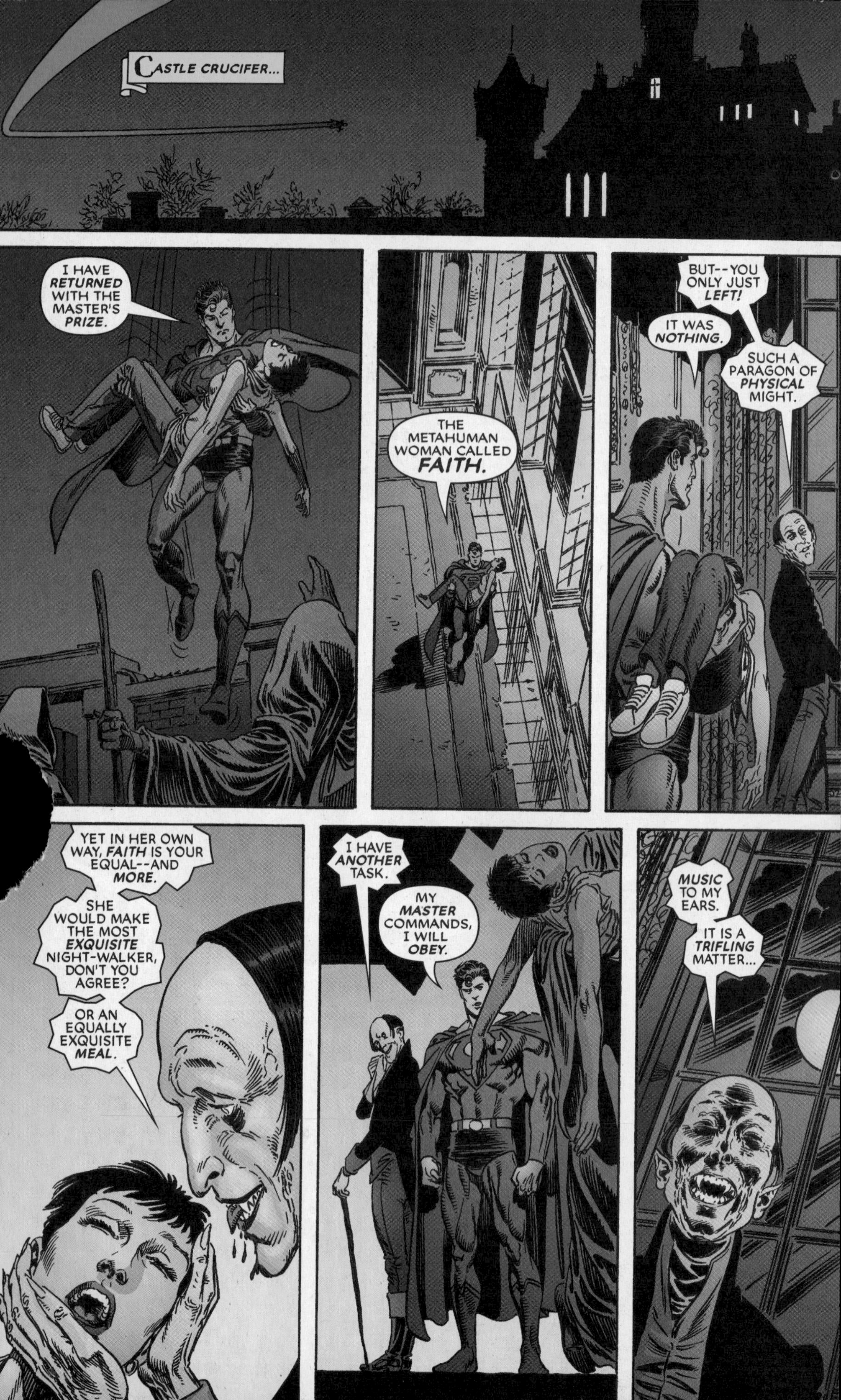
CASTLE CRUCIFER...
I HAVE RETURNED WITH THE MASTER'S PRIZE.
THE METAHUMAN WOMAN CALLED FAITH.
BUT--YOU ONLY JUST LEFT!
IT WAS NOTHING.
SUCH A PARAGON OF PHYSICAL MIGHT.
YET IN HER OWN WAY, FAITH IS YOUR EQUAL--AND MORE.
SHE WOULD MAKE THE MOST EXQUISITE NIGHT-WALKER, DON'T YOU AGREE?
OR AN EQUALLY EXQUISITE MEAL.
I HAVE ANOTHER TASK.
MY MASTER COMMANDS, I WILL OBEY.
MUSIC TO MY EARS.
IT IS A TRIFLING MATTER...

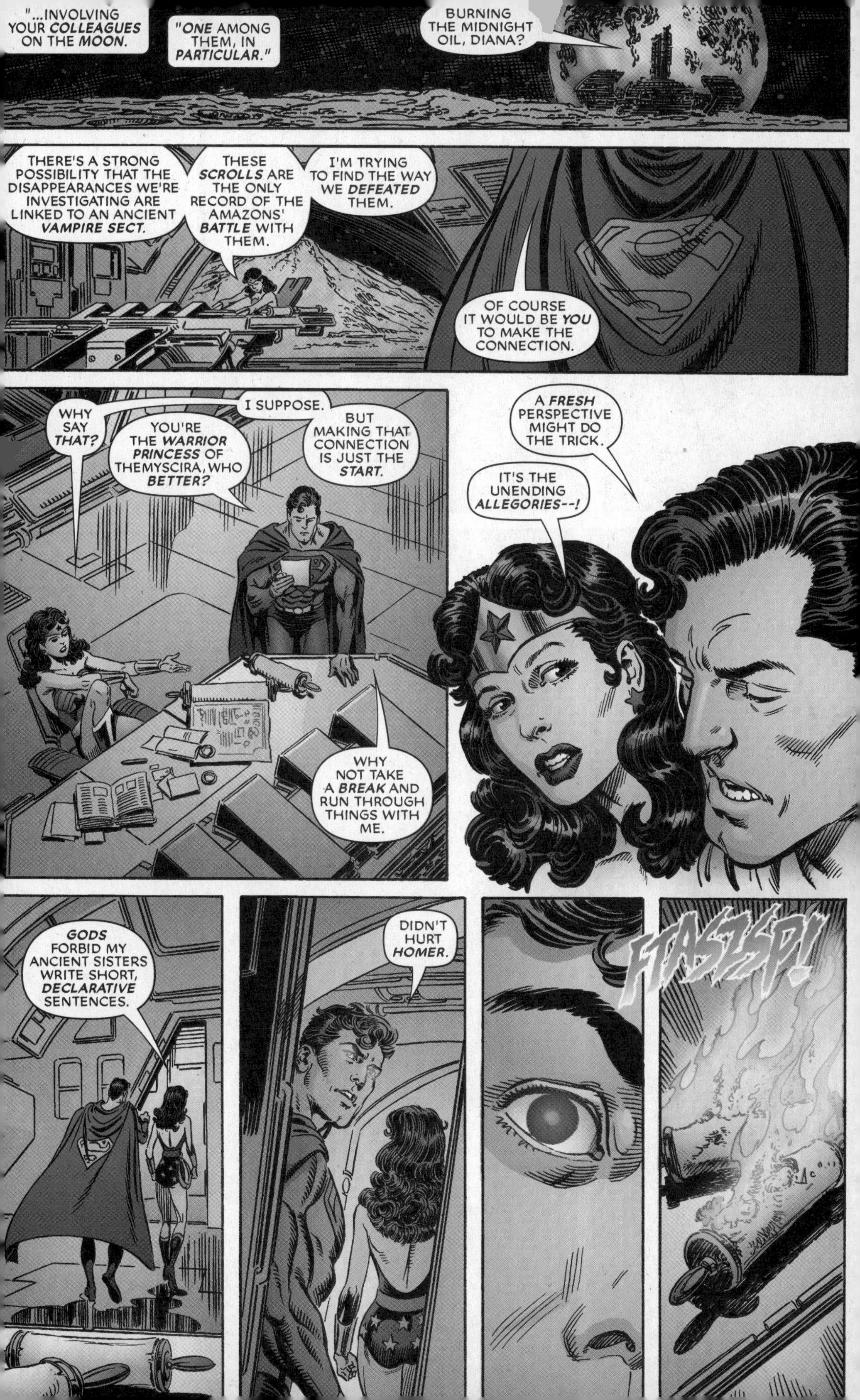
"...INVOLVING YOUR COLLEAGUES ON THE MOON.
"ONE AMONG THEM, IN PARTICULAR."
BURNING THE MIDNIGHT OIL, DIANA?
THERE'S A STRONG POSSIBILITY THAT THE DISAPPEARANCES WE'RE INVESTIGATING ARE LINKED TO AN ANCIENT VAMPIRE SECT.
THESE SCROLLS ARE THE ONLY RECORD OF THE AMAZONS' BATTLE WITH THEM.
I'M TRYING TO FIND THE WAY WE DEFEATED THEM.
OF COURSE IT WOULD BE YOU TO MAKE THE CONNECTION.
WHY SAY THAT?
YOU'RE THE WARRIOR PRINCESS OF THEMYSCIRA, WHO BETTER?
I SUPPOSE.
BUT MAKING THAT CONNECTION IS JUST THE START.
WHY NOT TAKE A BREAK AND RUN THROUGH THINGS WITH ME.
IT'S THE UNENDING ALLEGORIES--!
A FRESH PERSPECTIVE MIGHT DO THE TRICK.
GODS FORBID MY ANCIENT SISTERS WRITE SHORT, DECLARATIVE SENTENCES.
DIDN'T HURT HOMER.
FTASZSP!

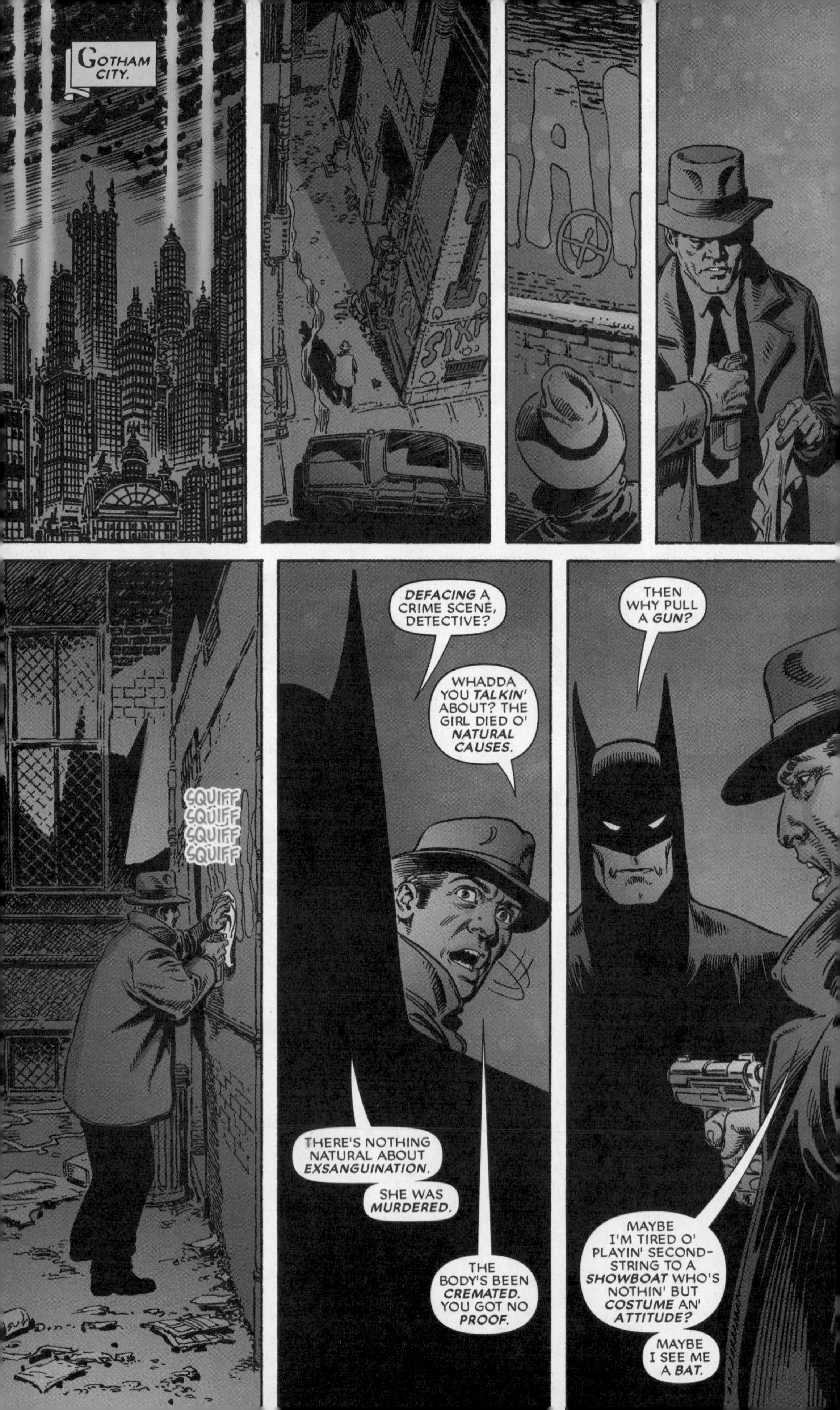
GOTHAM CITY.
SQUIFF SQUIFF SQUIFF SQUIFF
DEFACING A CRIME SCENE, DETECTIVE?
WHADDA YOU TALKIN' ABOUT? THE GIRL DIED O' NATURAL CAUSES.
THERE'S NOTHING NATURAL ABOUT EXSANGUINATION.
SHE WAS MURDERED.
THE BODY'S BEEN CREMATED. YOU GOT NO PROOF.
THEN WHY PULL A GUN?
MAYBE I'M TIRED O' PLAYIN' SECOND-STRING TO A SHOWBOAT WHO'S NOTHIN' BUT COSTUME AN' ATTITUDE?
MAYBE I SEE ME A BAT.

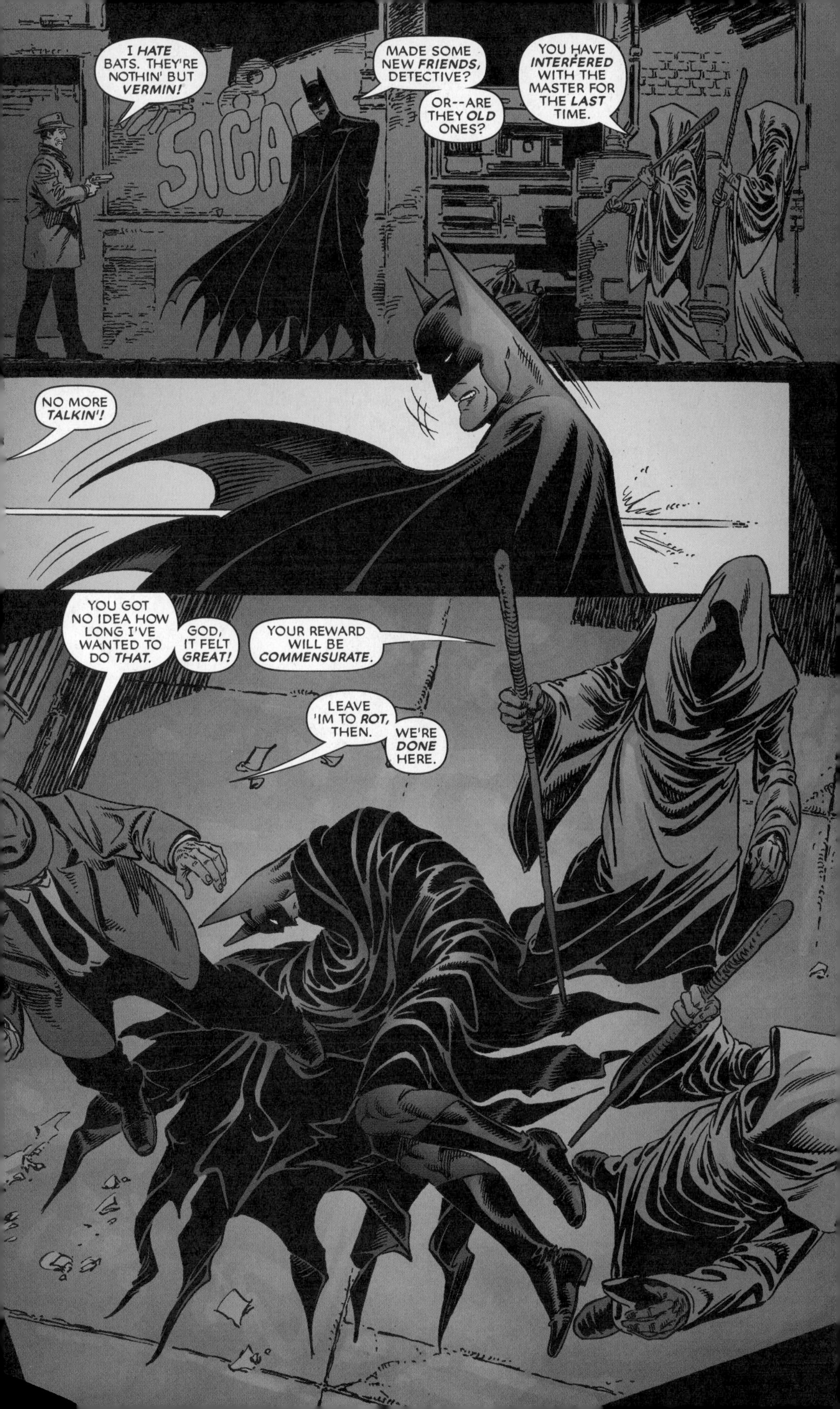
I HATE BATS. THEY'RE NOTHIN' BUT VERMIN!
MADE SOME NEW FRIENDS, DETECTIVE?
OR--ARE THEY OLD ONES?
YOU HAVE INTERFERED WITH THE MASTER FOR THE LAST TIME.
NO MORE TALKIN'!
YOU GOT NO IDEA HOW LONG I'VE WANTED TO DO THAT.
GOD, IT FELT GREAT!
YOUR REWARD WILL BE COMMENSURATE.
LEAVE 'IM TO ROT, THEN.
WE'RE DONE HERE.

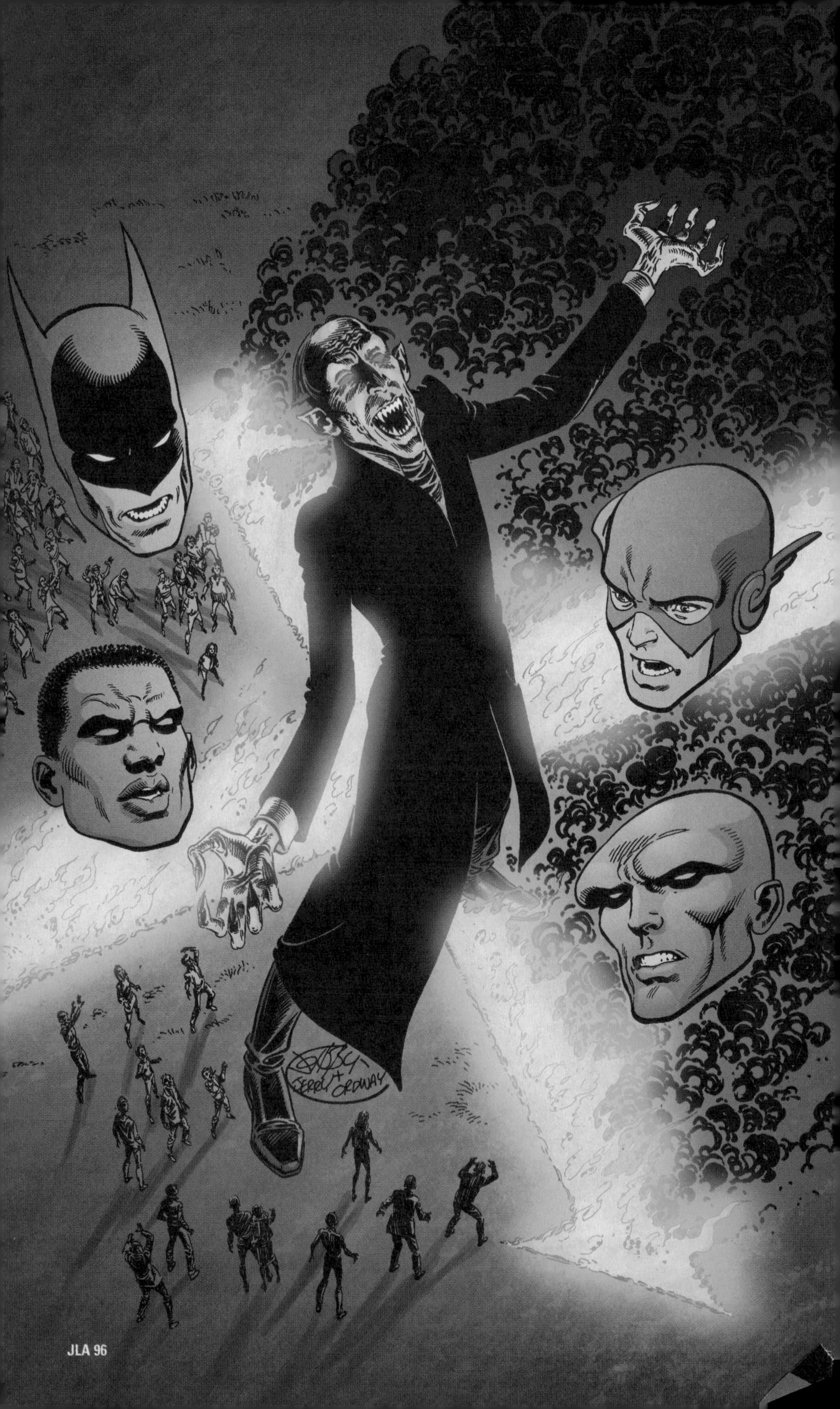

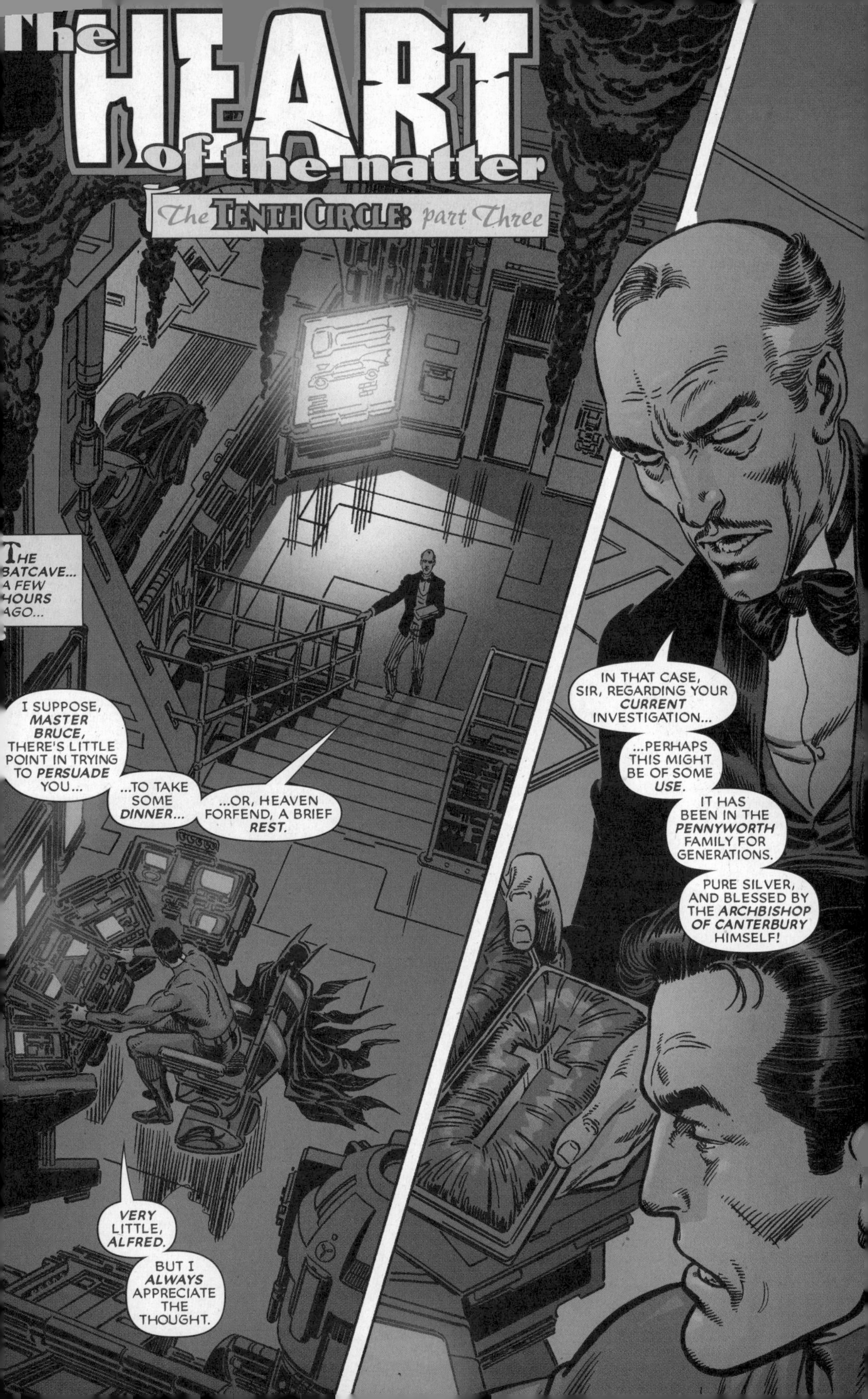
The HEART of the matter
The TENTH CIRCLE: part Three
THE BATCAVE... A FEW HOURS AGO...
I SUPPOSE, MASTER BRUCE, THERE'S LITTLE POINT IN TRYING TO PERSUADE YOU...
...TO TAKE SOME DINNER...
...OR, HEAVEN FORFEND, A BRIEF REST.
VERY LITTLE, ALFRED.
BUT I ALWAYS APPRECIATE THE THOUGHT.
IN THAT CASE, SIR, REGARDING YOUR CURRENT INVESTIGATION...
...PERHAPS THIS MIGHT BE OF SOME USE.
IT HAS BEEN IN THE PENNYWORTH FAMILY FOR GENERATIONS.
PURE SILVER, AND BLESSED BY THE ARCHBISHOP OF CANTERBURY HIMSELF!

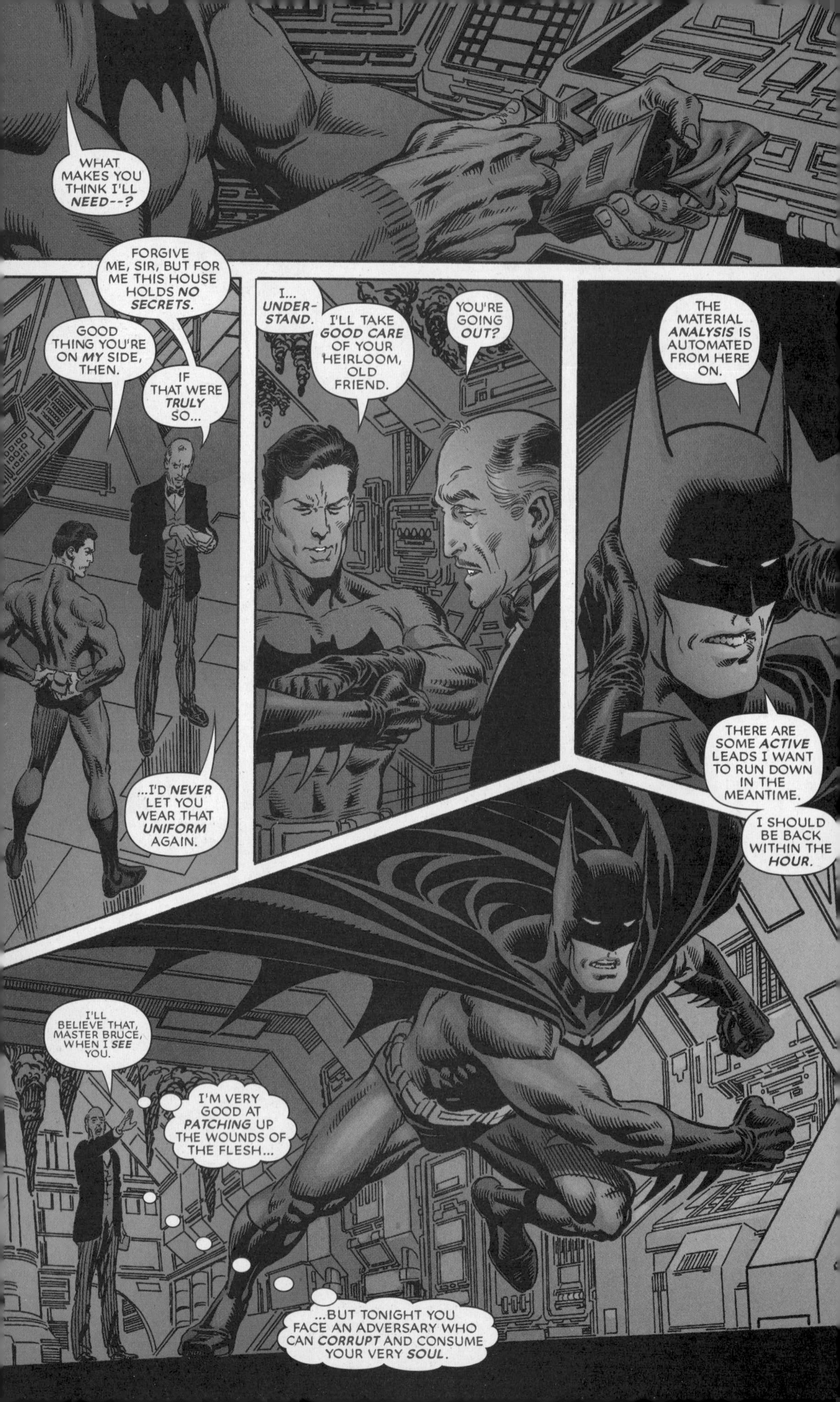

WHAT MAKES YOU THINK I'LL NEED--?
FORGIVE ME, SIR, BUT FOR ME THIS HOUSE HOLDS NO SECRETS.
GOOD THING YOU'RE ON MY SIDE, THEN.
IF THAT WERE TRULY SO...
...I'D NEVER LET YOU WEAR THAT UNIFORM AGAIN.
I... UNDER-STAND.
I'LL TAKE GOOD CARE OF YOUR HEIRLOOM, OLD FRIEND.
YOU'RE GOING OUT?
THE MATERIAL ANALYSIS IS AUTOMATED FROM HERE ON.
THERE ARE SOME ACTIVE LEADS I WANT TO RUN DOWN IN THE MEANTIME.
I SHOULD BE BACK WITHIN THE HOUR.
I'LL BELIEVE THAT, MASTER BRUCE, WHEN I SEE YOU.
I'M VERY GOOD AT PATCHING UP THE WOUNDS OF THE FLESH...
...BUT TONIGHT YOU FACE AN ADVERSARY WHO CAN CORRUPT AND CONSUME YOUR VERY SOUL.

JLA WATCHTOWER... THE MOON...

MANHUNTER?!?

HEY, J'ONN, YOU OKAY, BIG GUY?

LANTERN, ALERT THE OTHERS, MARTIAN MANHUNTER'S BEEN--!

FLASH-- SLOW DOWN!

SOMETIMES, MY FRIEND, YOUR MOUTH MOVES FASTER THAN YOUR FEET!

I HAVE NOT BEEN ATTACKED.

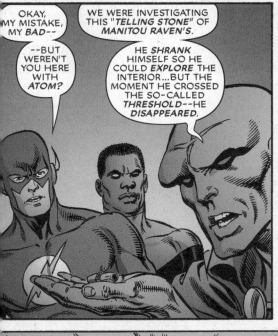

OKAY, MY MISTAKE, MY BAD--

--BUT WEREN'T YOU HERE WITH ATOM?

WE WERE INVESTIGATING THIS "TELLING STONE" OF MANITOU RAVEN'S.

HE SHRANK HIMSELF SO HE COULD EXPLORE THE INTERIOR...BUT THE MOMENT HE CROSSED THE SO-CALLED THRESHOLD--HE DISAPPEARED.

I HAVE BEEN UNABLE TO FIND HIM, EITHER WITH MY PHYSICAL OR TELEPATHIC ABILITIES.

MAYBE MY POWER RING CAN HELP?

HMMMM...NOT A TRACE OF HIM. BUT THAT ISN'T POSSIBLE.

WHERE COULD HE HAVE GONE?

Oohhhh

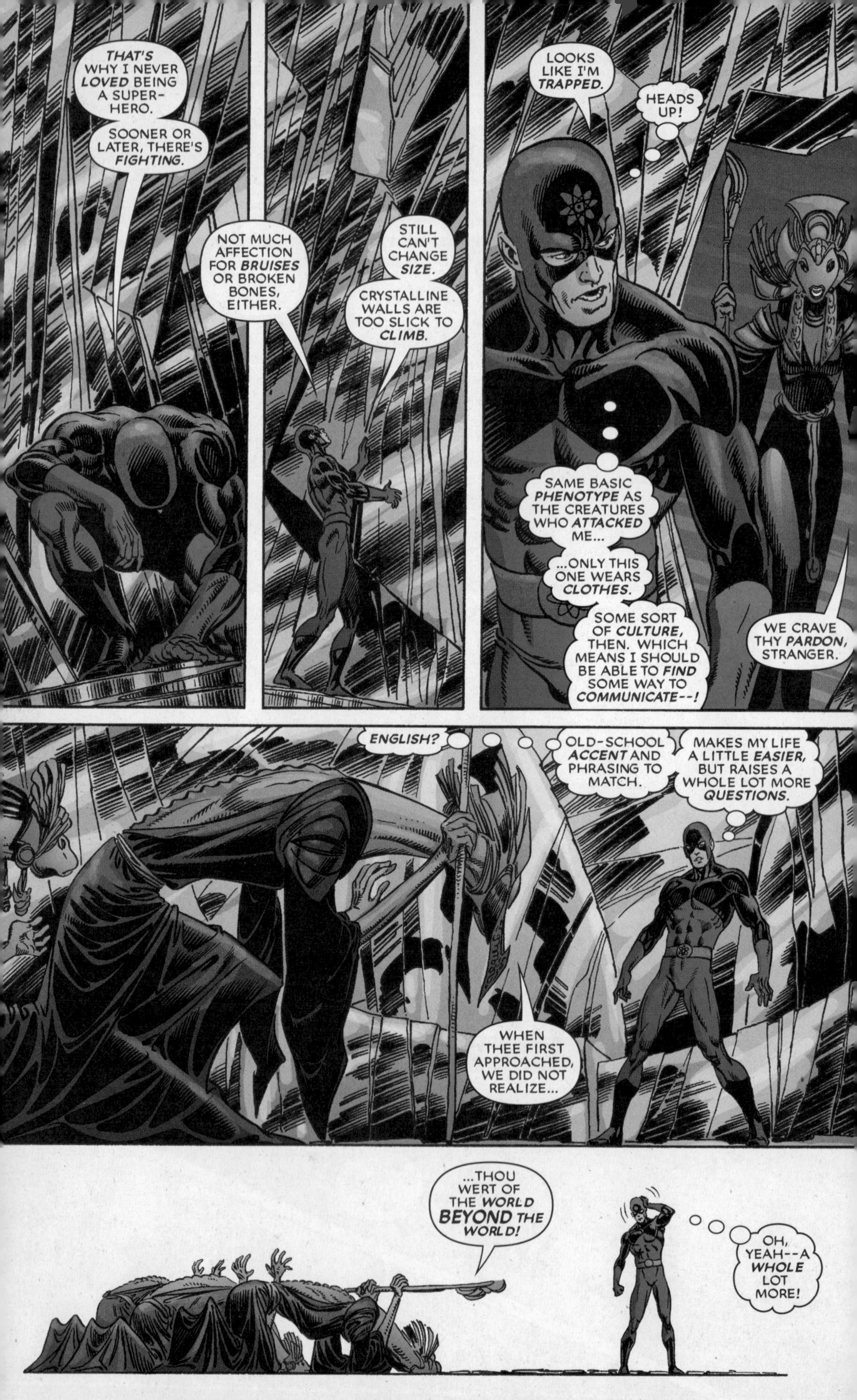
THAT'S WHY I NEVER LOVED BEING A SUPER-HERO.
SOONER OR LATER, THERE'S FIGHTING.
NOT MUCH AFFECTION FOR BRUISES OR BROKEN BONES, EITHER.
STILL CAN'T CHANGE SIZE.
CRYSTALLINE WALLS ARE TOO SLICK TO CLIMB.
LOOKS LIKE I'M TRAPPED.
HEADS UP!
SAME BASIC PHENOTYPE AS THE CREATURES WHO ATTACKED ME...
...ONLY THIS ONE WEARS CLOTHES.
SOME SORT OF CULTURE, THEN. WHICH MEANS I SHOULD BE ABLE TO FIND SOME WAY TO COMMUNICATE--!
WE CRAVE THY PARDON, STRANGER.
ENGLISH?
OLD-SCHOOL ACCENT AND PHRASING TO MATCH.
MAKES MY LIFE A LITTLE EASIER, BUT RAISES A WHOLE LOT MORE QUESTIONS.
WHEN THEE FIRST APPROACHED, WE DID NOT REALIZE...
...THOU WERT OF THE WORLD BEYOND THE WORLD!
OH, YEAH--A WHOLE LOT MORE!

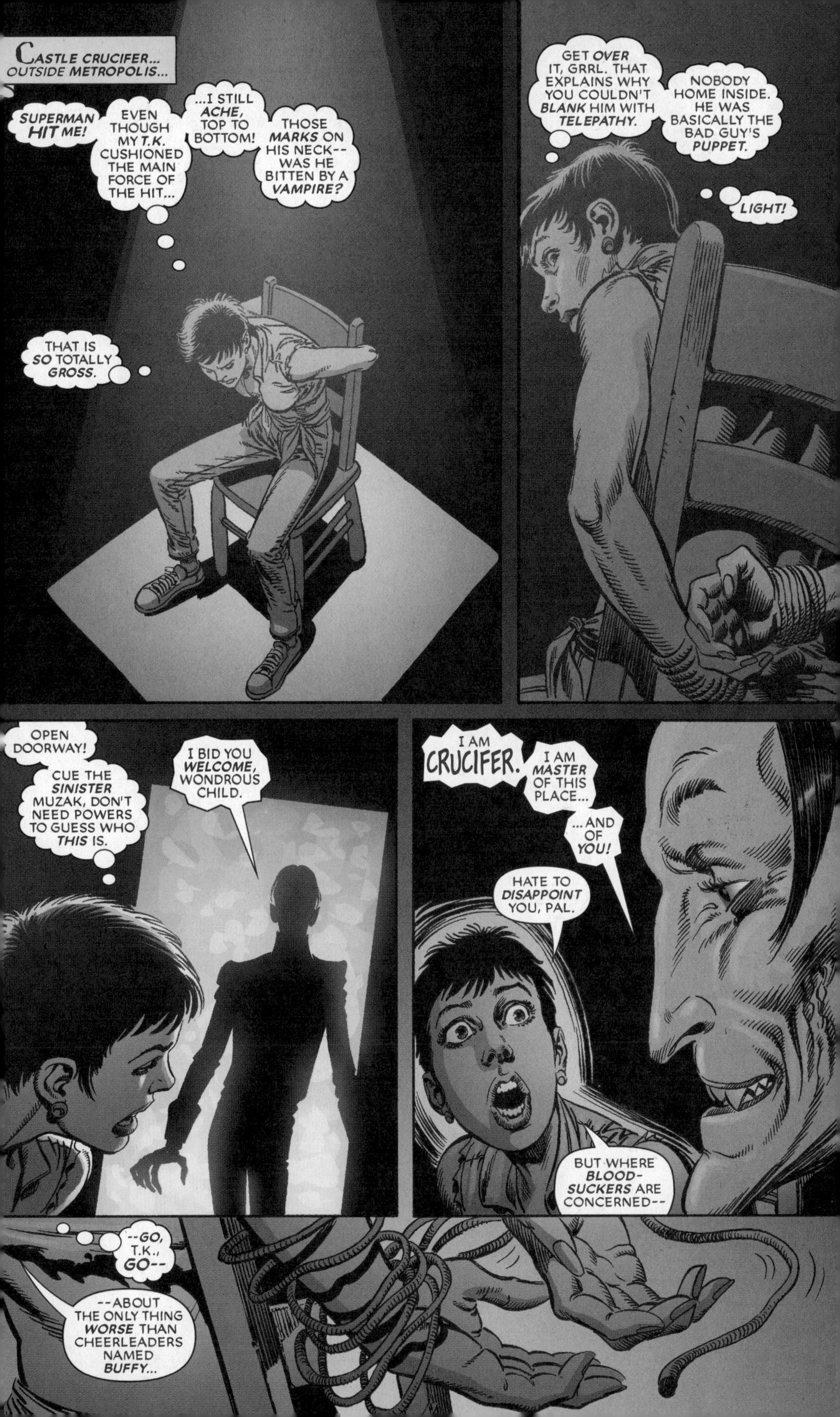

CASTLE CRUCIFER... OUTSIDE METROPOLIS...
SUPERMAN HIT ME!
EVEN THOUGH MY T.K. CUSHIONED THE MAIN FORCE OF THE HIT...
...I STILL ACHE, TOP TO BOTTOM!
THOSE MARKS ON HIS NECK--WAS HE BITTEN BY A VAMPIRE?
THAT IS SO TOTALLY GROSS.
GET OVER IT, GRRL. THAT EXPLAINS WHY YOU COULDN'T BLANK HIM WITH TELEPATHY.
NOBODY HOME INSIDE. HE WAS BASICALLY THE BAD GUY'S PUPPET.
LIGHT!
OPEN DOORWAY!
CUE THE SINISTER MUZAK, DON'T NEED POWERS TO GUESS WHO THIS IS.
I BID YOU WELCOME, WONDROUS CHILD.
I AM CRUCIFER.
I AM MASTER OF THIS PLACE...
...AND OF YOU!
HATE TO DISAPPOINT YOU, PAL.
BUT WHERE BLOOD-SUCKERS ARE CONCERNED--
--GO, T.K., GO--
--ABOUT THE ONLY THING WORSE THAN CHEERLEADERS NAMED BUFFY...

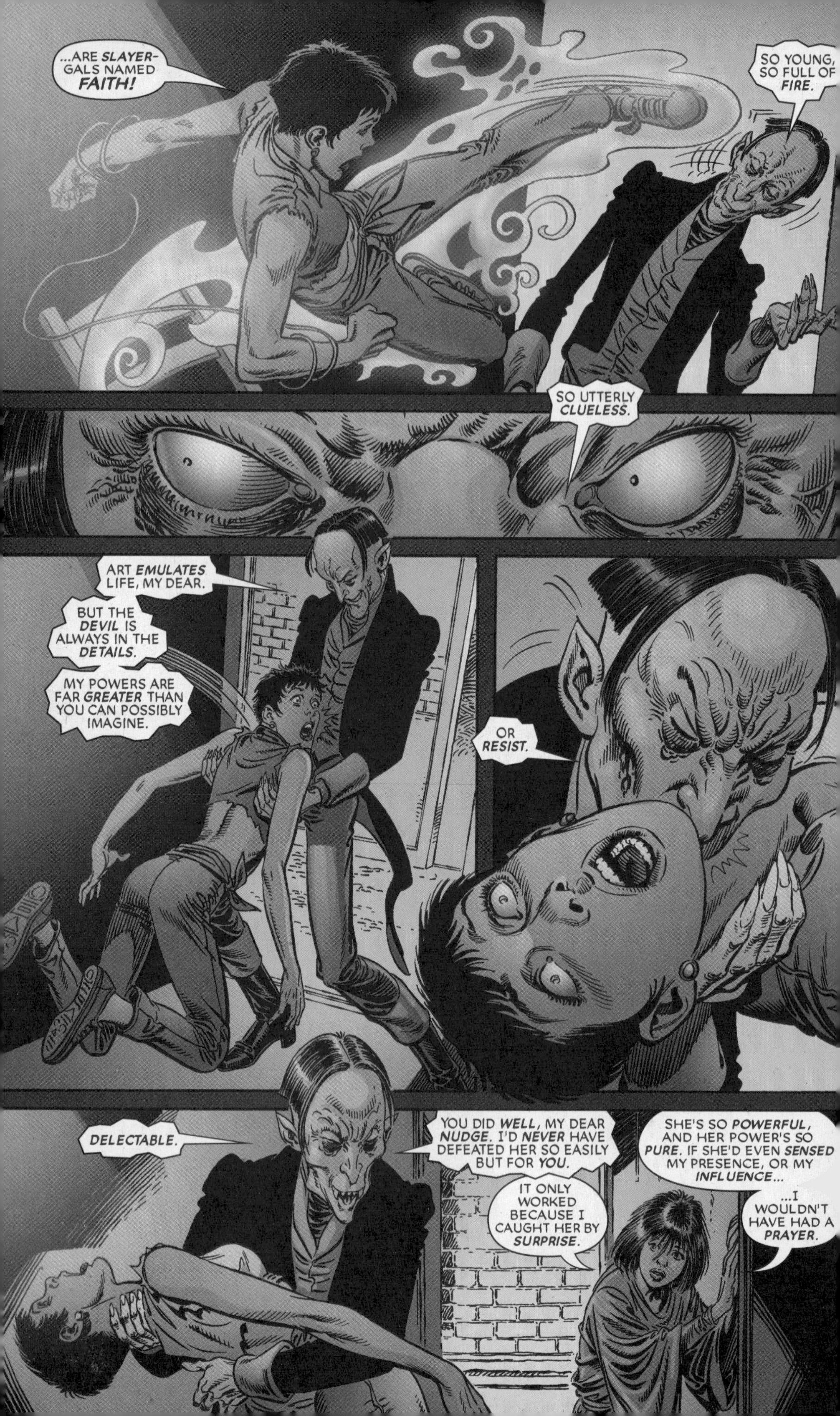

...ARE SLAYER-GALS NAMED FAITH!
SO YOUNG, SO FULL OF FIRE.
SO UTTERLY CLUELESS.
ART EMULATES LIFE, MY DEAR.
BUT THE DEVIL IS ALWAYS IN THE DETAILS.
MY POWERS ARE FAR GREATER THAN YOU CAN POSSIBLY IMAGINE.
OR RESIST.
DELECTABLE.
YOU DID WELL, MY DEAR NUDGE. I'D NEVER HAVE DEFEATED HER SO EASILY BUT FOR YOU.
IT ONLY WORKED BECAUSE I CAUGHT HER BY SURPRISE.
SHE'S SO POWERFUL, AND HER POWER'S SO PURE. IF SHE'D EVEN SENSED MY PRESENCE, OR MY INFLUENCE...
...I WOULDN'T HAVE HAD A PRAYER.

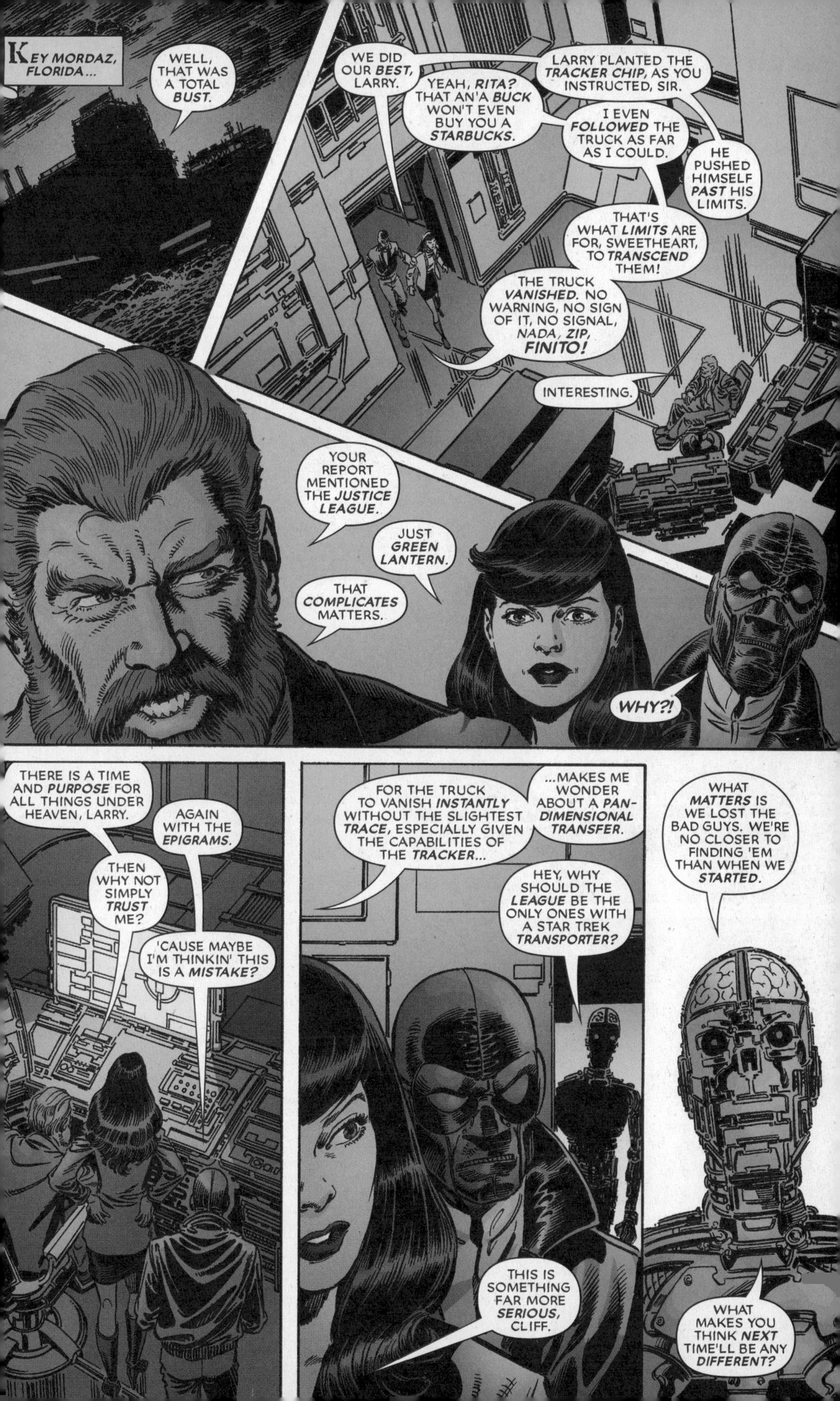
KEY MORDAZ, FLORIDA...
WELL, THAT WAS A TOTAL BUST.
WE DID OUR BEST, LARRY.
YEAH, RITA? THAT AN'A BUCK WON'T EVEN BUY YOU A STARBUCKS.
LARRY PLANTED THE TRACKER CHIP, AS YOU INSTRUCTED, SIR.
I EVEN FOLLOWED THE TRUCK AS FAR AS I COULD.
HE PUSHED HIMSELF PAST HIS LIMITS.
THAT'S WHAT LIMITS ARE FOR, SWEETHEART, TO TRANSCEND THEM!
THE TRUCK VANISHED. NO WARNING, NO SIGN OF IT, NO SIGNAL, NADA, ZIP, FINITO!
INTERESTING.
YOUR REPORT MENTIONED THE JUSTICE LEAGUE.
JUST GREEN LANTERN.
THAT COMPLICATES MATTERS.
WHY?!
THERE IS A TIME AND PURPOSE FOR ALL THINGS UNDER HEAVEN, LARRY.
AGAIN WITH THE EPIGRAMS.
THEN WHY NOT SIMPLY TRUST ME?
'CAUSE MAYBE I'M THINKIN' THIS IS A MISTAKE?
FOR THE TRUCK TO VANISH INSTANTLY WITHOUT THE SLIGHTEST TRACE, ESPECIALLY GIVEN THE CAPABILITIES OF THE TRACKER...
...MAKES ME WONDER ABOUT A PAN-DIMENSIONAL TRANSFER.
HEY, WHY SHOULD THE LEAGUE BE THE ONLY ONES WITH A STAR TREK TRANSPORTER?
THIS IS SOMETHING FAR MORE SERIOUS, CLIFF.
WHAT MATTERS IS WE LOST THE BAD GUYS. WE'RE NO CLOSER TO FINDING 'EM THAN WHEN WE STARTED.
WHAT MAKES YOU THINK NEXT TIME'LL BE ANY DIFFERENT?

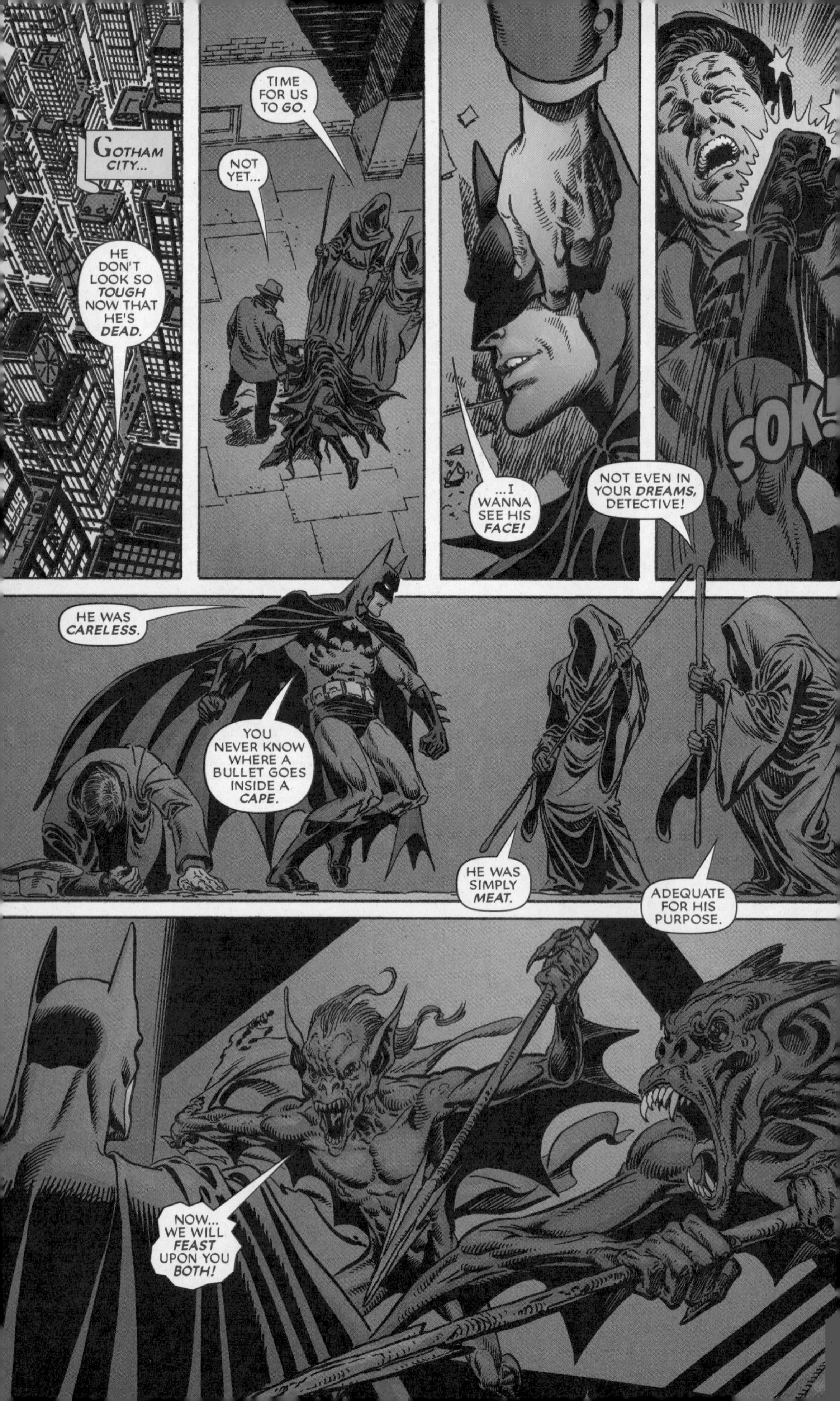

GOTHAM CITY...
HE DON'T LOOK SO TOUGH NOW THAT HE'S DEAD.
TIME FOR US TO GO.
NOT YET...
...I WANNA SEE HIS FACE!
NOT EVEN IN YOUR DREAMS, DETECTIVE!
SOK!
HE WAS CARELESS.
YOU NEVER KNOW WHERE A BULLET GOES INSIDE A CAPE.
HE WAS SIMPLY MEAT.
ADEQUATE FOR HIS PURPOSE.
NOW... WE WILL FEAST UPON YOU BOTH!

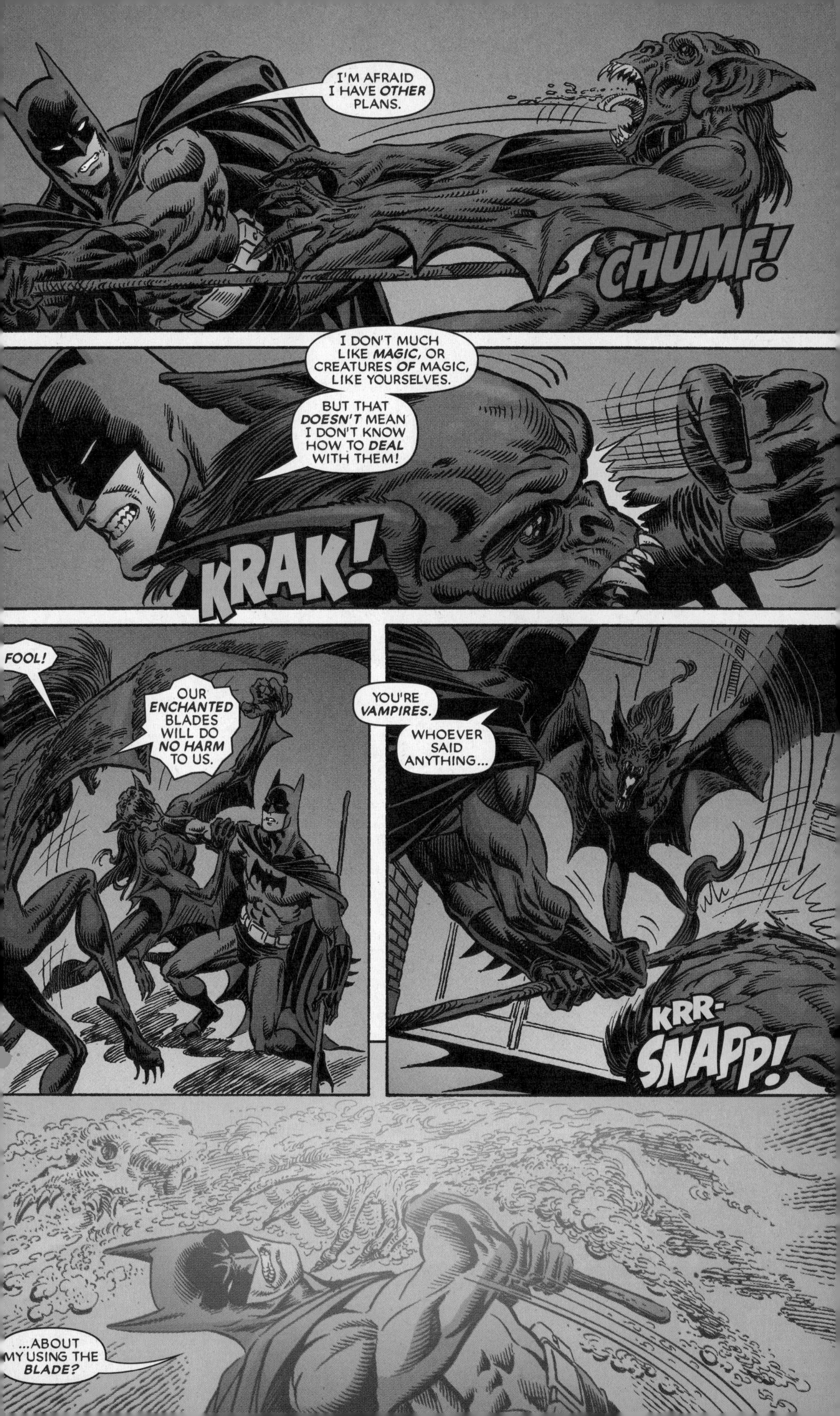
I'M AFRAID I HAVE OTHER PLANS.
CHUMF!
I DON'T MUCH LIKE MAGIC, OR CREATURES OF MAGIC, LIKE YOURSELVES.
BUT THAT DOESN'T MEAN I DON'T KNOW HOW TO DEAL WITH THEM!
KRAK!
FOOL!
OUR ENCHANTED BLADES WILL DO NO HARM TO US.
YOU'RE VAMPIRES.
WHOEVER SAID ANYTHING...
KRR-SNAPP!
...ABOUT MY USING THE BLADE?

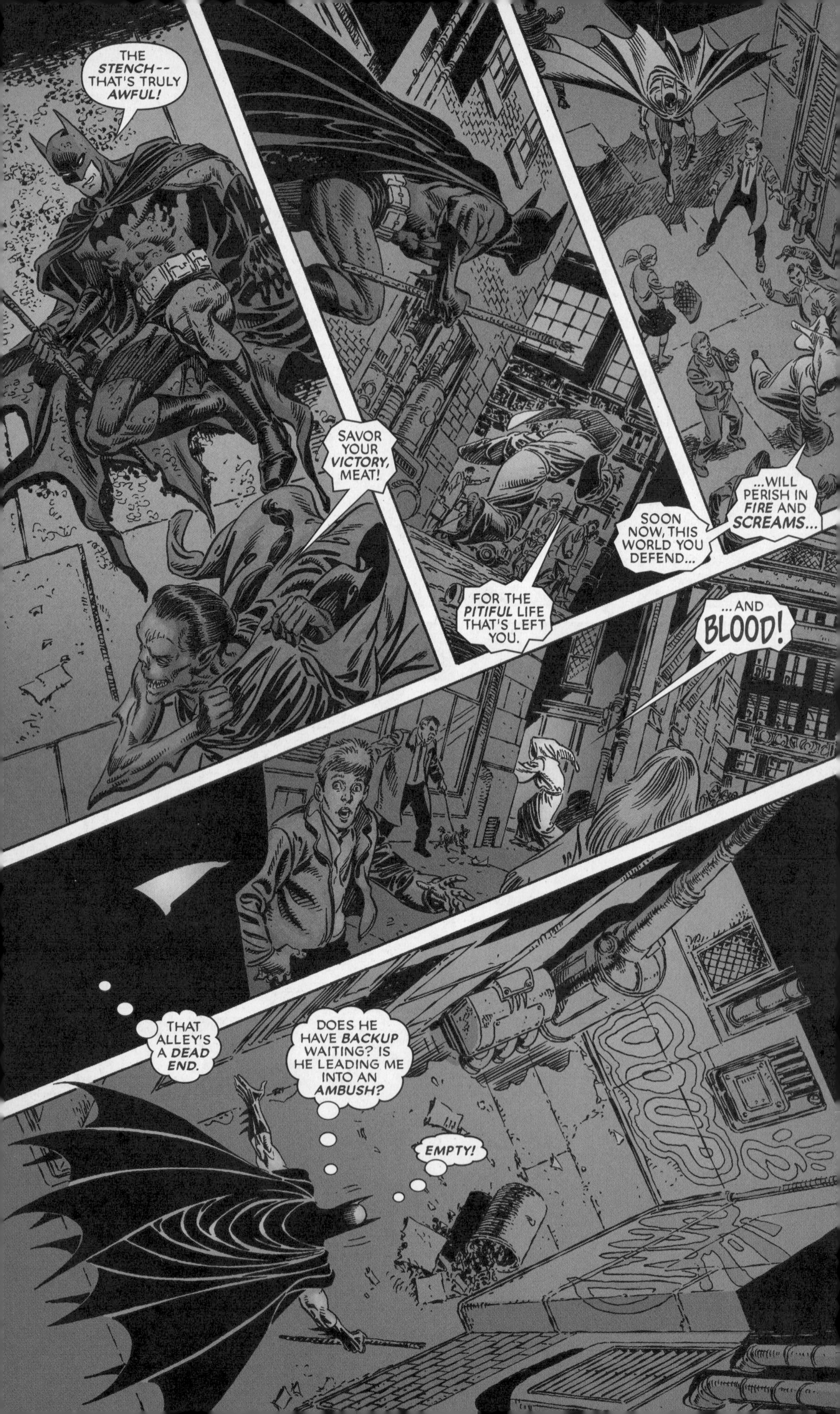
THE STENCH-- THAT'S TRULY AWFUL!
SAVOR YOUR VICTORY, MEAT!
FOR THE PITIFUL LIFE THAT'S LEFT YOU.
SOON NOW, THIS WORLD YOU DEFEND...
...WILL PERISH IN FIRE AND SCREAMS...
...AND BLOOD!
THAT ALLEY'S A DEAD END.
DOES HE HAVE BACKUP WAITING? IS HE LEADING ME INTO AN AMBUSH?
EMPTY!

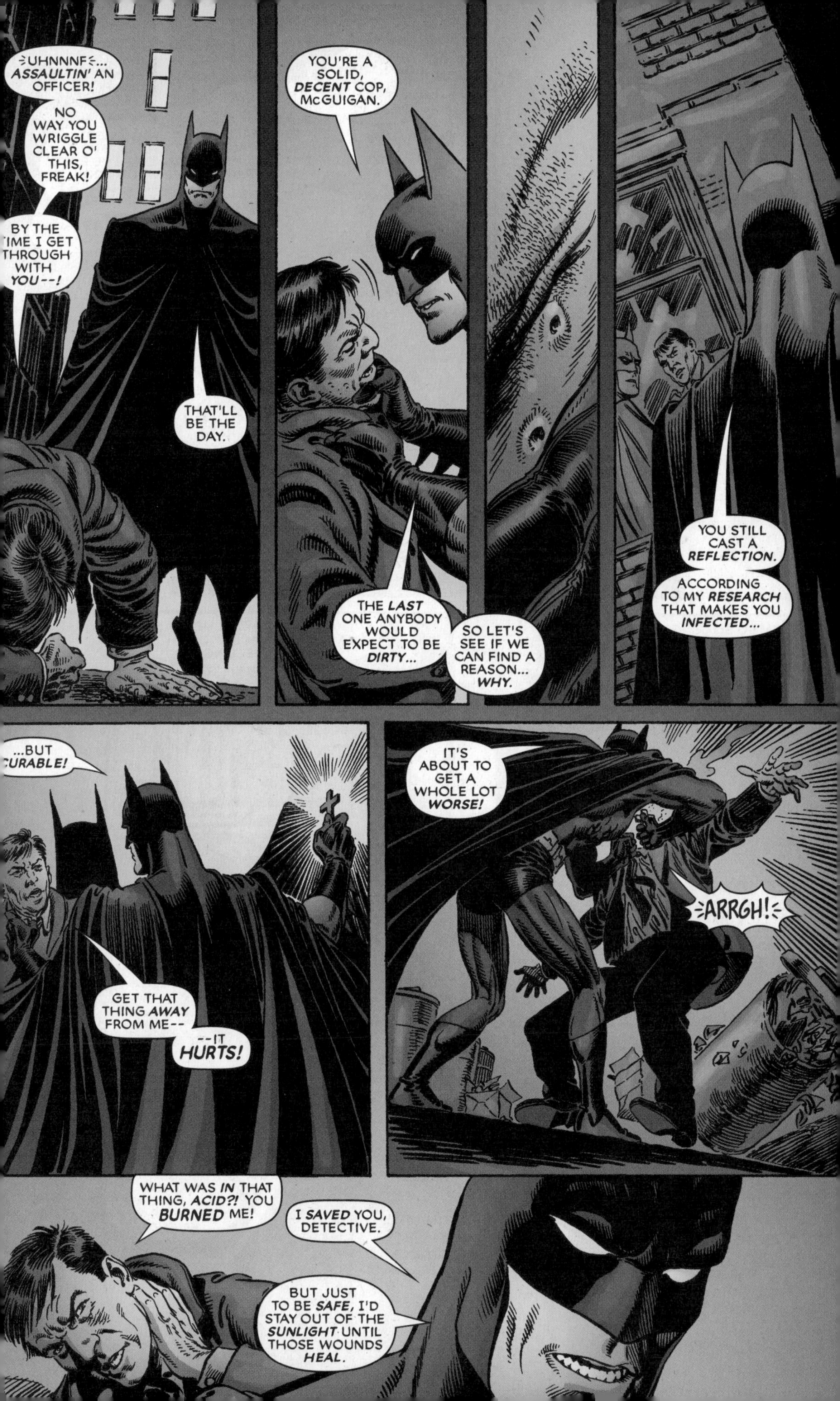
UHNNNF... ASSAULTIN' AN OFFICER!
NO WAY YOU WRIGGLE CLEAR O' THIS, FREAK!
BY THE TIME I GET THROUGH WITH YOU--!
THAT'LL BE THE DAY.
YOU'RE A SOLID, DECENT COP, McGUIGAN.
THE LAST ONE ANYBODY WOULD EXPECT TO BE DIRTY...
SO LET'S SEE IF WE CAN FIND A REASON... WHY.
YOU STILL CAST A REFLECTION.
ACCORDING TO MY RESEARCH THAT MAKES YOU INFECTED...
...BUT CURABLE!
GET THAT THING AWAY FROM ME--
--IT HURTS!
IT'S ABOUT TO GET A WHOLE LOT WORSE!
ARRGH!
WHAT WAS IN THAT THING, ACID?! YOU BURNED ME!
I SAVED YOU, DETECTIVE.
BUT JUST TO BE SAFE, I'D STAY OUT OF THE SUNLIGHT UNTIL THOSE WOUNDS HEAL.

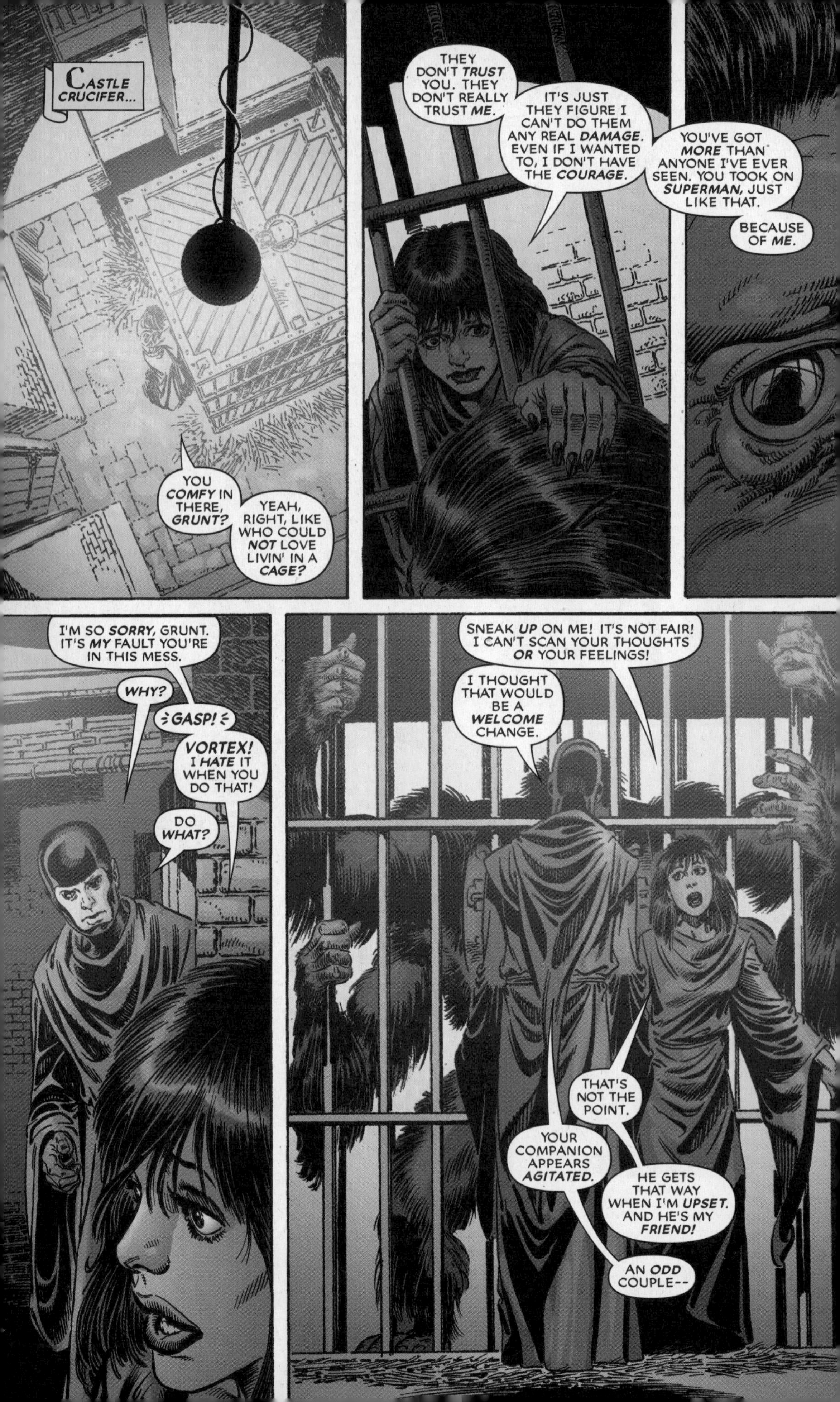
CASTLE CRUCIFER...
YOU COMFY IN THERE, GRUNT?
YEAH, RIGHT, LIKE WHO COULD NOT LOVE LIVIN' IN A CAGE?
THEY DON'T TRUST YOU. THEY DON'T REALLY TRUST ME.
IT'S JUST THEY FIGURE I CAN'T DO THEM ANY REAL DAMAGE. EVEN IF I WANTED TO, I DON'T HAVE THE COURAGE.
YOU'VE GOT MORE THAN ANYONE I'VE EVER SEEN. YOU TOOK ON SUPERMAN, JUST LIKE THAT.
BECAUSE OF ME.
I'M SO SORRY, GRUNT. IT'S MY FAULT YOU'RE IN THIS MESS.
WHY?
GASP!
VORTEX! I HATE IT WHEN YOU DO THAT!
DO WHAT?
SNEAK UP ON ME! IT'S NOT FAIR! I CAN'T SCAN YOUR THOUGHTS OR YOUR FEELINGS!
I THOUGHT THAT WOULD BE A WELCOME CHANGE.
THAT'S NOT THE POINT.
YOUR COMPANION APPEARS AGITATED.
HE GETS THAT WAY WHEN I'M UPSET. AND HE'S MY FRIEND!
AN ODD COUPLE--

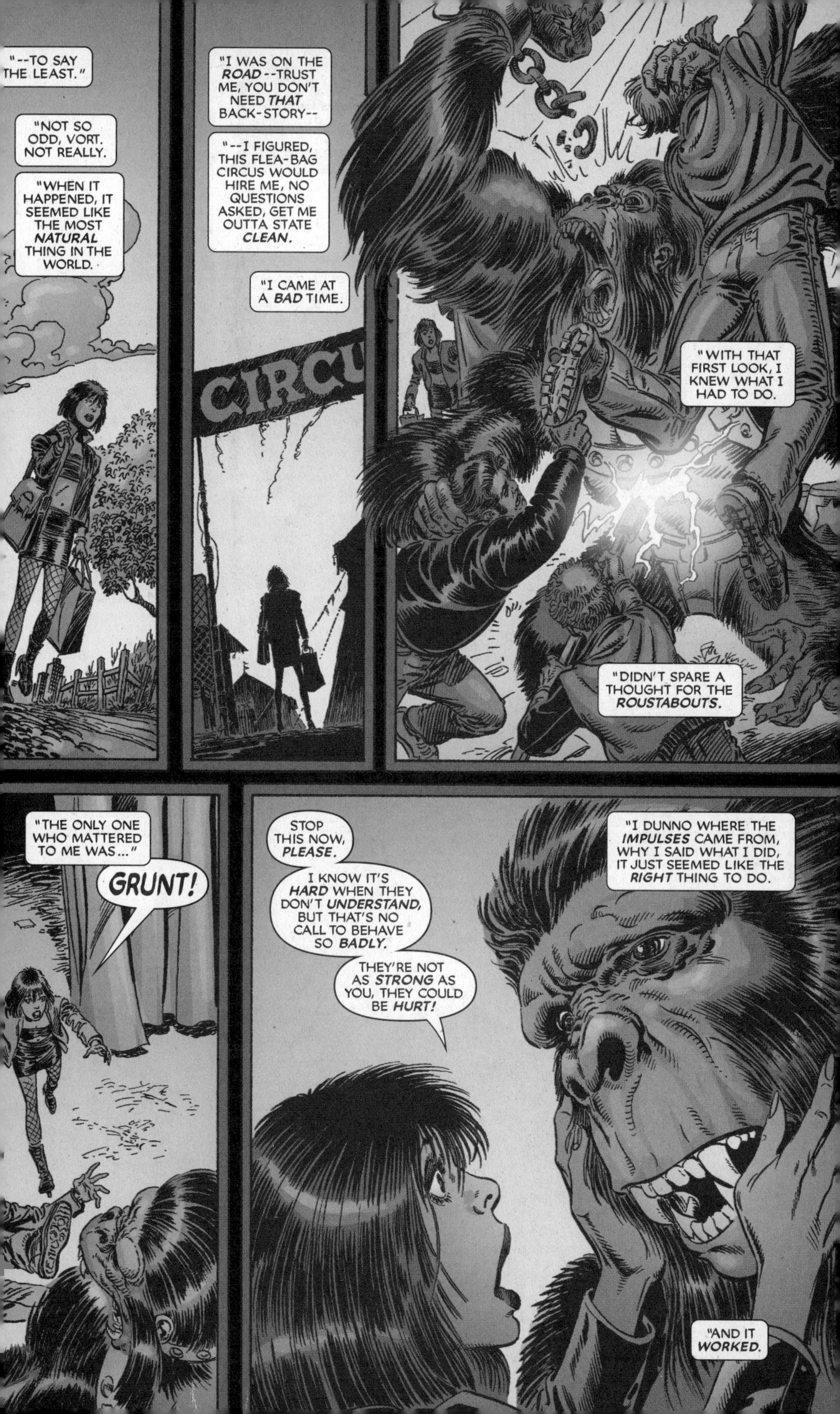
"--TO SAY THE LEAST."
"NOT SO ODD, VORT. NOT REALLY.
"WHEN IT HAPPENED, IT SEEMED LIKE THE MOST NATURAL THING IN THE WORLD.
"I WAS ON THE ROAD--TRUST ME, YOU DON'T NEED THAT BACK-STORY--
"--I FIGURED, THIS FLEA-BAG CIRCUS WOULD HIRE ME, NO QUESTIONS ASKED, GET ME OUTTA STATE CLEAN.
"I CAME AT A BAD TIME.
CIRCU
"WITH THAT FIRST LOOK, I KNEW WHAT I HAD TO DO.
"DIDN'T SPARE A THOUGHT FOR THE ROUSTABOUTS.
"THE ONLY ONE WHO MATTERED TO ME WAS..."
GRUNT!
STOP THIS NOW, PLEASE.
I KNOW IT'S HARD WHEN THEY DON'T UNDERSTAND, BUT THAT'S NO CALL TO BEHAVE SO BADLY.
THEY'RE NOT AS STRONG AS YOU, THEY COULD BE HURT!
"I DUNNO WHERE THE IMPULSES CAME FROM, WHY I SAID WHAT I DID, IT JUST SEEMED LIKE THE RIGHT THING TO DO.
"AND IT WORKED.

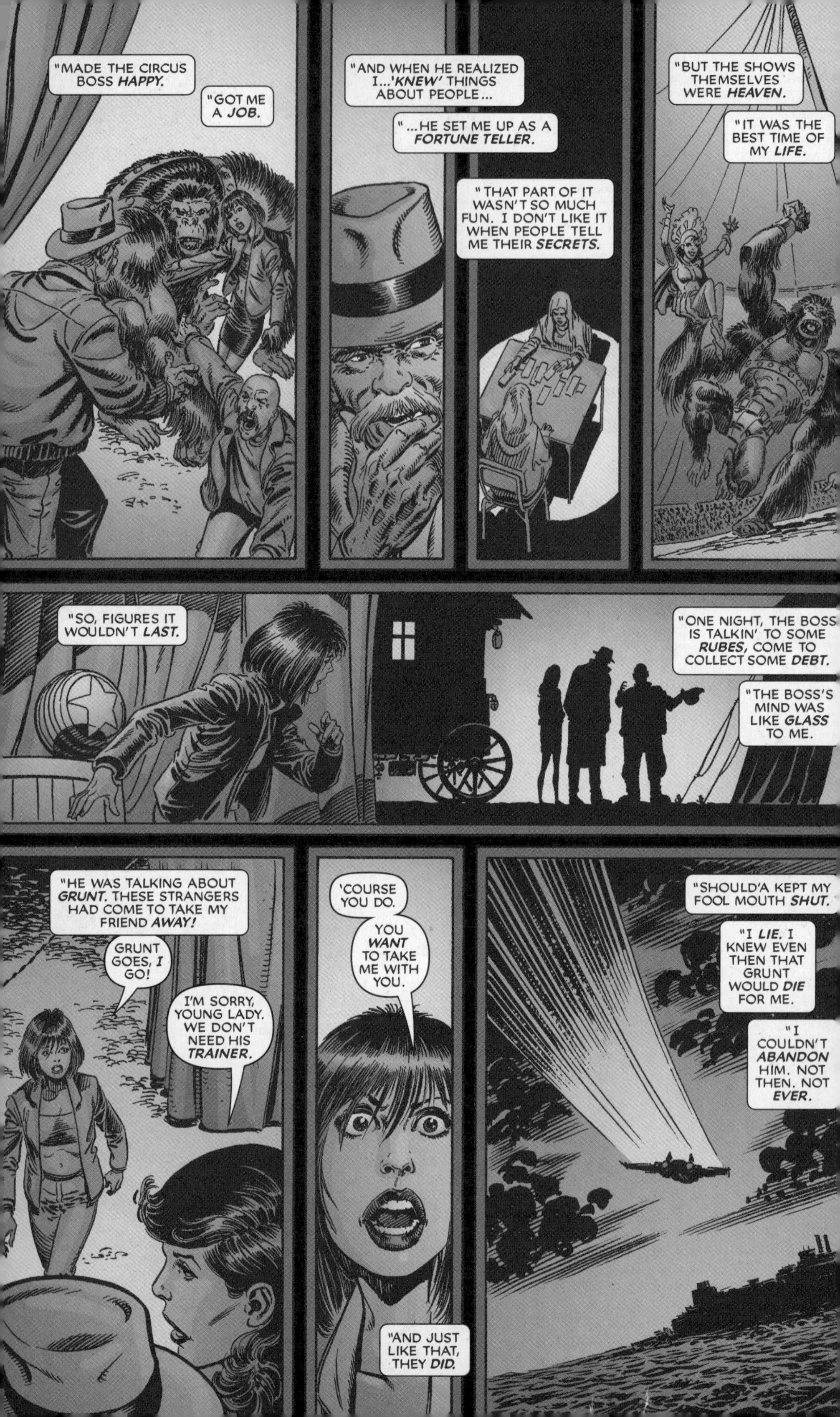

"MADE THE CIRCUS BOSS HAPPY.
"GOT ME A JOB.
"AND WHEN HE REALIZED I...'KNEW' THINGS ABOUT PEOPLE...
"...HE SET ME UP AS A FORTUNE TELLER.
"THAT PART OF IT WASN'T SO MUCH FUN. I DON'T LIKE IT WHEN PEOPLE TELL ME THEIR SECRETS.
"BUT THE SHOWS THEMSELVES WERE HEAVEN.
"IT WAS THE BEST TIME OF MY LIFE.
"SO, FIGURES IT WOULDN'T LAST.
"ONE NIGHT, THE BOSS IS TALKIN' TO SOME RUBES, COME TO COLLECT SOME DEBT.
"THE BOSS'S MIND WAS LIKE GLASS TO ME.
"HE WAS TALKING ABOUT GRUNT. THESE STRANGERS HAD COME TO TAKE MY FRIEND AWAY!
GRUNT GOES, I GO!
I'M SORRY, YOUNG LADY. WE DON'T NEED HIS TRAINER.
'COURSE YOU DO.
YOU WANT TO TAKE ME WITH YOU.
"AND JUST LIKE THAT, THEY DID.
"SHOULD'A KEPT MY FOOL MOUTH SHUT.
"I LIE. I KNEW EVEN THEN THAT GRUNT WOULD DIE FOR ME.
"I COULDN'T ABANDON HIM. NOT THEN. NOT EVER.

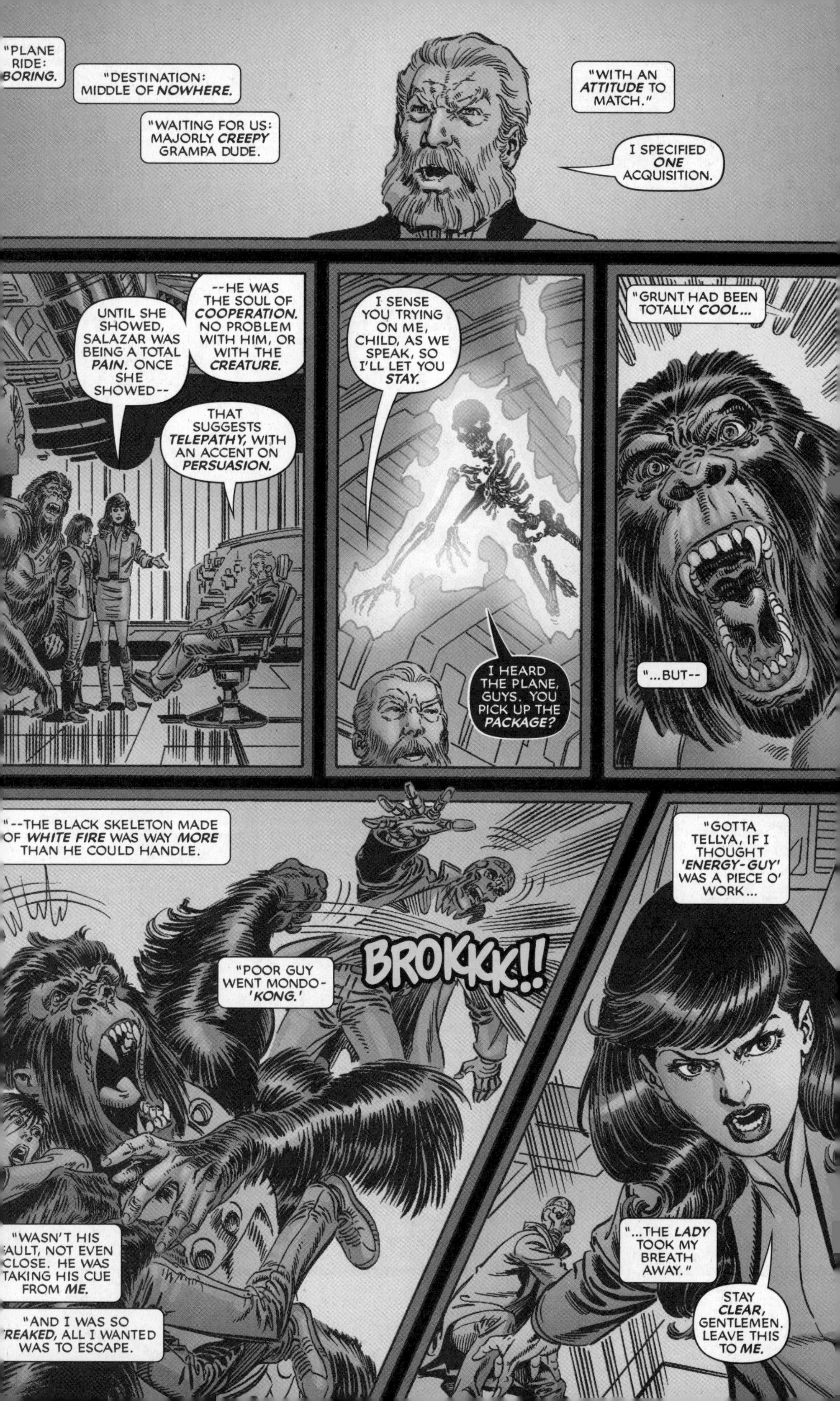
"PLANE RIDE: BORING.
"DESTINATION: MIDDLE OF NOWHERE.
"WAITING FOR US: MAJORLY CREEPY GRAMPA DUDE.
"WITH AN ATTITUDE TO MATCH."
I SPECIFIED ONE ACQUISITION.
UNTIL SHE SHOWED, SALAZAR WAS BEING A TOTAL PAIN. ONCE SHE SHOWED--
--HE WAS THE SOUL OF COOPERATION. NO PROBLEM WITH HIM, OR WITH THE CREATURE.
THAT SUGGESTS TELEPATHY, WITH AN ACCENT ON PERSUASION.
I SENSE YOU TRYING ON ME, CHILD, AS WE SPEAK, SO I'LL LET YOU STAY.
I HEARD THE PLANE, GUYS. YOU PICK UP THE PACKAGE?
"GRUNT HAD BEEN TOTALLY COOL...
"...BUT--
"--THE BLACK SKELETON MADE OF WHITE FIRE WAS WAY MORE THAN HE COULD HANDLE.
"POOR GUY WENT MONDO-'KONG.'
BROKKK!!
"WASN'T HIS FAULT, NOT EVEN CLOSE. HE WAS TAKING HIS CUE FROM ME.
"AND I WAS SO FREAKED, ALL I WANTED WAS TO ESCAPE.
"GOTTA TELLYA, IF I THOUGHT 'ENERGY-GUY' WAS A PIECE O' WORK...
"...THE LADY TOOK MY BREATH AWAY."
STAY CLEAR, GENTLEMEN. LEAVE THIS TO ME.

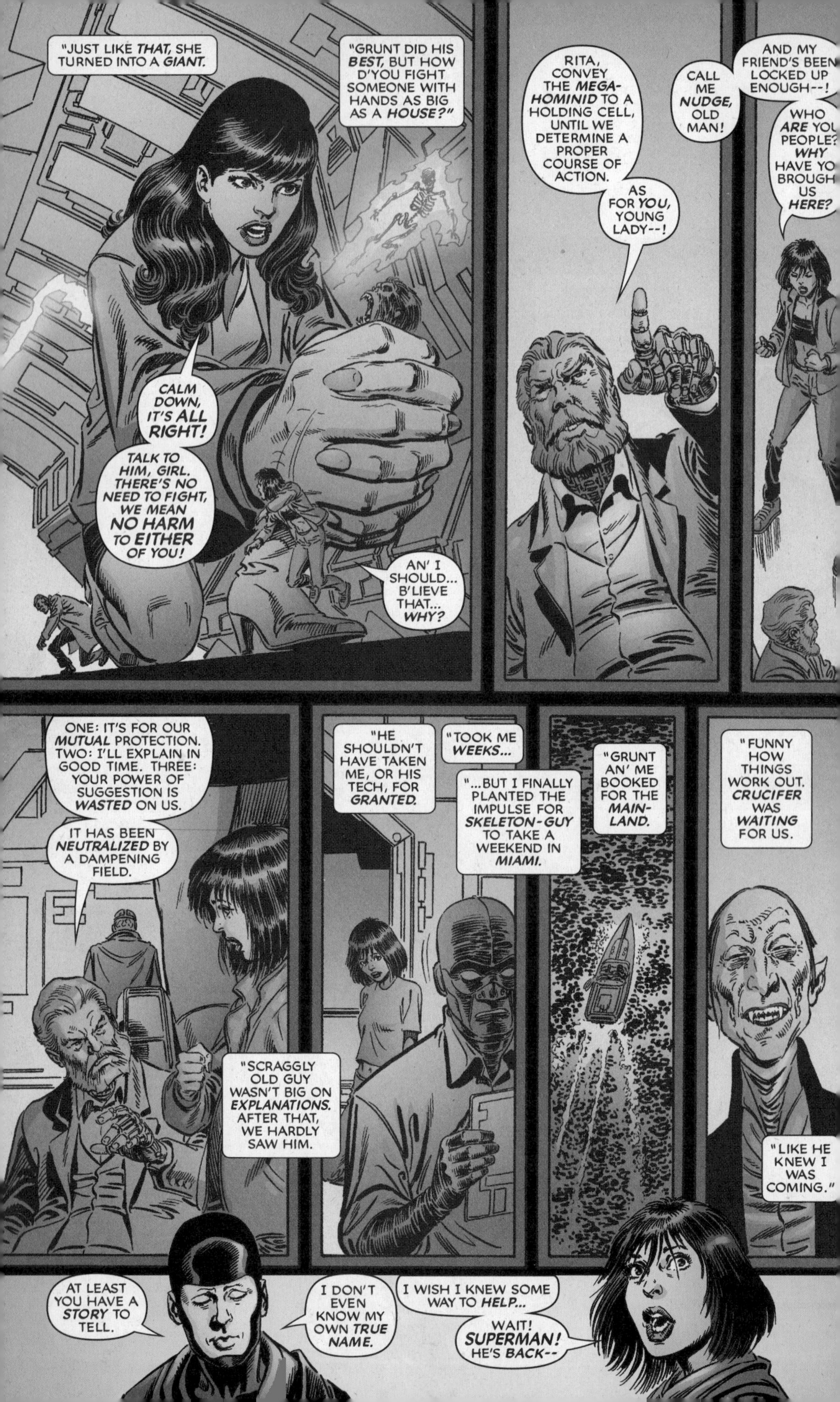

"JUST LIKE THAT, SHE TURNED INTO A GIANT.
"GRUNT DID HIS BEST, BUT HOW D'YOU FIGHT SOMEONE WITH HANDS AS BIG AS A HOUSE?"
CALM DOWN, IT'S ALL RIGHT!
TALK TO HIM, GIRL. THERE'S NO NEED TO FIGHT, WE MEAN NO HARM TO EITHER OF YOU!
AN' I SHOULD... B'LIEVE THAT... WHY?
RITA, CONVEY THE MEGA-HOMINID TO A HOLDING CELL, UNTIL WE DETERMINE A PROPER COURSE OF ACTION.
AS FOR YOU, YOUNG LADY--!
CALL ME NUDGE, OLD MAN!
AND MY FRIEND'S BEEN LOCKED UP ENOUGH--!
WHO ARE YOU PEOPLE? WHY HAVE YOU BROUGHT US HERE?
ONE: IT'S FOR OUR MUTUAL PROTECTION. TWO: I'LL EXPLAIN IN GOOD TIME. THREE: YOUR POWER OF SUGGESTION IS WASTED ON US.
IT HAS BEEN NEUTRALIZED BY A DAMPENING FIELD.
"SCRAGGLY OLD GUY WASN'T BIG ON EXPLANATIONS. AFTER THAT, WE HARDLY SAW HIM.
"HE SHOULDN'T HAVE TAKEN ME, OR HIS TECH, FOR GRANTED.
"TOOK ME WEEKS...
"...BUT I FINALLY PLANTED THE IMPULSE FOR SKELETON-GUY TO TAKE A WEEKEND IN MIAMI.
"GRUNT AN' ME BOOKED FOR THE MAIN-LAND.
"FUNNY HOW THINGS WORK OUT. CRUCIFER WAS WAITING FOR US.
"LIKE HE KNEW I WAS COMING."
AT LEAST YOU HAVE A STORY TO TELL.
I DON'T EVEN KNOW MY OWN TRUE NAME.
I WISH I KNEW SOME WAY TO HELP...
WAIT! SUPERMAN! HE'S BACK--

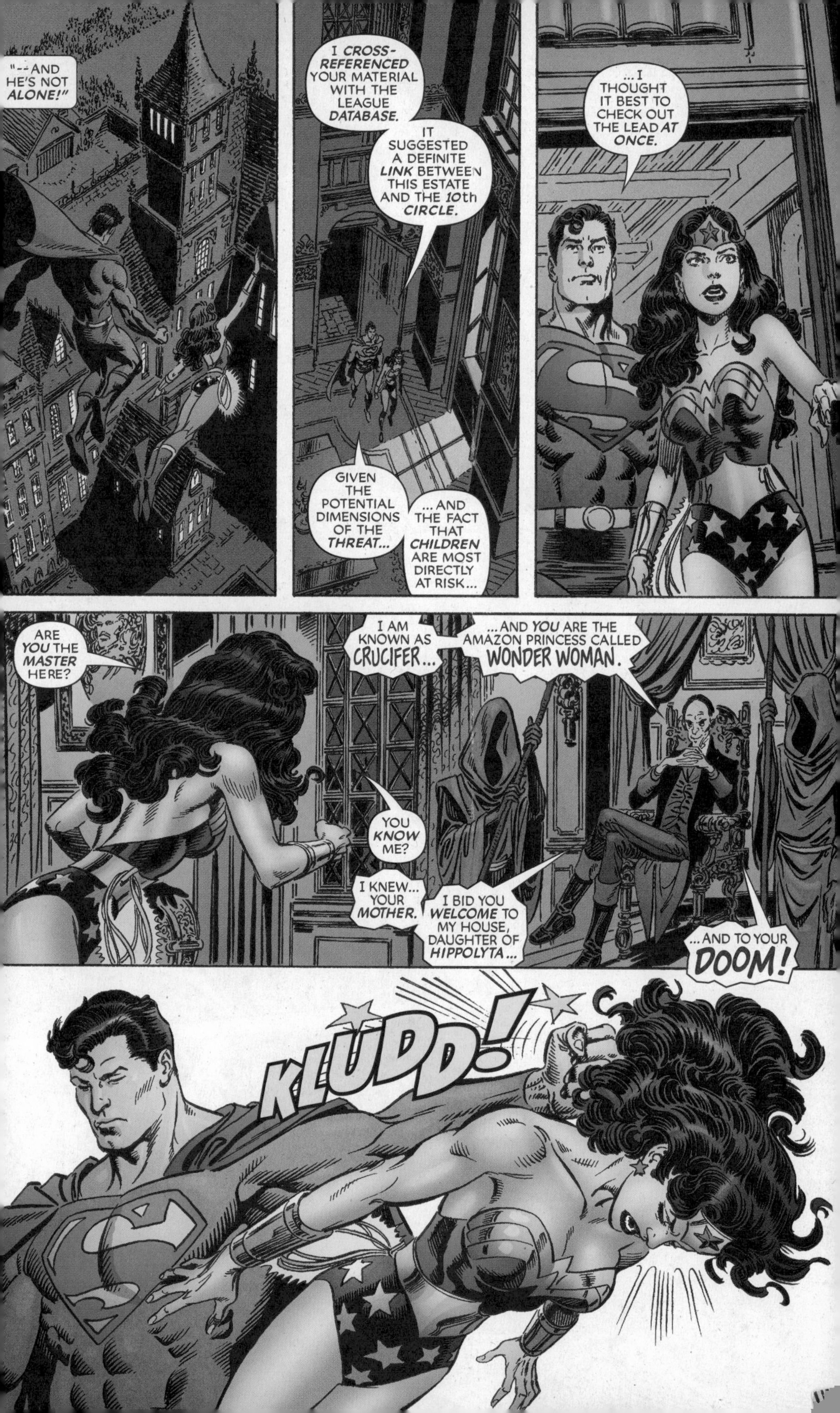
"-- AND HE'S NOT ALONE!"
I CROSS-REFERENCED YOUR MATERIAL WITH THE LEAGUE DATABASE.
IT SUGGESTED A DEFINITE LINK BETWEEN THIS ESTATE AND THE 10th CIRCLE.
GIVEN THE POTENTIAL DIMENSIONS OF THE THREAT...
...AND THE FACT THAT CHILDREN ARE MOST DIRECTLY AT RISK...
...I THOUGHT IT BEST TO CHECK OUT THE LEAD AT ONCE.
ARE YOU THE MASTER HERE?
I AM KNOWN AS CRUCIFER...
...AND YOU ARE THE AMAZON PRINCESS CALLED WONDER WOMAN.
YOU KNOW ME?
I KNEW... YOUR MOTHER.
I BID YOU WELCOME TO MY HOUSE, DAUGHTER OF HIPPOLYTA...
...AND TO YOUR DOOM!
KLUDD!

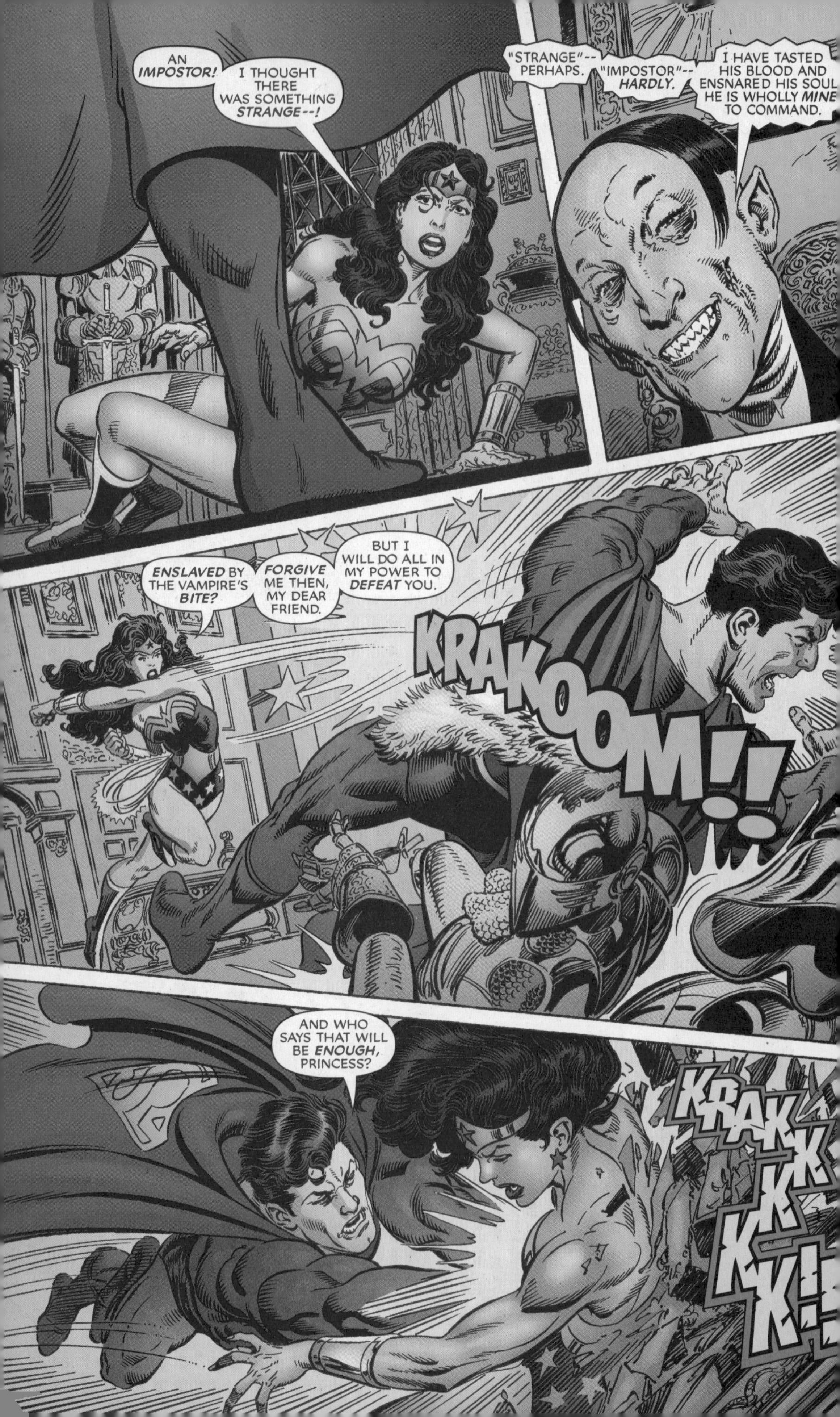
AN IMPOSTOR!
I THOUGHT THERE WAS SOMETHING STRANGE--!
"STRANGE"-- PERHAPS.
"IMPOSTOR"-- HARDLY.
I HAVE TASTED HIS BLOOD AND ENSNARED HIS SOUL. HE IS WHOLLY MINE TO COMMAND.
ENSLAVED BY THE VAMPIRE'S BITE?
FORGIVE ME THEN, MY DEAR FRIEND.
BUT I WILL DO ALL IN MY POWER TO DEFEAT YOU.
KRAKOOOM!!
AND WHO SAYS THAT WILL BE ENOUGH, PRINCESS?
KRAKKKK!

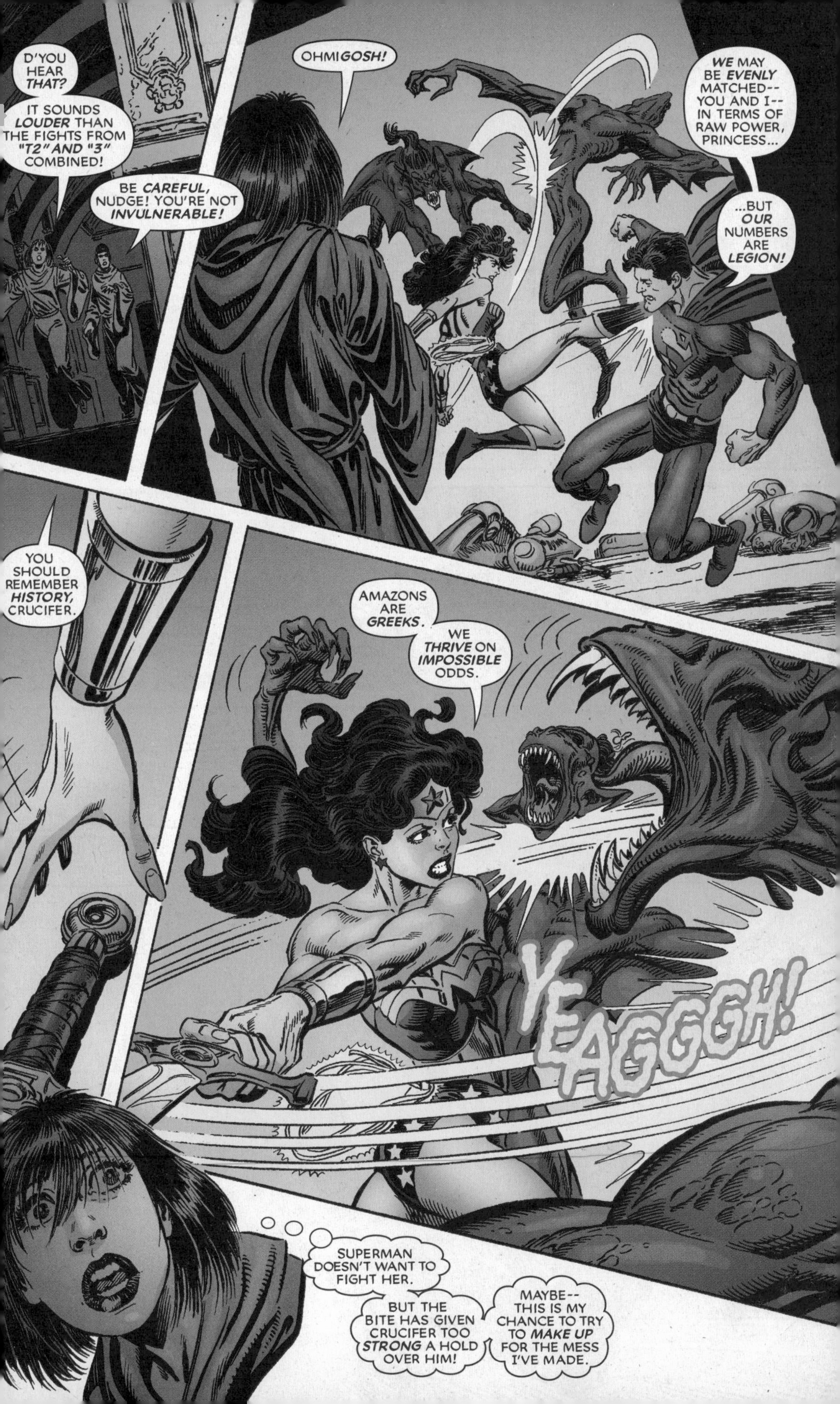

D'YOU HEAR THAT?
IT SOUNDS LOUDER THAN THE FIGHTS FROM "T2" AND "3" COMBINED!
BE CAREFUL, NUDGE! YOU'RE NOT INVULNERABLE!
OHMIGOSH!
WE MAY BE EVENLY MATCHED-- YOU AND I-- IN TERMS OF RAW POWER, PRINCESS...
...BUT OUR NUMBERS ARE LEGION!
YOU SHOULD REMEMBER HISTORY, CRUCIFER.
AMAZONS ARE GREEKS.
WE THRIVE ON IMPOSSIBLE ODDS.
YEAGGGH!
SUPERMAN DOESN'T WANT TO FIGHT HER.
BUT THE BITE HAS GIVEN CRUCIFER TOO STRONG A HOLD OVER HIM!
MAYBE-- THIS IS MY CHANCE TO TRY TO MAKE UP FOR THE MESS I'VE MADE.

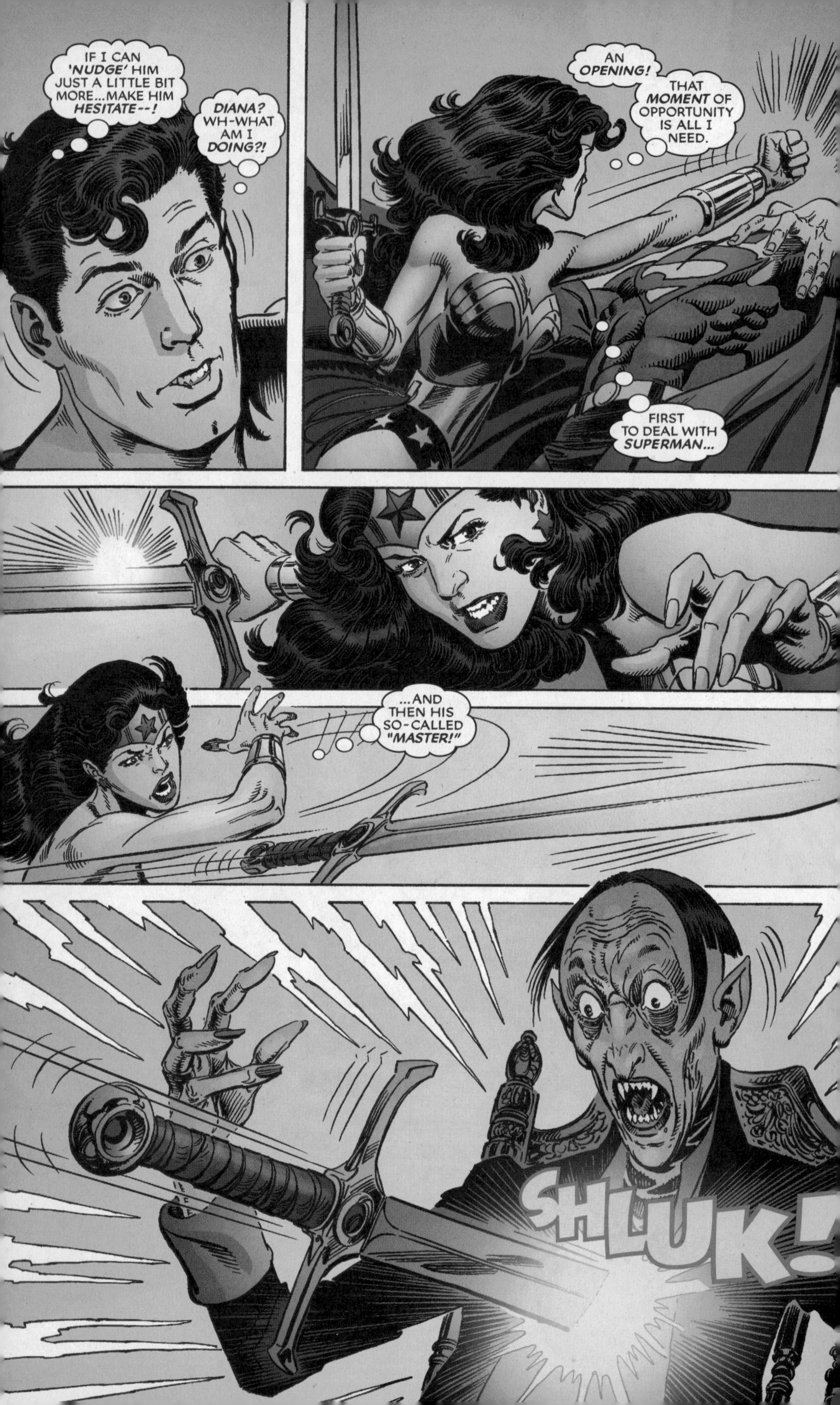
IF I CAN 'NUDGE' HIM JUST A LITTLE BIT MORE...MAKE HIM HESITATE--!
DIANA? WH-WHAT AM I DOING?!
AN OPENING!
THAT MOMENT OF OPPORTUNITY IS ALL I NEED.
FIRST TO DEAL WITH SUPERMAN...
...AND THEN HIS SO-CALLED "MASTER!"
SHLUK!

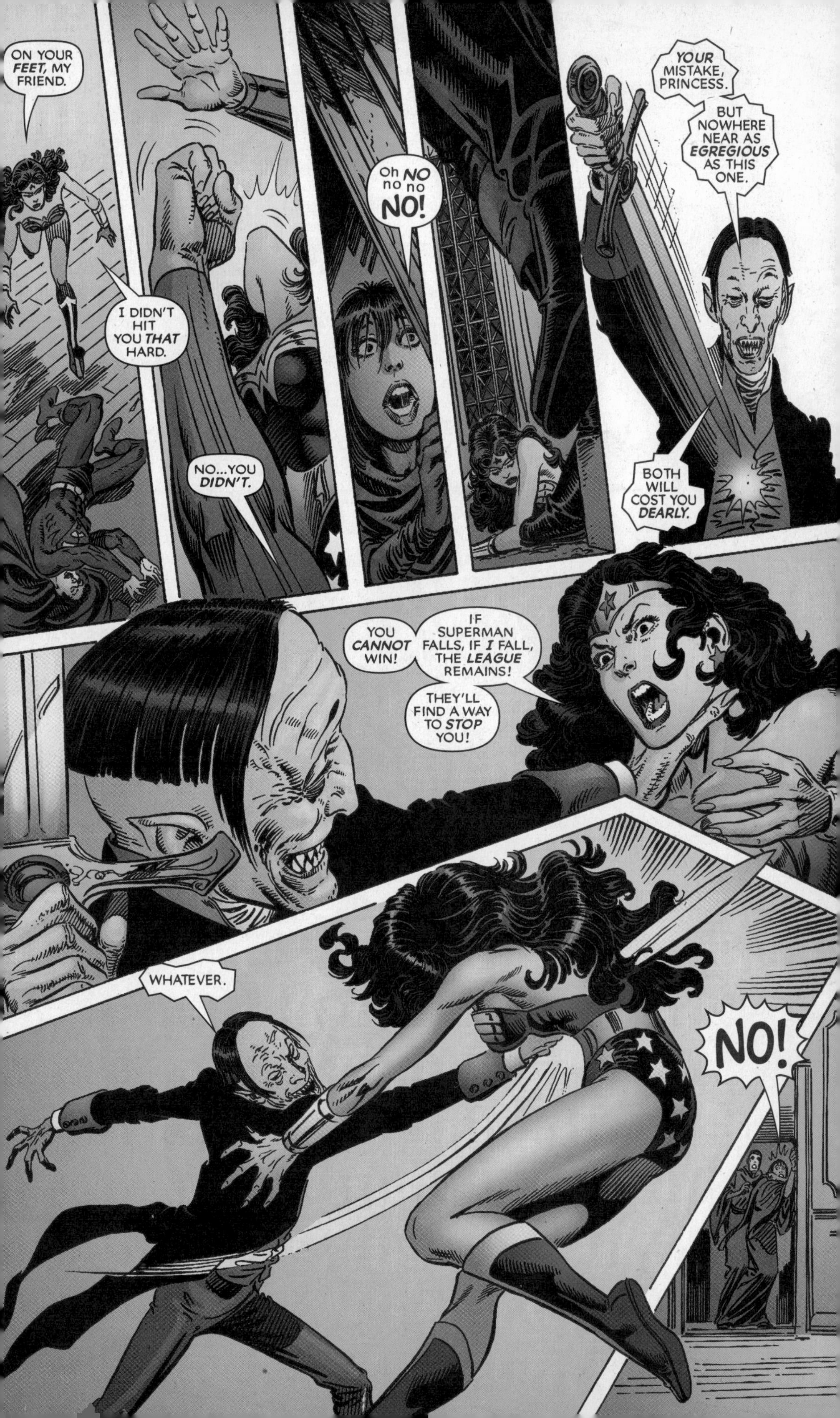
ON YOUR FEET, MY FRIEND.
I DIDN'T HIT YOU THAT HARD.
NO...YOU DIDN'T.
Oh NO no no no NO!
YOUR MISTAKE, PRINCESS.
BUT NOWHERE NEAR AS EGREGIOUS AS THIS ONE.
BOTH WILL COST YOU DEARLY.
YOU CANNOT WIN!
IF SUPERMAN FALLS, IF I FALL, THE LEAGUE REMAINS!
THEY'LL FIND A WAY TO STOP YOU!
WHATEVER.
NO!

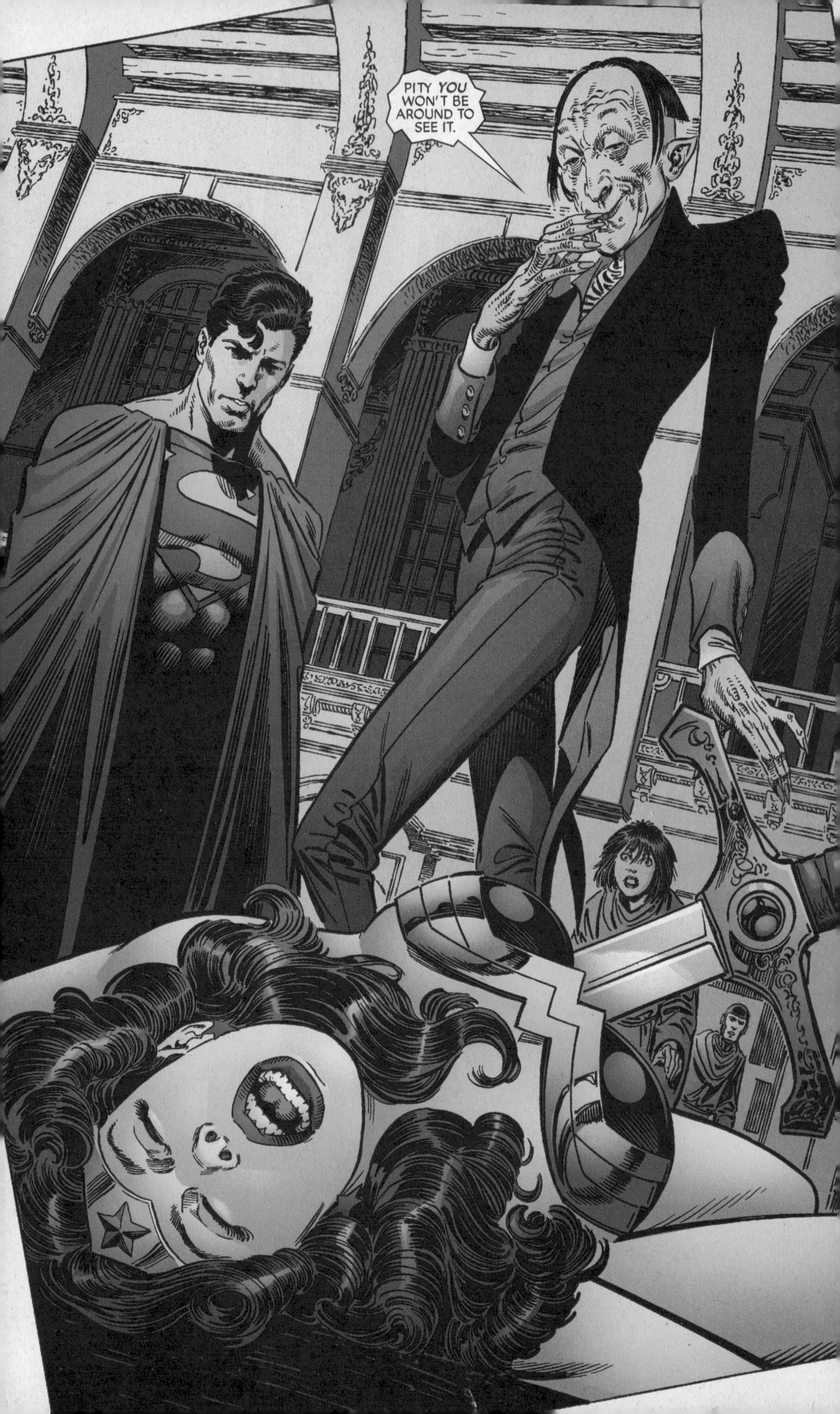
PITY YOU WON'T BE AROUND TO SEE IT.

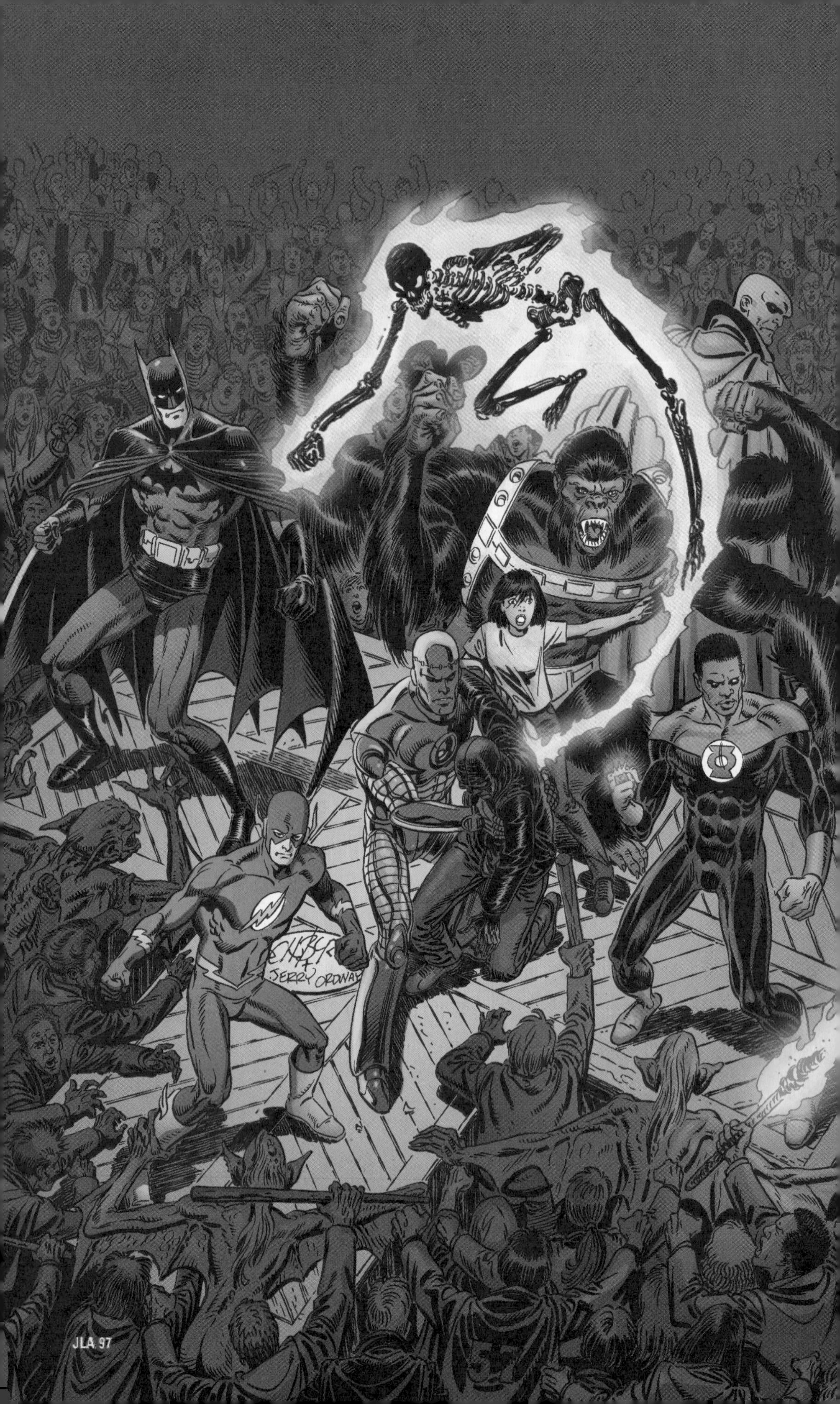
JERRY ORDWAY
JLA 97

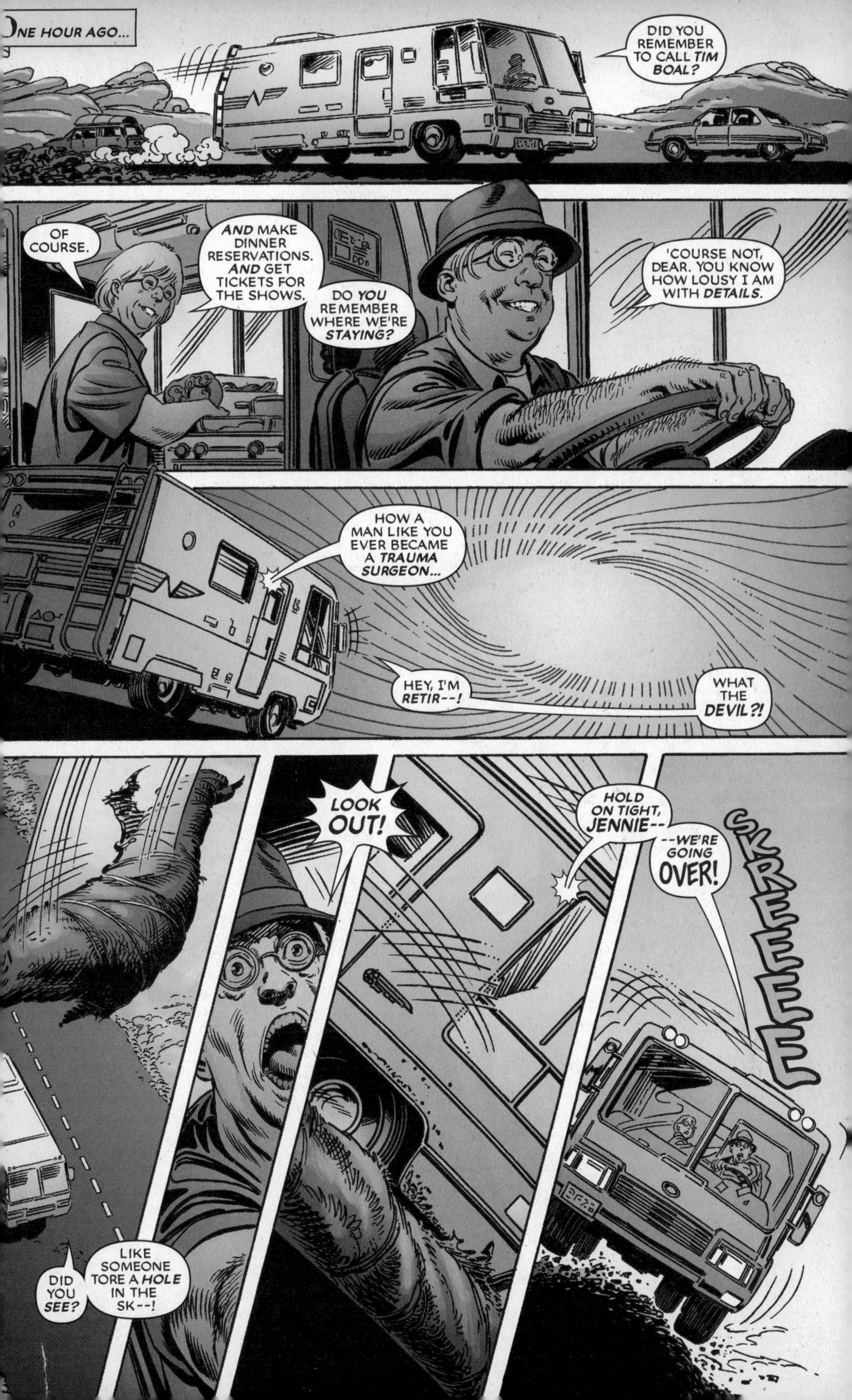

ONE HOUR AGO...
DID YOU REMEMBER TO CALL TIM BOAL?
OF COURSE.
AND MAKE DINNER RESERVATIONS. AND GET TICKETS FOR THE SHOWS.
DO YOU REMEMBER WHERE WE'RE STAYING?
'COURSE NOT, DEAR. YOU KNOW HOW LOUSY I AM WITH DETAILS.
HOW A MAN LIKE YOU EVER BECAME A TRAUMA SURGEON...
HEY, I'M RETIR--!
WHAT THE DEVIL?!
DID YOU SEE?
LIKE SOMEONE TORE A HOLE IN THE SK--!
LOOK OUT!
HOLD ON TIGHT, JENNIE--
--WE'RE GOING OVER!
SKREEEEE

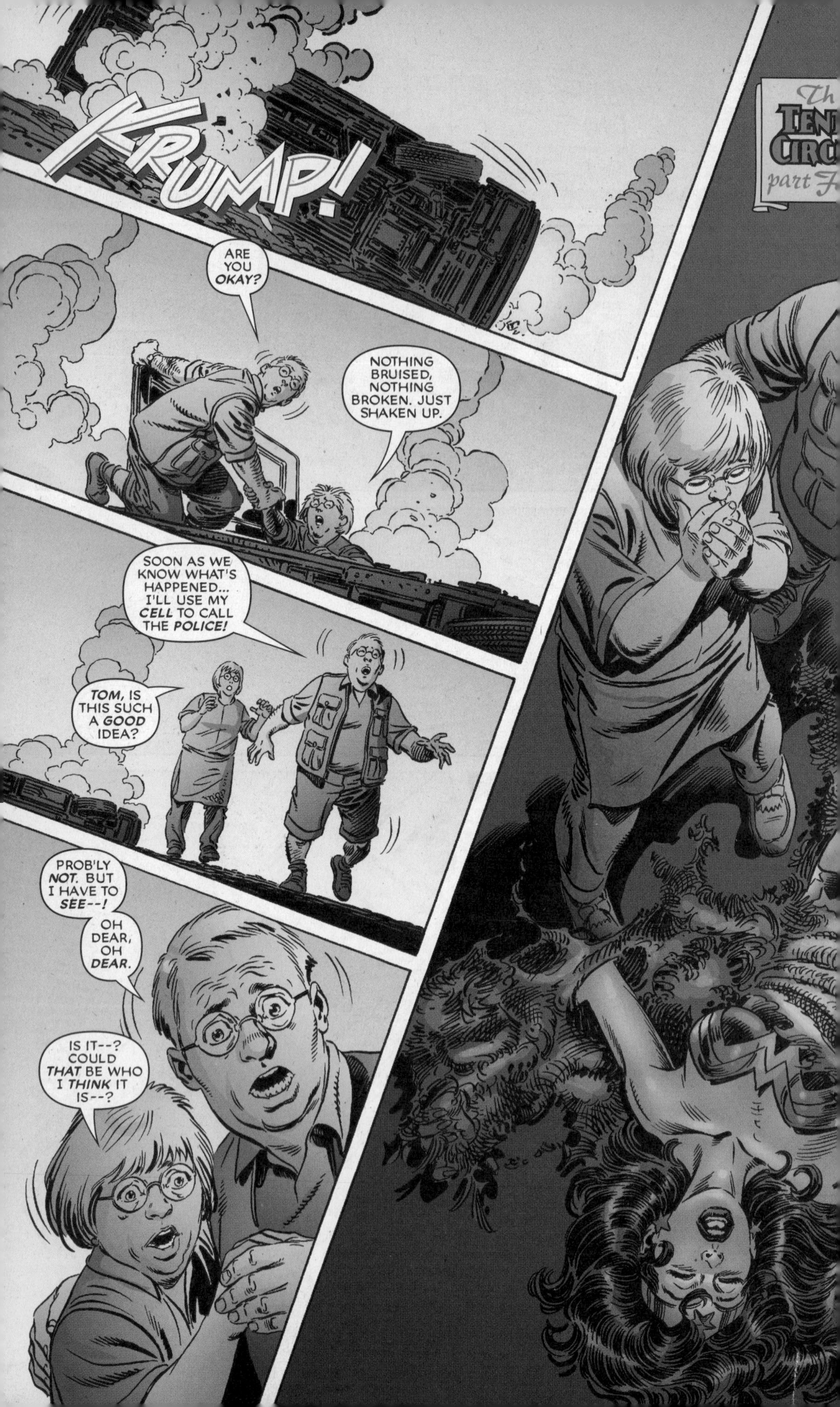

KRUMP!
The Tenth Circle part F
ARE YOU OKAY?
NOTHING BRUISED, NOTHING BROKEN. JUST SHAKEN UP.
SOON AS WE KNOW WHAT'S HAPPENED... I'LL USE MY CELL TO CALL THE POLICE!
TOM, IS THIS SUCH A GOOD IDEA?
PROB'LY NOT. BUT I HAVE TO SEE--!
OH DEAR, OH DEAR.
IS IT--? COULD THAT BE WHO I THINK IT IS--?

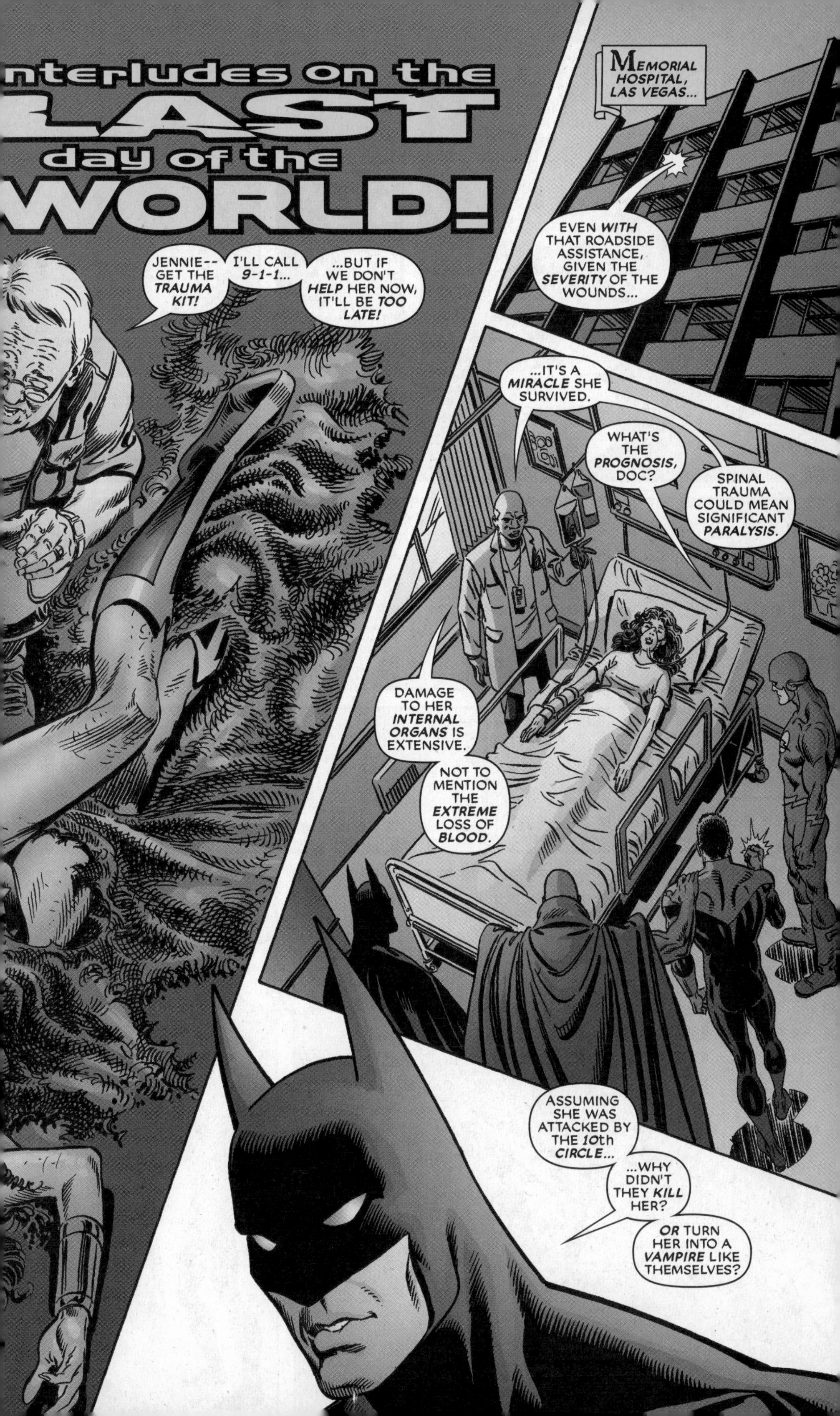

nterludes on the LAST day of the WORLD!
JENNIE-- GET THE TRAUMA KIT!
I'LL CALL 9-1-1...
...BUT IF WE DON'T HELP HER NOW, IT'LL BE TOO LATE!
MEMORIAL HOSPITAL, LAS VEGAS...
EVEN WITH THAT ROADSIDE ASSISTANCE, GIVEN THE SEVERITY OF THE WOUNDS...
...IT'S A MIRACLE SHE SURVIVED.
WHAT'S THE PROGNOSIS, DOC?
SPINAL TRAUMA COULD MEAN SIGNIFICANT PARALYSIS.
DAMAGE TO HER INTERNAL ORGANS IS EXTENSIVE.
NOT TO MENTION THE EXTREME LOSS OF BLOOD.
ASSUMING SHE WAS ATTACKED BY THE 10th CIRCLE...
...WHY DIDN'T THEY KILL HER?
OR TURN HER INTO A VAMPIRE LIKE THEMSELVES?

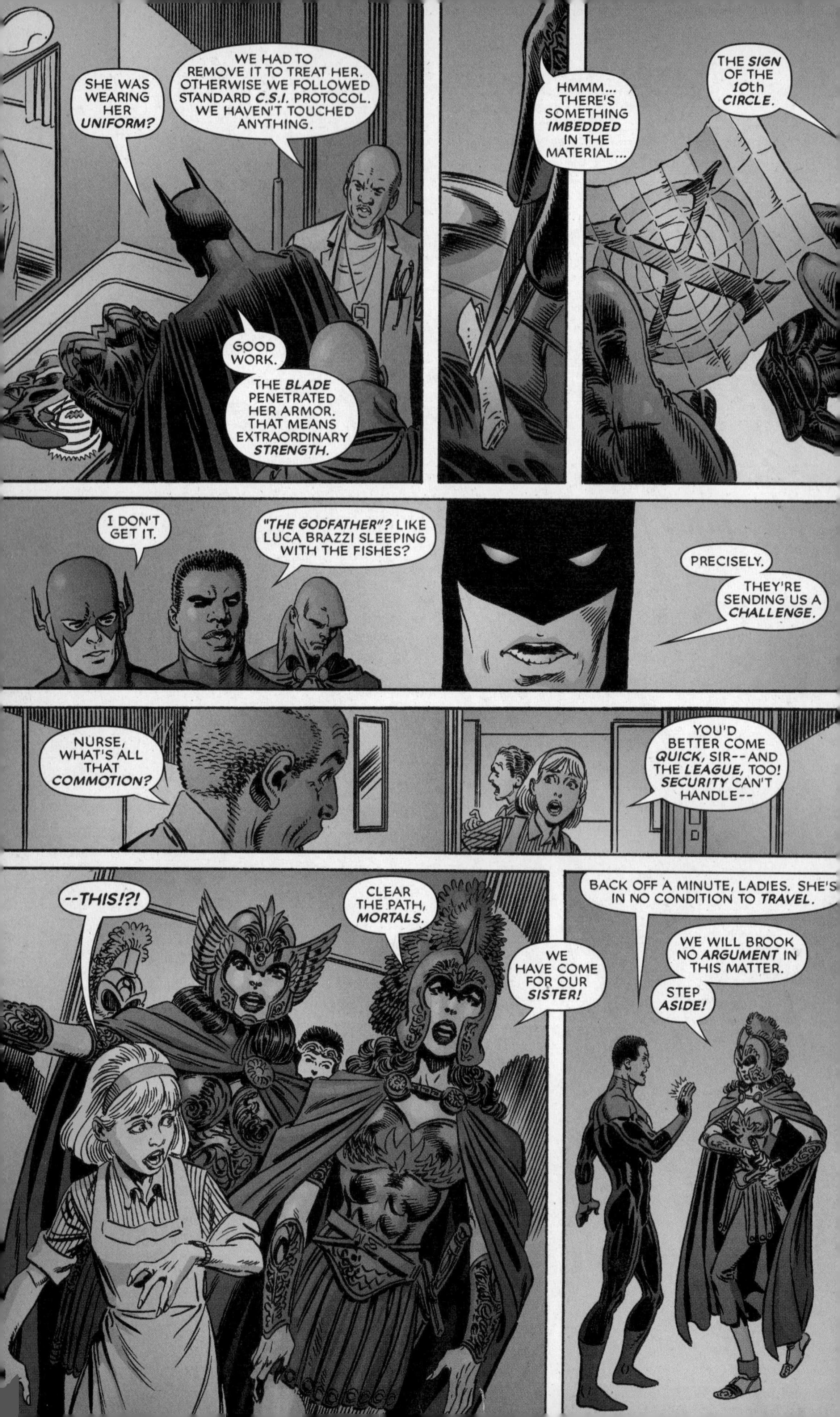
SHE WAS WEARING HER UNIFORM?
WE HAD TO REMOVE IT TO TREAT HER. OTHERWISE WE FOLLOWED STANDARD C.S.I. PROTOCOL. WE HAVEN'T TOUCHED ANYTHING.
GOOD WORK.
THE BLADE PENETRATED HER ARMOR. THAT MEANS EXTRAORDINARY STRENGTH.
HMMM... THERE'S SOMETHING IMBEDDED IN THE MATERIAL...
THE SIGN OF THE 10th CIRCLE.
I DON'T GET IT.
"THE GODFATHER"? LIKE LUCA BRAZZI SLEEPING WITH THE FISHES?
PRECISELY.
THEY'RE SENDING US A CHALLENGE.
NURSE, WHAT'S ALL THAT COMMOTION?
YOU'D BETTER COME QUICK, SIR--AND THE LEAGUE, TOO! SECURITY CAN'T HANDLE--
--THIS!?!
CLEAR THE PATH, MORTALS.
WE HAVE COME FOR OUR SISTER!
BACK OFF A MINUTE, LADIES. SHE'S IN NO CONDITION TO TRAVEL.
WE WILL BROOK NO ARGUMENT IN THIS MATTER.
STEP ASIDE!

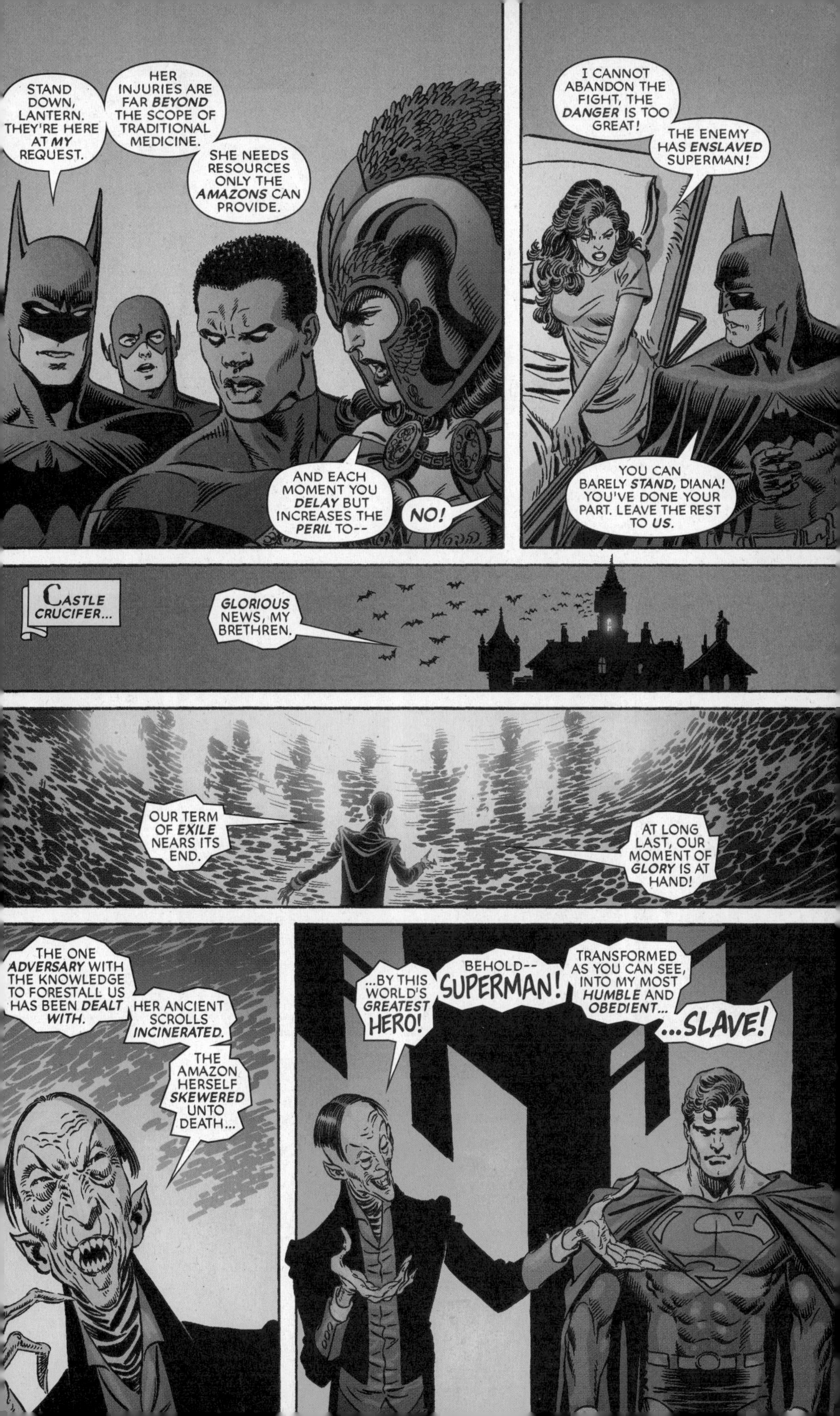
STAND DOWN, LANTERN. THEY'RE HERE AT MY REQUEST.
HER INJURIES ARE FAR BEYOND THE SCOPE OF TRADITIONAL MEDICINE.
SHE NEEDS RESOURCES ONLY THE AMAZONS CAN PROVIDE.
AND EACH MOMENT YOU DELAY BUT INCREASES THE PERIL TO--
NO!
I CANNOT ABANDON THE FIGHT, THE DANGER IS TOO GREAT!
THE ENEMY HAS ENSLAVED SUPERMAN!
YOU CAN BARELY STAND, DIANA! YOU'VE DONE YOUR PART. LEAVE THE REST TO US.
CASTLE CRUCIFER...
GLORIOUS NEWS, MY BRETHREN.
OUR TERM OF EXILE NEARS ITS END.
AT LONG LAST, OUR MOMENT OF GLORY IS AT HAND!
THE ONE ADVERSARY WITH THE KNOWLEDGE TO FORESTALL US HAS BEEN DEALT WITH.
HER ANCIENT SCROLLS INCINERATED.
THE AMAZON HERSELF SKEWERED UNTO DEATH...
...BY THIS WORLD'S GREATEST HERO!
BEHOLD-- SUPERMAN!
TRANSFORMED AS YOU CAN SEE, INTO MY MOST HUMBLE AND OBEDIENT...
...SLAVE!

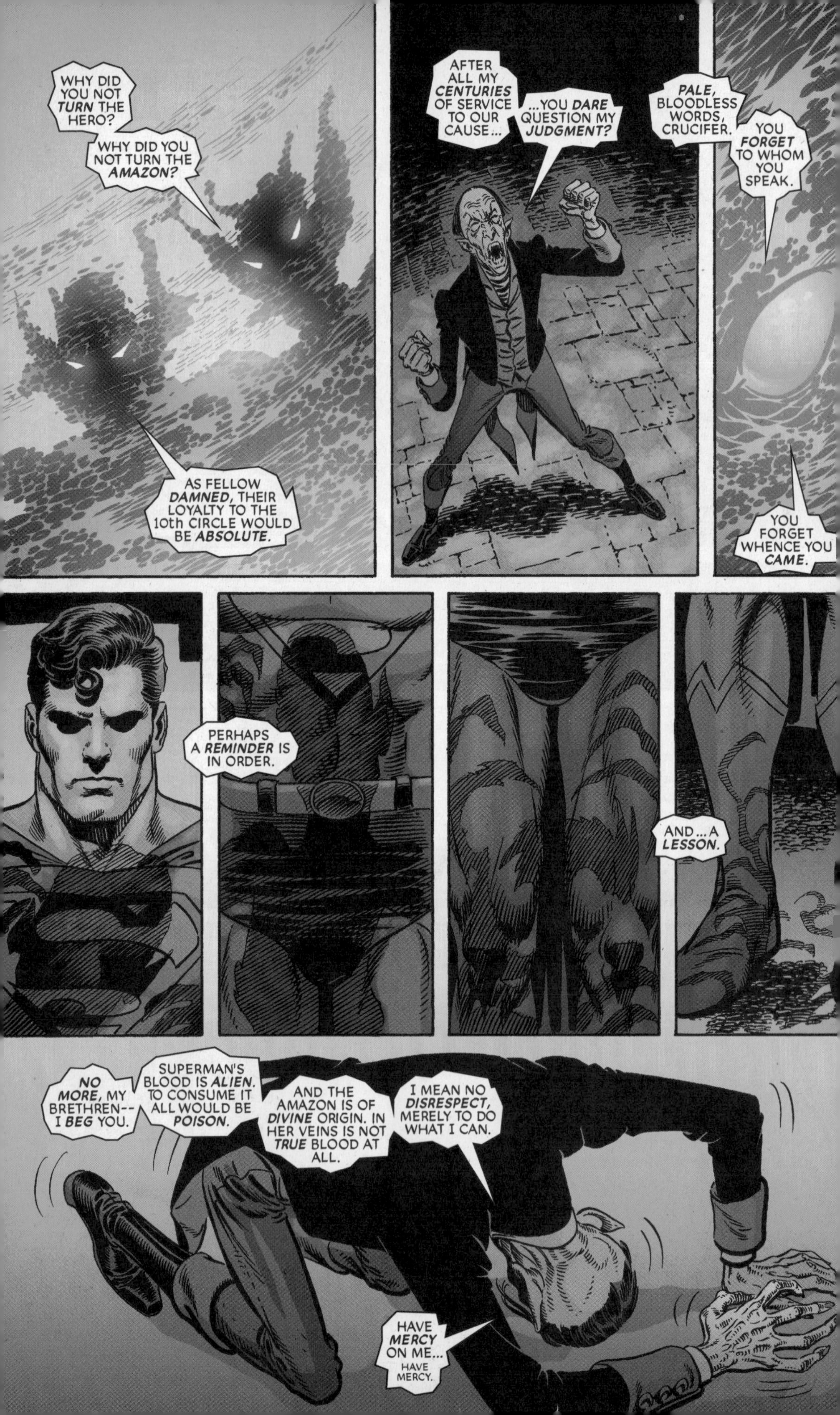

WHY DID YOU NOT TURN THE HERO?
WHY DID YOU NOT TURN THE AMAZON?
AS FELLOW DAMNED, THEIR LOYALTY TO THE 10th CIRCLE WOULD BE ABSOLUTE.
AFTER ALL MY CENTURIES OF SERVICE TO OUR CAUSE...
...YOU DARE QUESTION MY JUDGMENT?
PALE, BLOODLESS WORDS, CRUCIFER.
YOU FORGET TO WHOM YOU SPEAK.
YOU FORGET WHENCE YOU CAME.
PERHAPS A REMINDER IS IN ORDER.
AND...A LESSON.
NO MORE, MY BRETHREN-- I BEG YOU.
SUPERMAN'S BLOOD IS ALIEN. TO CONSUME IT ALL WOULD BE POISON.
AND THE AMAZON IS OF DIVINE ORIGIN. IN HER VEINS IS NOT TRUE BLOOD AT ALL.
I MEAN NO DISRESPECT, MERELY TO DO WHAT I CAN.
HAVE MERCY ON ME... HAVE MERCY.

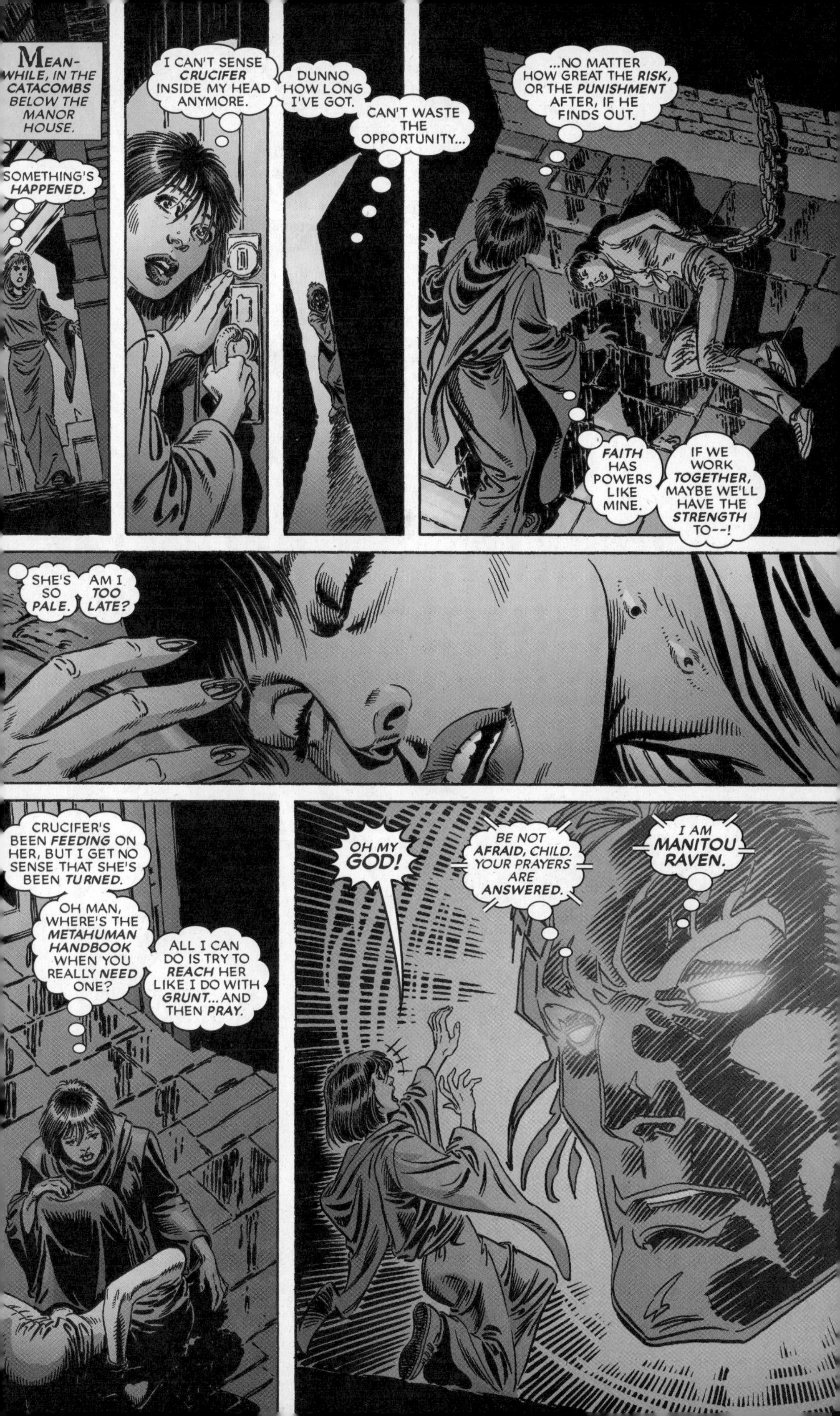
MEANWHILE, IN THE CATACOMBS BELOW THE MANOR HOUSE.
SOMETHING'S HAPPENED.
I CAN'T SENSE CRUCIFER INSIDE MY HEAD ANYMORE.
DUNNO HOW LONG I'VE GOT.
CAN'T WASTE THE OPPORTUNITY...
...NO MATTER HOW GREAT THE RISK, OR THE PUNISHMENT AFTER, IF HE FINDS OUT.
FAITH HAS POWERS LIKE MINE.
IF WE WORK TOGETHER, MAYBE WE'LL HAVE THE STRENGTH TO--!
SHE'S SO PALE.
AM I TOO LATE?
CRUCIFER'S BEEN FEEDING ON HER, BUT I GET NO SENSE THAT SHE'S BEEN TURNED.
OH MAN, WHERE'S THE METAHUMAN HANDBOOK WHEN YOU REALLY NEED ONE?
ALL I CAN DO IS TRY TO REACH HER LIKE I DO WITH GRUNT... AND THEN PRAY.
OH MY GOD!
BE NOT AFRAID, CHILD. YOUR PRAYERS ARE ANSWERED.
I AM MANITOU RAVEN.

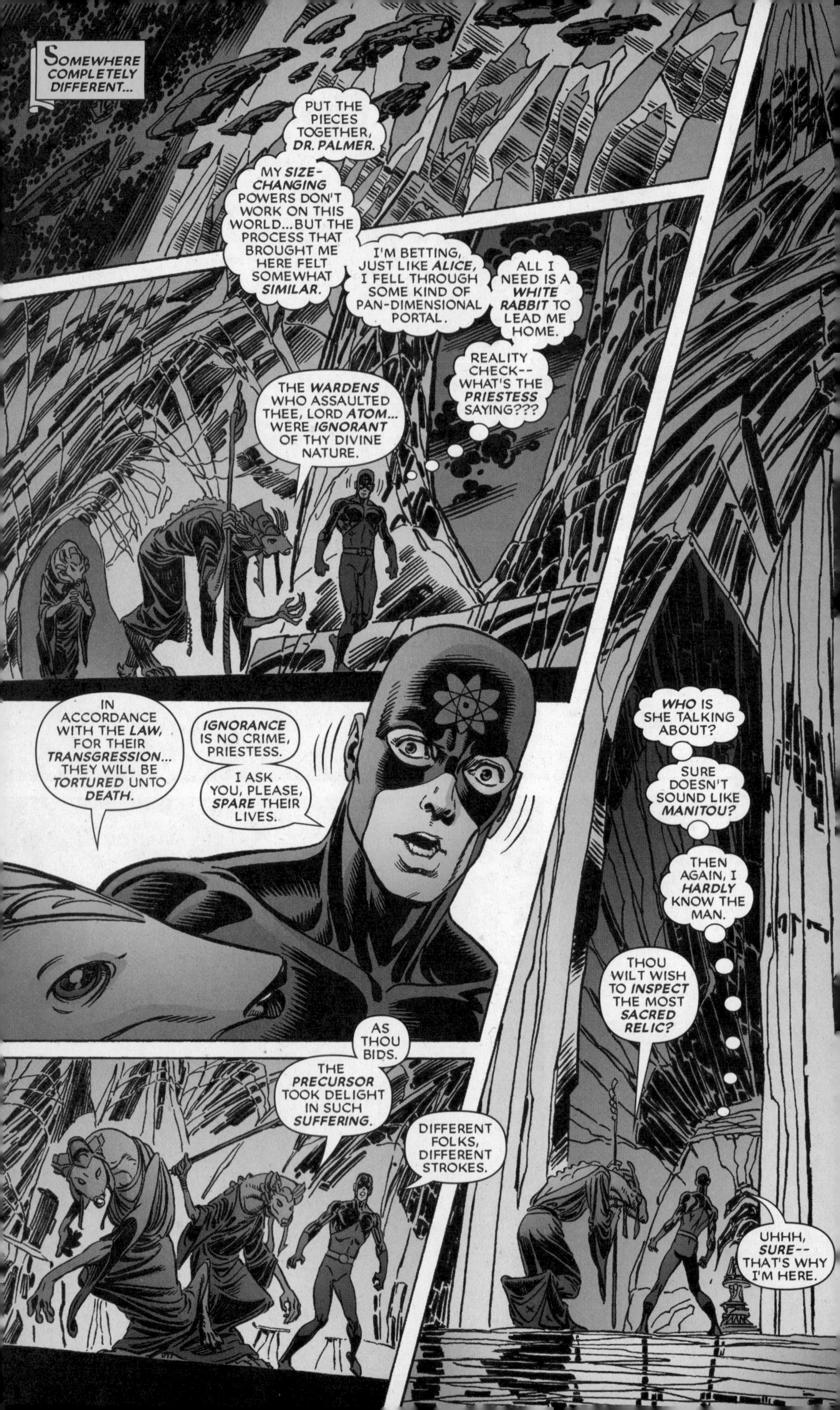
SOMEWHERE COMPLETELY DIFFERENT...
PUT THE PIECES TOGETHER, DR. PALMER.
MY SIZE-CHANGING POWERS DON'T WORK ON THIS WORLD...BUT THE PROCESS THAT BROUGHT ME HERE FELT SOMEWHAT SIMILAR.
I'M BETTING, JUST LIKE ALICE, I FELL THROUGH SOME KIND OF PAN-DIMENSIONAL PORTAL.
ALL I NEED IS A WHITE RABBIT TO LEAD ME HOME.
REALITY CHECK-- WHAT'S THE PRIESTESS SAYING???
THE WARDENS WHO ASSAULTED THEE, LORD ATOM... WERE IGNORANT OF THY DIVINE NATURE.
IN ACCORDANCE WITH THE LAW, FOR THEIR TRANSGRESSION... THEY WILL BE TORTURED UNTO DEATH.
IGNORANCE IS NO CRIME, PRIESTESS.
I ASK YOU, PLEASE, SPARE THEIR LIVES.
AS THOU BIDS.
THE PRECURSOR TOOK DELIGHT IN SUCH SUFFERING.
DIFFERENT FOLKS, DIFFERENT STROKES.
WHO IS SHE TALKING ABOUT?
SURE DOESN'T SOUND LIKE MANITOU?
THEN AGAIN, I HARDLY KNOW THE MAN.
THOU WILT WISH TO INSPECT THE MOST SACRED RELIC?
UHHH, SURE-- THAT'S WHY I'M HERE.

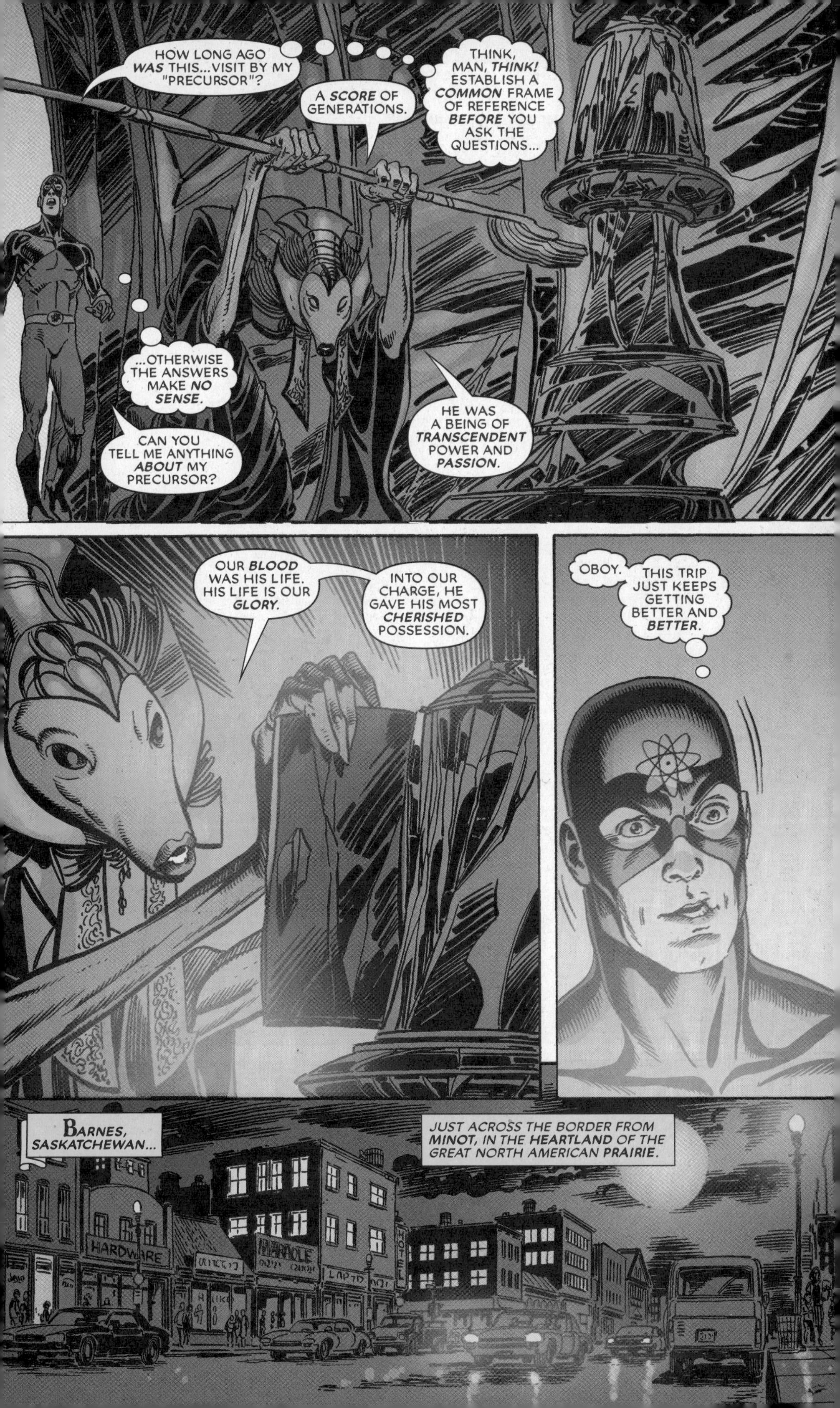
HOW LONG AGO WAS THIS...VISIT BY MY "PRECURSOR"?
A SCORE OF GENERATIONS.
THINK, MAN, THINK! ESTABLISH A COMMON FRAME OF REFERENCE BEFORE YOU ASK THE QUESTIONS...
...OTHERWISE THE ANSWERS MAKE NO SENSE.
CAN YOU TELL ME ANYTHING ABOUT MY PRECURSOR?
HE WAS A BEING OF TRANSCENDENT POWER AND PASSION.
OUR BLOOD WAS HIS LIFE. HIS LIFE IS OUR GLORY.
INTO OUR CHARGE, HE GAVE HIS MOST CHERISHED POSSESSION.
OBOY.
THIS TRIP JUST KEEPS GETTING BETTER AND BETTER.
BARNES, SASKATCHEWAN...
JUST ACROSS THE BORDER FROM MINOT, IN THE HEARTLAND OF THE GREAT NORTH AMERICAN PRAIRIE.
HARDWARE
HOTEL

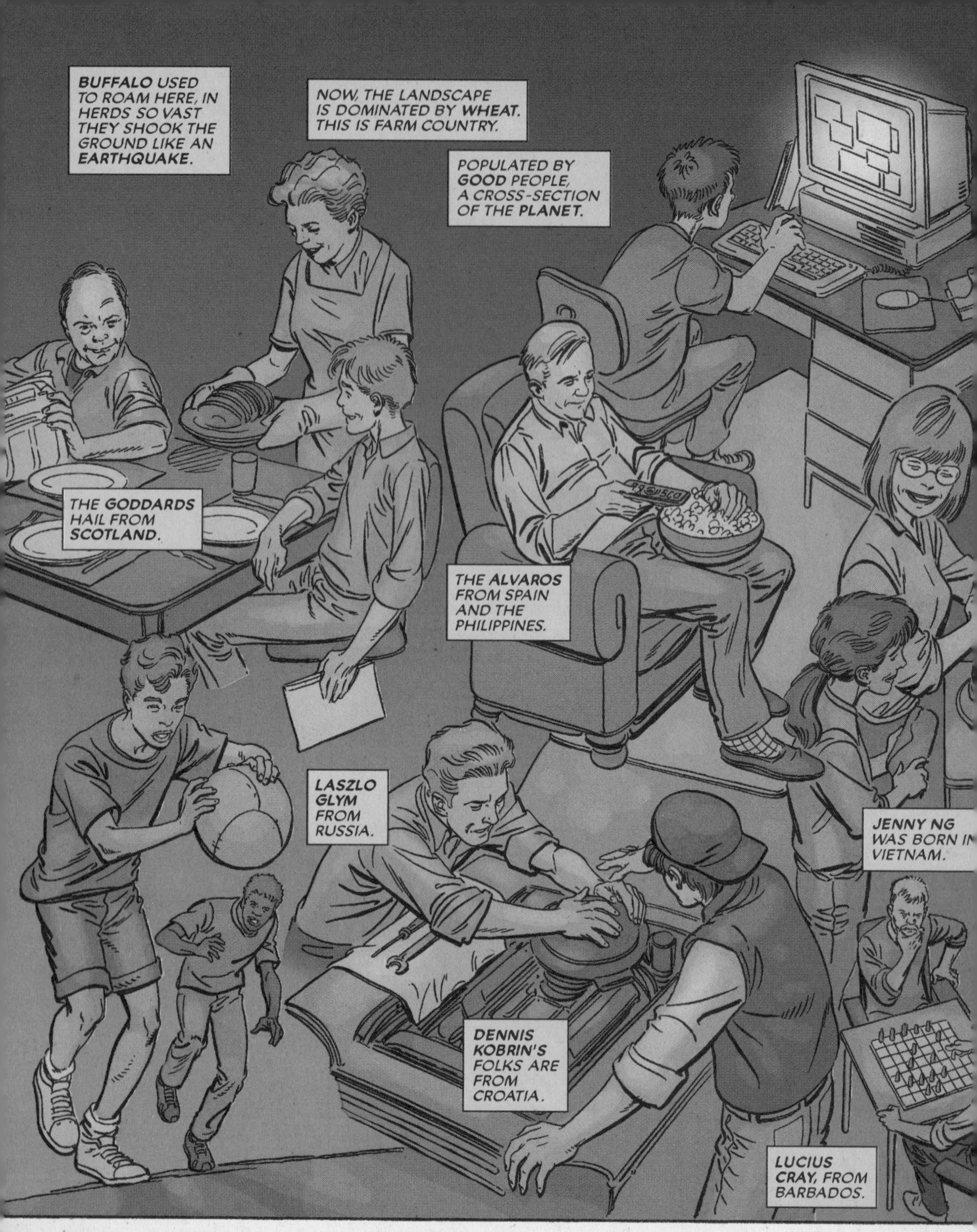
BUFFALO USED TO ROAM HERE, IN HERDS SO VAST THEY SHOOK THE GROUND LIKE AN EARTHQUAKE.
NOW, THE LANDSCAPE IS DOMINATED BY WHEAT. THIS IS FARM COUNTRY.
POPULATED BY GOOD PEOPLE, A CROSS-SECTION OF THE PLANET.
THE GODDARDS HAIL FROM SCOTLAND.
THE ALVAROS FROM SPAIN AND THE PHILIPPINES.
LASZLO GLYM FROM RUSSIA.
JENNY NG WAS BORN IN VIETNAM.
DENNIS KOBRIN'S FOLKS ARE FROM CROATIA.
LUCIUS CRAY, FROM BARBADOS.

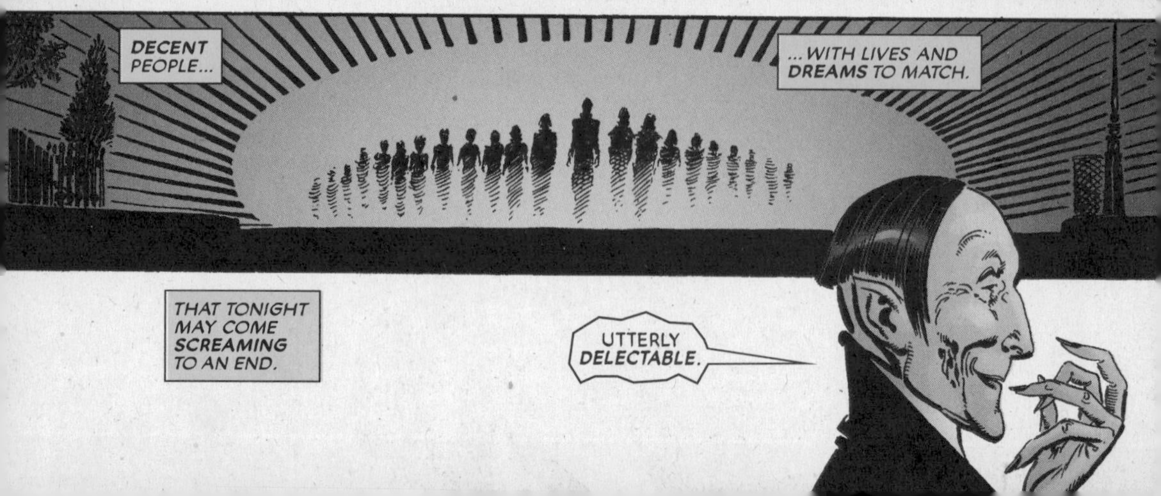
DECENT PEOPLE...
...WITH LIVES AND DREAMS TO MATCH.
THAT TONIGHT MAY COME SCREAMING TO AN END.
UTTERLY DELECTABLE.

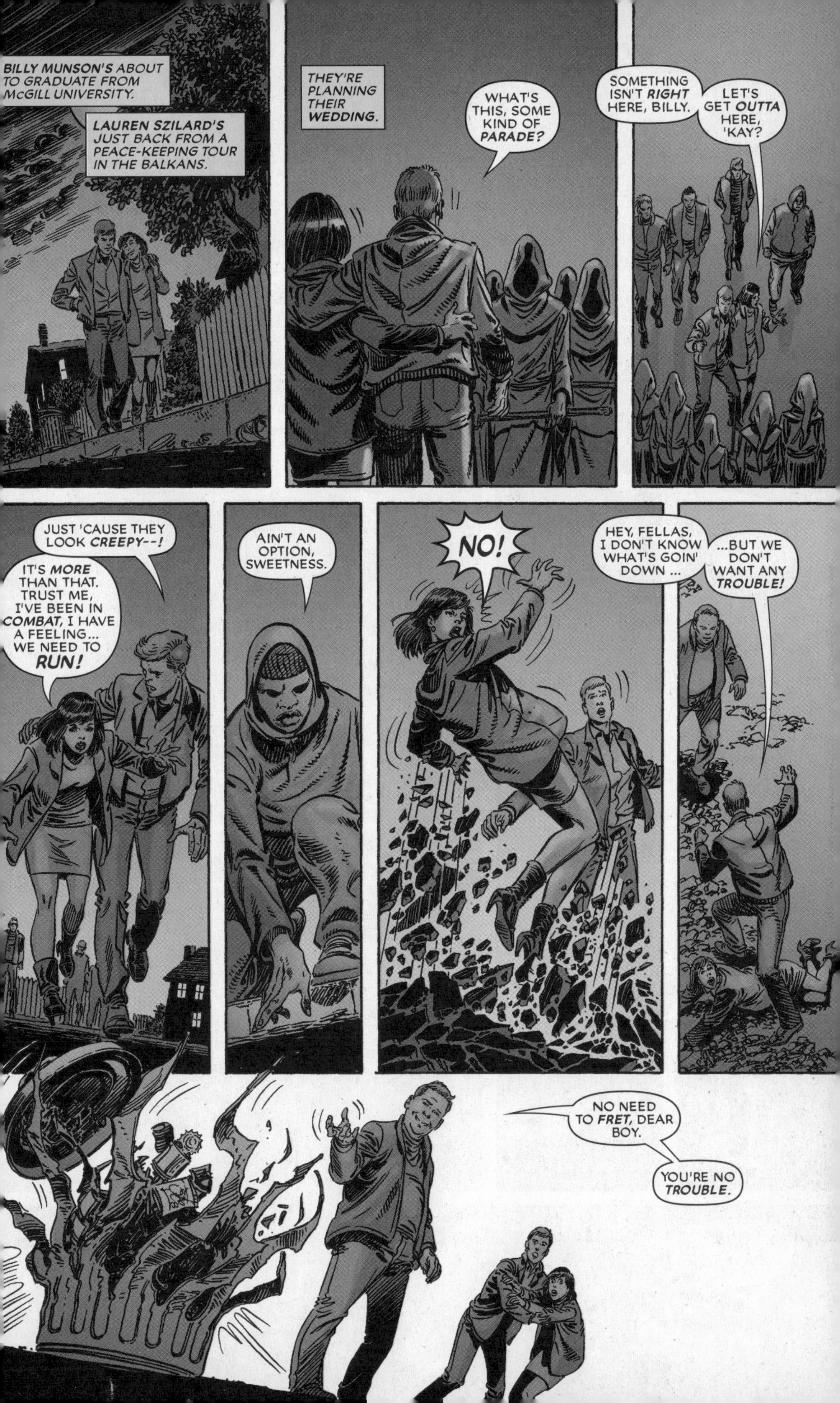

BILLY MUNSON'S ABOUT TO GRADUATE FROM McGILL UNIVERSITY.
LAUREN SZILARD'S JUST BACK FROM A PEACE-KEEPING TOUR IN THE BALKANS.
THEY'RE PLANNING THEIR WEDDING.
WHAT'S THIS, SOME KIND OF PARADE?
SOMETHING ISN'T RIGHT HERE, BILLY.
LET'S GET OUTTA HERE, 'KAY?
JUST 'CAUSE THEY LOOK CREEPY--!
IT'S MORE THAN THAT. TRUST ME, I'VE BEEN IN COMBAT, I HAVE A FEELING... WE NEED TO RUN!
AIN'T AN OPTION, SWEETNESS.
NO!
HEY, FELLAS, I DON'T KNOW WHAT'S GOIN' DOWN ...
...BUT WE DON'T WANT ANY TROUBLE!
NO NEED TO FRET, DEAR BOY.
YOU'RE NO TROUBLE.

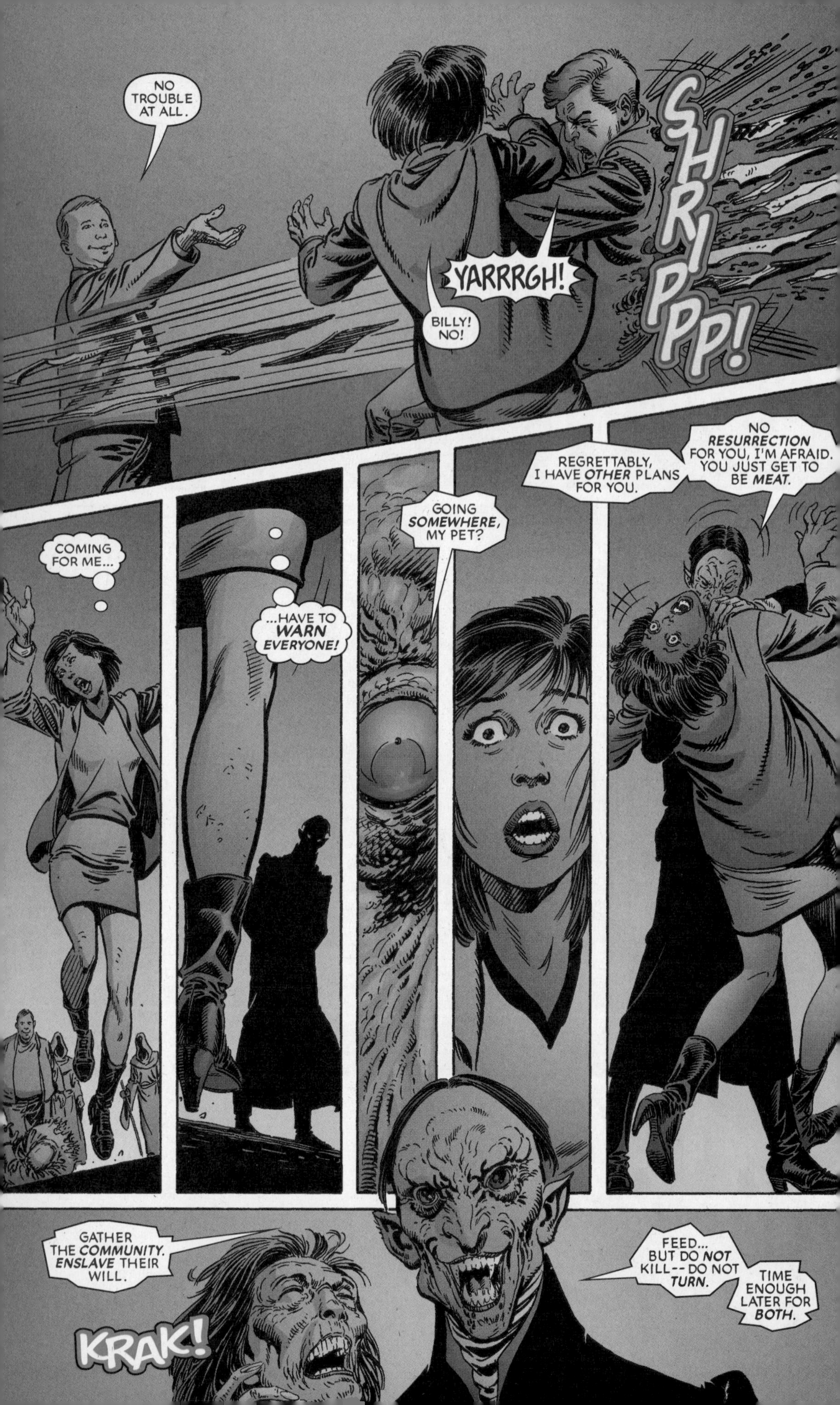

NO TROUBLE AT ALL.
YARRRGH!
BILLY! NO!
SHRIPPP!
COMING FOR ME...
...HAVE TO WARN EVERYONE!
GOING SOMEWHERE, MY PET?
REGRETTABLY, I HAVE OTHER PLANS FOR YOU.
NO RESURRECTION FOR YOU, I'M AFRAID. YOU JUST GET TO BE MEAT.
GATHER THE COMMUNITY. ENSLAVE THEIR WILL.
FEED... BUT DO NOT KILL-- DO NOT TURN.
TIME ENOUGH LATER FOR BOTH.
KRAK!

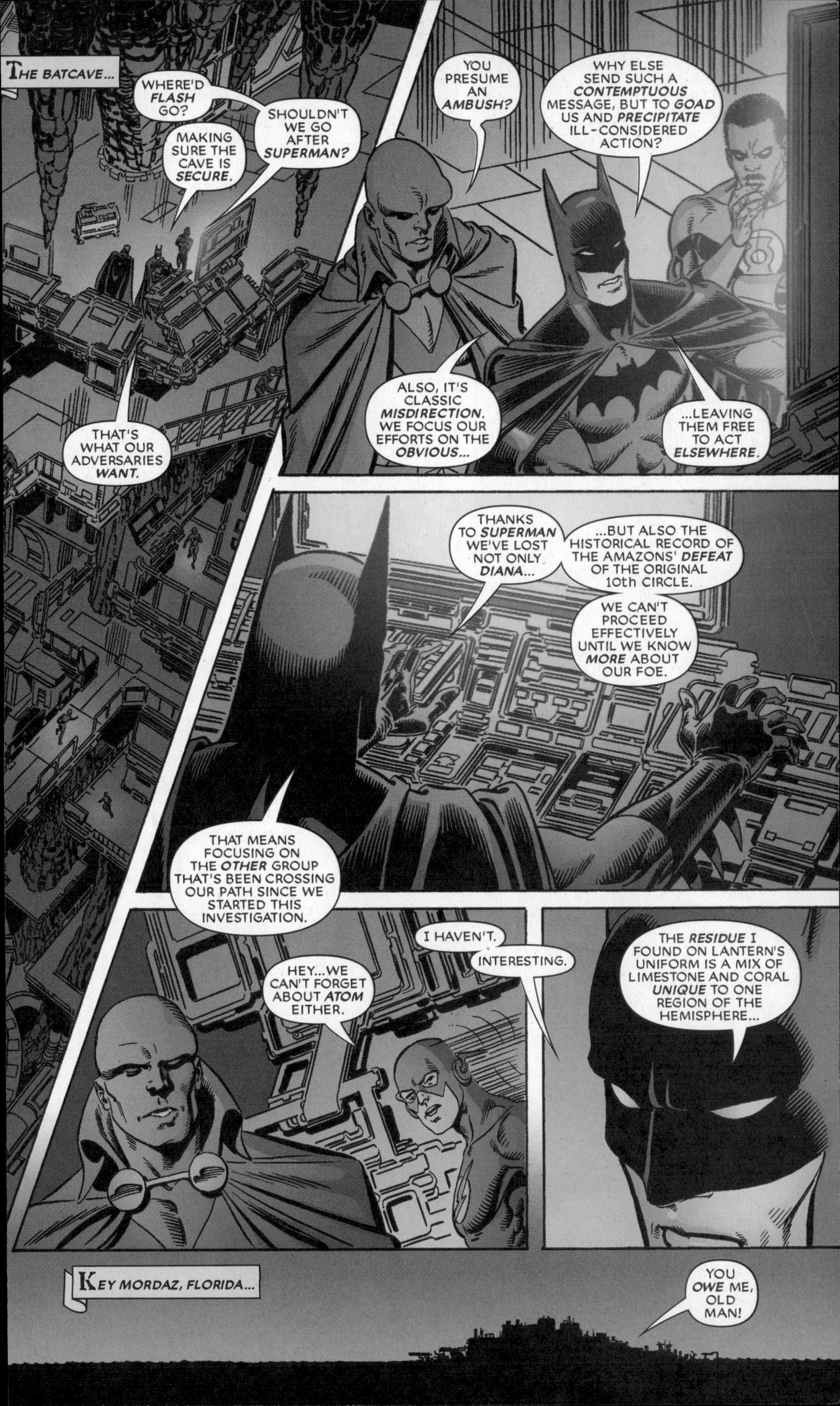

THE BATCAVE...
WHERE'D FLASH GO?
MAKING SURE THE CAVE IS SECURE.
SHOULDN'T WE GO AFTER SUPERMAN?
THAT'S WHAT OUR ADVERSARIES WANT.
YOU PRESUME AN AMBUSH?
WHY ELSE SEND SUCH A CONTEMPTUOUS MESSAGE, BUT TO GOAD US AND PRECIPITATE ILL-CONSIDERED ACTION?
ALSO, IT'S CLASSIC MISDIRECTION. WE FOCUS OUR EFFORTS ON THE OBVIOUS...
...LEAVING THEM FREE TO ACT ELSEWHERE.
THANKS TO SUPERMAN WE'VE LOST NOT ONLY DIANA...
...BUT ALSO THE HISTORICAL RECORD OF THE AMAZONS' DEFEAT OF THE ORIGINAL 10th CIRCLE.
WE CAN'T PROCEED EFFECTIVELY UNTIL WE KNOW MORE ABOUT OUR FOE.
THAT MEANS FOCUSING ON THE OTHER GROUP THAT'S BEEN CROSSING OUR PATH SINCE WE STARTED THIS INVESTIGATION.
HEY...WE CAN'T FORGET ABOUT ATOM EITHER.
I HAVEN'T.
INTERESTING.
THE RESIDUE I FOUND ON LANTERN'S UNIFORM IS A MIX OF LIMESTONE AND CORAL UNIQUE TO ONE REGION OF THE HEMISPHERE...
KEY MORDAZ, FLORIDA...
YOU OWE ME, OLD MAN!

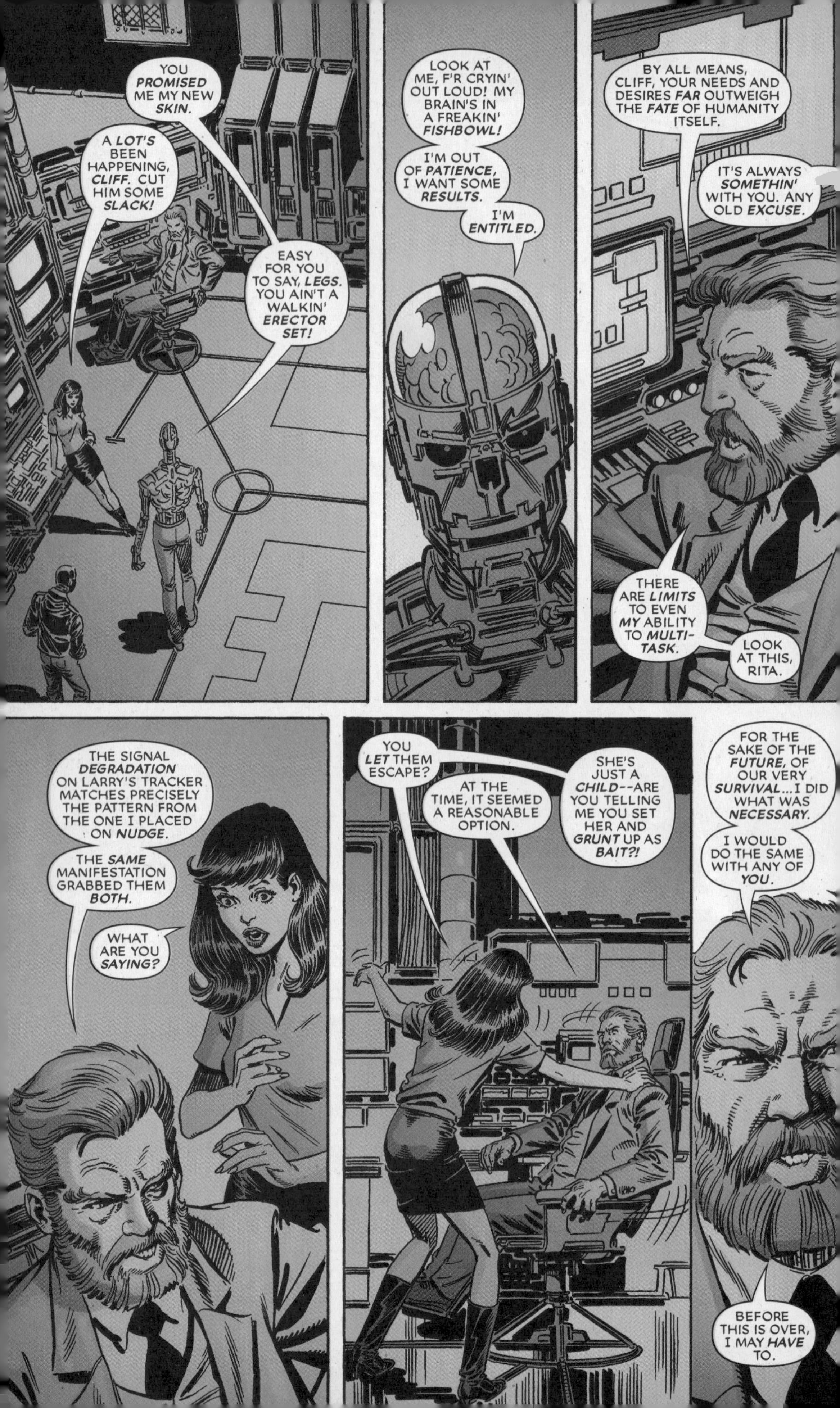
YOU PROMISED ME MY NEW SKIN.
A LOT'S BEEN HAPPENING, CLIFF. CUT HIM SOME SLACK!
EASY FOR YOU TO SAY, LEGS. YOU AIN'T A WALKIN' ERECTOR SET!
LOOK AT ME, F'R CRYIN' OUT LOUD! MY BRAIN'S IN A FREAKIN' FISHBOWL!
I'M OUT OF PATIENCE, I WANT SOME RESULTS.
I'M ENTITLED.
BY ALL MEANS, CLIFF, YOUR NEEDS AND DESIRES FAR OUTWEIGH THE FATE OF HUMANITY ITSELF.
IT'S ALWAYS SOMETHIN' WITH YOU. ANY OLD EXCUSE.
THERE ARE LIMITS TO EVEN MY ABILITY TO MULTI-TASK.
LOOK AT THIS, RITA.
THE SIGNAL DEGRADATION ON LARRY'S TRACKER MATCHES PRECISELY THE PATTERN FROM THE ONE I PLACED ON NUDGE.
THE SAME MANIFESTATION GRABBED THEM BOTH.
WHAT ARE YOU SAYING?
YOU LET THEM ESCAPE?
AT THE TIME, IT SEEMED A REASONABLE OPTION.
SHE'S JUST A CHILD--ARE YOU TELLING ME YOU SET HER AND GRUNT UP AS BAIT?!
FOR THE SAKE OF THE FUTURE, OF OUR VERY SURVIVAL...I DID WHAT WAS NECESSARY.
I WOULD DO THE SAME WITH ANY OF YOU.
BEFORE THIS IS OVER, I MAY HAVE TO.

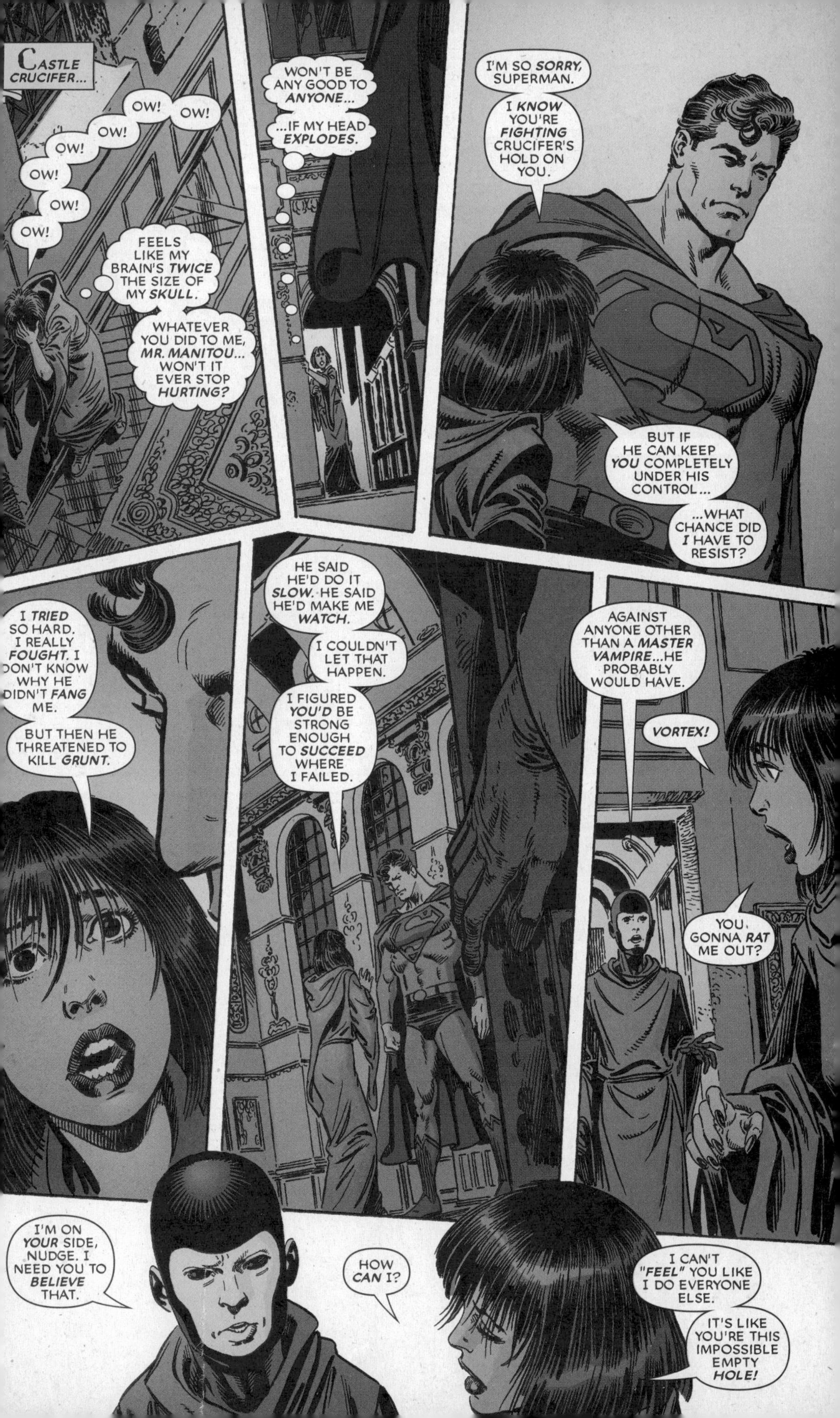
CASTLE CRUCIFER...
OW!
OW!
OW!
OW!
OW!
OW!
OW!
FEELS LIKE MY BRAIN'S TWICE THE SIZE OF MY SKULL.
WHATEVER YOU DID TO ME, MR. MANITOU... WON'T IT EVER STOP HURTING?
WON'T BE ANY GOOD TO ANYONE...
...IF MY HEAD EXPLODES.
I'M SO SORRY, SUPERMAN.
I KNOW YOU'RE FIGHTING CRUCIFER'S HOLD ON YOU.
BUT IF HE CAN KEEP YOU COMPLETELY UNDER HIS CONTROL...
...WHAT CHANCE DID I HAVE TO RESIST?
I TRIED SO HARD. I REALLY FOUGHT. I DON'T KNOW WHY HE DIDN'T FANG ME.
BUT THEN HE THREATENED TO KILL GRUNT.
HE SAID HE'D DO IT SLOW. HE SAID HE'D MAKE ME WATCH.
I COULDN'T LET THAT HAPPEN.
I FIGURED YOU'D BE STRONG ENOUGH TO SUCCEED WHERE I FAILED.
AGAINST ANYONE OTHER THAN A MASTER VAMPIRE...HE PROBABLY WOULD HAVE.
VORTEX!
YOU GONNA RAT ME OUT?
I'M ON YOUR SIDE, NUDGE. I NEED YOU TO BELIEVE THAT.
HOW CAN I?
I CAN'T "FEEL" YOU LIKE I DO EVERYONE ELSE.
IT'S LIKE YOU'RE THIS IMPOSSIBLE EMPTY HOLE!

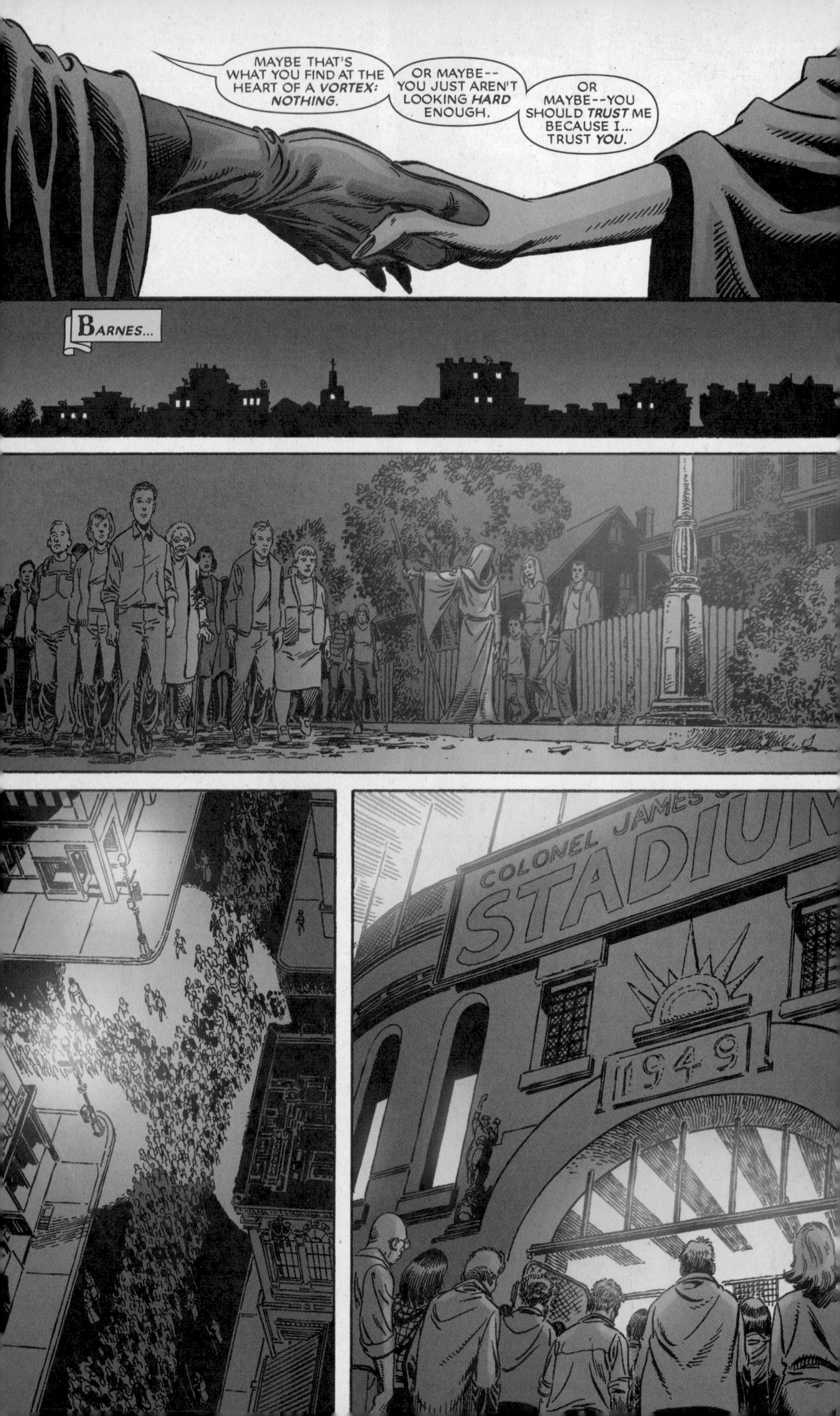
MAYBE THAT'S WHAT YOU FIND AT THE HEART OF A VORTEX: NOTHING.
OR MAYBE-- YOU JUST AREN'T LOOKING HARD ENOUGH.
OR MAYBE--YOU SHOULD TRUST ME BECAUSE I... TRUST YOU.
BARNES...
COLONEL JAMES
STADIUM
1949

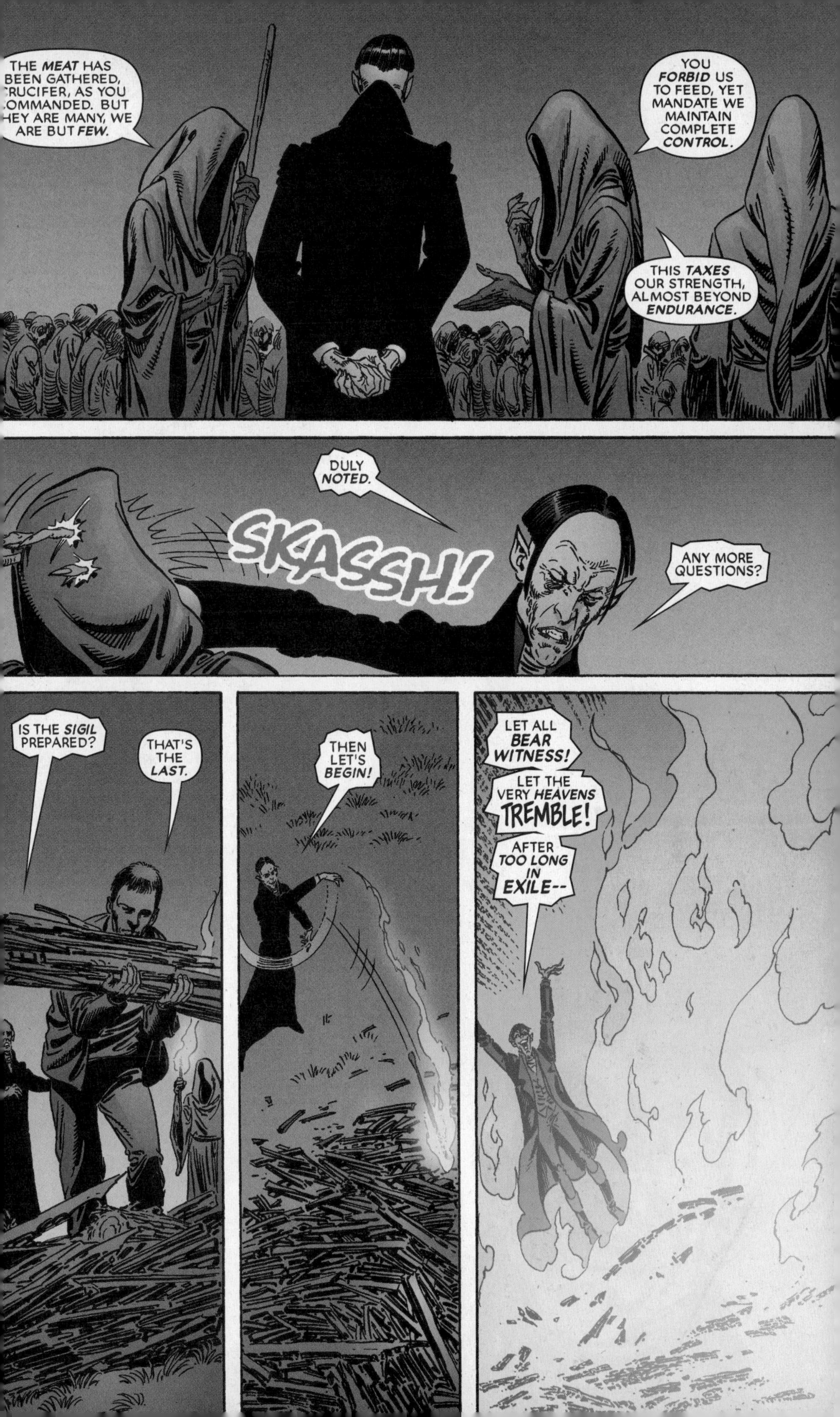
THE MEAT HAS BEEN GATHERED, CRUCIFER, AS YOU COMMANDED. BUT THEY ARE MANY, WE ARE BUT FEW.
YOU FORBID US TO FEED, YET MANDATE WE MAINTAIN COMPLETE CONTROL.
THIS TAXES OUR STRENGTH, ALMOST BEYOND ENDURANCE.
DULY NOTED.
SKASSH!
ANY MORE QUESTIONS?
IS THE SIGIL PREPARED?
THAT'S THE LAST.
THEN LET'S BEGIN!
LET ALL BEAR WITNESS!
LET THE VERY HEAVENS TREMBLE!
AFTER TOO LONG IN EXILE--

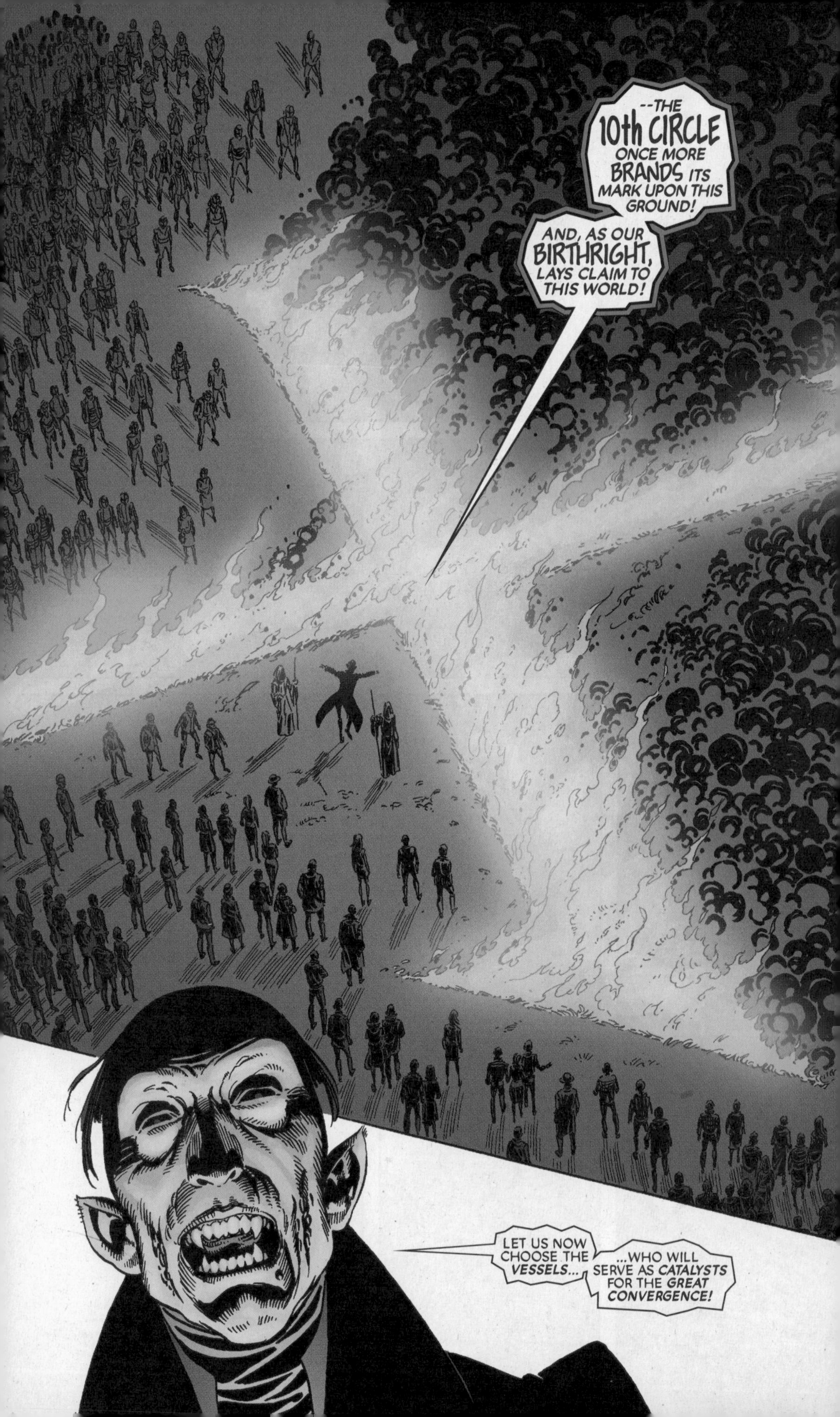
--THE 10th CIRCLE ONCE MORE BRANDS ITS MARK UPON THIS GROUND!
AND, AS OUR BIRTHRIGHT, LAYS CLAIM TO THIS WORLD!
LET US NOW CHOOSE THE VESSELS...
...WHO WILL SERVE AS CATALYSTS FOR THE GREAT CONVERGENCE!

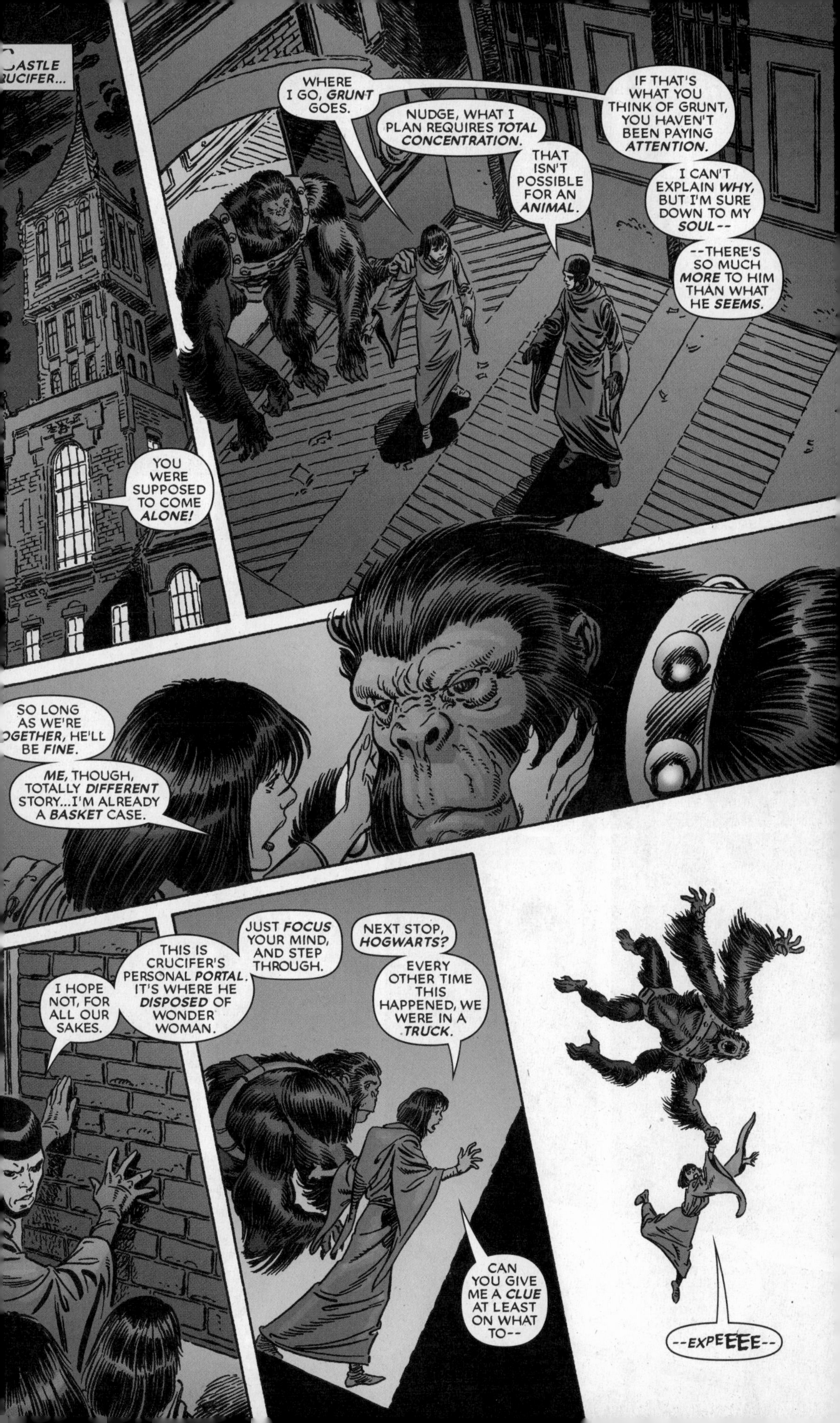
CASTLE
RUCIFER...
WHERE I GO, GRUNT GOES.
NUDGE, WHAT I PLAN REQUIRES TOTAL CONCENTRATION.
THAT ISN'T POSSIBLE FOR AN ANIMAL.
IF THAT'S WHAT YOU THINK OF GRUNT, YOU HAVEN'T BEEN PAYING ATTENTION.
I CAN'T EXPLAIN WHY, BUT I'M SURE DOWN TO MY SOUL--
--THERE'S SO MUCH MORE TO HIM THAN WHAT HE SEEMS.
YOU WERE SUPPOSED TO COME ALONE!
SO LONG AS WE'RE OGETHER, HE'LL BE FINE.
ME, THOUGH, TOTALLY DIFFERENT STORY...I'M ALREADY A BASKET CASE.
THIS IS CRUCIFER'S PERSONAL PORTAL. IT'S WHERE HE DISPOSED OF WONDER WOMAN.
I HOPE NOT, FOR ALL OUR SAKES.
JUST FOCUS YOUR MIND, AND STEP THROUGH.
NEXT STOP, HOGWARTS?
EVERY OTHER TIME THIS HAPPENED, WE WERE IN A TRUCK.
CAN YOU GIVE ME A CLUE AT LEAST ON WHAT TO--
--EXPEEEE--

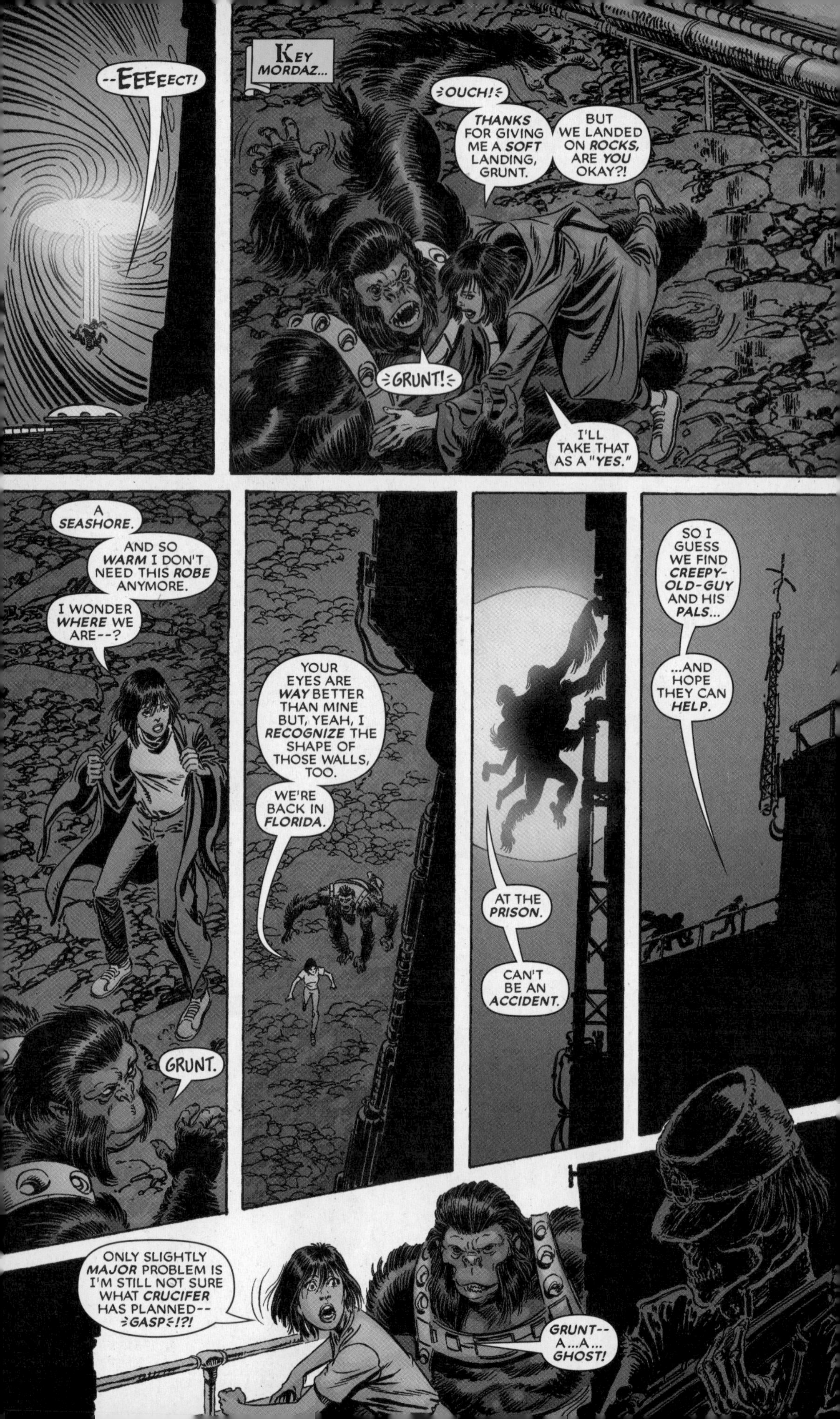
--EEEEECT!
KEY MORDAZ...
OUCH!
THANKS FOR GIVING ME A SOFT LANDING, GRUNT.
BUT WE LANDED ON ROCKS, ARE YOU OKAY?!
GRUNT!
I'LL TAKE THAT AS A "YES."
A SEASHORE.
AND SO WARM I DON'T NEED THIS ROBE ANYMORE.
I WONDER WHERE WE ARE--?
GRUNT.
YOUR EYES ARE WAY BETTER THAN MINE BUT, YEAH, I RECOGNIZE THE SHAPE OF THOSE WALLS, TOO.
WE'RE BACK IN FLORIDA.
AT THE PRISON.
CAN'T BE AN ACCIDENT.
SO I GUESS WE FIND CREEPY-OLD-GUY AND HIS PALS...
...AND HOPE THEY CAN HELP.
ONLY SLIGHTLY MAJOR PROBLEM IS I'M STILL NOT SURE WHAT CRUCIFER HAS PLANNED-- GASP!?!
GRUNT-- A...A... GHOST!

I *UNDERESTIMATED* THE CAPABILITIES OF OUR ADVERSARY. FOR THAT, I TAKE *FULL RESPONSIBILITY.*

BUT I SUSPECT I ALSO UNDERESTIMATED THOSE OF *NUDGE* AND HER COMPANION.

AH-- *CLIFFORD--* YOU WERE IMPATIENT FOR YOUR *SKIN?*

CHANGIN' THE SUBJECT, OLD MAN?

QUITE THE CONTRARY...

...THE *LENS* ON YOUR CHEST IS A *HOLOGRAPHIC TRANSCEIVER* AND MULTI-SPECTRUM *SCANNER ARRAY*...

...THAT WILL ALLOW US TO REMAIN IN CONSTANT *CONTACT.*

BETTER HAVE AN *"OFF"* SWITCH.

THE *FLEXI-METAL* WILL PROTECT YOU AGAINST A BROAD ARRAY OF PROJECTILE AND ENERGY *WEAPONS.*

THE ENHANCED MUSCULATURE WILL INCREASE YOUR ALREADY EXCEPTIONAL STRENGTH BY *1000-FOLD.*

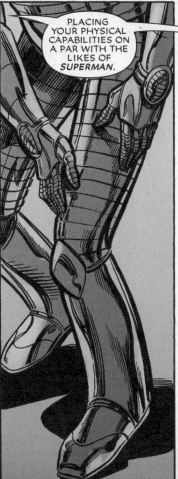

PLACING YOUR PHYSICAL CAPABILITIES ON A PAR WITH THE LIKES OF *SUPERMAN.*

SIGHT, HEARING, TOUCH, ALL HAVE BEEN BROADENED TO AN *EQUIVALENT* DEGREE.

AND OF COURSE, THAT SAME FLEXI-METAL WILL GIVE YOUR *FACE*... A MUCH GREATER RANGE OF *EXPRESSION.*

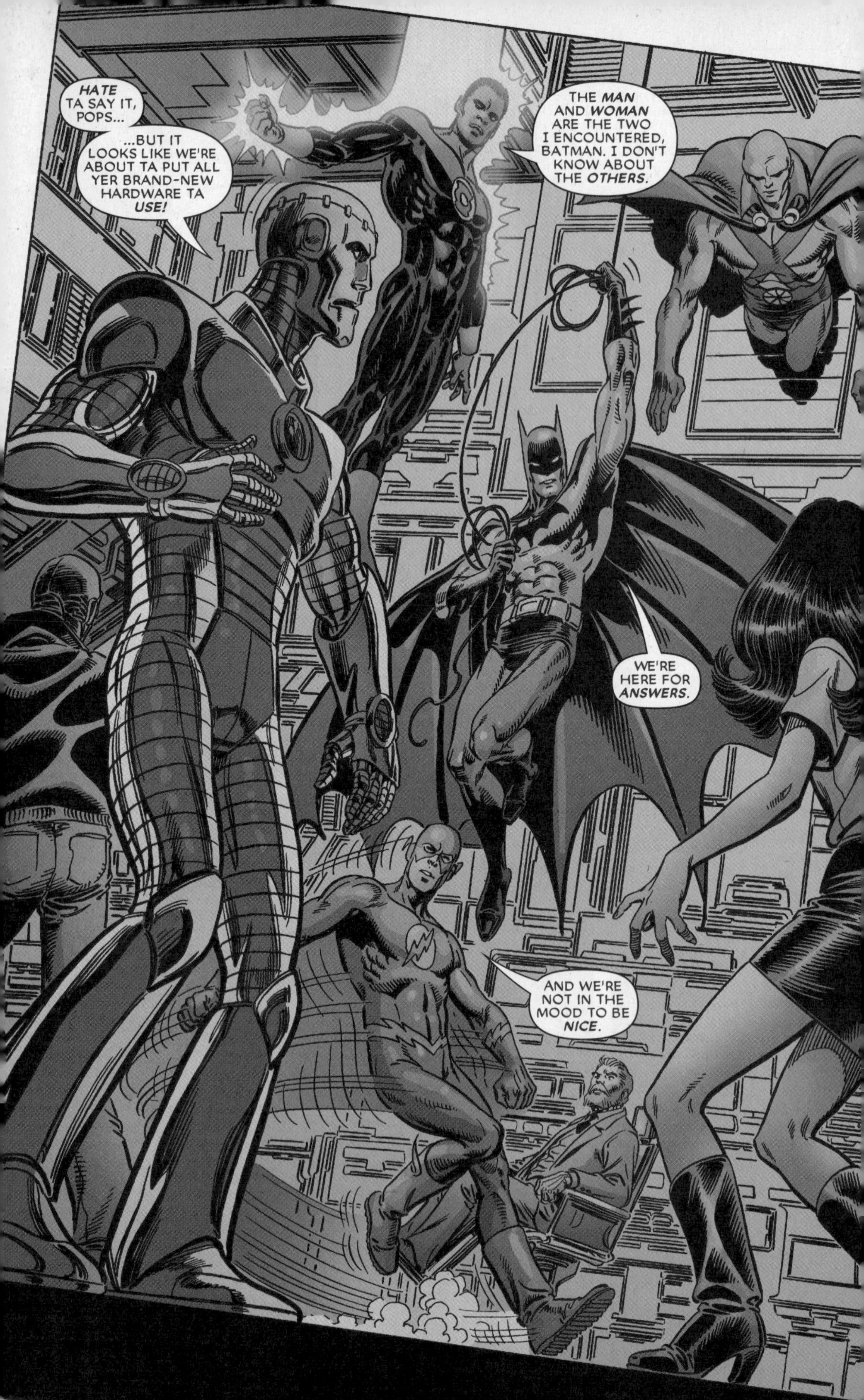
HATE TA SAY IT, POPS...
...BUT IT LOOKS LIKE WE'RE ABOUT TA PUT ALL YER BRAND-NEW HARDWARE TA USE!
THE MAN AND WOMAN ARE THE TWO I ENCOUNTERED, BATMAN. I DON'T KNOW ABOUT THE OTHERS.
WE'RE HERE FOR ANSWERS.
AND WE'RE NOT IN THE MOOD TO BE NICE.

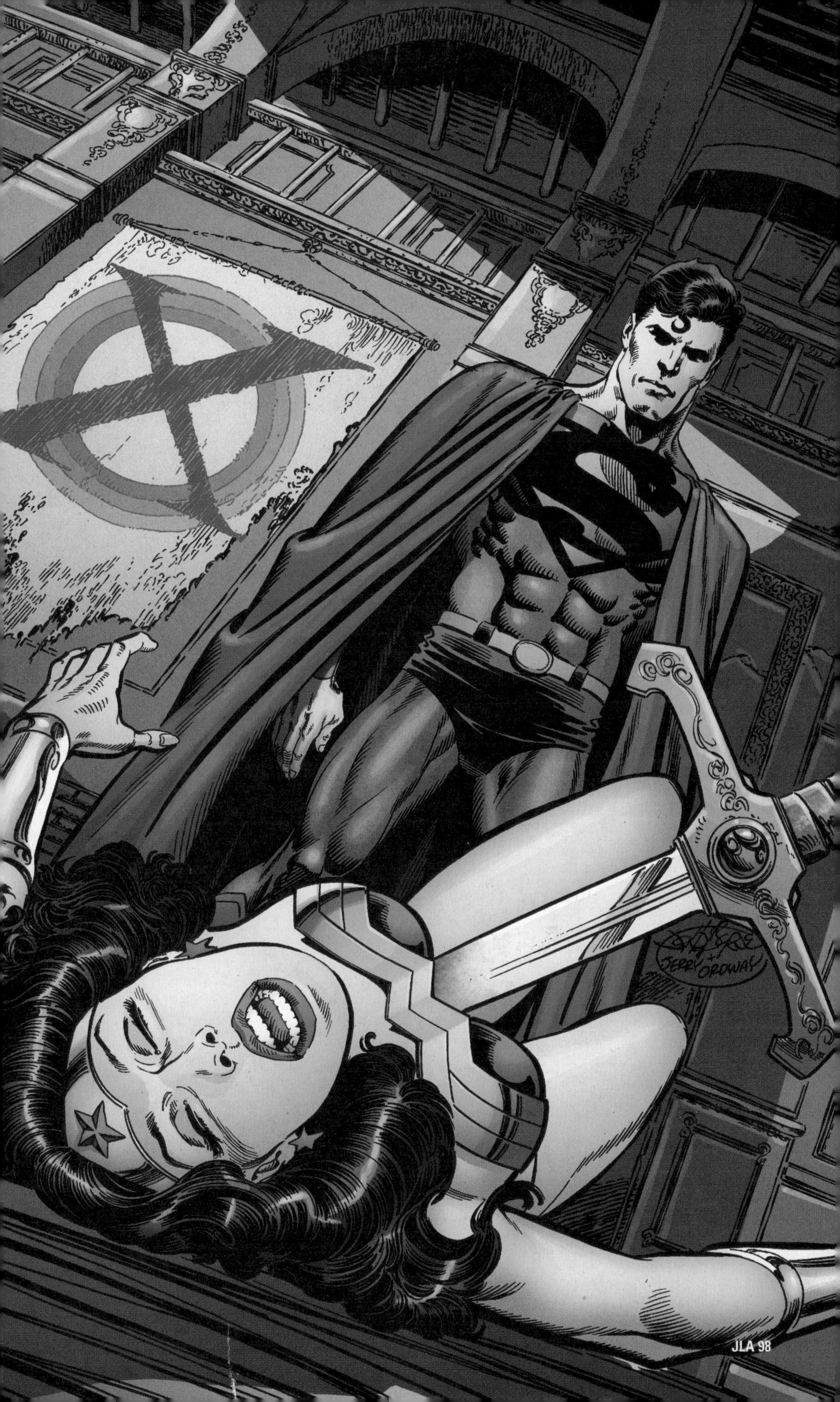
JERRY ORDWAY
JLA 98

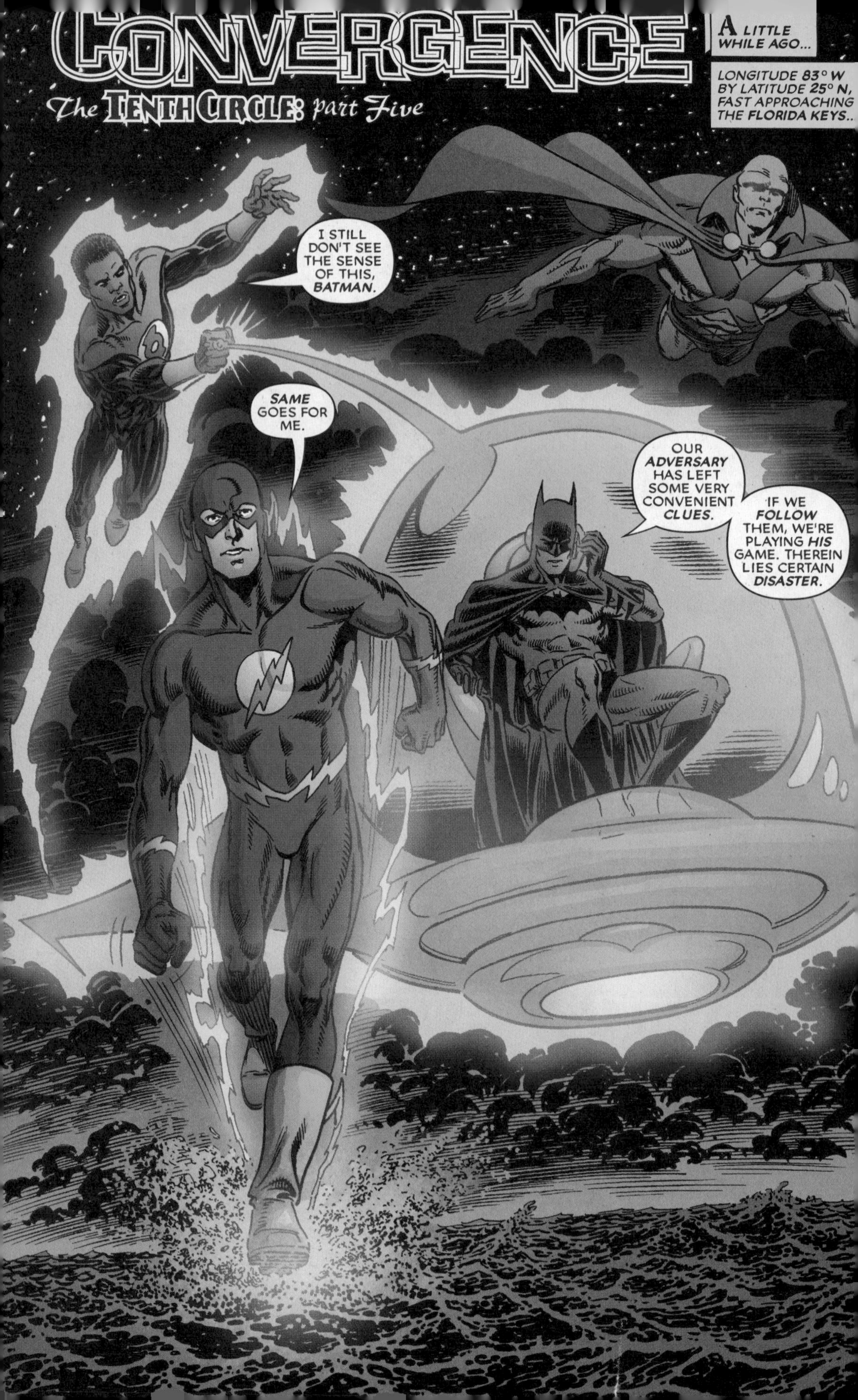
CONVERGENCE
The TENTH CIRCLE: part Five
A LITTLE WHILE AGO...
LONGITUDE 83° W BY LATITUDE 25° N, FAST APPROACHING THE FLORIDA KEYS..
I STILL DON'T SEE THE SENSE OF THIS, BATMAN.
SAME GOES FOR ME.
OUR ADVERSARY HAS LEFT SOME VERY CONVENIENT CLUES.
IF WE FOLLOW THEM, WE'RE PLAYING HIS GAME. THEREIN LIES CERTAIN DISASTER.

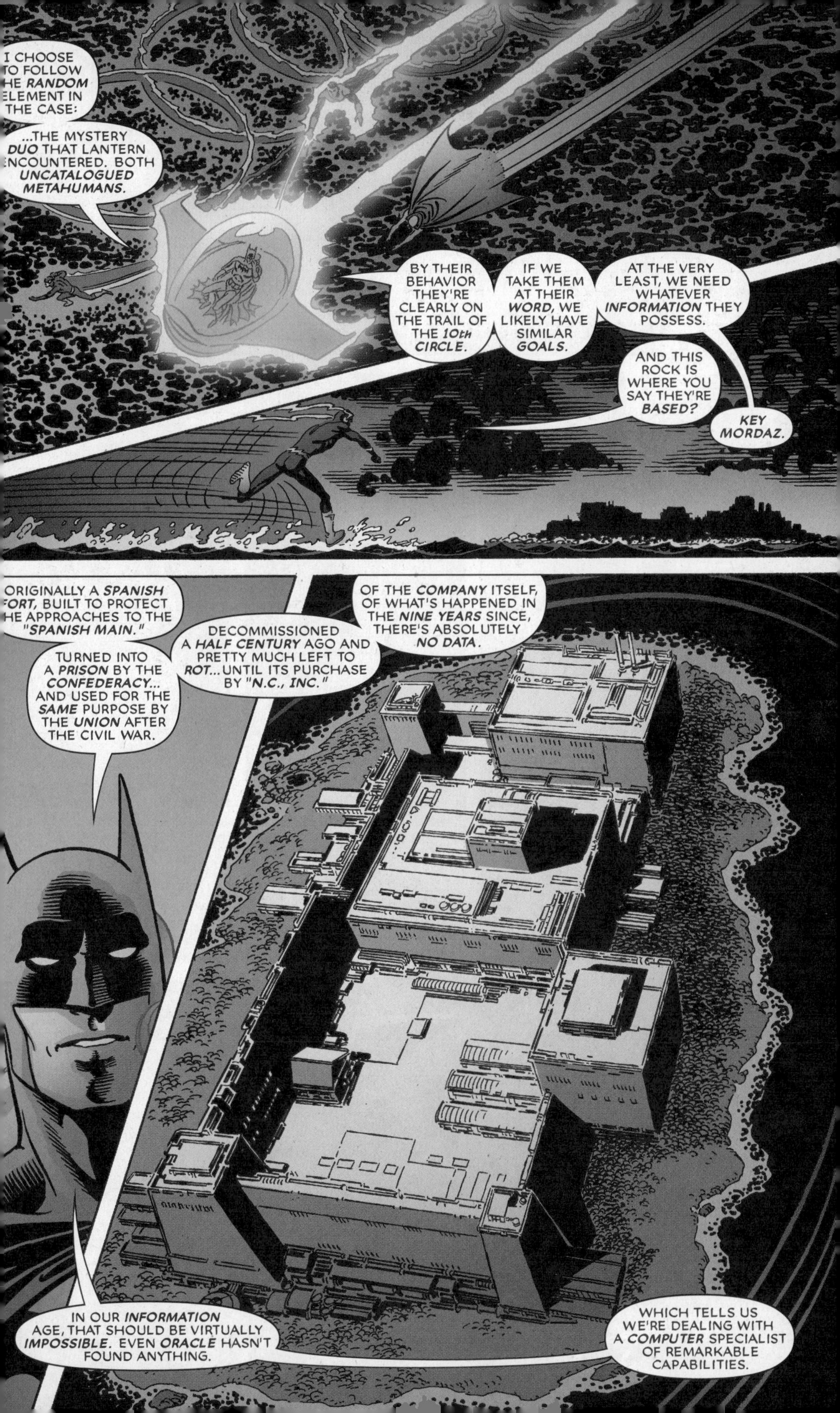

I CHOOSE TO FOLLOW HE RANDOM ELEMENT IN THE CASE:
...THE MYSTERY DUO THAT LANTERN NCOUNTERED. BOTH UNCATALOGUED METAHUMANS.
BY THEIR BEHAVIOR THEY'RE CLEARLY ON THE TRAIL OF THE 10th CIRCLE.
IF WE TAKE THEM AT THEIR WORD, WE LIKELY HAVE SIMILAR GOALS.
AT THE VERY LEAST, WE NEED WHATEVER INFORMATION THEY POSSESS.
AND THIS ROCK IS WHERE YOU SAY THEY'RE BASED?
KEY MORDAZ.
ORIGINALLY A SPANISH FORT, BUILT TO PROTECT HE APPROACHES TO THE "SPANISH MAIN."
TURNED INTO A PRISON BY THE CONFEDERACY... AND USED FOR THE SAME PURPOSE BY THE UNION AFTER THE CIVIL WAR.
DECOMMISSIONED A HALF CENTURY AGO AND PRETTY MUCH LEFT TO ROT... UNTIL ITS PURCHASE BY "N.C., INC."
OF THE COMPANY ITSELF, OF WHAT'S HAPPENED IN THE NINE YEARS SINCE, THERE'S ABSOLUTELY NO DATA.
IN OUR INFORMATION AGE, THAT SHOULD BE VIRTUALLY IMPOSSIBLE. EVEN ORACLE HASN'T FOUND ANYTHING.
WHICH TELLS US WE'RE DEALING WITH A COMPUTER SPECIALIST OF REMARKABLE CAPABILITIES.

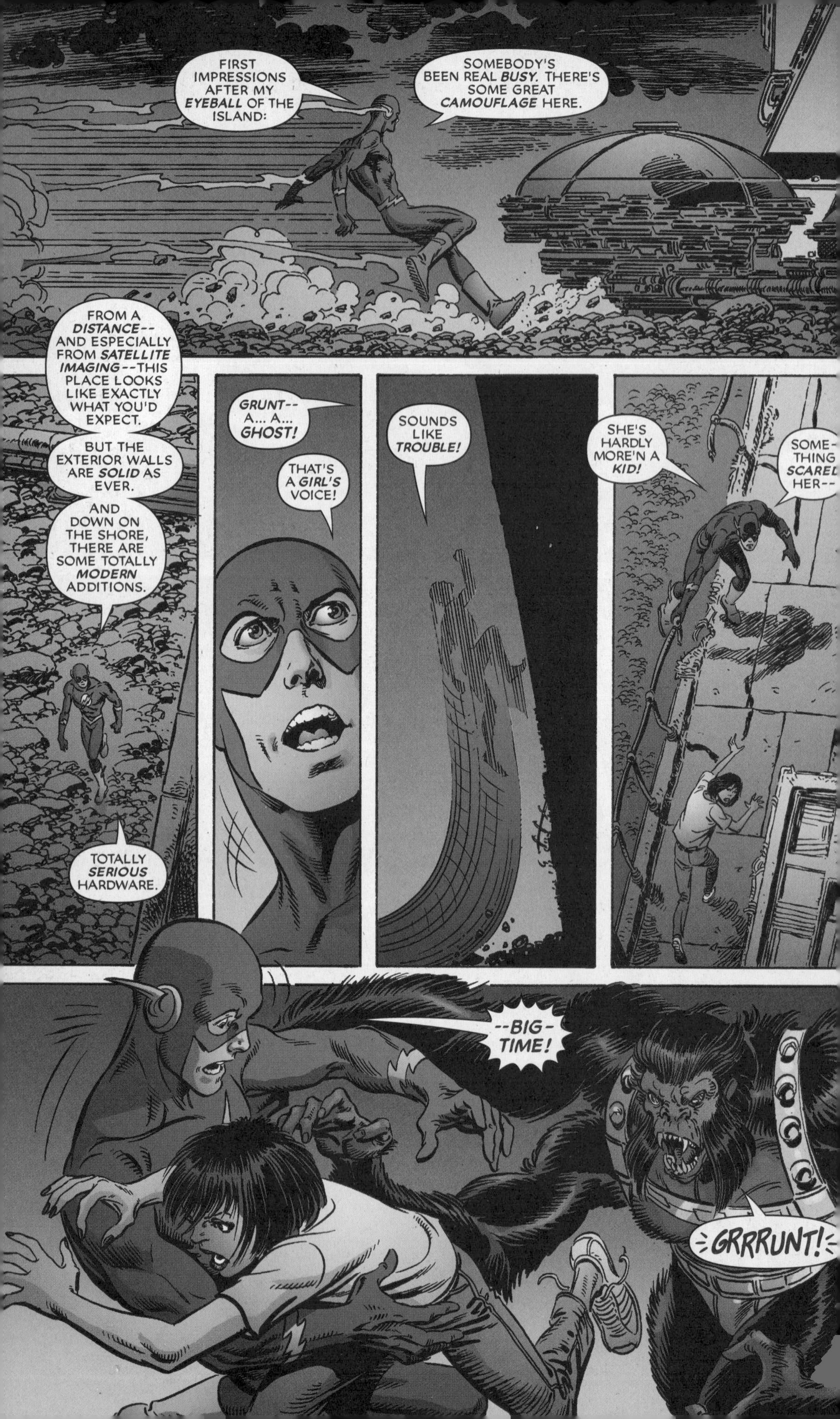

FIRST IMPRESSIONS AFTER MY EYEBALL OF THE ISLAND:
SOMEBODY'S BEEN REAL BUSY. THERE'S SOME GREAT CAMOUFLAGE HERE.
FROM A DISTANCE-- AND ESPECIALLY FROM SATELLITE IMAGING--THIS PLACE LOOKS LIKE EXACTLY WHAT YOU'D EXPECT.
BUT THE EXTERIOR WALLS ARE SOLID AS EVER.
AND DOWN ON THE SHORE, THERE ARE SOME TOTALLY MODERN ADDITIONS.
TOTALLY SERIOUS HARDWARE.
GRUNT-- A... A... GHOST!
THAT'S A GIRL'S VOICE!
SOUNDS LIKE TROUBLE!
SHE'S HARDLY MORE'N A KID!
SOME-THING SCARED HER--
--BIG TIME!
GRRRUNT!

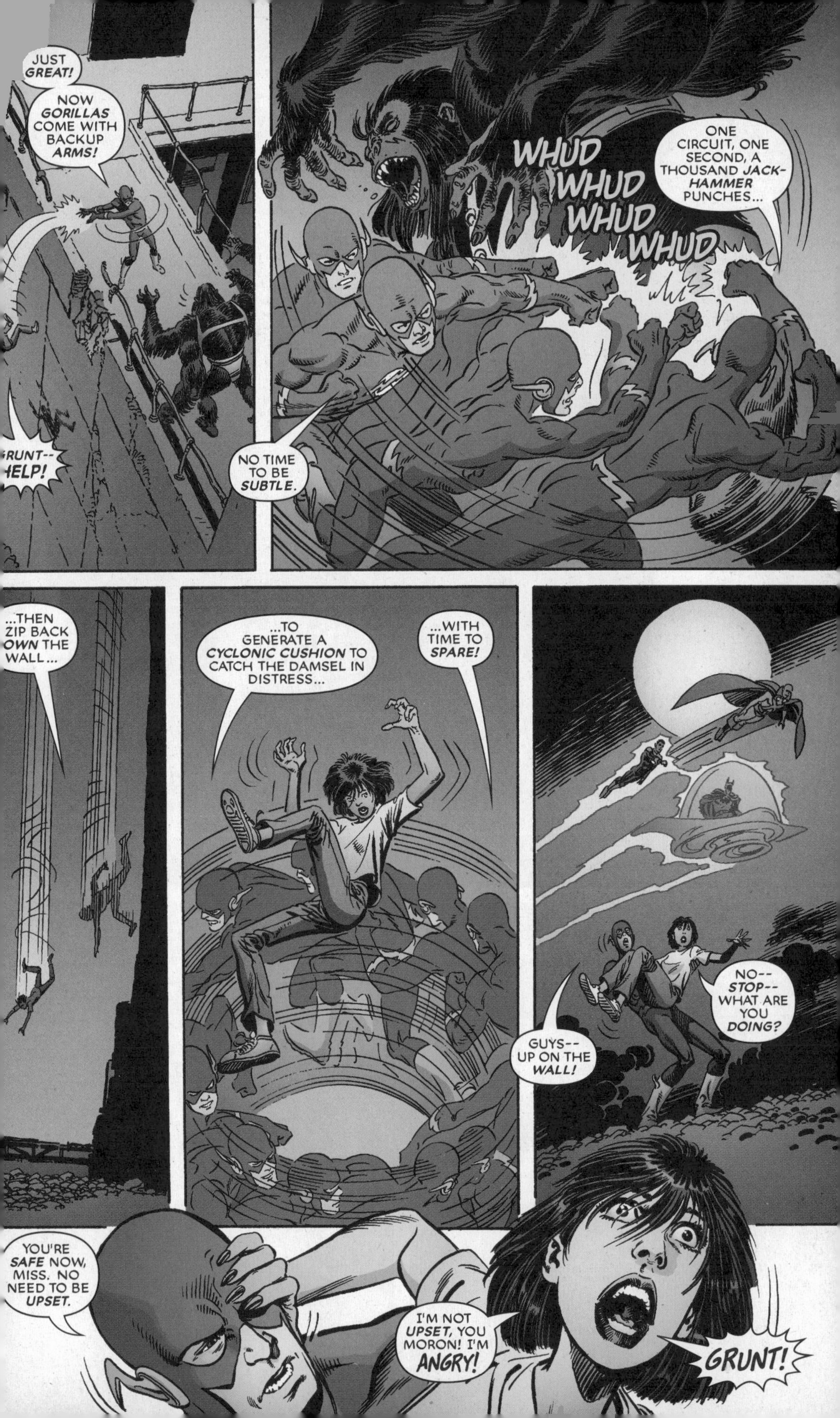
JUST GREAT!
NOW GORILLAS COME WITH BACKUP ARMS!
RUNT-- HELP!
WHUD WHUD WHUD WHUD
ONE CIRCUIT, ONE SECOND, A THOUSAND JACK-HAMMER PUNCHES...
NO TIME TO BE SUBTLE.
...THEN ZIP BACK OWN THE WALL...
...TO GENERATE A CYCLONIC CUSHION TO CATCH THE DAMSEL IN DISTRESS...
...WITH TIME TO SPARE!
GUYS-- UP ON THE WALL!
NO-- STOP-- WHAT ARE YOU DOING?
YOU'RE SAFE NOW, MISS. NO NEED TO BE UPSET.
I'M NOT UPSET, YOU MORON! I'M ANGRY!
GRUNT!

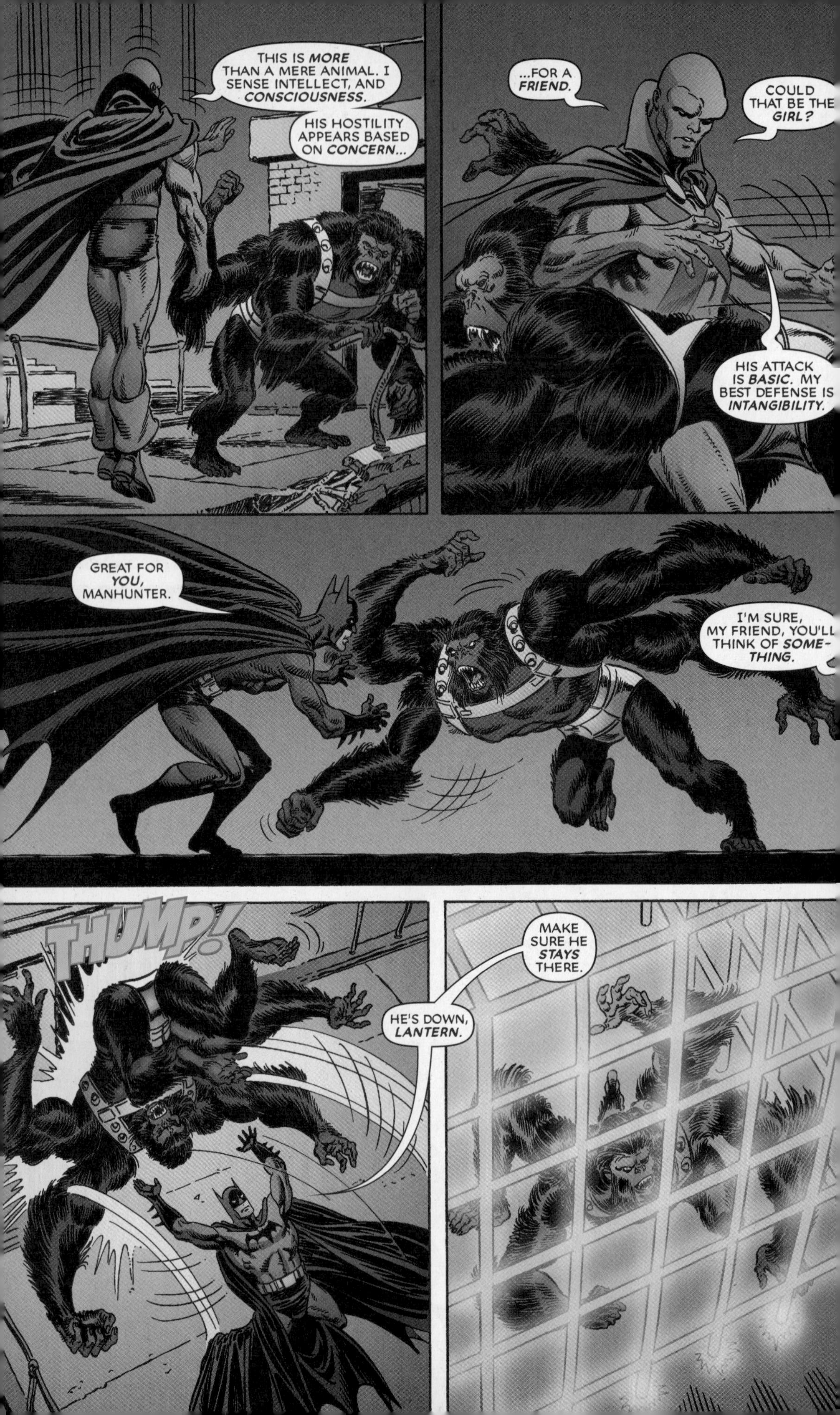
THIS IS MORE THAN A MERE ANIMAL. I SENSE INTELLECT, AND CONSCIOUSNESS.
HIS HOSTILITY APPEARS BASED ON CONCERN...
...FOR A FRIEND.
COULD THAT BE THE GIRL?
HIS ATTACK IS BASIC. MY BEST DEFENSE IS INTANGIBILITY.
GREAT FOR YOU, MANHUNTER.
I'M SURE, MY FRIEND, YOU'LL THINK OF SOME-THING.
THUMP!
HE'S DOWN, LANTERN.
MAKE SURE HE STAYS THERE.

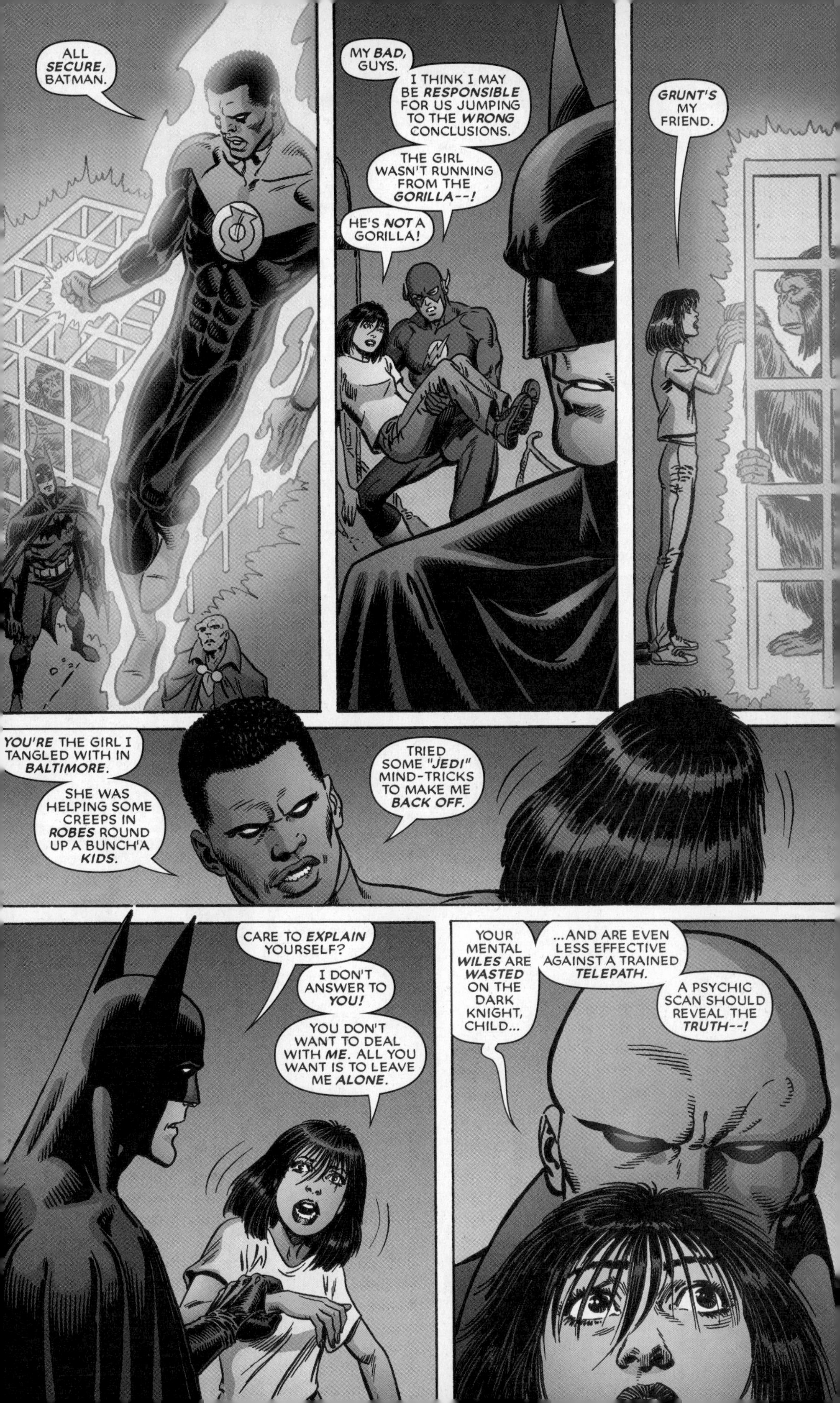
ALL SECURE, BATMAN.
MY BAD, GUYS.
I THINK I MAY BE RESPONSIBLE FOR US JUMPING TO THE WRONG CONCLUSIONS.
THE GIRL WASN'T RUNNING FROM THE GORILLA--!
HE'S NOT A GORILLA!
GRUNT'S MY FRIEND.
YOU'RE THE GIRL I TANGLED WITH IN BALTIMORE.
SHE WAS HELPING SOME CREEPS IN ROBES ROUND UP A BUNCH'A KIDS.
TRIED SOME "JEDI" MIND-TRICKS TO MAKE ME BACK OFF.
CARE TO EXPLAIN YOURSELF?
I DON'T ANSWER TO YOU!
YOU DON'T WANT TO DEAL WITH ME. ALL YOU WANT IS TO LEAVE ME ALONE.
YOUR MENTAL WILES ARE WASTED ON THE DARK KNIGHT, CHILD...
...AND ARE EVEN LESS EFFECTIVE AGAINST A TRAINED TELEPATH.
A PSYCHIC SCAN SHOULD REVEAL THE TRUTH--!

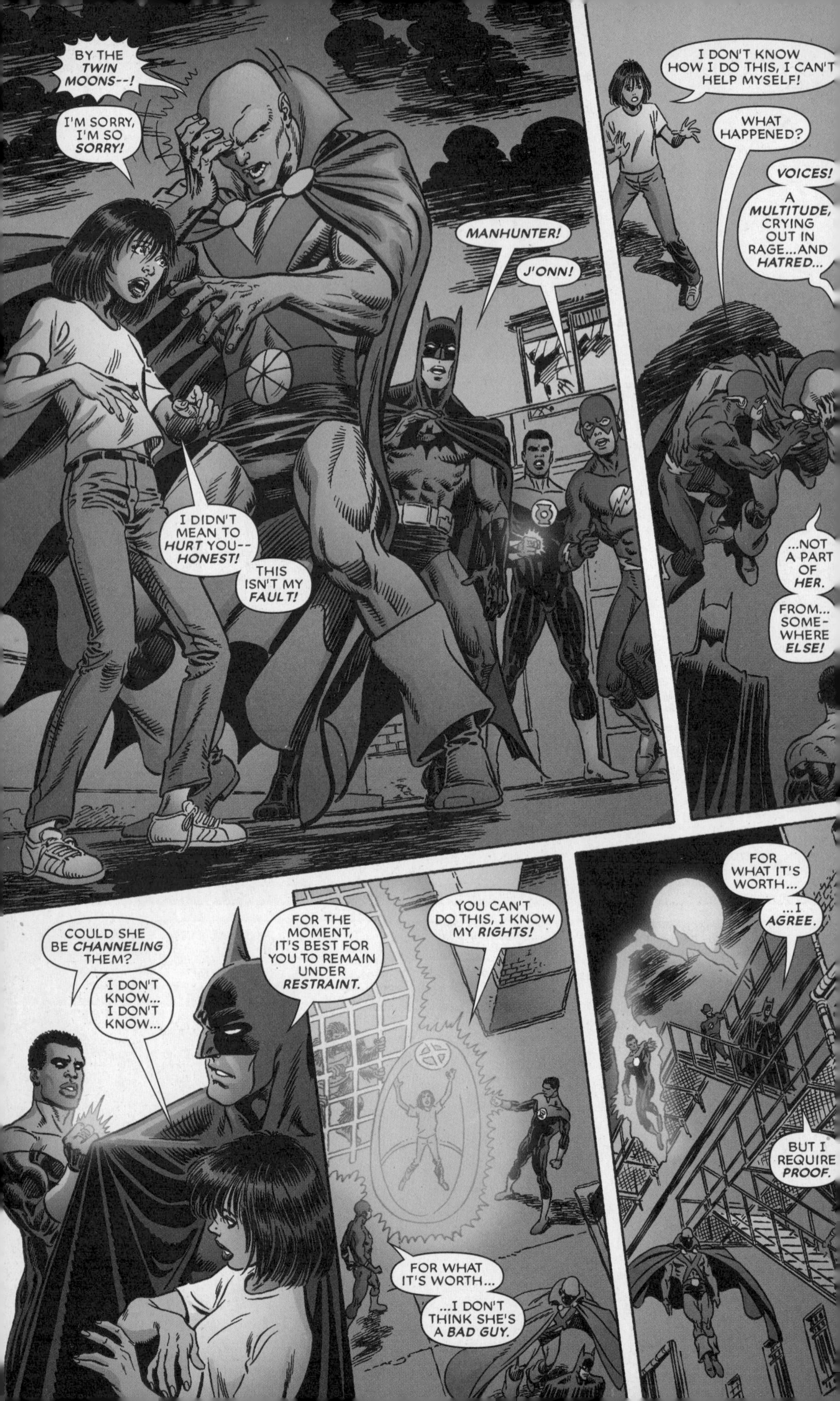
BY THE TWIN MOONS--!
I'M SORRY, I'M SO SORRY!
MANHUNTER!
J'ONN!
I DIDN'T MEAN TO HURT YOU-- HONEST!
THIS ISN'T MY FAULT!
I DON'T KNOW HOW I DO THIS, I CAN'T HELP MYSELF!
WHAT HAPPENED?
VOICES!
A MULTITUDE, CRYING OUT IN RAGE...AND HATRED...
...NOT A PART OF HER.
FROM... SOME-WHERE ELSE!
COULD SHE BE CHANNELING THEM?
I DON'T KNOW... I DON'T KNOW...
FOR THE MOMENT, IT'S BEST FOR YOU TO REMAIN UNDER RESTRAINT.
YOU CAN'T DO THIS, I KNOW MY RIGHTS!
FOR WHAT IT'S WORTH...
...I DON'T THINK SHE'S A BAD GUY.
FOR WHAT IT'S WORTH...
...I AGREE.
BUT I REQUIRE PROOF.

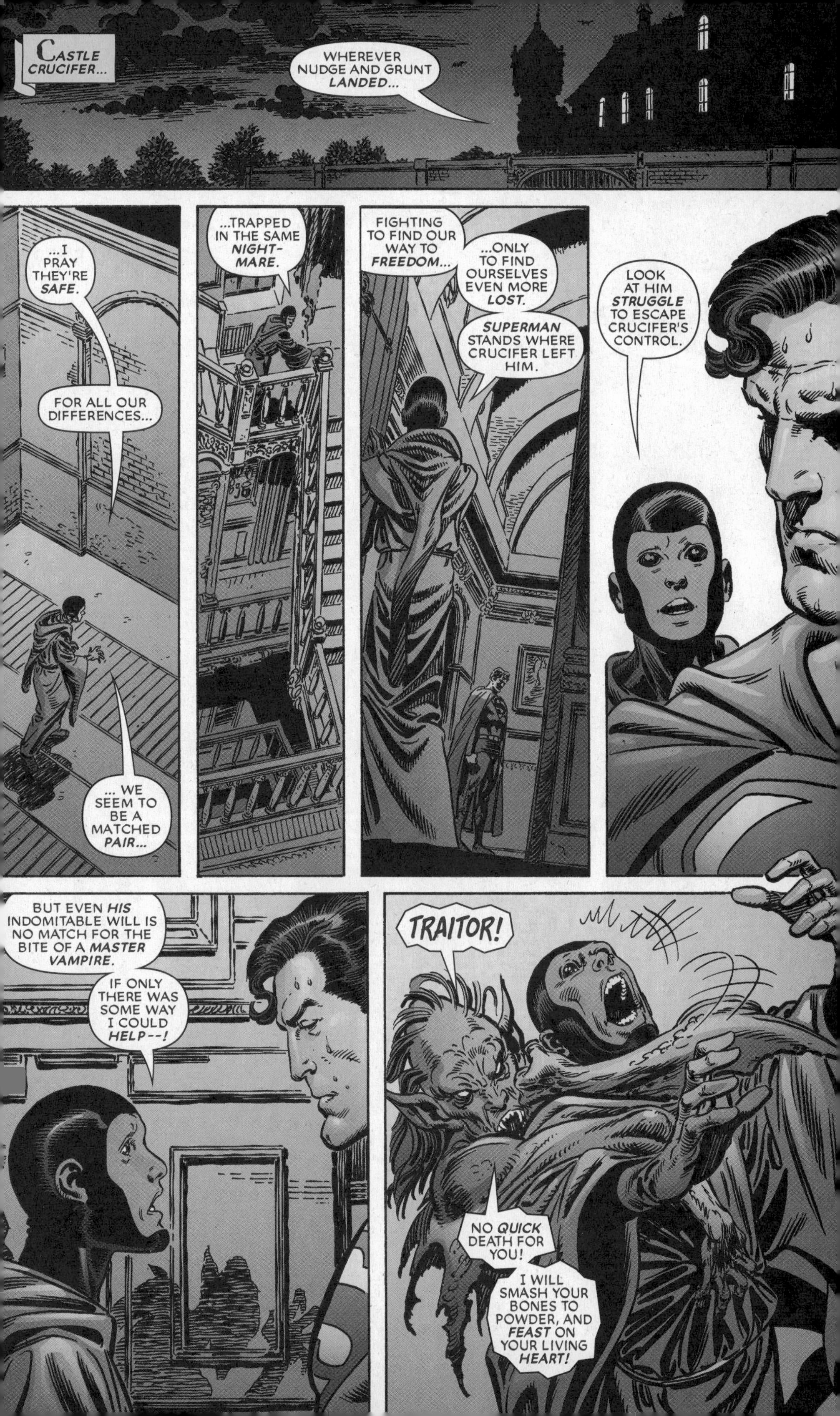
CASTLE CRUCIFER...
WHEREVER NUDGE AND GRUNT LANDED...
...I PRAY THEY'RE SAFE.
FOR ALL OUR DIFFERENCES...
... WE SEEM TO BE A MATCHED PAIR...
...TRAPPED IN THE SAME NIGHT-MARE.
FIGHTING TO FIND OUR WAY TO FREEDOM...
...ONLY TO FIND OURSELVES EVEN MORE LOST.
SUPERMAN STANDS WHERE CRUCIFER LEFT HIM.
LOOK AT HIM STRUGGLE TO ESCAPE CRUCIFER'S CONTROL.
BUT EVEN HIS INDOMITABLE WILL IS NO MATCH FOR THE BITE OF A MASTER VAMPIRE.
IF ONLY THERE WAS SOME WAY I COULD HELP--!
TRAITOR!
NO QUICK DEATH FOR YOU!
I WILL SMASH YOUR BONES TO POWDER, AND FEAST ON YOUR LIVING HEART!

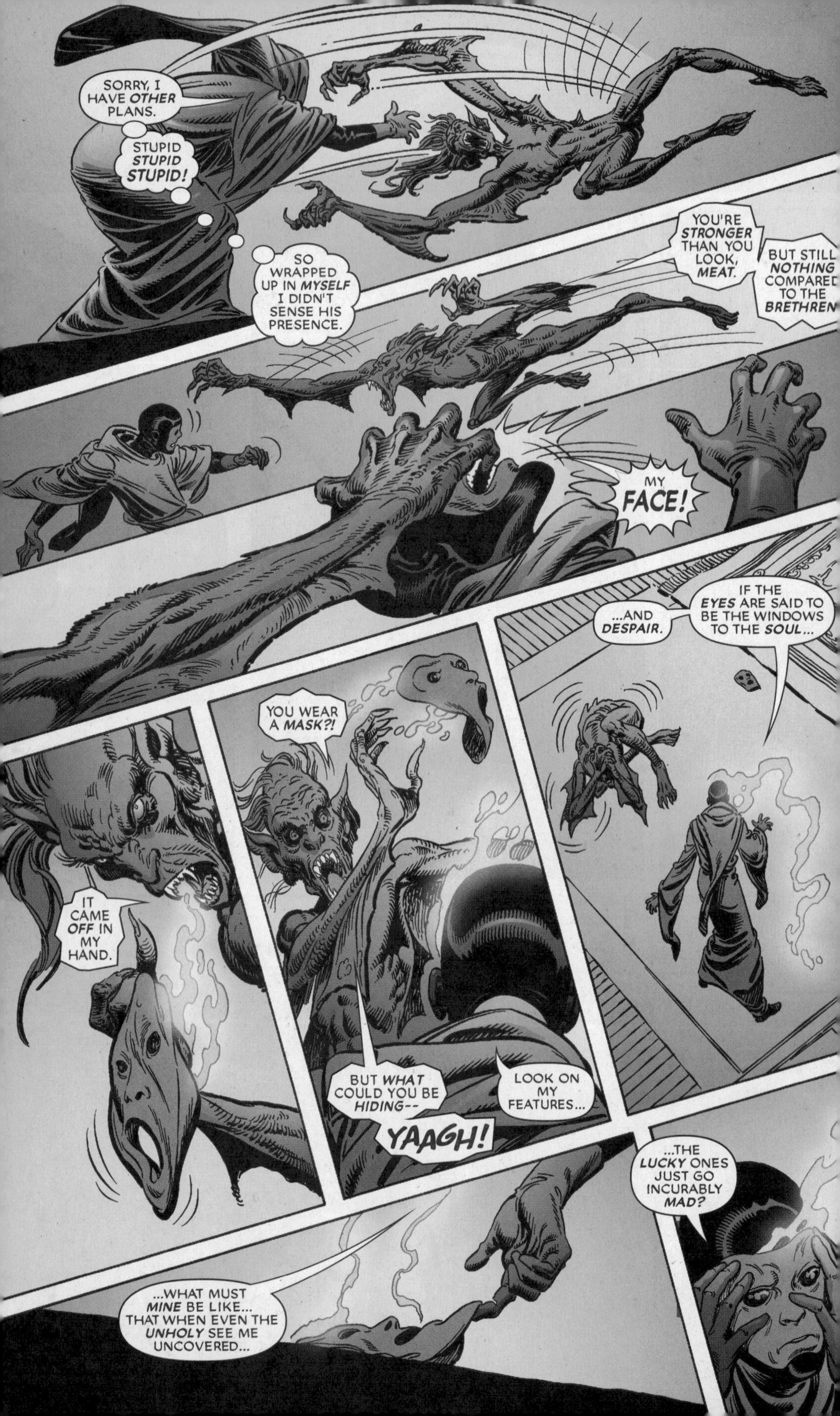

SORRY, I HAVE *OTHER* PLANS.
STUPID *STUPID* **STUPID!**
SO WRAPPED UP IN *MYSELF* I DIDN'T SENSE HIS PRESENCE.
YOU'RE *STRONGER* THAN YOU LOOK, *MEAT.*
BUT STILL *NOTHING* COMPARED TO THE *BRETHREN*
MY **FACE!**
IT CAME *OFF* IN MY HAND.
YOU WEAR A *MASK?!*
BUT *WHAT* COULD YOU BE *HIDING--*
YAAGH!
...AND *DESPAIR.*
IF THE *EYES* ARE SAID TO BE THE WINDOWS TO THE *SOUL*...
LOOK ON MY FEATURES...
...WHAT MUST *MINE* BE LIKE... THAT WHEN EVEN THE *UNHOLY* SEE ME UNCOVERED...
...THE *LUCKY* ONES JUST GO INCURABLY *MAD?*

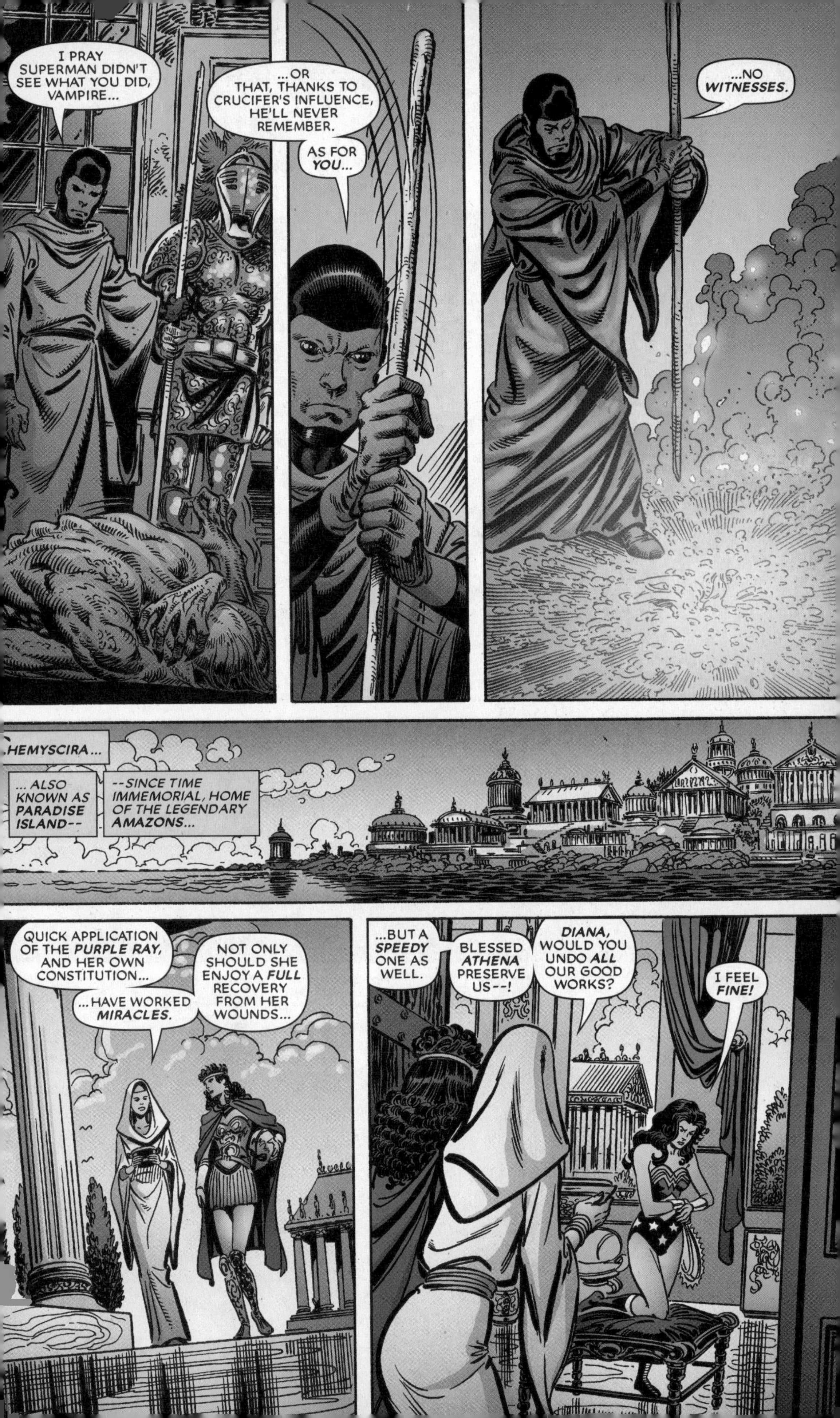
I PRAY SUPERMAN DIDN'T SEE WHAT YOU DID, VAMPIRE...
...OR THAT, THANKS TO CRUCIFER'S INFLUENCE, HE'LL NEVER REMEMBER.
AS FOR YOU...
...NO WITNESSES.
HEMYSCIRA...
... ALSO KNOWN AS PARADISE ISLAND--
--SINCE TIME IMMEMORIAL, HOME OF THE LEGENDARY AMAZONS...
QUICK APPLICATION OF THE PURPLE RAY, AND HER OWN CONSTITUTION...
...HAVE WORKED MIRACLES.
NOT ONLY SHOULD SHE ENJOY A FULL RECOVERY FROM HER WOUNDS...
...BUT A SPEEDY ONE AS WELL.
BLESSED ATHENA PRESERVE US--!
DIANA, WOULD YOU UNDO ALL OUR GOOD WORKS?
I FEEL FINE!

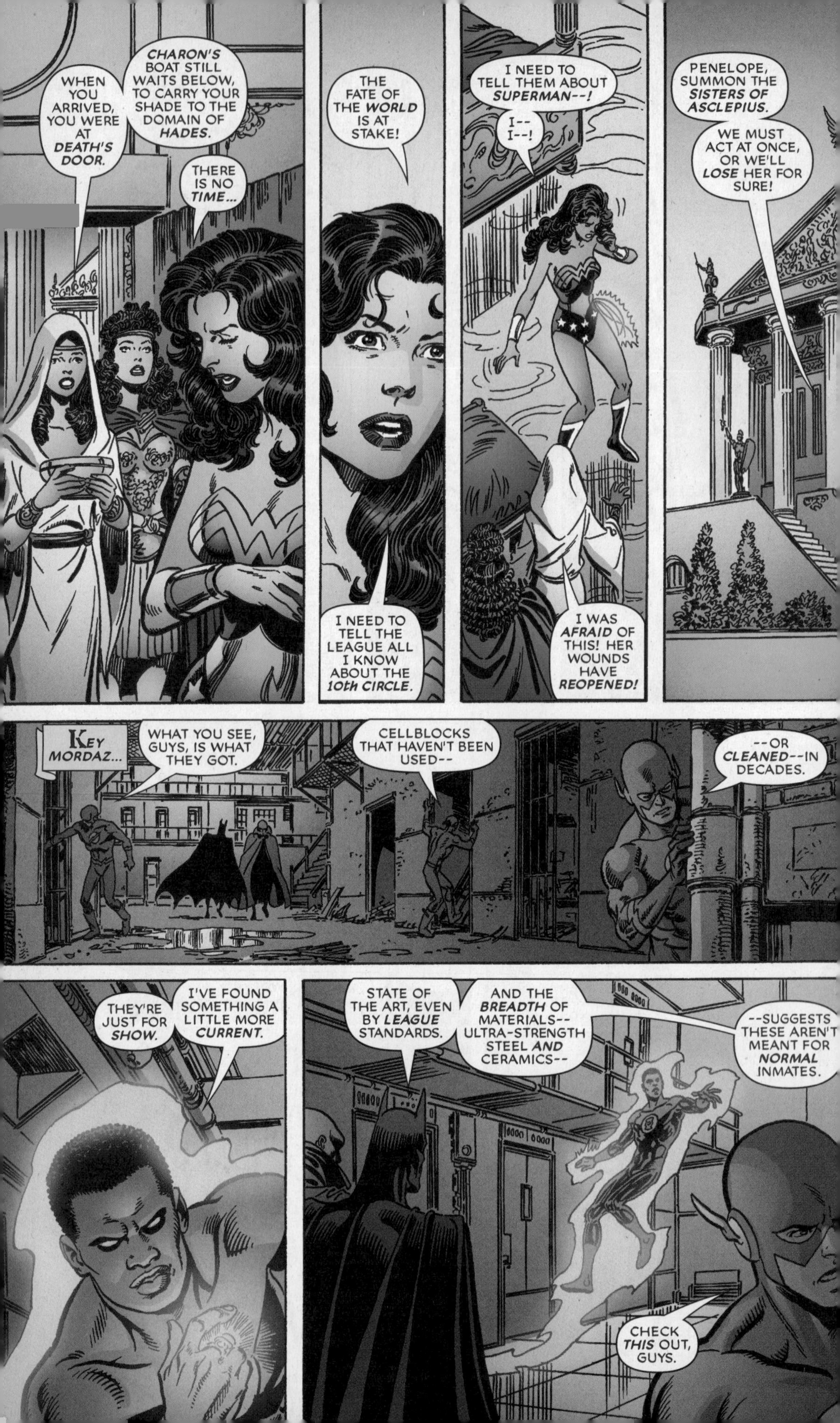

WHEN YOU ARRIVED, YOU WERE AT DEATH'S DOOR.
CHARON'S BOAT STILL WAITS BELOW, TO CARRY YOUR SHADE TO THE DOMAIN OF HADES.
THERE IS NO TIME...
THE FATE OF THE WORLD IS AT STAKE!
I NEED TO TELL THE LEAGUE ALL I KNOW ABOUT THE 10th CIRCLE.
I NEED TO TELL THEM ABOUT SUPERMAN--!
I-- I--!
I WAS AFRAID OF THIS! HER WOUNDS HAVE REOPENED!
PENELOPE, SUMMON THE SISTERS OF ASCLEPIUS.
WE MUST ACT AT ONCE, OR WE'LL LOSE HER FOR SURE!
KEY MORDAZ...
WHAT YOU SEE, GUYS, IS WHAT THEY GOT.
CELLBLOCKS THAT HAVEN'T BEEN USED--
--OR CLEANED--IN DECADES.
THEY'RE JUST FOR SHOW.
I'VE FOUND SOMETHING A LITTLE MORE CURRENT.
STATE OF THE ART, EVEN BY LEAGUE STANDARDS.
AND THE BREADTH OF MATERIALS--ULTRA-STRENGTH STEEL AND CERAMICS--
--SUGGESTS THESE AREN'T MEANT FOR NORMAL INMATES.
CHECK THIS OUT, GUYS.

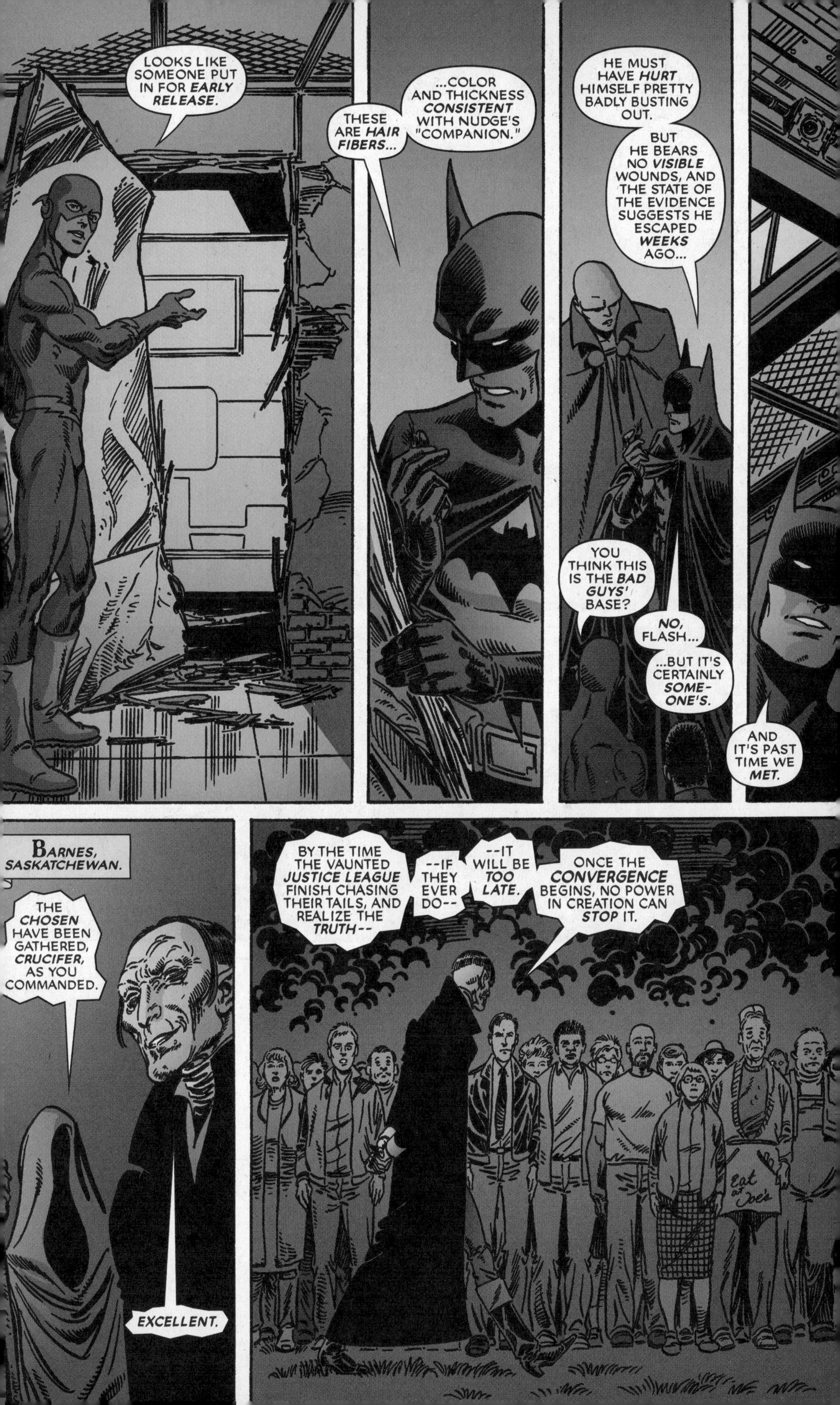
LOOKS LIKE SOMEONE PUT IN FOR EARLY RELEASE.
THESE ARE HAIR FIBERS...
...COLOR AND THICKNESS CONSISTENT WITH NUDGE'S "COMPANION."
HE MUST HAVE HURT HIMSELF PRETTY BADLY BUSTING OUT.
BUT HE BEARS NO VISIBLE WOUNDS, AND THE STATE OF THE EVIDENCE SUGGESTS HE ESCAPED WEEKS AGO...
YOU THINK THIS IS THE BAD GUYS' BASE?
NO, FLASH...
...BUT IT'S CERTAINLY SOME-ONE'S.
AND IT'S PAST TIME WE MET.
BARNES, SASKATCHEWAN.
THE CHOSEN HAVE BEEN GATHERED, CRUCIFER, AS YOU COMMANDED.
EXCELLENT.
BY THE TIME THE VAUNTED JUSTICE LEAGUE FINISH CHASING THEIR TAILS, AND REALIZE THE TRUTH--
--IF THEY EVER DO--
--IT WILL BE TOO LATE.
ONCE THE CONVERGENCE BEGINS, NO POWER IN CREATION CAN STOP IT.
Eat at Joe's

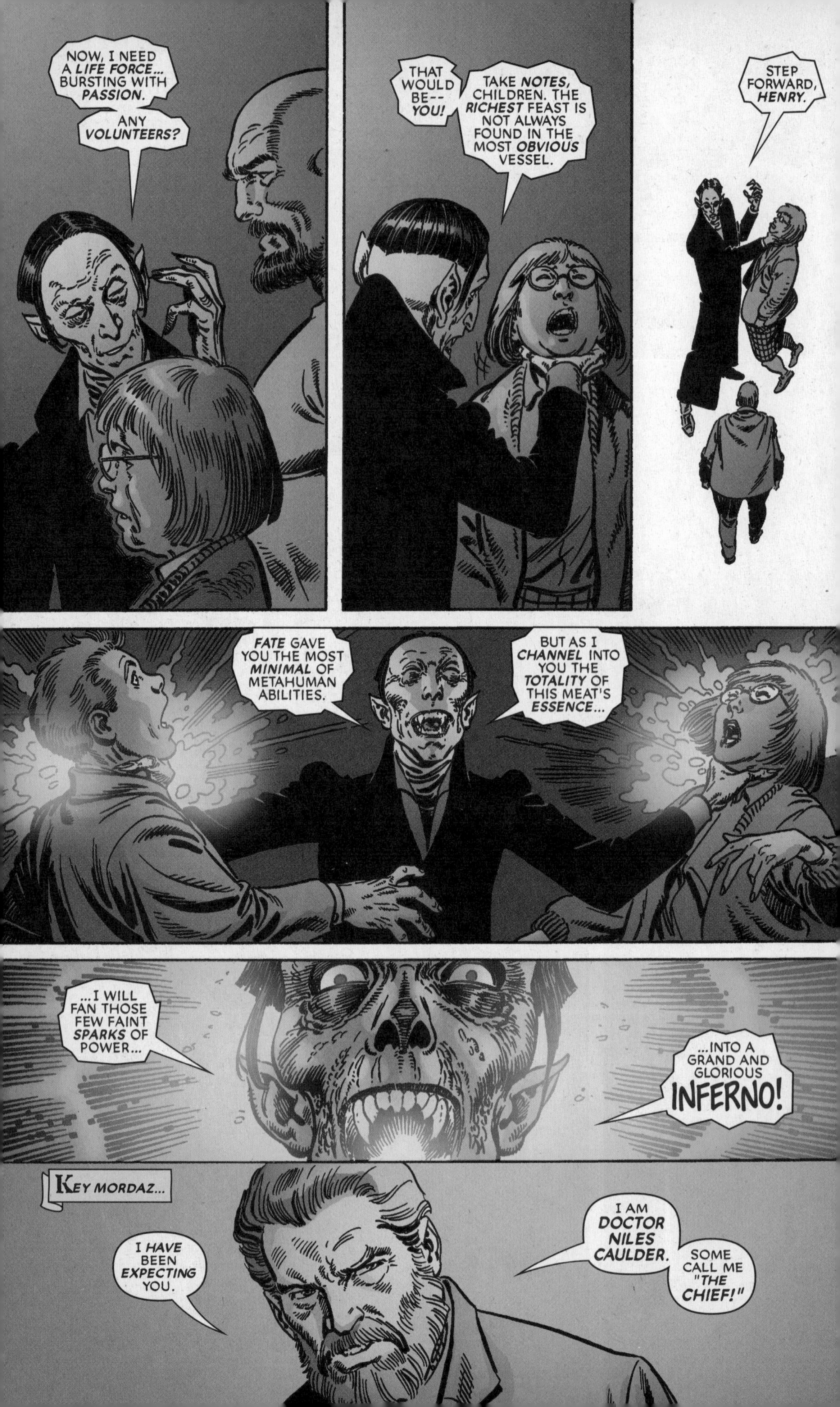
NOW, I NEED A LIFE FORCE... BURSTING WITH PASSION.
ANY VOLUNTEERS?
THAT WOULD BE-- YOU!
TAKE NOTES, CHILDREN. THE RICHEST FEAST IS NOT ALWAYS FOUND IN THE MOST OBVIOUS VESSEL.
STEP FORWARD, HENRY.
FATE GAVE YOU THE MOST MINIMAL OF METAHUMAN ABILITIES.
BUT AS I CHANNEL INTO YOU THE TOTALITY OF THIS MEAT'S ESSENCE...
...I WILL FAN THOSE FEW FAINT SPARKS OF POWER...
...INTO A GRAND AND GLORIOUS INFERNO!
KEY MORDAZ...
I HAVE BEEN EXPECTING YOU.
I AM DOCTOR NILES CAULDER.
SOME CALL ME "THE CHIEF!"

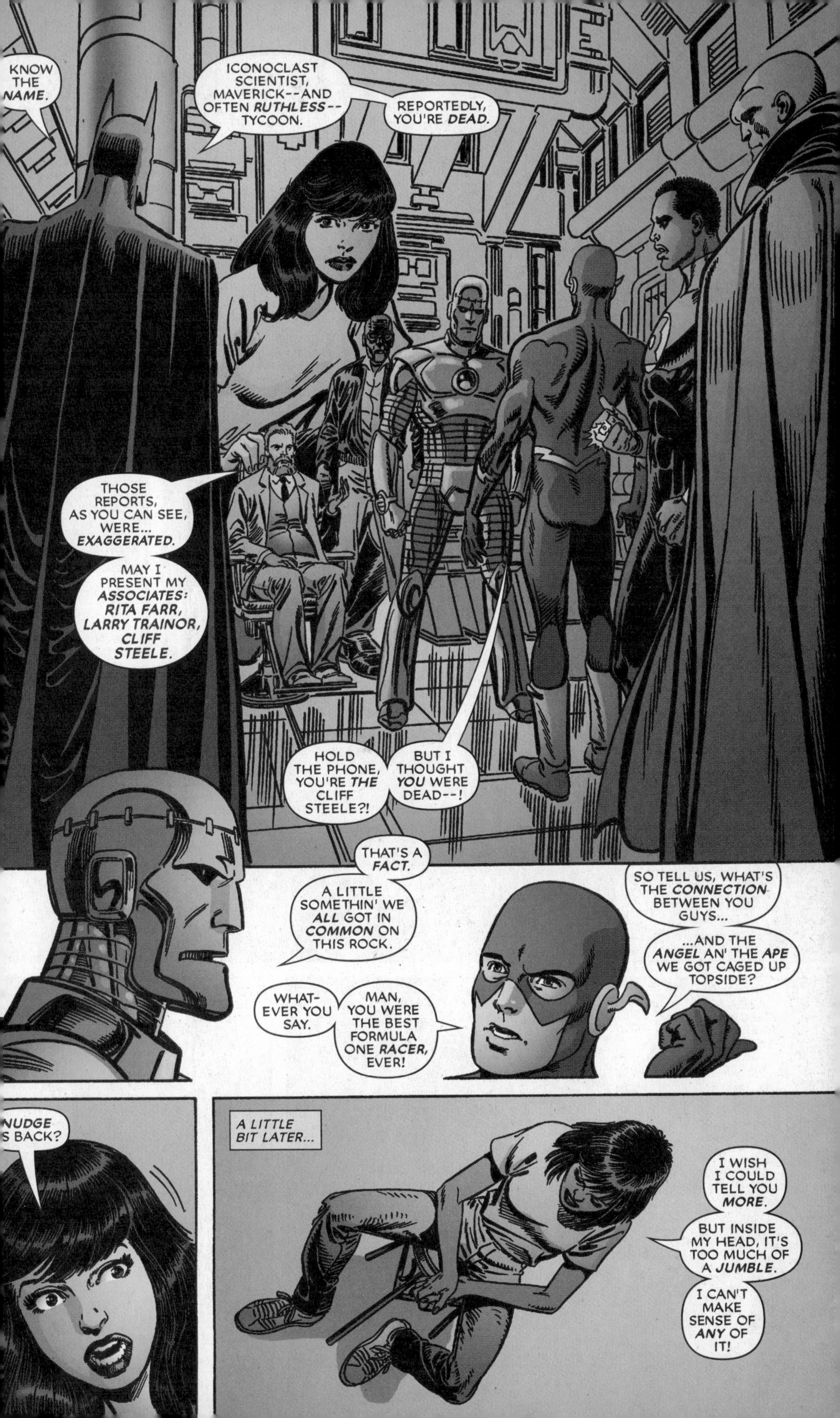
KNOW THE NAME.
ICONOCLAST SCIENTIST, MAVERICK--AND OFTEN RUTHLESS--TYCOON.
REPORTEDLY, YOU'RE DEAD.
THOSE REPORTS, AS YOU CAN SEE, WERE... EXAGGERATED.
MAY I PRESENT MY ASSOCIATES: RITA FARR, LARRY TRAINOR, CLIFF STEELE.
HOLD THE PHONE, YOU'RE THE CLIFF STEELE?!
BUT I THOUGHT YOU WERE DEAD--!
THAT'S A FACT.
A LITTLE SOMETHIN' WE ALL GOT IN COMMON ON THIS ROCK.
MAN, YOU WERE THE BEST FORMULA ONE RACER, EVER!
WHAT-EVER YOU SAY.
SO TELL US, WHAT'S THE CONNECTION BETWEEN YOU GUYS...
...AND THE ANGEL AN' THE APE WE GOT CAGED UP TOPSIDE?
NUDGE S BACK?
A LITTLE BIT LATER...
I WISH I COULD TELL YOU MORE.
BUT INSIDE MY HEAD, IT'S TOO MUCH OF A JUMBLE.
I CAN'T MAKE SENSE OF ANY OF IT!

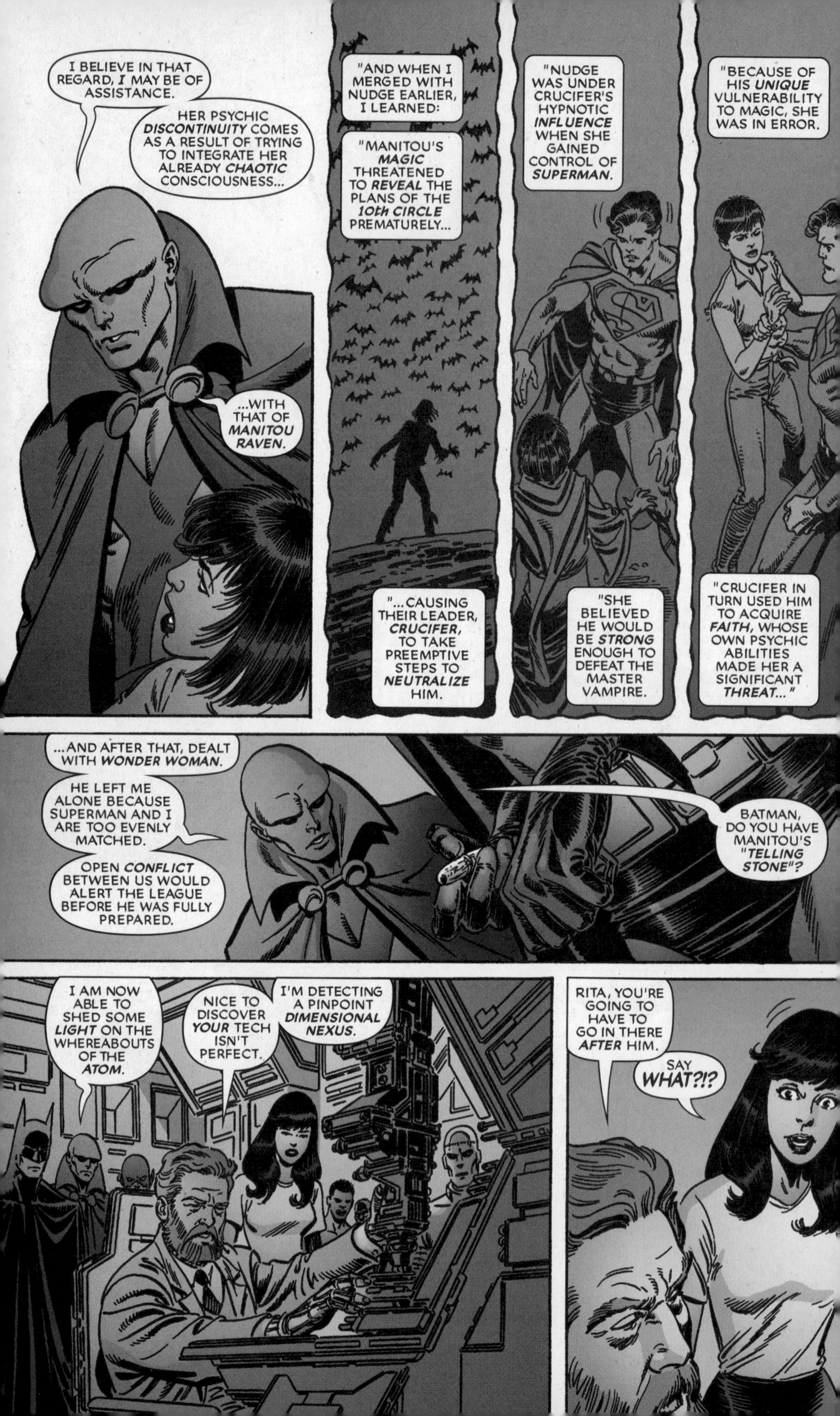

I BELIEVE IN THAT REGARD, *I* MAY BE OF ASSISTANCE.
HER PSYCHIC *DISCONTINUITY* COMES AS A RESULT OF TRYING TO INTEGRATE HER ALREADY *CHAOTIC* CONSCIOUSNESS...
...WITH THAT OF *MANITOU RAVEN.*
"AND WHEN I MERGED WITH NUDGE EARLIER, I LEARNED:
"MANITOU'S *MAGIC* THREATENED TO *REVEAL* THE PLANS OF THE *10th CIRCLE* PREMATURELY...
"...CAUSING THEIR LEADER, *CRUCIFER,* TO TAKE PREEMPTIVE STEPS TO *NEUTRALIZE* HIM.
"NUDGE WAS UNDER CRUCIFER'S HYPNOTIC *INFLUENCE* WHEN SHE GAINED CONTROL OF *SUPERMAN.*
"SHE BELIEVED HE WOULD BE *STRONG* ENOUGH TO DEFEAT THE MASTER VAMPIRE.
"BECAUSE OF HIS *UNIQUE* VULNERABILITY TO MAGIC, SHE WAS IN ERROR.
"CRUCIFER IN TURN USED HIM TO ACQUIRE *FAITH,* WHOSE OWN PSYCHIC ABILITIES MADE HER A SIGNIFICANT *THREAT...*"
...AND AFTER THAT, DEALT WITH *WONDER WOMAN.*
HE LEFT ME ALONE BECAUSE SUPERMAN AND I ARE TOO EVENLY MATCHED.
OPEN *CONFLICT* BETWEEN US WOULD ALERT THE LEAGUE BEFORE HE WAS FULLY PREPARED.
BATMAN, DO YOU HAVE MANITOU'S "*TELLING STONE*"?
I AM NOW ABLE TO SHED SOME *LIGHT* ON THE WHEREABOUTS OF THE *ATOM.*
NICE TO DISCOVER *YOUR* TECH ISN'T PERFECT.
I'M DETECTING A PINPOINT *DIMENSIONAL NEXUS.*
RITA, YOU'RE GOING TO HAVE TO GO IN THERE *AFTER* HIM.
SAY *WHAT?!?*

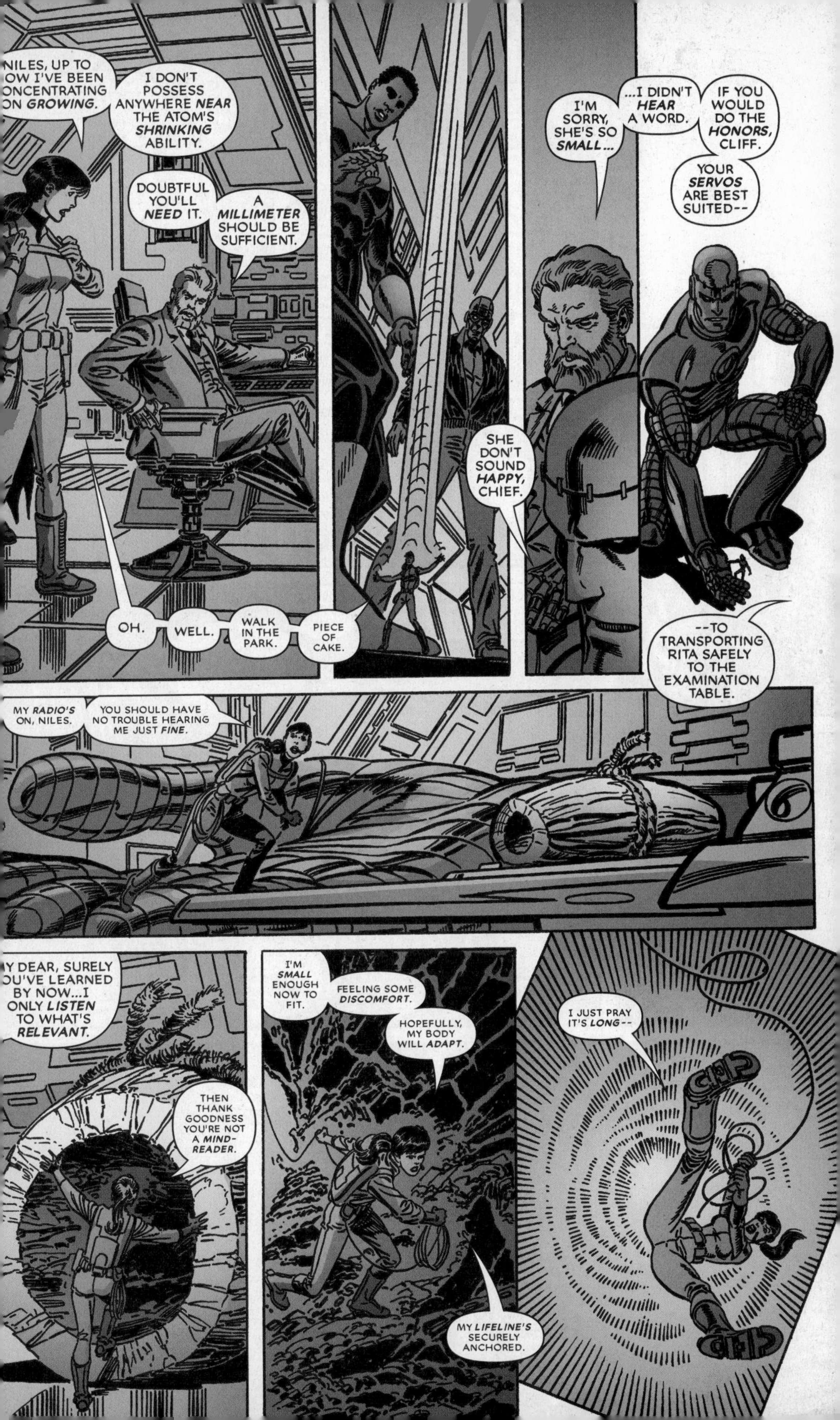
NILES, UP TO
OW I'VE BEEN
ONCENTRATING
ON GROWING.
I DON'T POSSESS ANYWHERE NEAR THE ATOM'S SHRINKING ABILITY.
DOUBTFUL YOU'LL NEED IT.
A MILLIMETER SHOULD BE SUFFICIENT.
OH.
WELL.
WALK IN THE PARK.
PIECE OF CAKE.
SHE DON'T SOUND HAPPY, CHIEF.
I'M SORRY, SHE'S SO SMALL...
...I DIDN'T HEAR A WORD.
IF YOU WOULD DO THE HONORS, CLIFF.
YOUR SERVOS ARE BEST SUITED--
--TO TRANSPORTING RITA SAFELY TO THE EXAMINATION TABLE.
MY RADIO'S ON, NILES.
YOU SHOULD HAVE NO TROUBLE HEARING ME JUST FINE.
Y DEAR, SURELY OU'VE LEARNED BY NOW...I ONLY LISTEN TO WHAT'S RELEVANT.
THEN THANK GOODNESS YOU'RE NOT A MIND-READER.
I'M SMALL ENOUGH NOW TO FIT.
FEELING SOME DISCOMFORT.
HOPEFULLY, MY BODY WILL ADAPT.
MY LIFELINE'S SECURELY ANCHORED.
I JUST PRAY IT'S LONG--

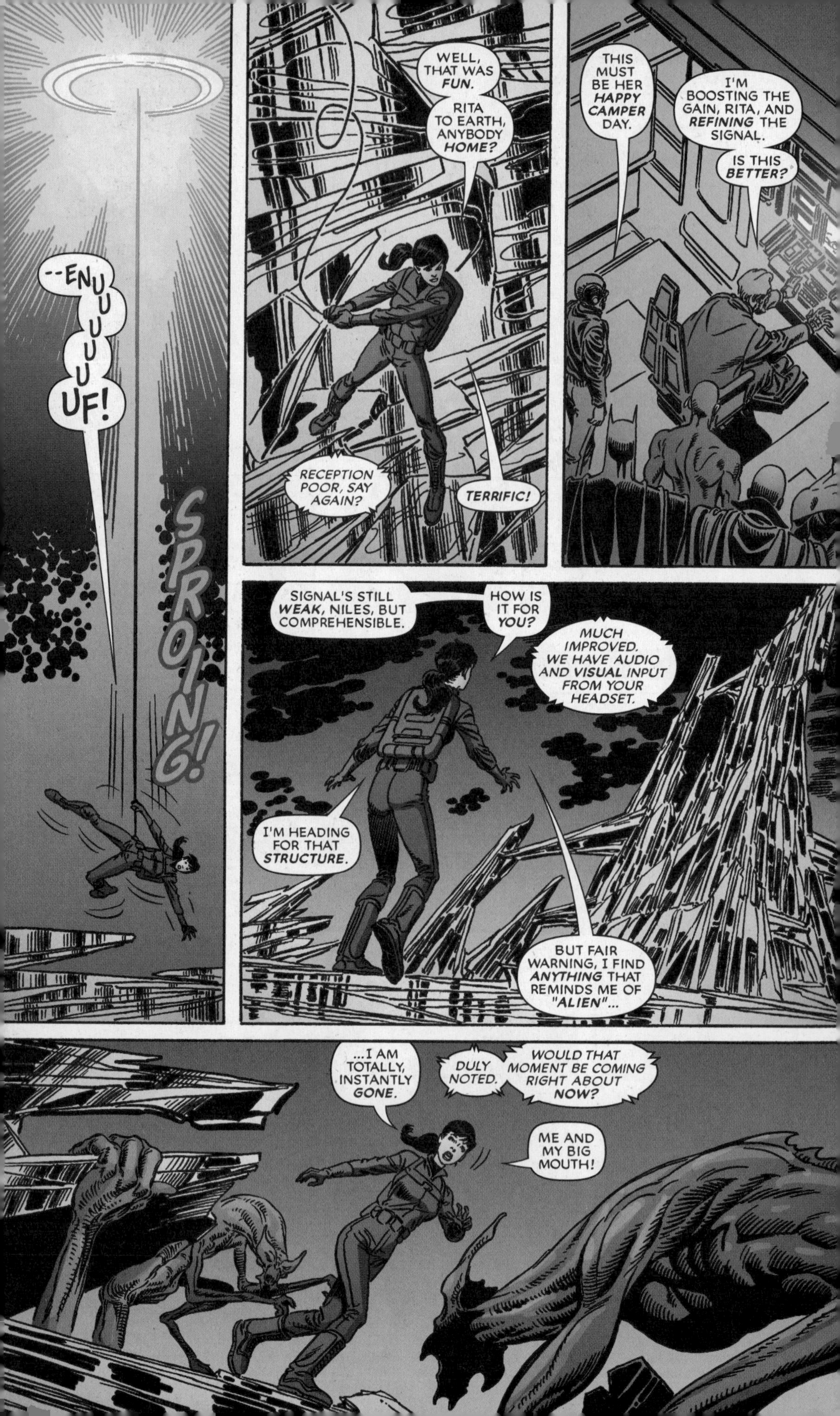
--ENUUUUUUF!
SPROING!
WELL, THAT WAS FUN.
RITA TO EARTH, ANYBODY HOME?
RECEPTION POOR, SAY AGAIN?
TERRIFIC!
THIS MUST BE HER HAPPY CAMPER DAY.
I'M BOOSTING THE GAIN, RITA, AND REFINING THE SIGNAL.
IS THIS BETTER?
SIGNAL'S STILL WEAK, NILES, BUT COMPREHENSIBLE.
HOW IS IT FOR YOU?
MUCH IMPROVED. WE HAVE AUDIO AND VISUAL INPUT FROM YOUR HEADSET.
I'M HEADING FOR THAT STRUCTURE.
BUT FAIR WARNING, I FIND ANYTHING THAT REMINDS ME OF "ALIEN"...
...I AM TOTALLY, INSTANTLY GONE.
DULY NOTED.
WOULD THAT MOMENT BE COMING RIGHT ABOUT NOW?
ME AND MY BIG MOUTH!

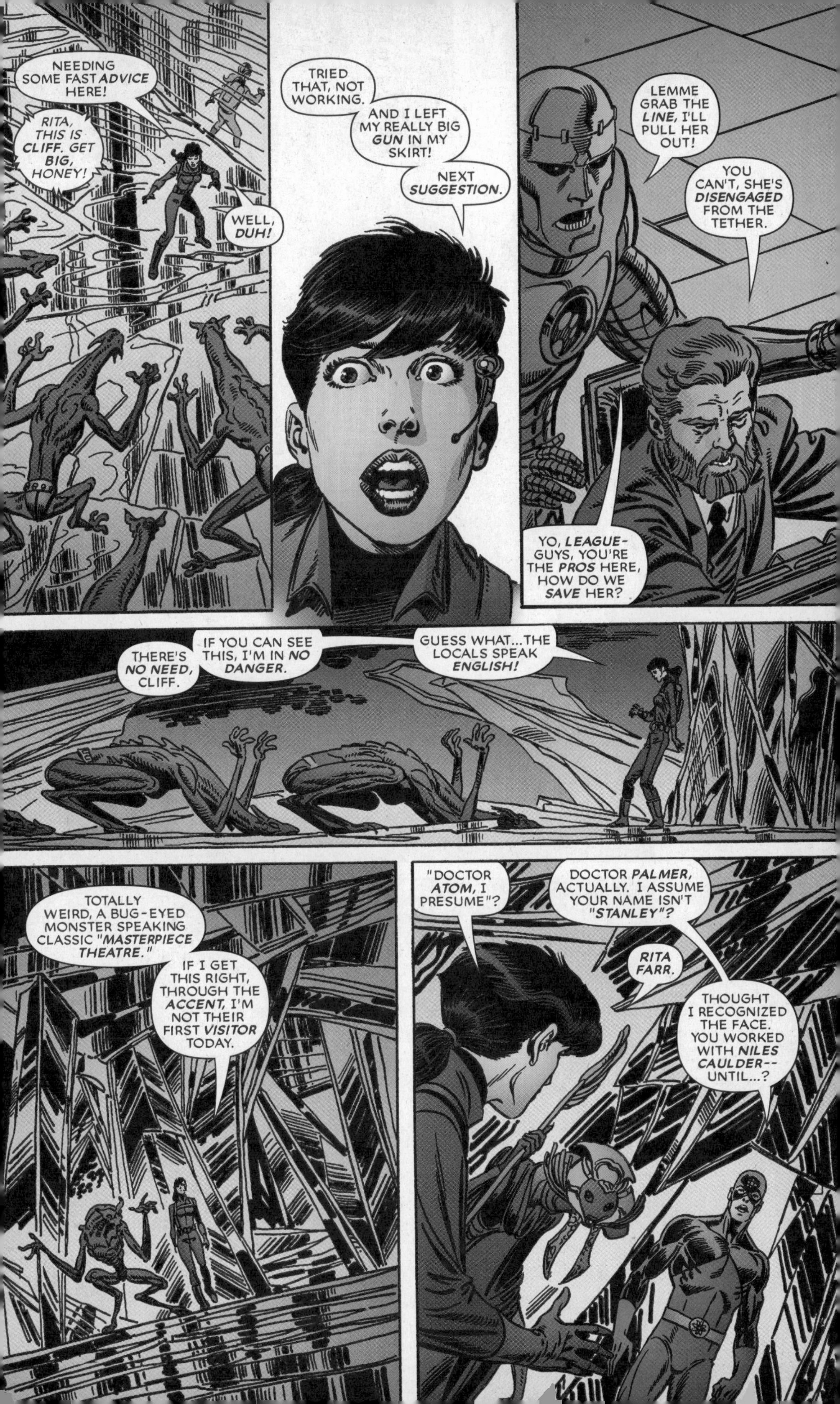
NEEDING SOME FAST ADVICE HERE!
RITA, THIS IS CLIFF. GET BIG, HONEY!
WELL, DUH!
TRIED THAT, NOT WORKING.
AND I LEFT MY REALLY BIG GUN IN MY SKIRT!
NEXT SUGGESTION.
LEMME GRAB THE LINE, I'LL PULL HER OUT!
YOU CAN'T, SHE'S DISENGAGED FROM THE TETHER.
YO, LEAGUE-GUYS, YOU'RE THE PROS HERE, HOW DO WE SAVE HER?
THERE'S NO NEED, CLIFF.
IF YOU CAN SEE THIS, I'M IN NO DANGER.
GUESS WHAT...THE LOCALS SPEAK ENGLISH!
TOTALLY WEIRD, A BUG-EYED MONSTER SPEAKING CLASSIC "MASTERPIECE THEATRE."
IF I GET THIS RIGHT, THROUGH THE ACCENT, I'M NOT THEIR FIRST VISITOR TODAY.
"DOCTOR ATOM, I PRESUME"?
DOCTOR PALMER, ACTUALLY. I ASSUME YOUR NAME ISN'T "STANLEY"?
RITA FARR.
THOUGHT I RECOGNIZED THE FACE. YOU WORKED WITH NILES CAULDER--UNTIL...?

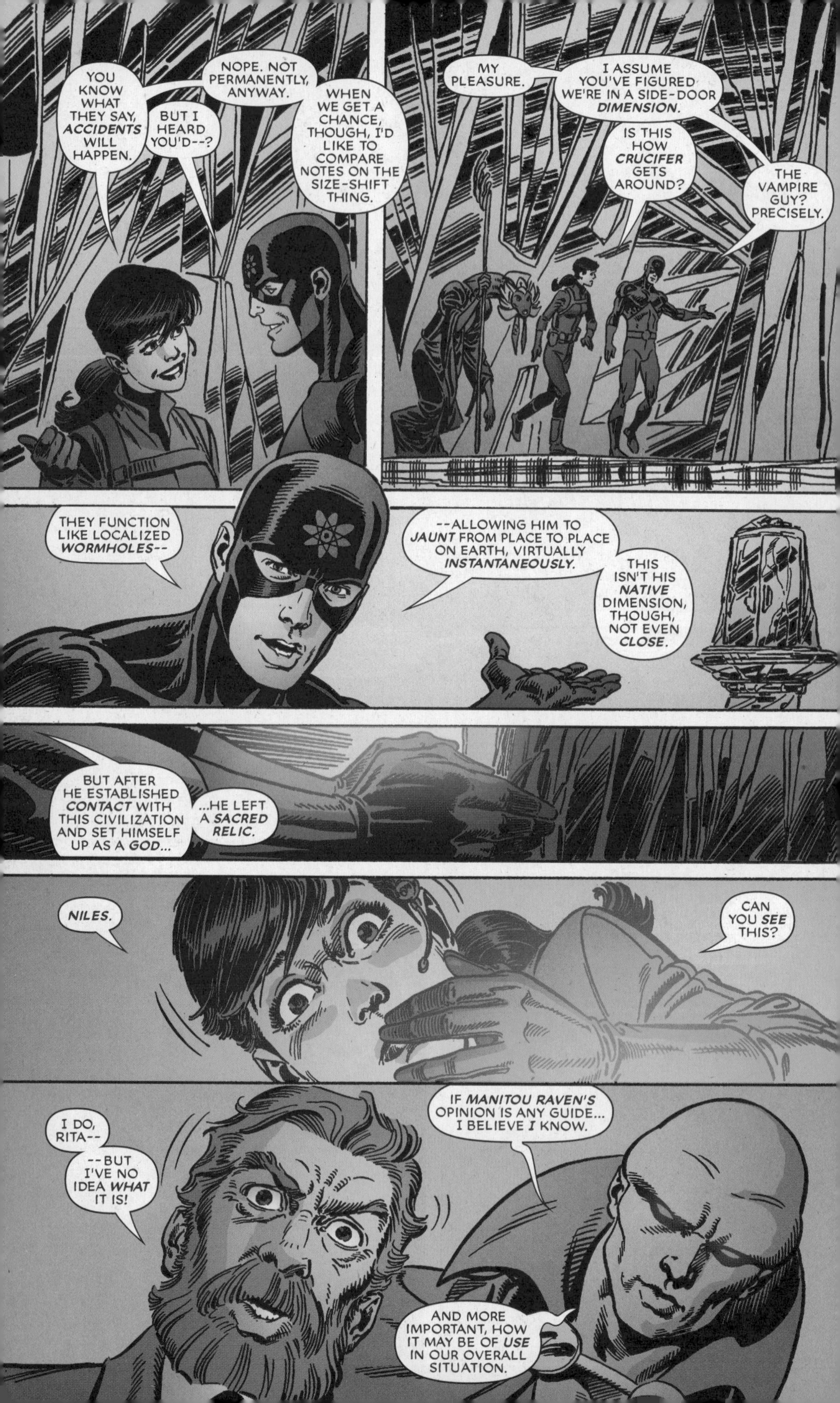

YOU KNOW WHAT THEY SAY, ACCIDENTS WILL HAPPEN.
NOPE. NOT PERMANENTLY, ANYWAY.
BUT I HEARD YOU'D--?
WHEN WE GET A CHANCE, THOUGH, I'D LIKE TO COMPARE NOTES ON THE SIZE-SHIFT THING.
MY PLEASURE.
I ASSUME YOU'VE FIGURED WE'RE IN A SIDE-DOOR DIMENSION.
IS THIS HOW CRUCIFER GETS AROUND?
THE VAMPIRE GUY? PRECISELY.
THEY FUNCTION LIKE LOCALIZED WORMHOLES--
--ALLOWING HIM TO JAUNT FROM PLACE TO PLACE ON EARTH, VIRTUALLY INSTANTANEOUSLY.
THIS ISN'T HIS NATIVE DIMENSION, THOUGH, NOT EVEN CLOSE.
BUT AFTER HE ESTABLISHED CONTACT WITH THIS CIVILIZATION AND SET HIMSELF UP AS A GOD...
...HE LEFT A SACRED RELIC.
NILES.
CAN YOU SEE THIS?
I DO, RITA--
--BUT I'VE NO IDEA WHAT IT IS!
IF MANITOU RAVEN'S OPINION IS ANY GUIDE... I BELIEVE I KNOW.
AND MORE IMPORTANT, HOW IT MAY BE OF USE IN OUR OVERALL SITUATION.

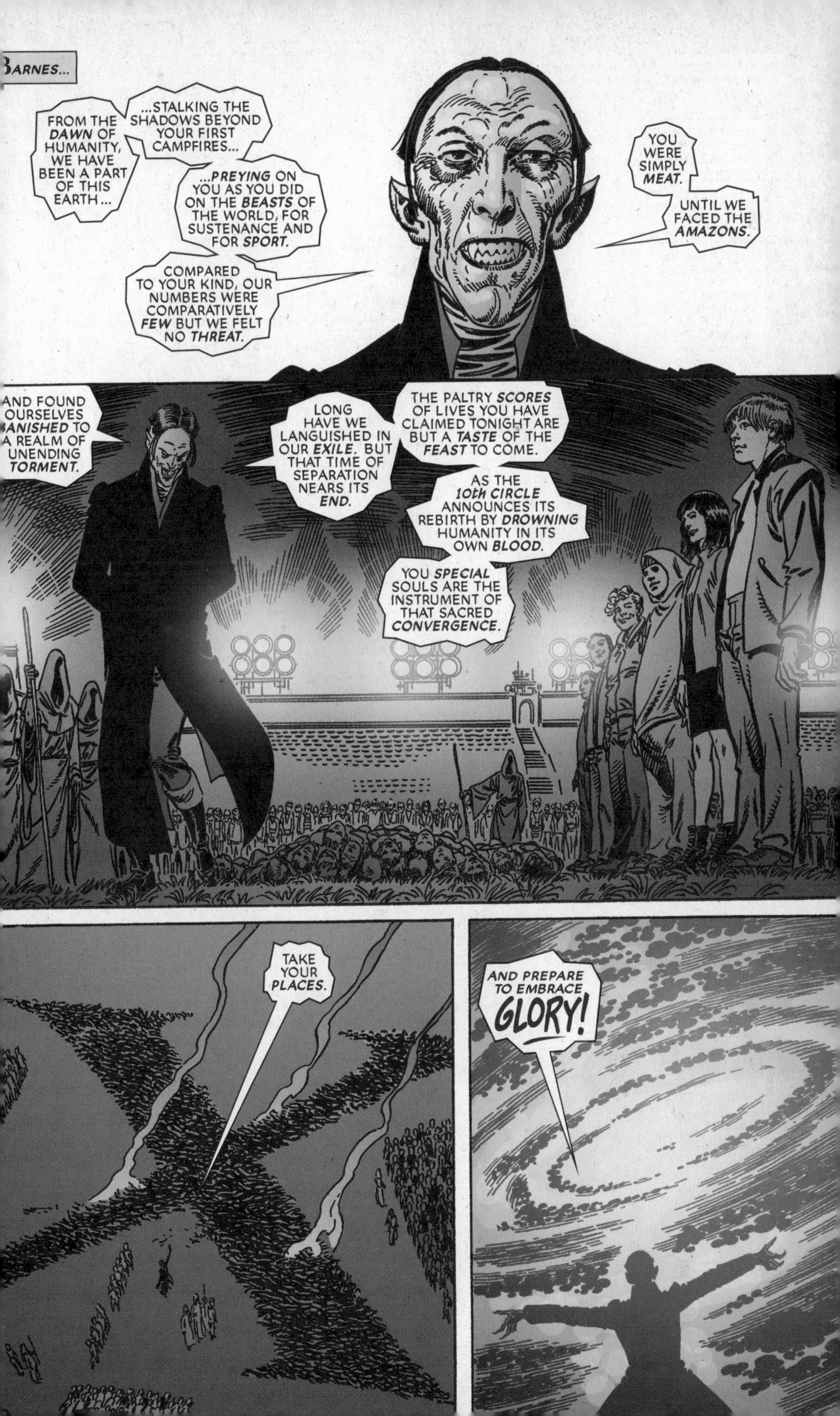

BARNES...
FROM THE DAWN OF HUMANITY, WE HAVE BEEN A PART OF THIS EARTH...
...STALKING THE SHADOWS BEYOND YOUR FIRST CAMPFIRES...
...PREYING ON YOU AS YOU DID ON THE BEASTS OF THE WORLD, FOR SUSTENANCE AND FOR SPORT.
COMPARED TO YOUR KIND, OUR NUMBERS WERE COMPARATIVELY FEW BUT WE FELT NO THREAT.
YOU WERE SIMPLY MEAT.
UNTIL WE FACED THE AMAZONS.
AND FOUND OURSELVES BANISHED TO A REALM OF UNENDING TORMENT.
LONG HAVE WE LANGUISHED IN OUR EXILE. BUT THAT TIME OF SEPARATION NEARS ITS END.
THE PALTRY SCORES OF LIVES YOU HAVE CLAIMED TONIGHT ARE BUT A TASTE OF THE FEAST TO COME.
AS THE 10th CIRCLE ANNOUNCES ITS REBIRTH BY DROWNING HUMANITY IN ITS OWN BLOOD.
YOU SPECIAL SOULS ARE THE INSTRUMENT OF THAT SACRED CONVERGENCE.
TAKE YOUR PLACES.
AND PREPARE TO EMBRACE GLORY!

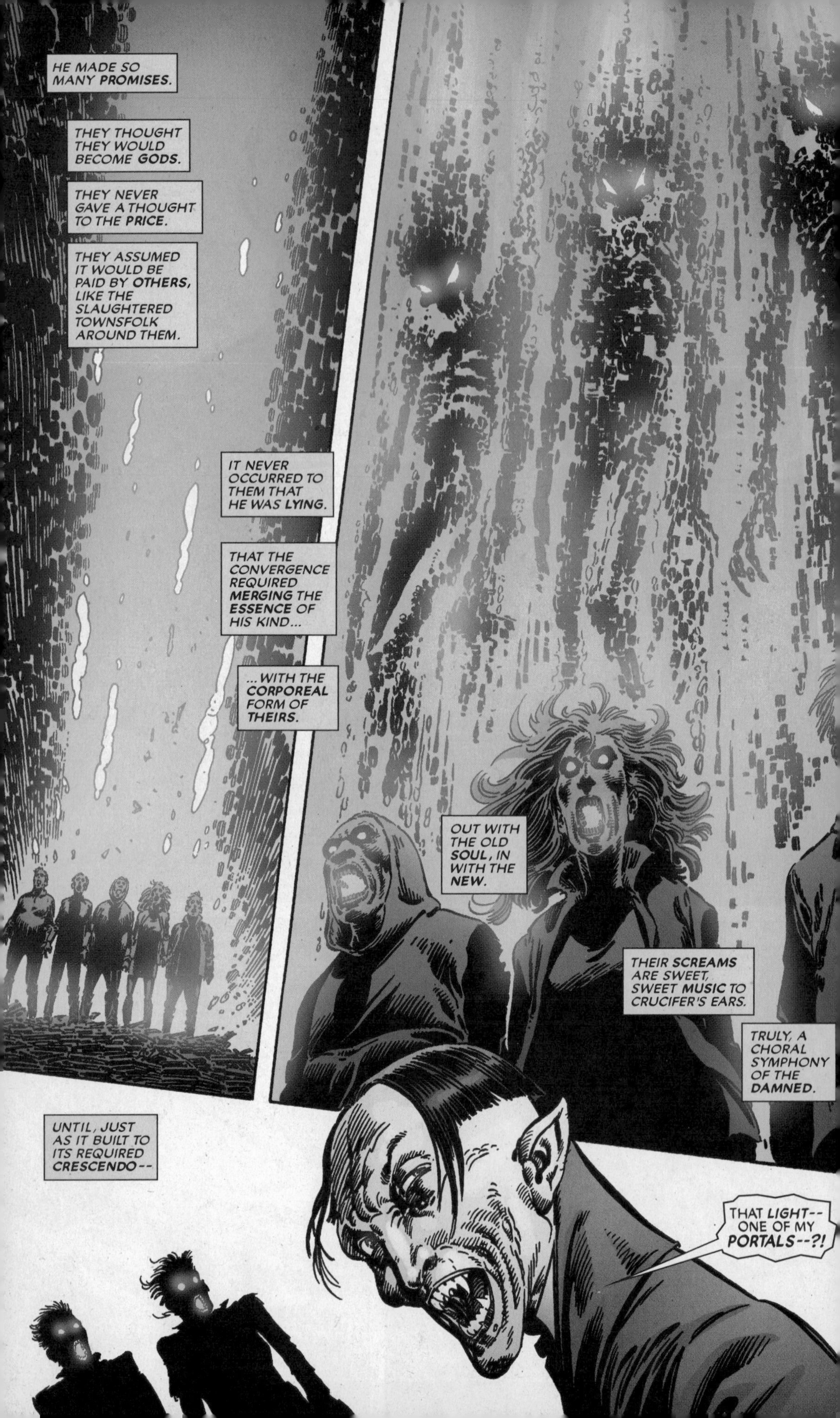
HE MADE SO MANY PROMISES.
THEY THOUGHT THEY WOULD BECOME GODS.
THEY NEVER GAVE A THOUGHT TO THE PRICE.
THEY ASSUMED IT WOULD BE PAID BY OTHERS, LIKE THE SLAUGHTERED TOWNSFOLK AROUND THEM.
IT NEVER OCCURRED TO THEM THAT HE WAS LYING.
THAT THE CONVERGENCE REQUIRED MERGING THE ESSENCE OF HIS KIND...
...WITH THE CORPOREAL FORM OF THEIRS.
OUT WITH THE OLD SOUL, IN WITH THE NEW.
THEIR SCREAMS ARE SWEET, SWEET MUSIC TO CRUCIFER'S EARS.
TRULY, A CHORAL SYMPHONY OF THE DAMNED.
UNTIL, JUST AS IT BUILT TO ITS REQUIRED CRESCENDO--
THAT LIGHT-- ONE OF MY PORTALS--?!

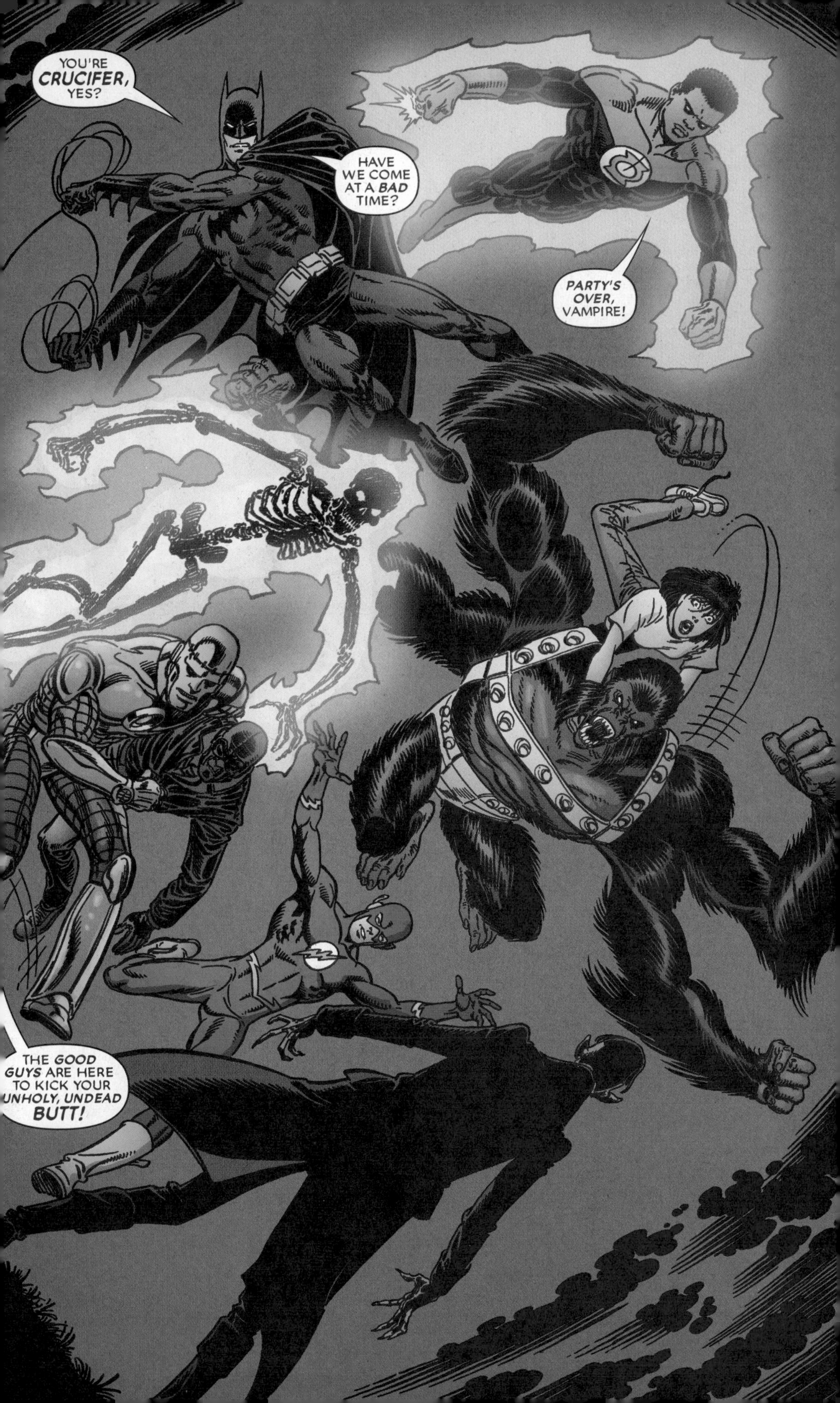
YOU'RE *CRUCIFER,* YES?
HAVE WE COME AT A *BAD* TIME?
PARTY'S OVER, VAMPIRE!
THE *GOOD GUYS* ARE HERE TO KICK YOUR *UNHOLY, UNDEAD* **BUTT!**

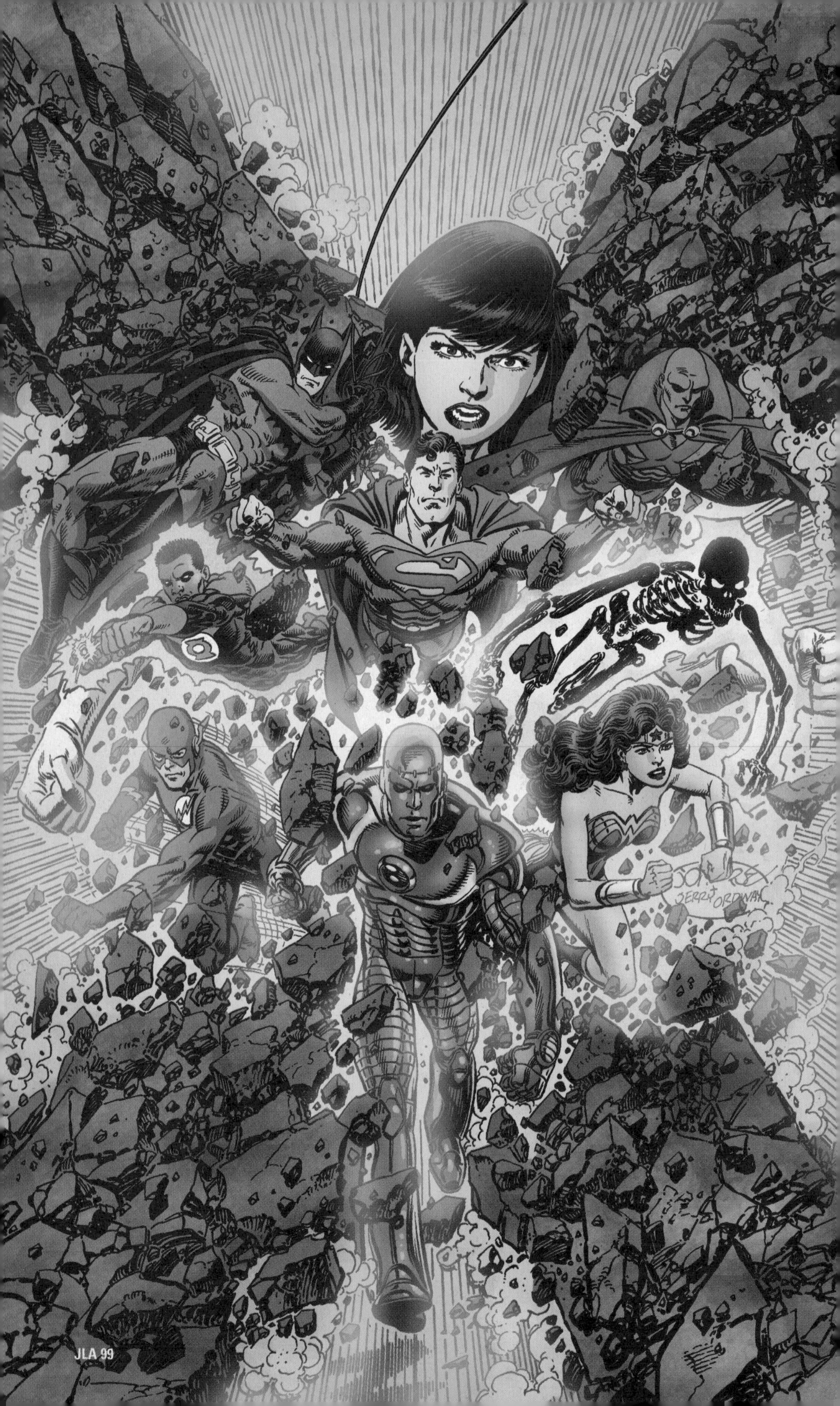
JERRY ORDWAY

JLA 99

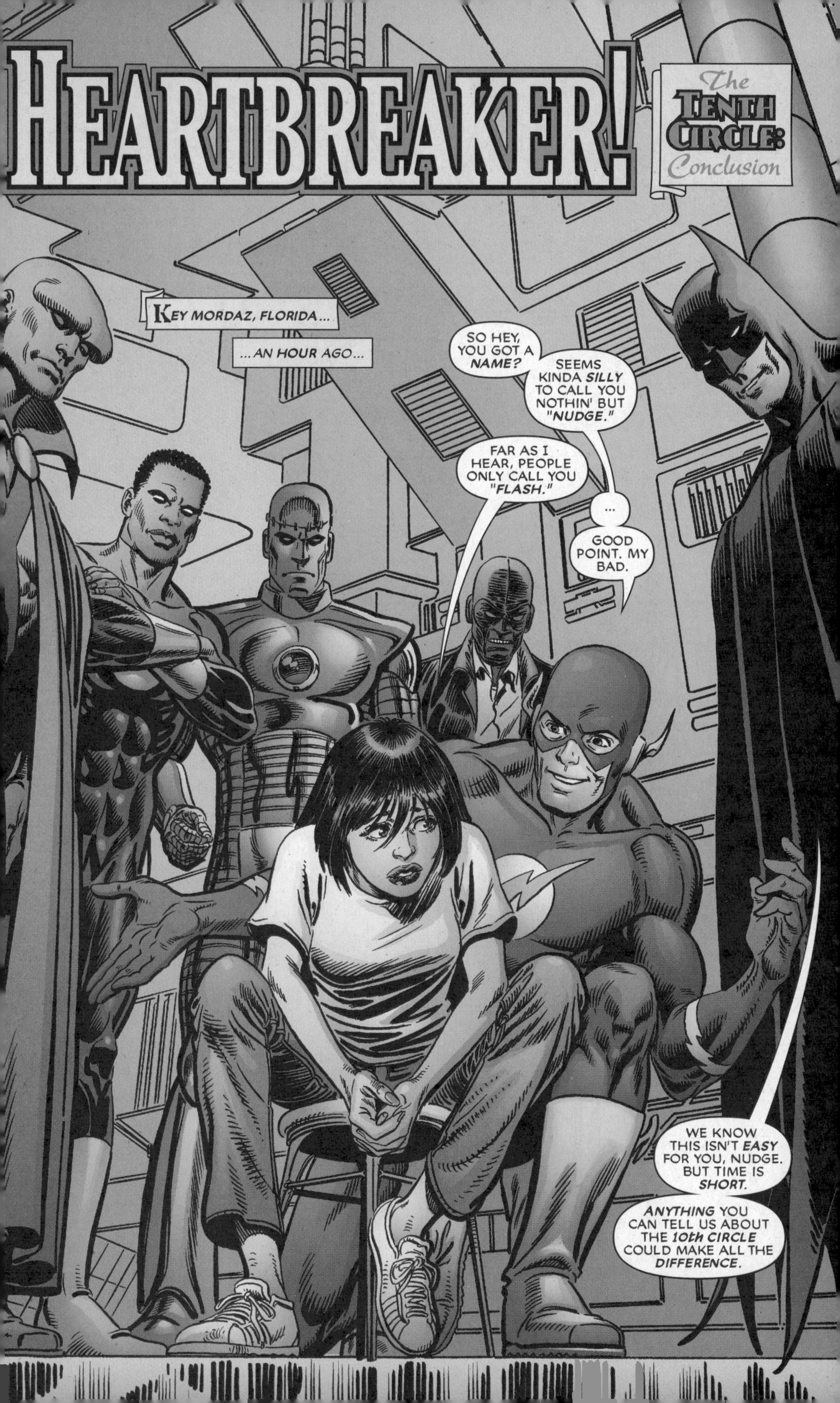
HEARTBREAKER!
The TENTH CIRCLE: Conclusion
KEY MORDAZ, FLORIDA...
...AN HOUR AGO...
SO HEY, YOU GOT A NAME?
SEEMS KINDA SILLY TO CALL YOU NOTHIN' BUT "NUDGE."
FAR AS I HEAR, PEOPLE ONLY CALL YOU "FLASH."
...
GOOD POINT. MY BAD.
WE KNOW THIS ISN'T EASY FOR YOU, NUDGE. BUT TIME IS SHORT.
ANYTHING YOU CAN TELL US ABOUT THE 10th CIRCLE COULD MAKE ALL THE DIFFERENCE.

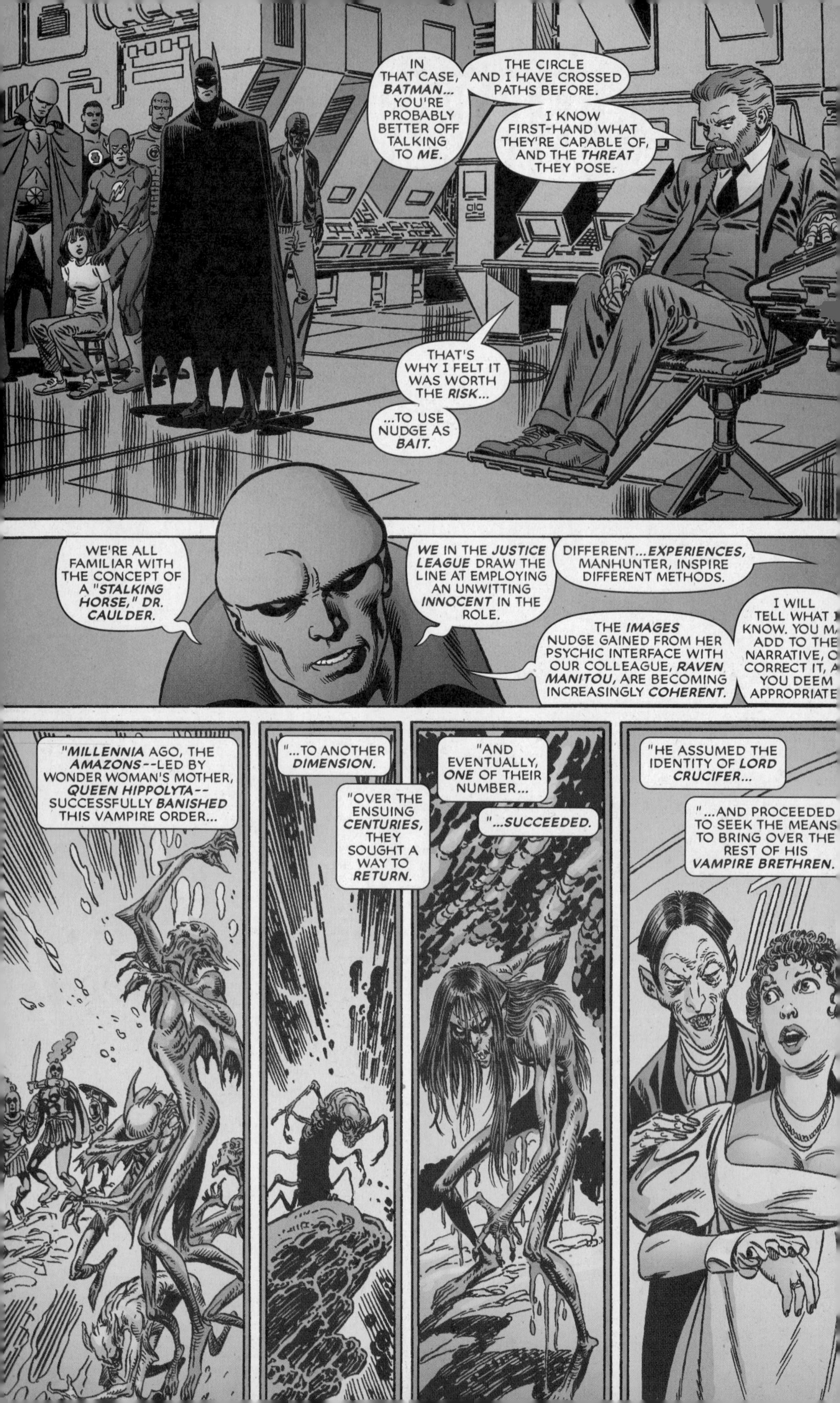
IN THAT CASE, BATMAN... YOU'RE PROBABLY BETTER OFF TALKING TO ME.
THE CIRCLE AND I HAVE CROSSED PATHS BEFORE.
I KNOW FIRST-HAND WHAT THEY'RE CAPABLE OF, AND THE THREAT THEY POSE.
THAT'S WHY I FELT IT WAS WORTH THE RISK...
...TO USE NUDGE AS BAIT.
WE'RE ALL FAMILIAR WITH THE CONCEPT OF A "STALKING HORSE," DR. CAULDER.
WE IN THE JUSTICE LEAGUE DRAW THE LINE AT EMPLOYING AN UNWITTING INNOCENT IN THE ROLE.
DIFFERENT...EXPERIENCES, MANHUNTER, INSPIRE DIFFERENT METHODS.
THE IMAGES NUDGE GAINED FROM HER PSYCHIC INTERFACE WITH OUR COLLEAGUE, RAVEN MANITOU, ARE BECOMING INCREASINGLY COHERENT.
I WILL TELL WHAT KNOW. YOU ADD TO THE NARRATIVE, CORRECT IT, YOU DEEM APPROPRIATE
"MILLENNIA AGO, THE AMAZONS--LED BY WONDER WOMAN'S MOTHER, QUEEN HIPPOLYTA--SUCCESSFULLY BANISHED THIS VAMPIRE ORDER...
"...TO ANOTHER DIMENSION.
"OVER THE ENSUING CENTURIES, THEY SOUGHT A WAY TO RETURN.
"AND EVENTUALLY, ONE OF THEIR NUMBER...
"...SUCCEEDED.
"HE ASSUMED THE IDENTITY OF LORD CRUCIFER...
"...AND PROCEEDED TO SEEK THE MEANS TO BRING OVER THE REST OF HIS VAMPIRE BRETHREN.

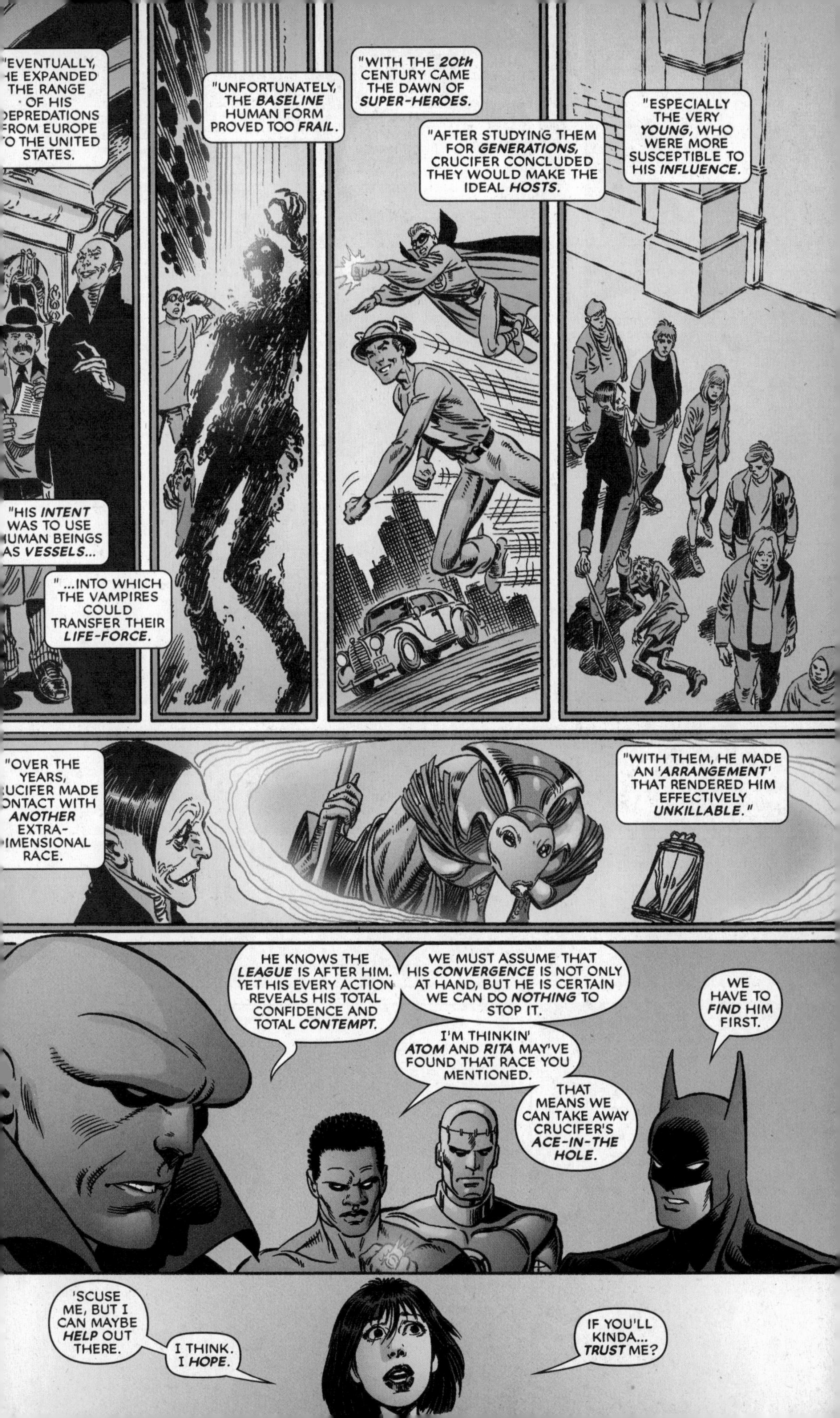
"EVENTUALLY, HE EXPANDED THE RANGE OF HIS DEPREDATIONS FROM EUROPE TO THE UNITED STATES.
"HIS *INTENT* WAS TO USE HUMAN BEINGS AS *VESSELS*...
" ...INTO WHICH THE VAMPIRES COULD TRANSFER THEIR *LIFE-FORCE*.
"UNFORTUNATELY, THE *BASELINE* HUMAN FORM PROVED TOO *FRAIL*.
"WITH THE *20th* CENTURY CAME THE DAWN OF *SUPER-HEROES*.
"AFTER STUDYING THEM FOR *GENERATIONS*, CRUCIFER CONCLUDED THEY WOULD MAKE THE IDEAL *HOSTS*.
"ESPECIALLY THE VERY *YOUNG*, WHO WERE MORE SUSCEPTIBLE TO HIS *INFLUENCE*.
"OVER THE YEARS, CRUCIFER MADE CONTACT WITH *ANOTHER* EXTRA-DIMENSIONAL RACE.
"WITH THEM, HE MADE AN '*ARRANGEMENT*' THAT RENDERED HIM EFFECTIVELY *UNKILLABLE*."
HE KNOWS THE *LEAGUE* IS AFTER HIM. YET HIS EVERY ACTION REVEALS HIS TOTAL CONFIDENCE AND TOTAL *CONTEMPT*.
WE MUST ASSUME THAT HIS *CONVERGENCE* IS NOT ONLY AT HAND, BUT HE IS CERTAIN WE CAN DO *NOTHING* TO STOP IT.
WE HAVE TO *FIND* HIM FIRST.
I'M THINKIN' *ATOM* AND *RITA* MAY'VE FOUND THAT RACE YOU MENTIONED.
THAT MEANS WE CAN TAKE AWAY CRUCIFER'S *ACE-IN-THE HOLE*.
'SCUSE ME, BUT I CAN MAYBE *HELP* OUT THERE.
I THINK. I *HOPE*.
IF YOU'LL KINDA... *TRUST* ME?

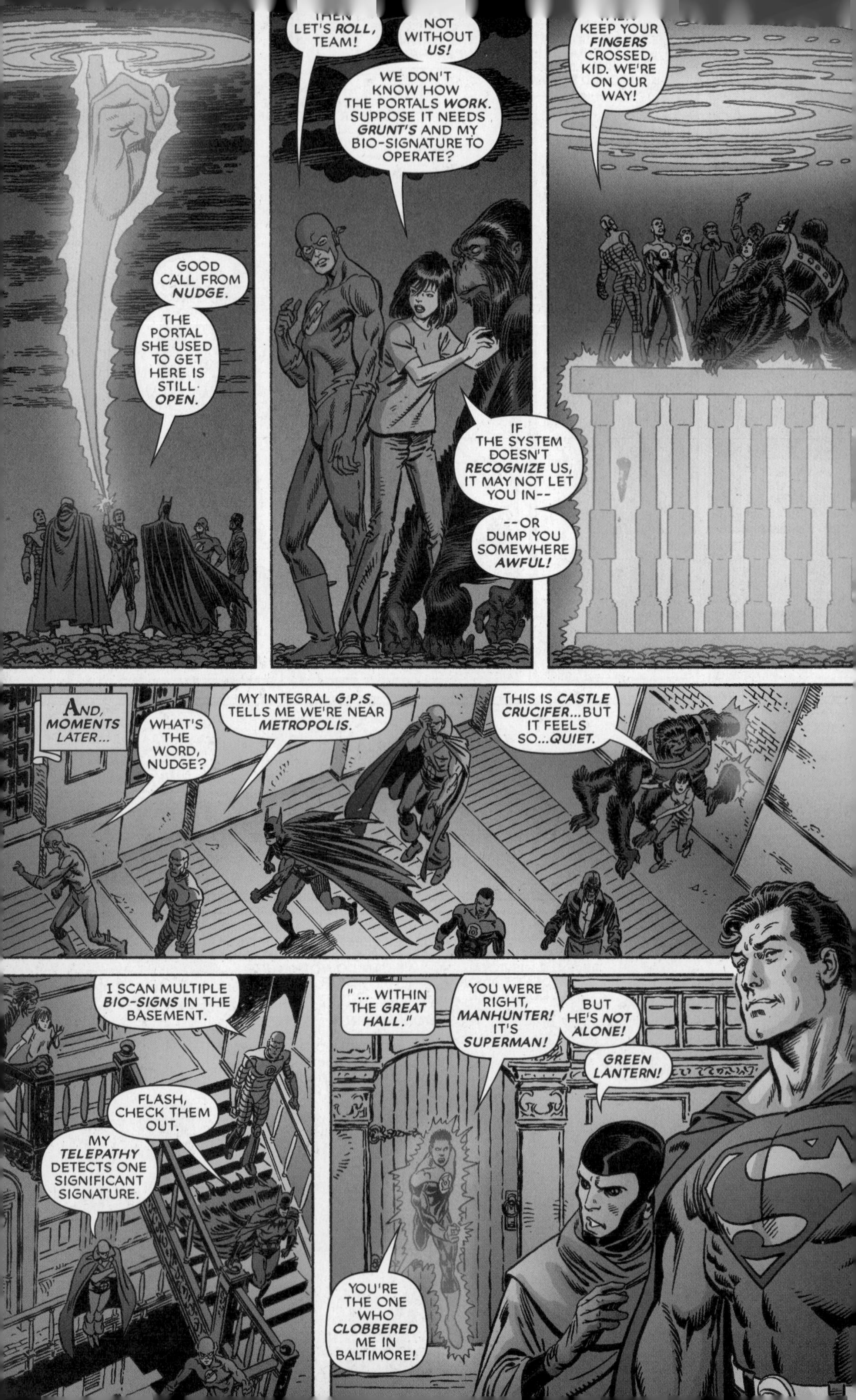
GOOD CALL FROM NUDGE.
THE PORTAL SHE USED TO GET HERE IS STILL OPEN.
LET'S ROLL, TEAM!
NOT WITHOUT US!
WE DON'T KNOW HOW THE PORTALS WORK. SUPPOSE IT NEEDS GRUNT'S AND MY BIO-SIGNATURE TO OPERATE?
IF THE SYSTEM DOESN'T RECOGNIZE US, IT MAY NOT LET YOU IN--
--OR DUMP YOU SOMEWHERE AWFUL!
KEEP YOUR FINGERS CROSSED, KID. WE'RE ON OUR WAY!
AND, MOMENTS LATER...
WHAT'S THE WORD, NUDGE?
MY INTEGRAL G.P.S. TELLS ME WE'RE NEAR METROPOLIS.
THIS IS CASTLE CRUCIFER...BUT IT FEELS SO...QUIET.
I SCAN MULTIPLE BIO-SIGNS IN THE BASEMENT.
FLASH, CHECK THEM OUT.
MY TELEPATHY DETECTS ONE SIGNIFICANT SIGNATURE.
"... WITHIN THE GREAT HALL."
YOU WERE RIGHT, MANHUNTER! IT'S SUPERMAN!
BUT HE'S NOT ALONE!
GREEN LANTERN!
YOU'RE THE ONE WHO CLOBBERED ME IN BALTIMORE!

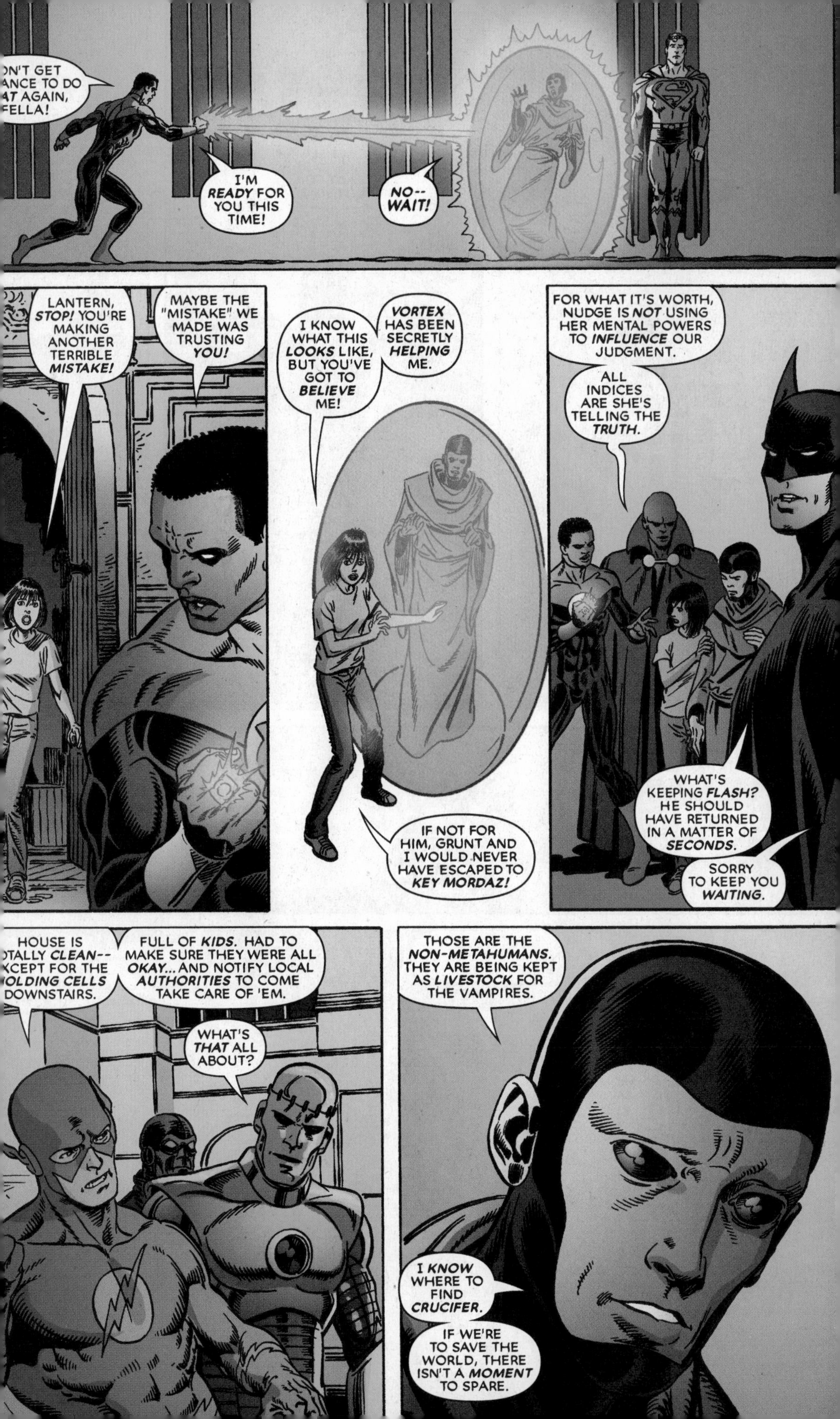

ON'T GET ANCE TO DO AT AGAIN, FELLA!
I'M READY FOR YOU THIS TIME!
NO-- WAIT!
LANTERN, STOP! YOU'RE MAKING ANOTHER TERRIBLE MISTAKE!
MAYBE THE "MISTAKE" WE MADE WAS TRUSTING YOU!
I KNOW WHAT THIS LOOKS LIKE, BUT YOU'VE GOT TO BELIEVE ME!
VORTEX HAS BEEN SECRETLY HELPING ME.
IF NOT FOR HIM, GRUNT AND I WOULD NEVER HAVE ESCAPED TO KEY MORDAZ!
FOR WHAT IT'S WORTH, NUDGE IS NOT USING HER MENTAL POWERS TO INFLUENCE OUR JUDGMENT.
ALL INDICES ARE SHE'S TELLING THE TRUTH.
WHAT'S KEEPING FLASH? HE SHOULD HAVE RETURNED IN A MATTER OF SECONDS.
SORRY TO KEEP YOU WAITING.
HOUSE IS OTALLY CLEAN-- XCEPT FOR THE OLDING CELLS DOWNSTAIRS.
FULL OF KIDS. HAD TO MAKE SURE THEY WERE ALL OKAY... AND NOTIFY LOCAL AUTHORITIES TO COME TAKE CARE OF 'EM.
WHAT'S THAT ALL ABOUT?
THOSE ARE THE NON-METAHUMANS. THEY ARE BEING KEPT AS LIVESTOCK FOR THE VAMPIRES.
I KNOW WHERE TO FIND CRUCIFER.
IF WE'RE TO SAVE THE WORLD, THERE ISN'T A MOMENT TO SPARE.

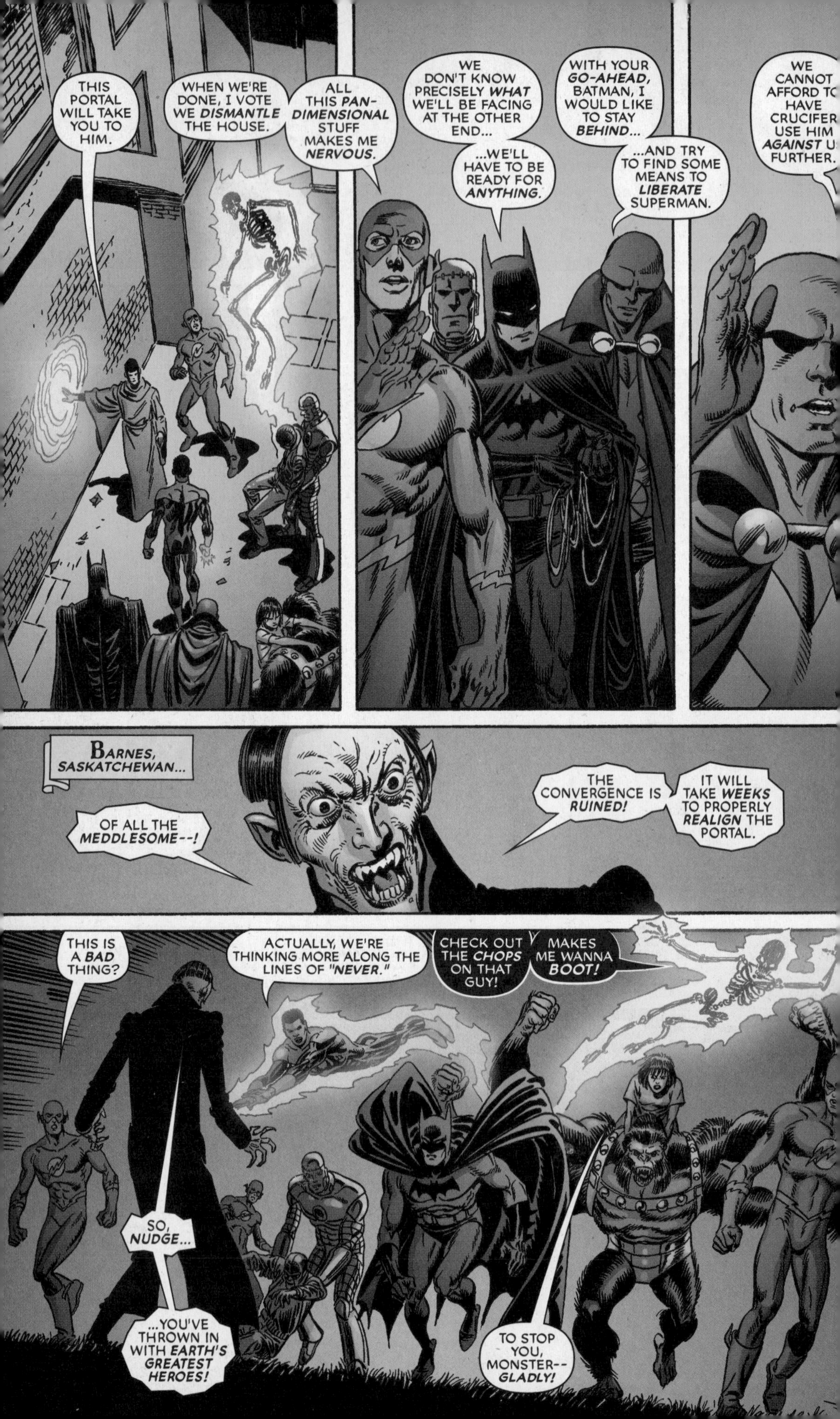
THIS PORTAL WILL TAKE YOU TO HIM.
WHEN WE'RE DONE, I VOTE WE DISMANTLE THE HOUSE.
ALL THIS PAN-DIMENSIONAL STUFF MAKES ME NERVOUS.
WE DON'T KNOW PRECISELY WHAT WE'LL BE FACING AT THE OTHER END...
...WE'LL HAVE TO BE READY FOR ANYTHING.
WITH YOUR GO-AHEAD, BATMAN, I WOULD LIKE TO STAY BEHIND...
...AND TRY TO FIND SOME MEANS TO LIBERATE SUPERMAN.
WE CANNOT AFFORD TO HAVE CRUCIFER USE HIM AGAINST US FURTHER.
BARNES, SASKATCHEWAN...
OF ALL THE MEDDLESOME--!
THE CONVERGENCE IS RUINED!
IT WILL TAKE WEEKS TO PROPERLY REALIGN THE PORTAL.
THIS IS A BAD THING?
ACTUALLY, WE'RE THINKING MORE ALONG THE LINES OF "NEVER."
CHECK OUT THE CHOPS ON THAT GUY!
MAKES ME WANNA BOOT!
SO, NUDGE...
...YOU'VE THROWN IN WITH EARTH'S GREATEST HEROES!
TO STOP YOU, MONSTER--GLADLY!

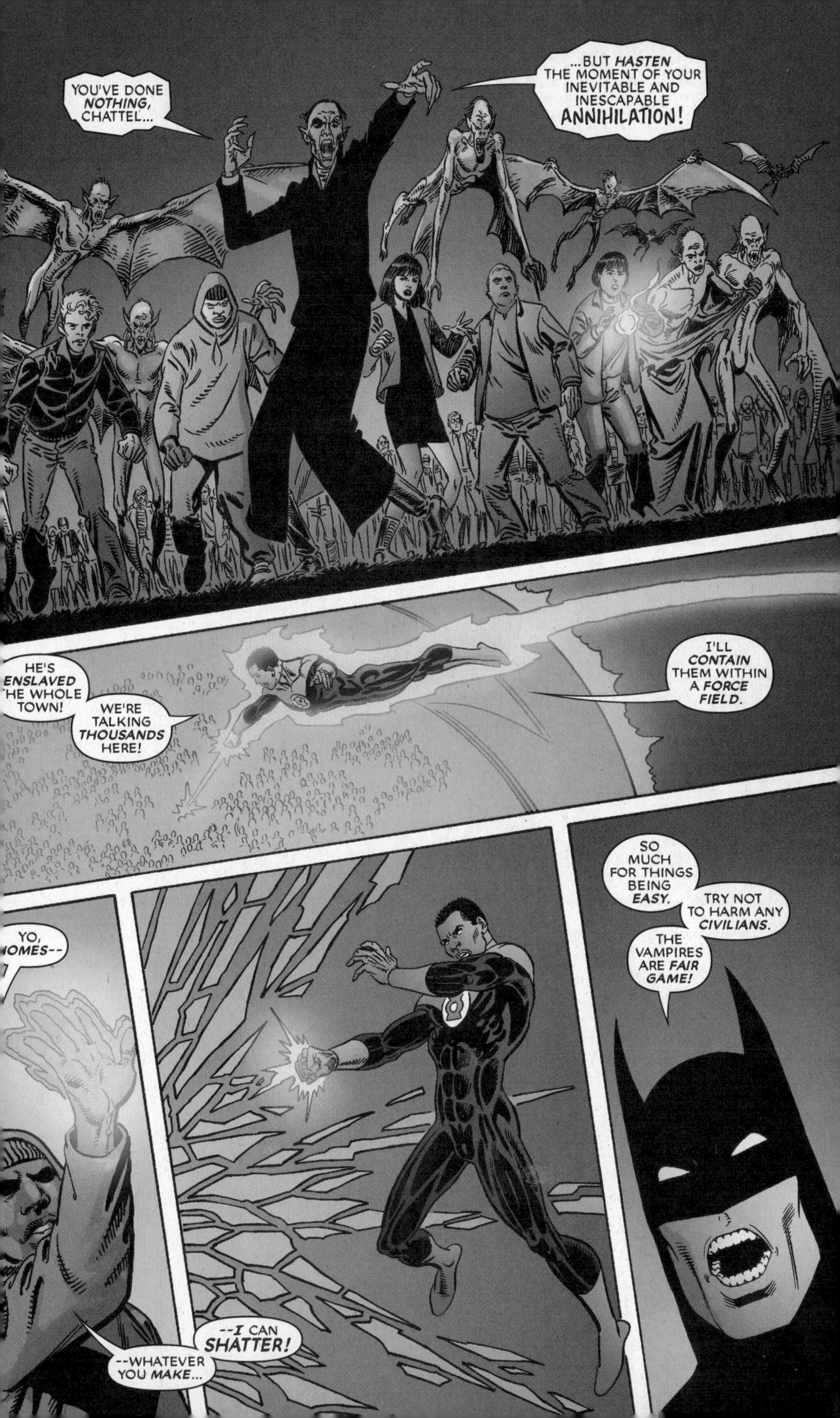
YOU'VE DONE NOTHING, CHATTEL...
...BUT HASTEN THE MOMENT OF YOUR INEVITABLE AND INESCAPABLE ANNIHILATION!
HE'S ENSLAVED THE WHOLE TOWN!
WE'RE TALKING THOUSANDS HERE!
I'LL CONTAIN THEM WITHIN A FORCE FIELD.
YO, HOMES--
--WHATEVER YOU MAKE...
--I CAN SHATTER!
SO MUCH FOR THINGS BEING EASY.
TRY NOT TO HARM ANY CIVILIANS.
THE VAMPIRES ARE FAIR GAME!

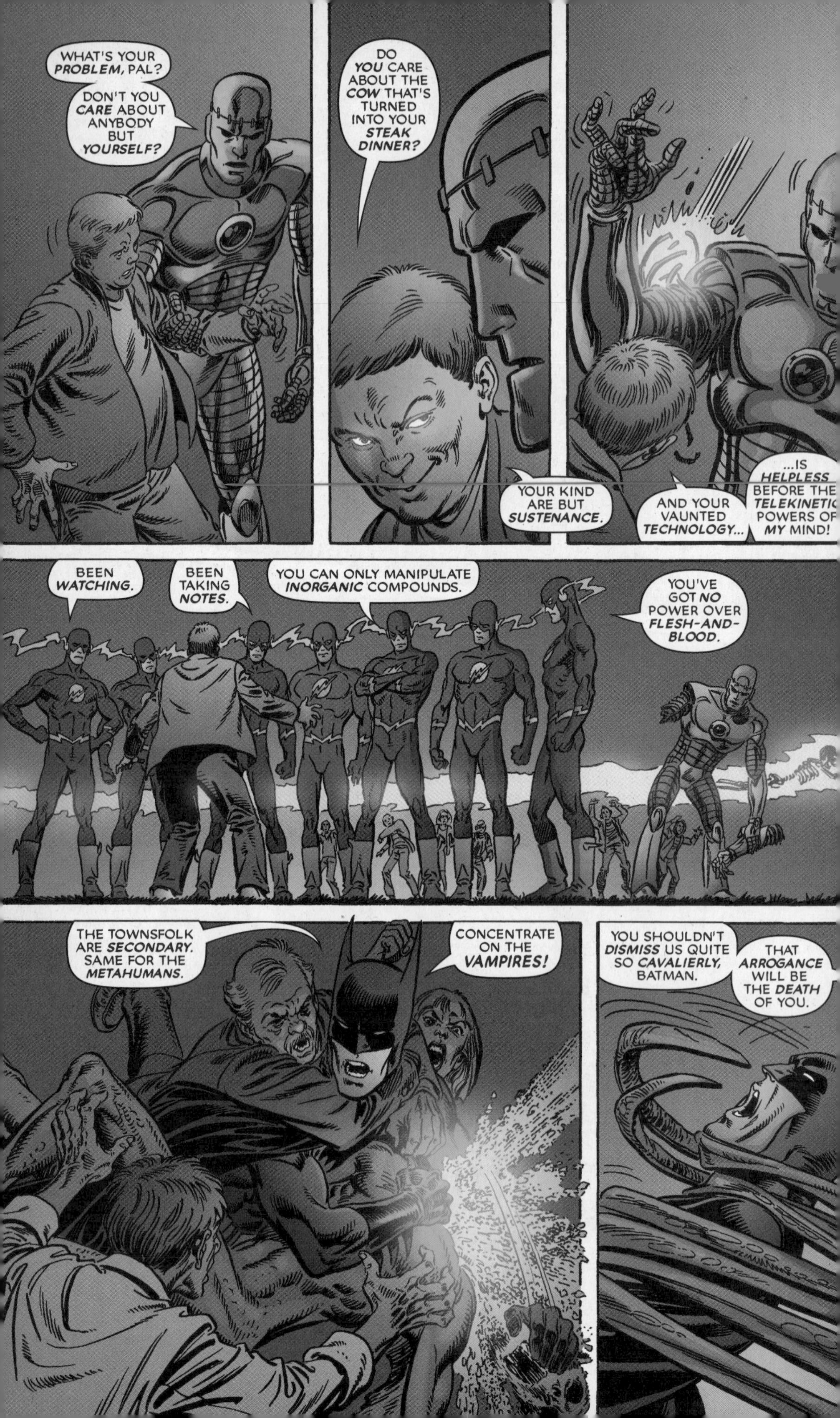
WHAT'S YOUR PROBLEM, PAL?
DON'T YOU CARE ABOUT ANYBODY BUT YOURSELF?
DO YOU CARE ABOUT THE COW THAT'S TURNED INTO YOUR STEAK DINNER?
YOUR KIND ARE BUT SUSTENANCE.
AND YOUR VAUNTED TECHNOLOGY...
...IS HELPLESS BEFORE THE TELEKINETIC POWERS OF MY MIND!
BEEN WATCHING.
BEEN TAKING NOTES.
YOU CAN ONLY MANIPULATE INORGANIC COMPOUNDS.
YOU'VE GOT NO POWER OVER FLESH-AND-BLOOD.
THE TOWNSFOLK ARE SECONDARY. SAME FOR THE METAHUMANS.
CONCENTRATE ON THE VAMPIRES!
YOU SHOULDN'T DISMISS US QUITE SO CAVALIERLY, BATMAN.
THAT ARROGANCE WILL BE THE DEATH OF YOU.

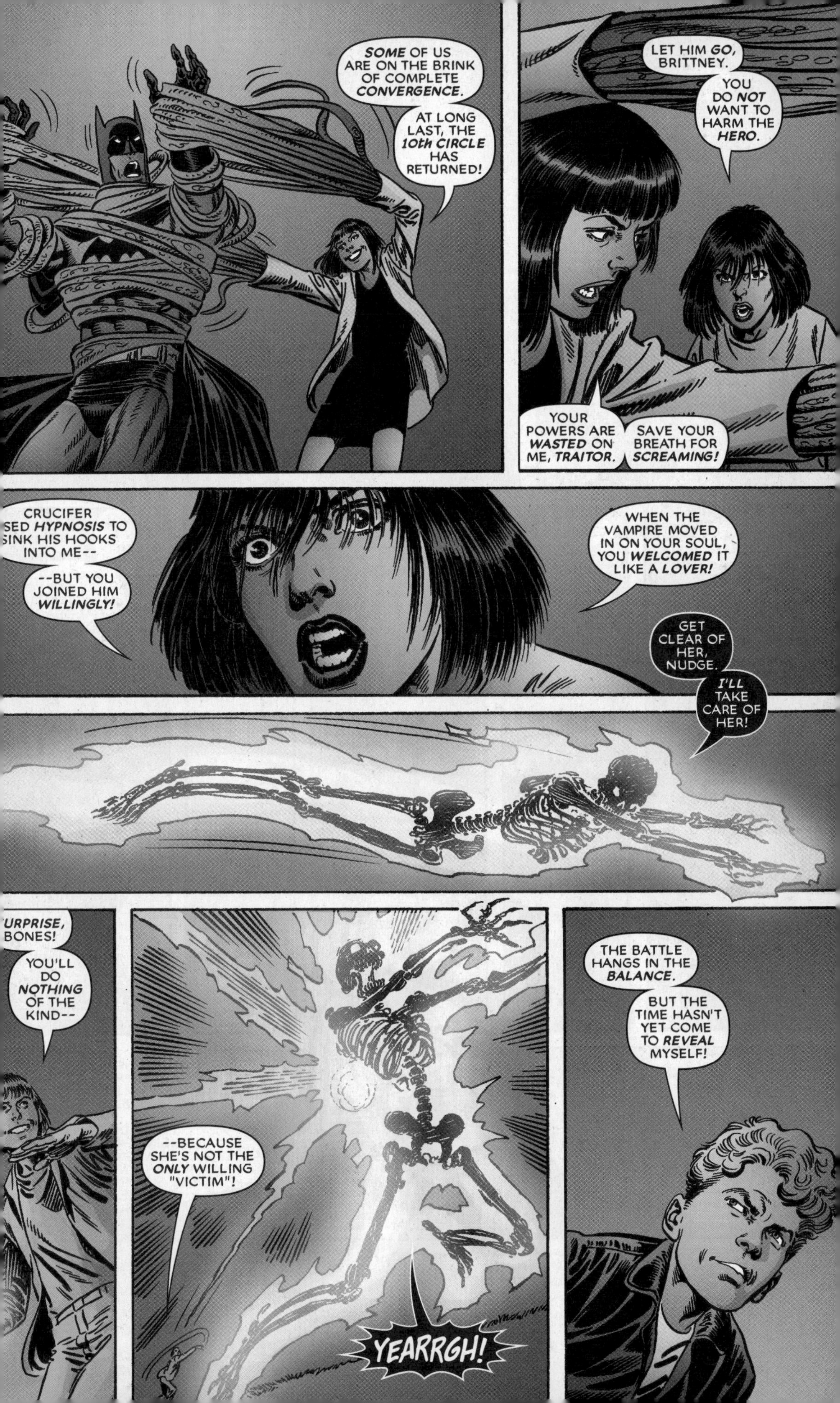
SOME OF US ARE ON THE BRINK OF COMPLETE CONVERGENCE.
AT LONG LAST, THE 10th CIRCLE HAS RETURNED!
LET HIM GO, BRITTNEY.
YOU DO NOT WANT TO HARM THE HERO.
YOUR POWERS ARE WASTED ON ME, TRAITOR.
SAVE YOUR BREATH FOR SCREAMING!
CRUCIFER SED HYPNOSIS TO SINK HIS HOOKS INTO ME--
--BUT YOU JOINED HIM WILLINGLY!
WHEN THE VAMPIRE MOVED IN ON YOUR SOUL, YOU WELCOMED IT LIKE A LOVER!
GET CLEAR OF HER, NUDGE.
I'LL TAKE CARE OF HER!
URPRISE, BONES!
YOU'LL DO NOTHING OF THE KIND--
--BECAUSE SHE'S NOT THE ONLY WILLING "VICTIM"!
YEARRGH!
THE BATTLE HANGS IN THE BALANCE.
BUT THE TIME HASN'T YET COME TO REVEAL MYSELF!

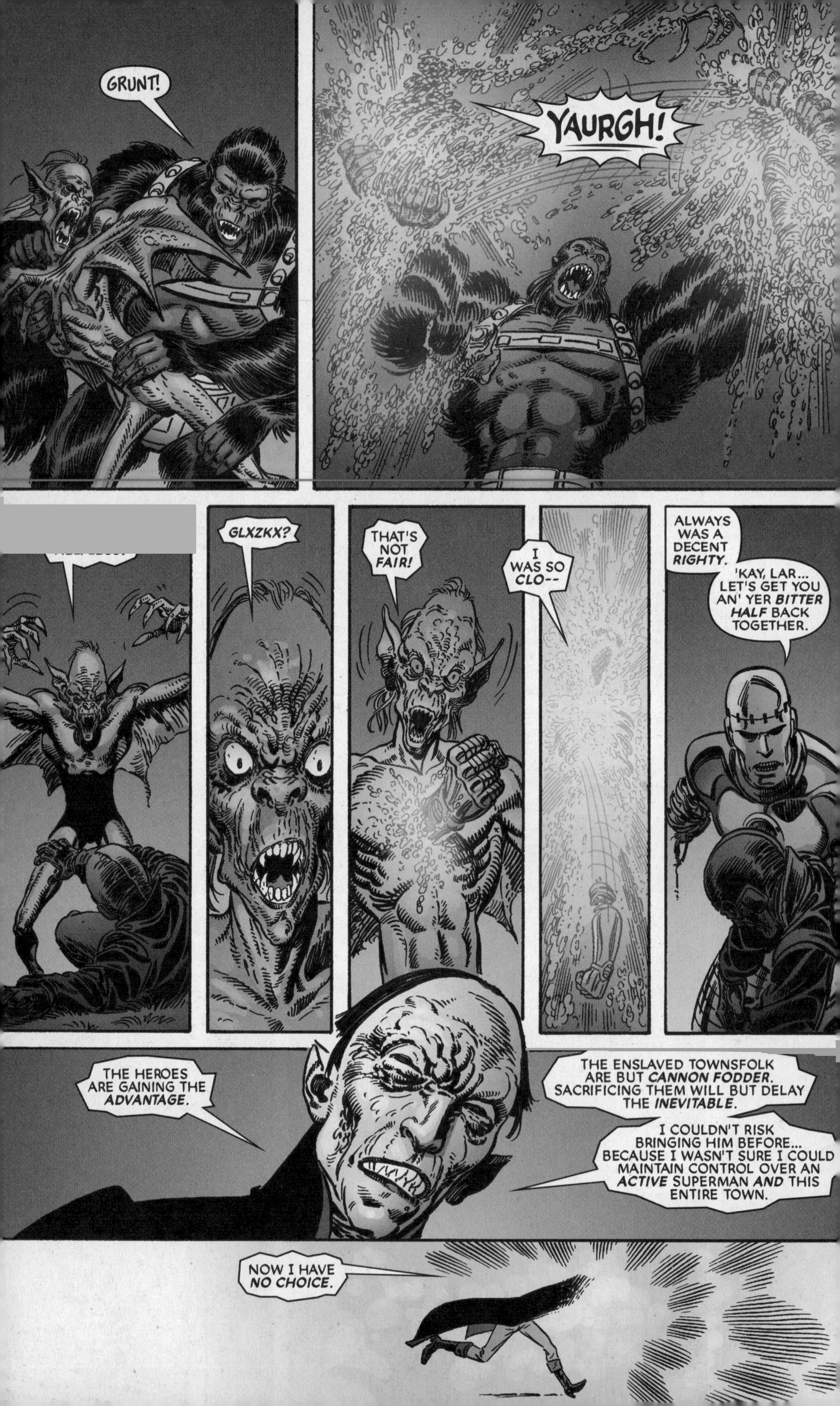

GRUNT!
YAURGH!
GLXZKX?
THAT'S NOT FAIR!
I WAS SO CLO--
ALWAYS WAS A DECENT RIGHTY.
'KAY, LAR... LET'S GET YOU AN' YER BITTER HALF BACK TOGETHER.
THE HEROES ARE GAINING THE ADVANTAGE.
THE ENSLAVED TOWNSFOLK ARE BUT CANNON FODDER. SACRIFICING THEM WILL BUT DELAY THE INEVITABLE.
I COULDN'T RISK BRINGING HIM BEFORE... BECAUSE I WASN'T SURE I COULD MAINTAIN CONTROL OVER AN ACTIVE SUPERMAN AND THIS ENTIRE TOWN.
NOW I HAVE NO CHOICE.

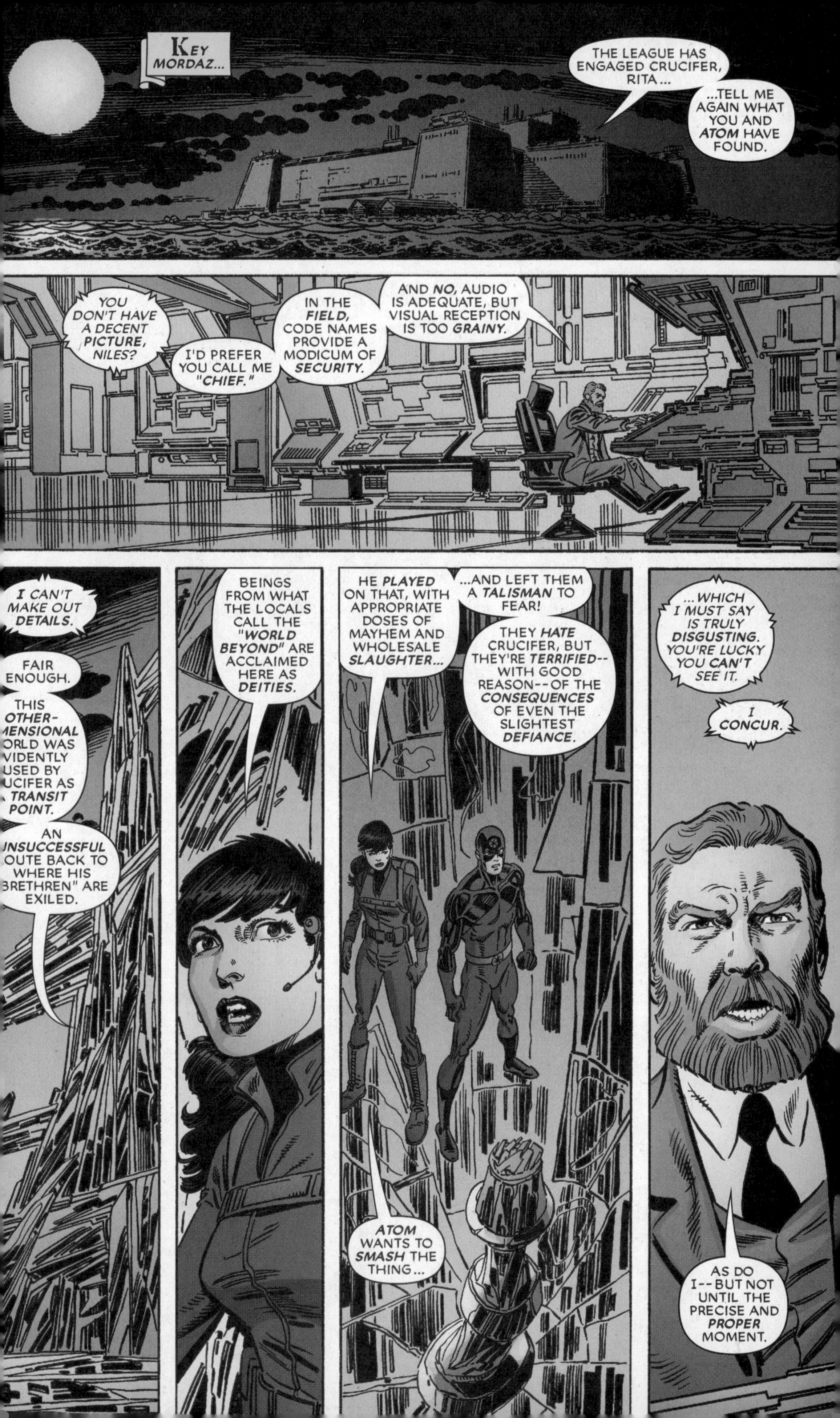
KEY MORDAZ...
THE LEAGUE HAS ENGAGED CRUCIFER, RITA...
...TELL ME AGAIN WHAT YOU AND ATOM HAVE FOUND.
YOU DON'T HAVE A DECENT PICTURE, NILES?
I'D PREFER YOU CALL ME "CHIEF."
IN THE FIELD, CODE NAMES PROVIDE A MODICUM OF SECURITY.
AND NO, AUDIO IS ADEQUATE, BUT VISUAL RECEPTION IS TOO GRAINY.
I CAN'T MAKE OUT DETAILS.
FAIR ENOUGH.
THIS OTHER-MENSIONAL ORLD WAS VIDENTLY USED BY UCIFER AS TRANSIT POINT.
AN UNSUCCESSFUL OUTE BACK TO WHERE HIS BRETHREN" ARE EXILED.
BEINGS FROM WHAT THE LOCALS CALL THE "WORLD BEYOND" ARE ACCLAIMED HERE AS DEITIES.
HE PLAYED ON THAT, WITH APPROPRIATE DOSES OF MAYHEM AND WHOLESALE SLAUGHTER...
...AND LEFT THEM A TALISMAN TO FEAR!
THEY HATE CRUCIFER, BUT THEY'RE TERRIFIED--WITH GOOD REASON--OF THE CONSEQUENCES OF EVEN THE SLIGHTEST DEFIANCE.
ATOM WANTS TO SMASH THE THING...
...WHICH I MUST SAY IS TRULY DISGUSTING. YOU'RE LUCKY YOU CAN'T SEE IT.
I CONCUR.
AS DO I--BUT NOT UNTIL THE PRECISE AND PROPER MOMENT.

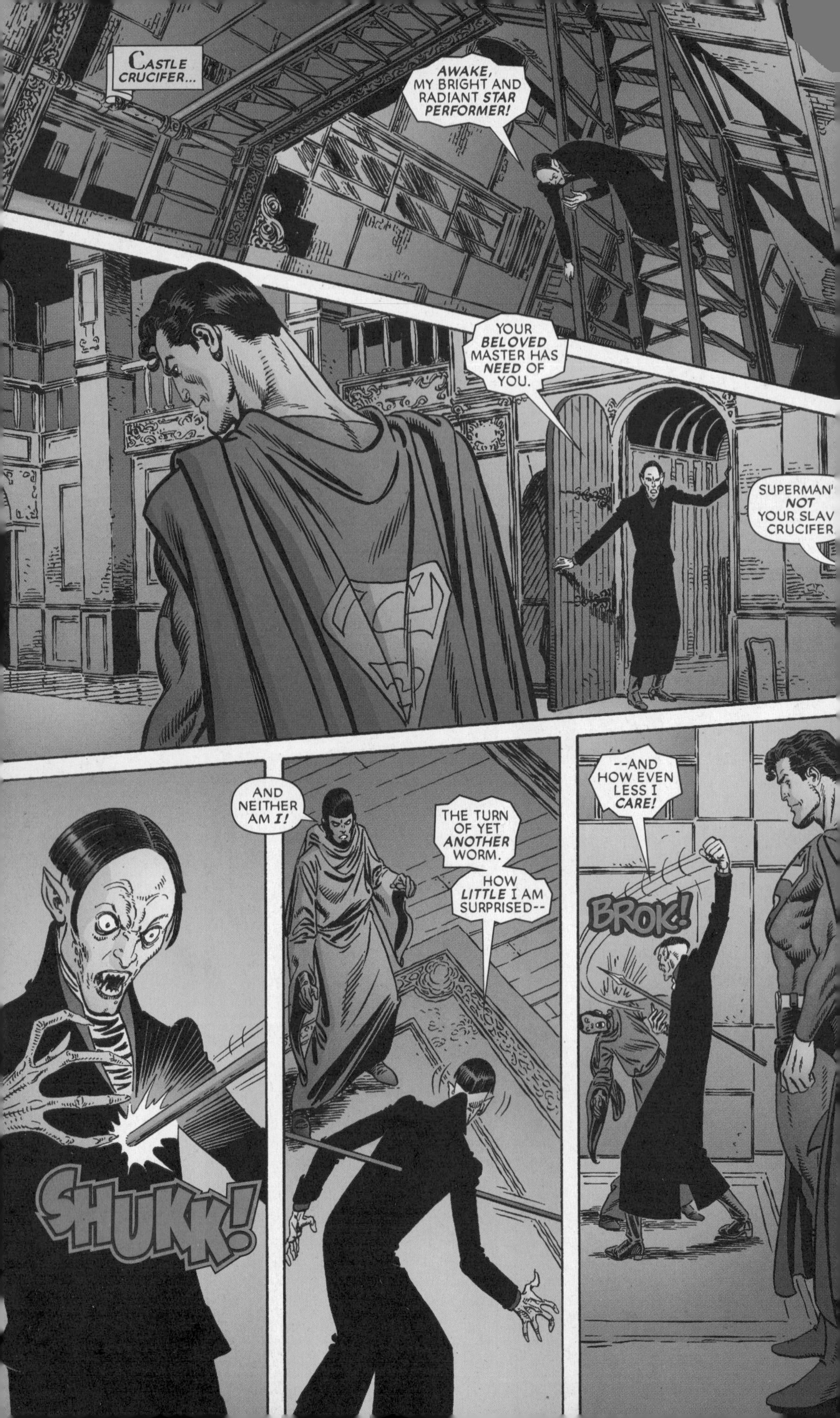
CASTLE CRUCIFER...
AWAKE, MY BRIGHT AND RADIANT STAR PERFORMER!
YOUR BELOVED MASTER HAS NEED OF YOU.
SUPERMAN' NOT YOUR SLAV CRUCIFER
AND NEITHER AM I!
SHUKK!
THE TURN OF YET ANOTHER WORM.
HOW LITTLE I AM SURPRISED--
--AND HOW EVEN LESS I CARE!
BROK!

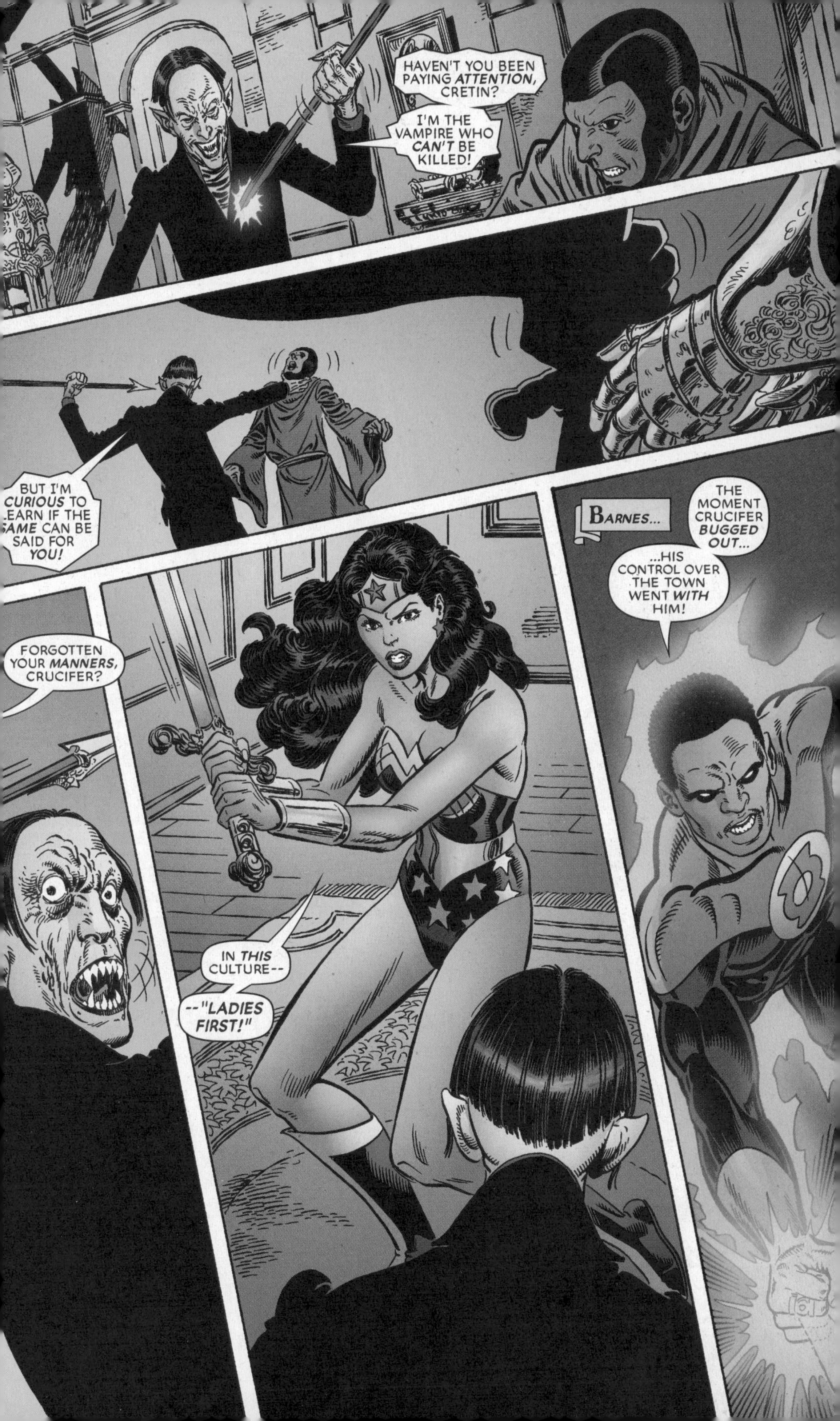
HAVEN'T YOU BEEN PAYING ATTENTION, CRETIN?
I'M THE VAMPIRE WHO CAN'T BE KILLED!
BUT I'M CURIOUS TO LEARN IF THE SAME CAN BE SAID FOR YOU!
BARNES...
THE MOMENT CRUCIFER BUGGED OUT...
...HIS CONTROL OVER THE TOWN WENT WITH HIM!
FORGOTTEN YOUR MANNERS, CRUCIFER?
IN THIS CULTURE--
--"LADIES FIRST!"

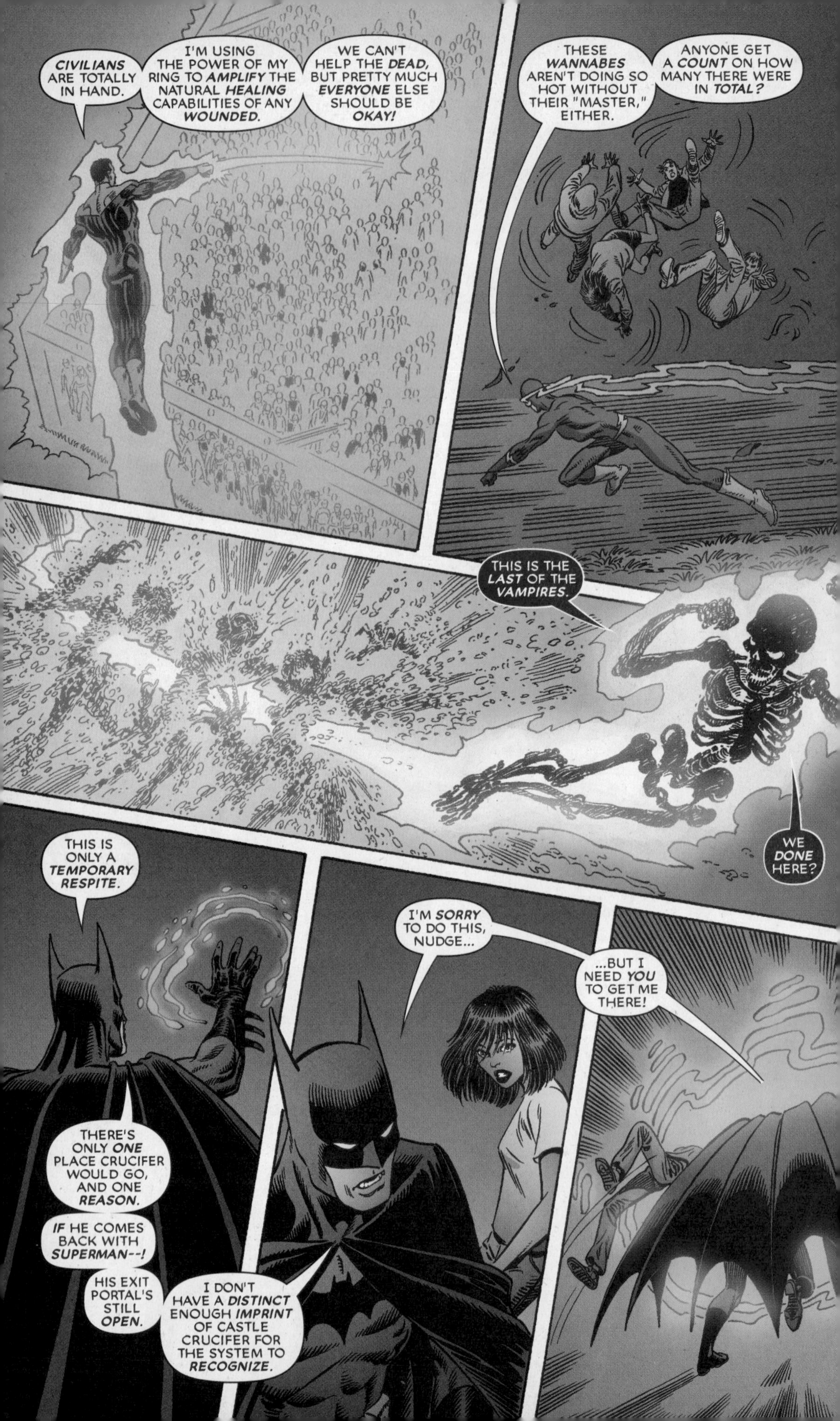
CIVILIANS ARE TOTALLY IN HAND.
I'M USING THE POWER OF MY RING TO AMPLIFY THE NATURAL HEALING CAPABILITIES OF ANY WOUNDED.
WE CAN'T HELP THE DEAD, BUT PRETTY MUCH EVERYONE ELSE SHOULD BE OKAY!
THESE WANNABES AREN'T DOING SO HOT WITHOUT THEIR "MASTER," EITHER.
ANYONE GET A COUNT ON HOW MANY THERE WERE IN TOTAL?
THIS IS THE LAST OF THE VAMPIRES.
WE DONE HERE?
THIS IS ONLY A TEMPORARY RESPITE.
THERE'S ONLY ONE PLACE CRUCIFER WOULD GO, AND ONE REASON.
IF HE COMES BACK WITH SUPERMAN--!
HIS EXIT PORTAL'S STILL OPEN.
I DON'T HAVE A DISTINCT ENOUGH IMPRINT OF CASTLE CRUCIFER FOR THE SYSTEM TO RECOGNIZE.
I'M SORRY TO DO THIS, NUDGE...
...BUT I NEED YOU TO GET ME THERE!

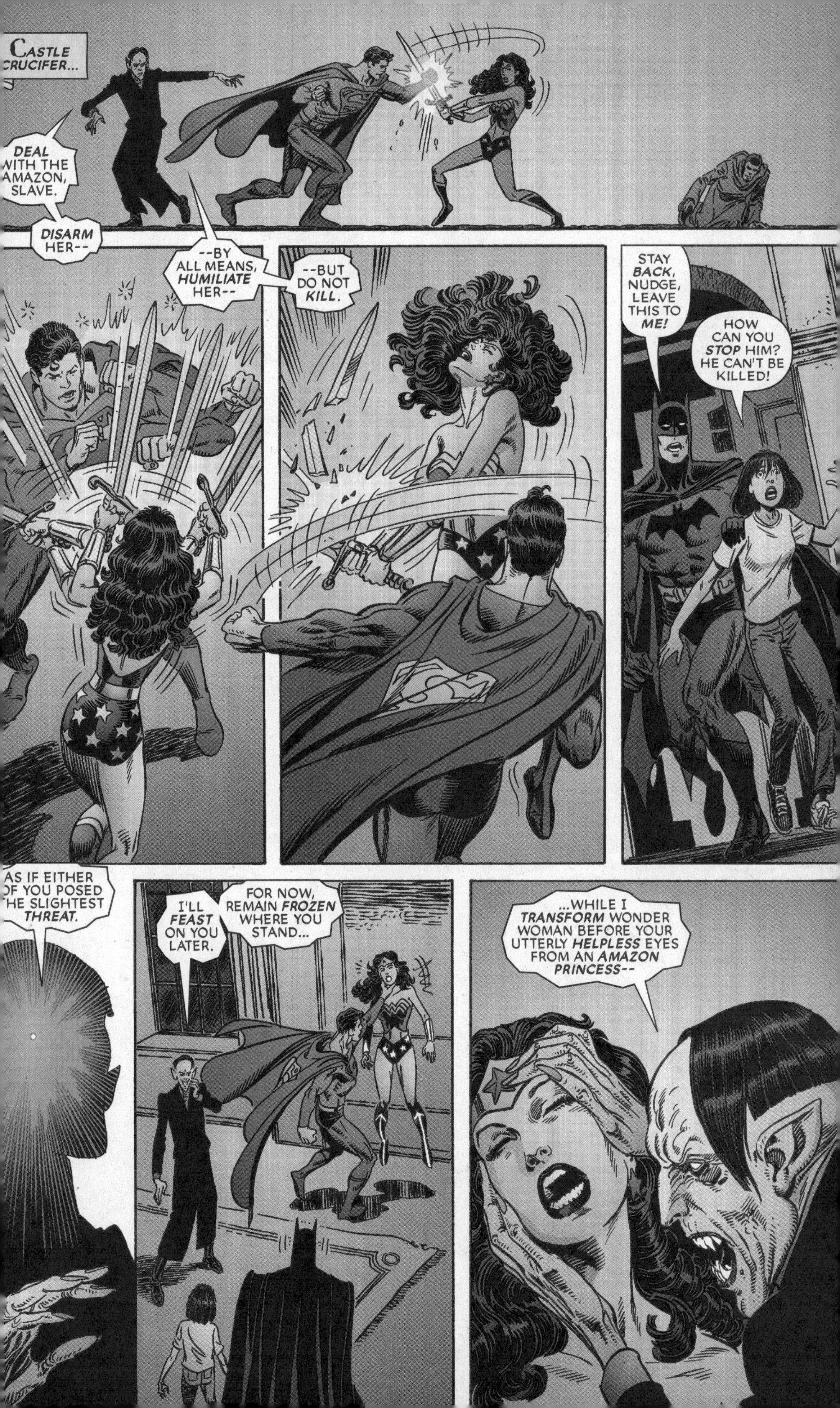

CASTLE CRUCIFER...
DEAL WITH THE AMAZON, SLAVE.
DISARM HER--
--BY ALL MEANS, HUMILIATE HER--
--BUT DO NOT KILL.
STAY BACK, NUDGE, LEAVE THIS TO ME!
HOW CAN YOU STOP HIM? HE CAN'T BE KILLED!
AS IF EITHER OF YOU POSED THE SLIGHTEST THREAT.
I'LL FEAST ON YOU LATER.
FOR NOW, REMAIN FROZEN WHERE YOU STAND...
...WHILE I TRANSFORM WONDER WOMAN BEFORE YOUR UTTERLY HELPLESS EYES FROM AN AMAZON PRINCESS--

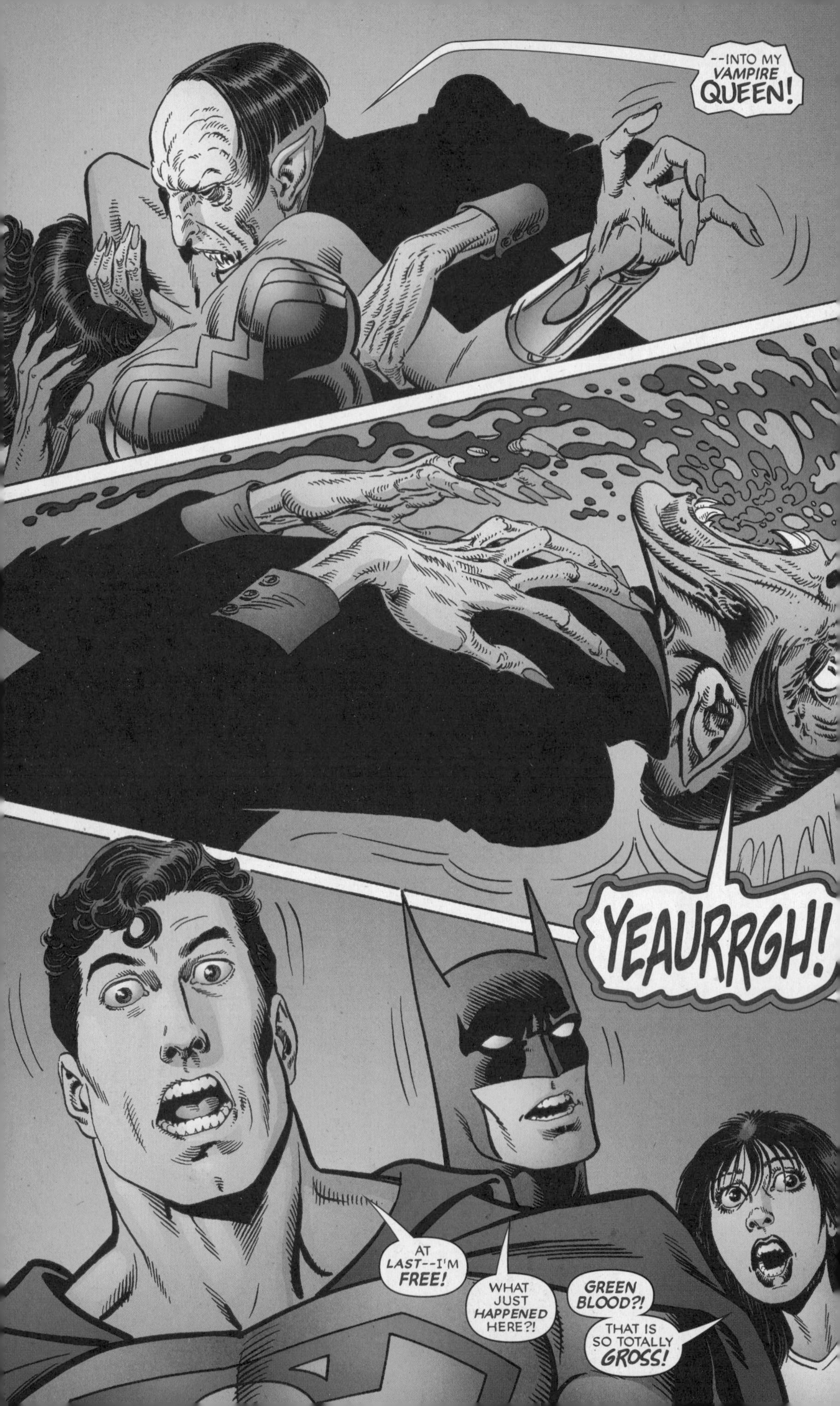
--INTO MY VAMPIRE QUEEN!
YEAURRGH!
AT LAST--I'M FREE!
WHAT JUST HAPPENED HERE?!
GREEN BLOOD?!
THAT IS SO TOTALLY GROSS!

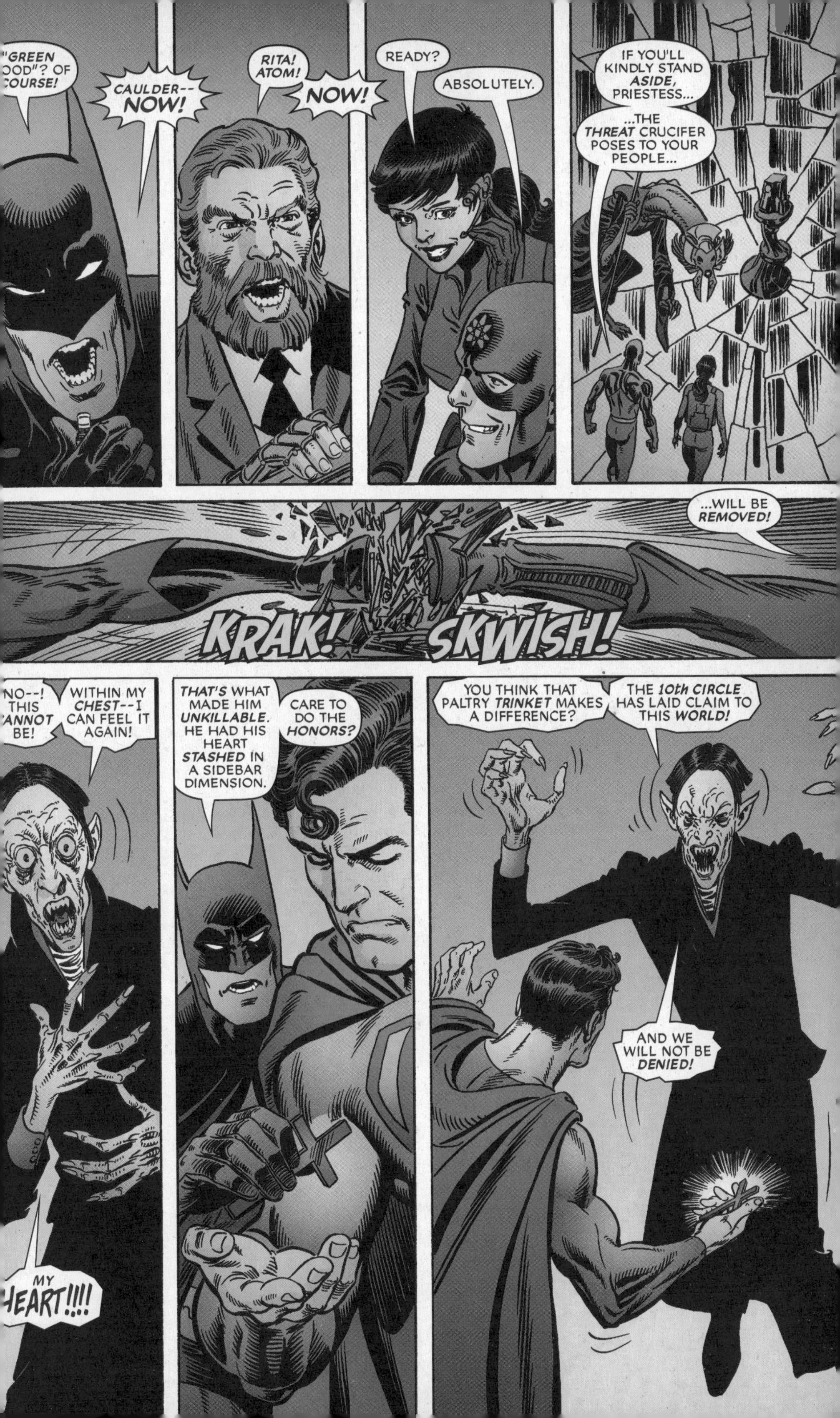
"GREEN
OOD"? OF
COURSE!
CAULDER--
NOW!
RITA!
ATOM!
NOW!
READY?
ABSOLUTELY.
IF YOU'LL KINDLY STAND ASIDE, PRIESTESS...
...THE THREAT CRUCIFER POSES TO YOUR PEOPLE...
...WILL BE REMOVED!
KRAK!
SKWISH!
NO--! THIS CANNOT BE!
WITHIN MY CHEST--I CAN FEEL IT AGAIN!
MY HEART!!!!
THAT'S WHAT MADE HIM UNKILLABLE. HE HAD HIS HEART STASHED IN A SIDEBAR DIMENSION.
CARE TO DO THE HONORS?
YOU THINK THAT PALTRY TRINKET MAKES A DIFFERENCE?
THE 10th CIRCLE HAS LAID CLAIM TO THIS WORLD!
AND WE WILL NOT BE DENIED!

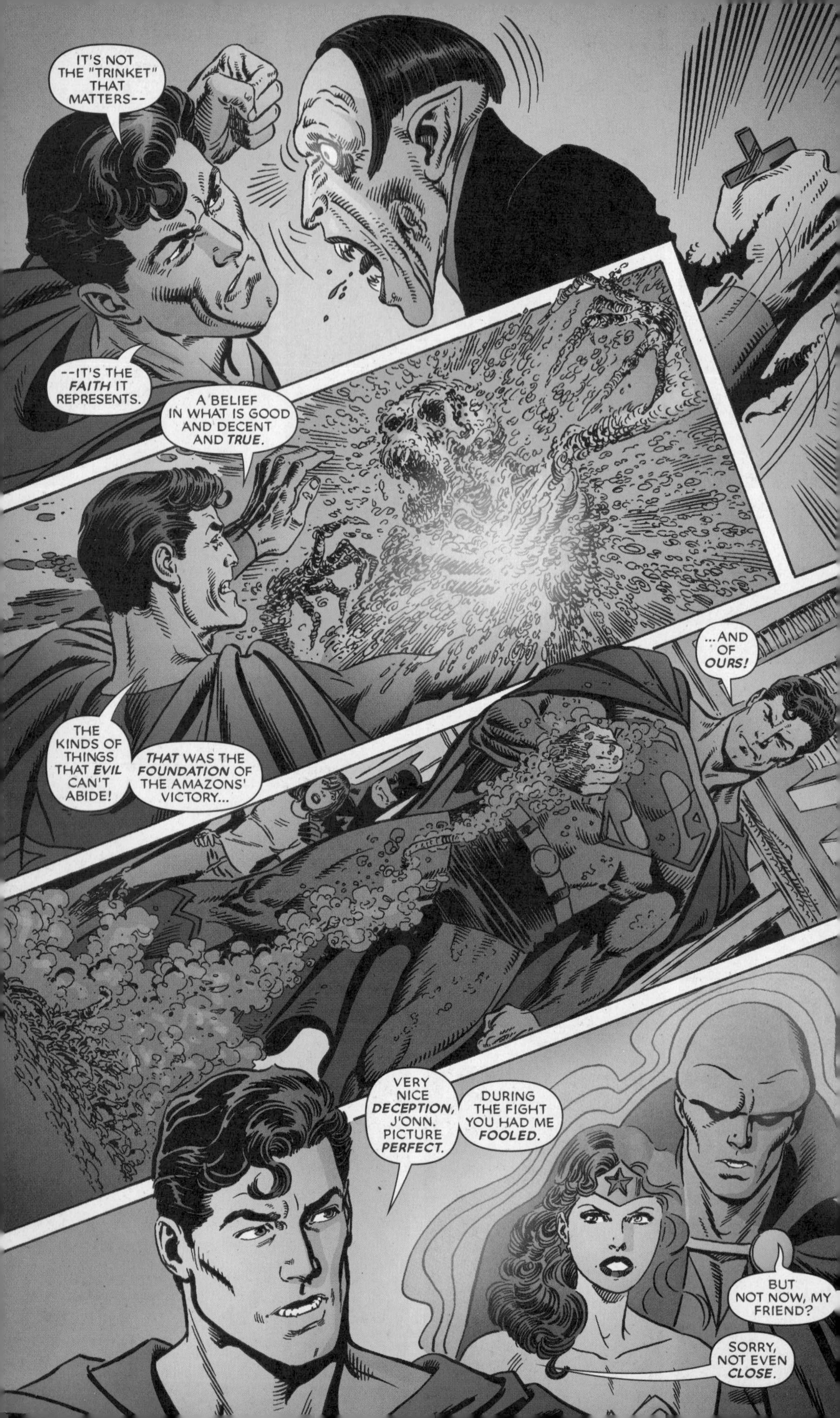
IT'S NOT THE "TRINKET" THAT MATTERS--
--IT'S THE FAITH IT REPRESENTS.
A BELIEF IN WHAT IS GOOD AND DECENT AND TRUE.
THE KINDS OF THINGS THAT EVIL CAN'T ABIDE!
THAT WAS THE FOUNDATION OF THE AMAZONS' VICTORY...
...AND OF OURS!
VERY NICE DECEPTION, J'ONN. PICTURE PERFECT.
DURING THE FIGHT YOU HAD ME FOOLED.
BUT NOT NOW, MY FRIEND?
SORRY, NOT EVEN CLOSE.

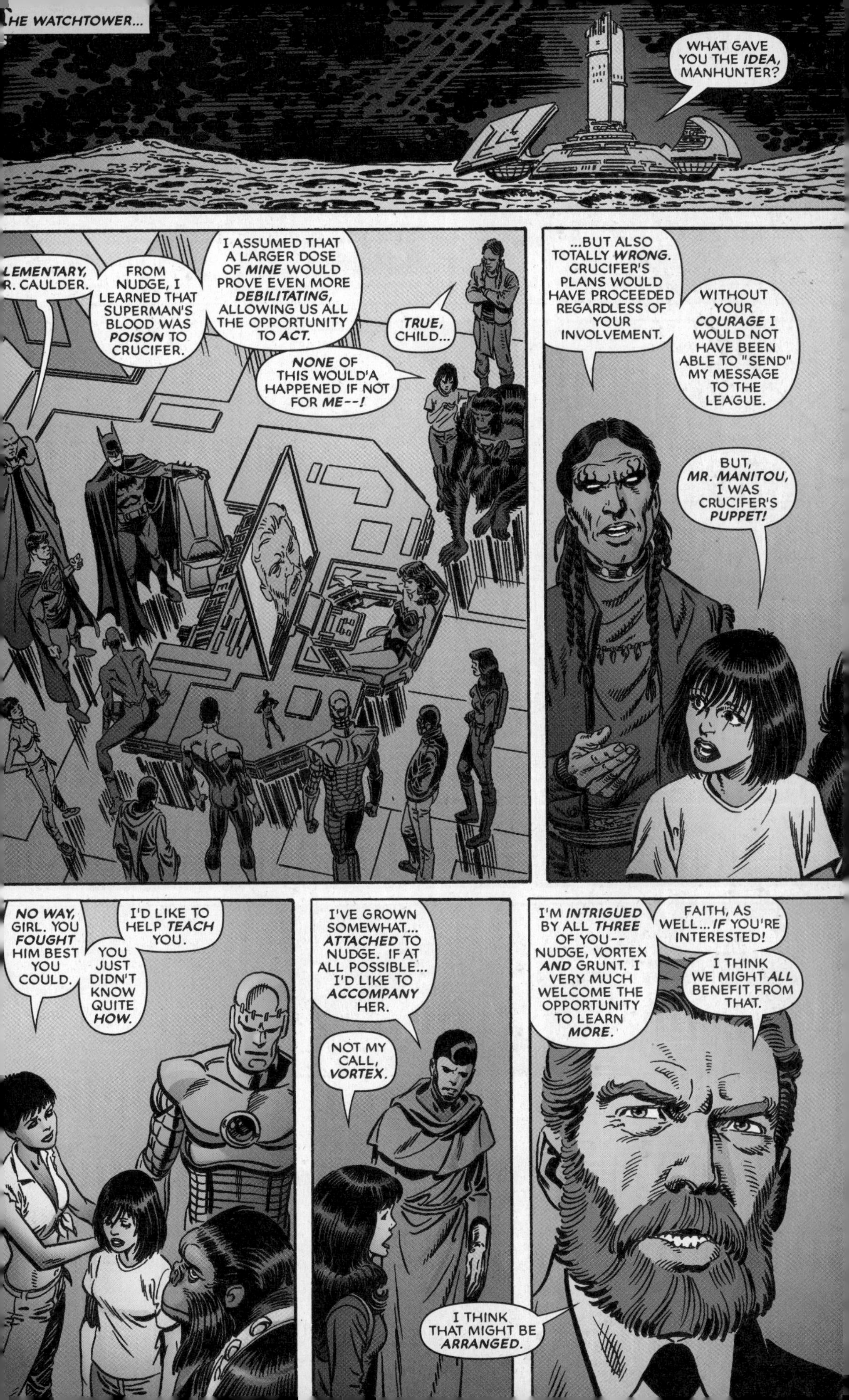
HE WATCHTOWER...
WHAT GAVE YOU THE *IDEA*, MANHUNTER?
LEMENTARY, R. CAULDER.
FROM NUDGE, I LEARNED THAT SUPERMAN'S BLOOD WAS *POISON* TO CRUCIFER.
I ASSUMED THAT A LARGER DOSE OF *MINE* WOULD PROVE EVEN MORE *DEBILITATING*, ALLOWING US ALL THE OPPORTUNITY TO *ACT*.
NONE OF THIS WOULD'A HAPPENED IF NOT FOR *ME--!*
TRUE, CHILD...
...BUT ALSO TOTALLY *WRONG*. CRUCIFER'S PLANS WOULD HAVE PROCEEDED REGARDLESS OF YOUR INVOLVEMENT.
WITHOUT YOUR *COURAGE* I WOULD NOT HAVE BEEN ABLE TO "SEND" MY MESSAGE TO THE LEAGUE.
BUT, *MR. MANITOU*, I WAS CRUCIFER'S *PUPPET!*
NO WAY, GIRL. YOU *FOUGHT* HIM BEST YOU COULD.
YOU JUST DIDN'T KNOW QUITE *HOW*.
I'D LIKE TO HELP *TEACH* YOU.
I'VE GROWN SOMEWHAT... *ATTACHED* TO NUDGE. IF AT ALL POSSIBLE... I'D LIKE TO *ACCOMPANY* HER.
NOT MY CALL, *VORTEX*.
I'M *INTRIGUED* BY ALL *THREE* OF YOU-- NUDGE, VORTEX *AND* GRUNT. I VERY MUCH WELCOME THE OPPORTUNITY TO LEARN *MORE*.
FAITH, AS WELL... *IF* YOU'RE INTERESTED!
I THINK WE MIGHT *ALL* BENEFIT FROM THAT.
I THINK THAT MIGHT BE *ARRANGED*.

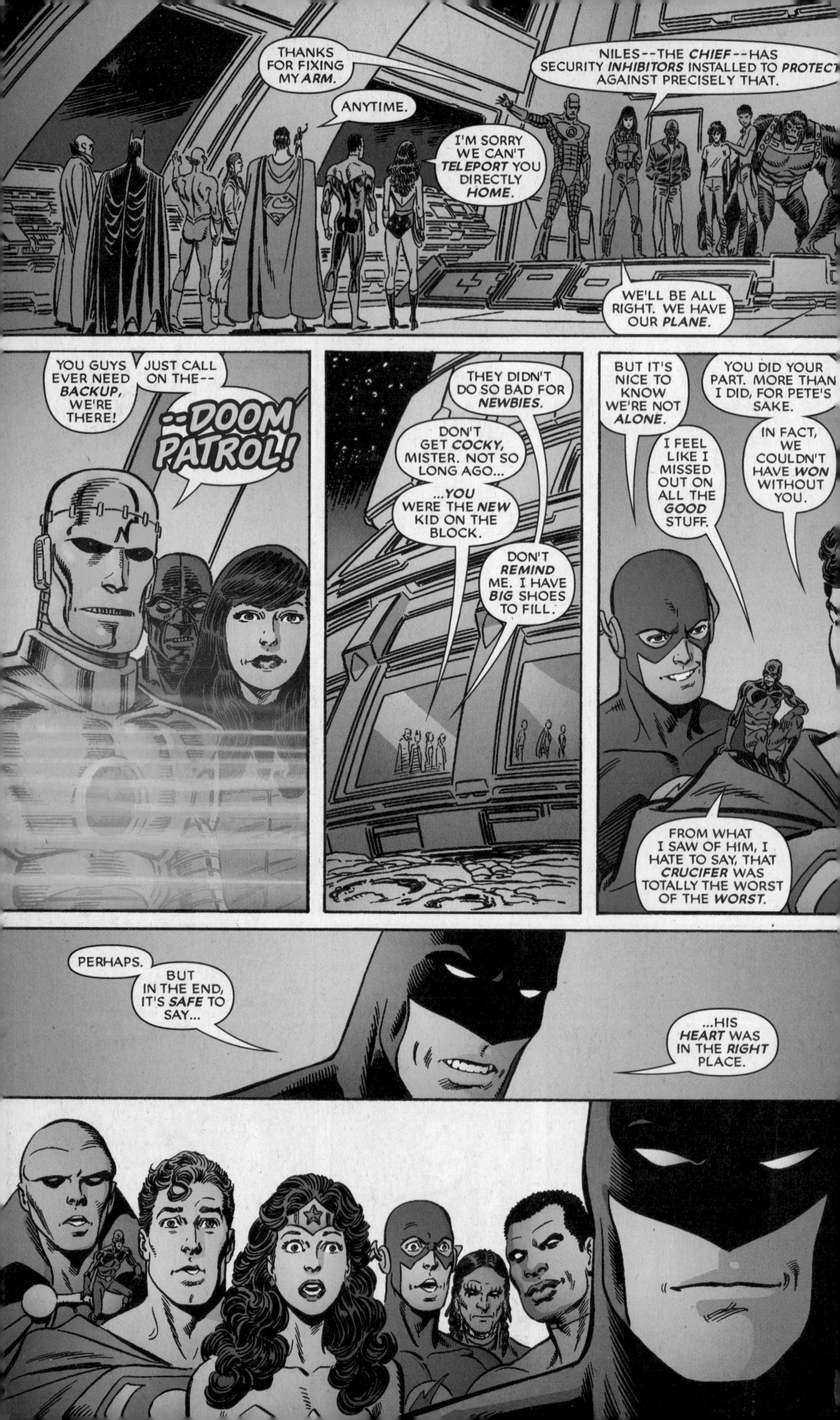
THANKS FOR FIXING MY ARM.
ANYTIME.
NILES--THE CHIEF--HAS SECURITY INHIBITORS INSTALLED TO PROTECT AGAINST PRECISELY THAT.
I'M SORRY WE CAN'T TELEPORT YOU DIRECTLY HOME.
WE'LL BE ALL RIGHT. WE HAVE OUR PLANE.
YOU GUYS EVER NEED BACKUP, WE'RE THERE!
JUST CALL ON THE--
--DOOM PATROL!
THEY DIDN'T DO SO BAD FOR NEWBIES.
DON'T GET COCKY, MISTER. NOT SO LONG AGO...
...YOU WERE THE NEW KID ON THE BLOCK.
DON'T REMIND ME. I HAVE BIG SHOES TO FILL.
BUT IT'S NICE TO KNOW WE'RE NOT ALONE.
I FEEL LIKE I MISSED OUT ON ALL THE GOOD STUFF.
YOU DID YOUR PART. MORE THAN I DID, FOR PETE'S SAKE.
IN FACT, WE COULDN'T HAVE WON WITHOUT YOU.
FROM WHAT I SAW OF HIM, I HATE TO SAY, THAT CRUCIFER WAS TOTALLY THE WORST OF THE WORST.
PERHAPS.
BUT IN THE END, IT'S SAFE TO SAY...
...HIS HEART WAS IN THE RIGHT PLACE.

JLA DON'T MISS A SINGLE VOLUME FEATURING THE WORLD'S GREATEST SUPER-HEROES

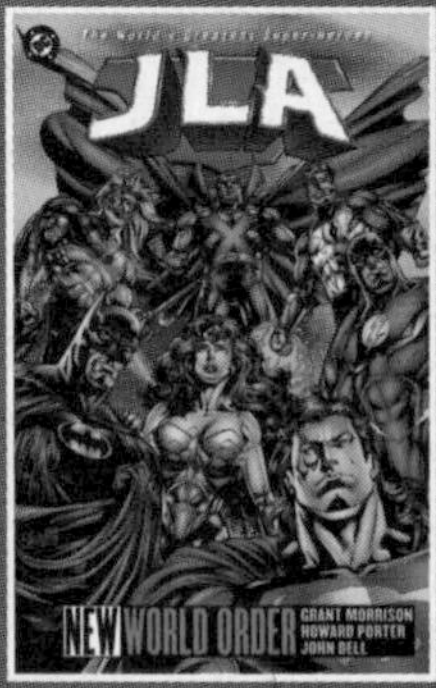
JLA
NEW WORLD ORDER
GRANT MORRISON
HOWARD PORTER
JOHN DELL

VOLUME 1:
NEW WORLD ORDER
Morrison/Porter/Dell

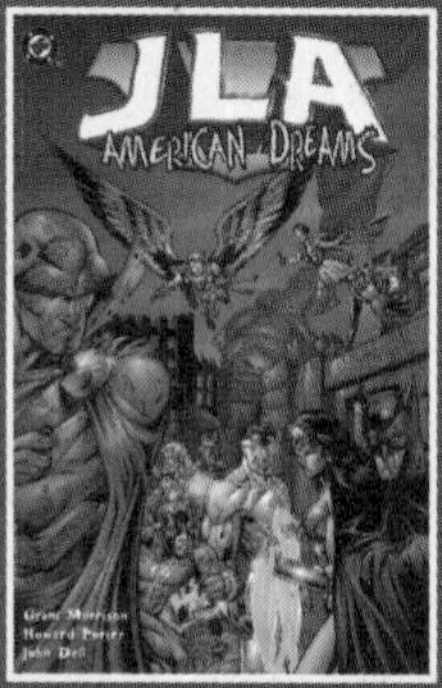
JLA
AMERICAN DREAMS

VOLUME 2:
AMERICAN DREAMS
Morrison/Porter/Dell/various

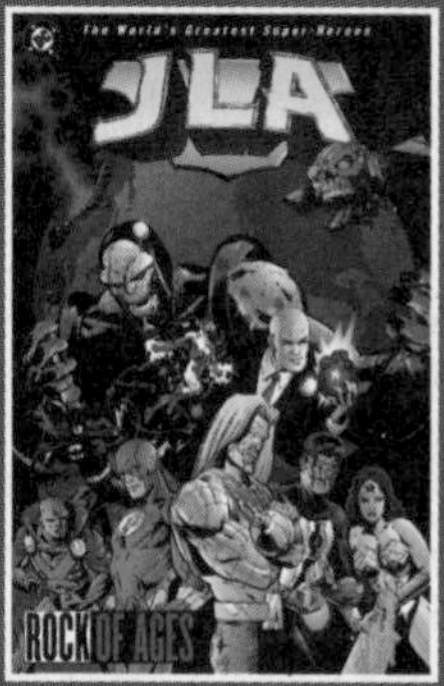
The World's Greatest Super-Heroes
JLA
ROCK OF AGES

VOLUME 3:
ROCK OF AGES
Morrison/Porter/Dell/various

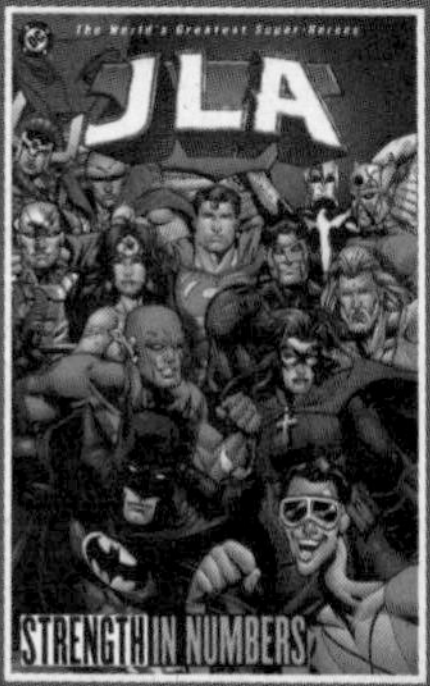
The World's Greatest Super-Heroes
JLA
STRENGTH IN NUMBERS

VOLUME 4:
STRENGTH IN NUMBERS
Morrison/Porter/Dell/various

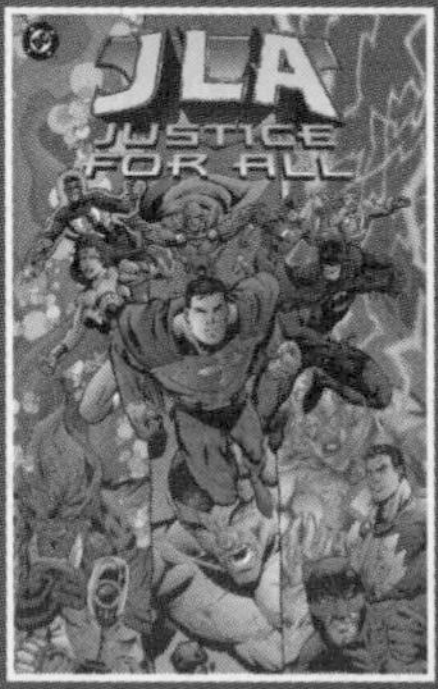
JLA
JUSTICE FOR ALL

VOLUME 5:
JUSTICE FOR ALL
Morrison/Waid/Porter/various

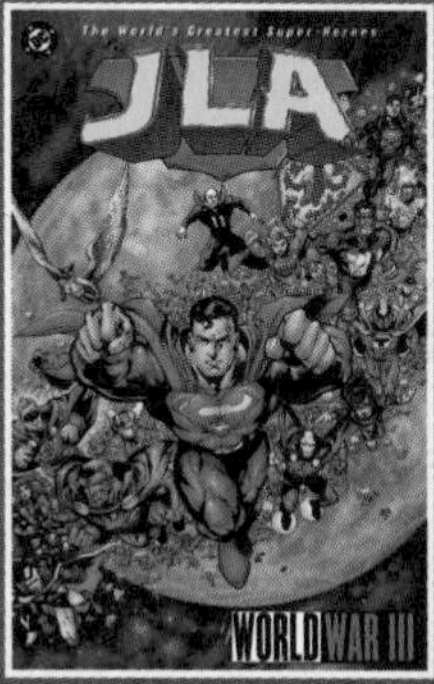
The World's Greatest Super-Heroes
JLA
WORLD WAR III

VOLUME 6:
WORLD WAR III
Morrison/DeMatteis/Porter/various

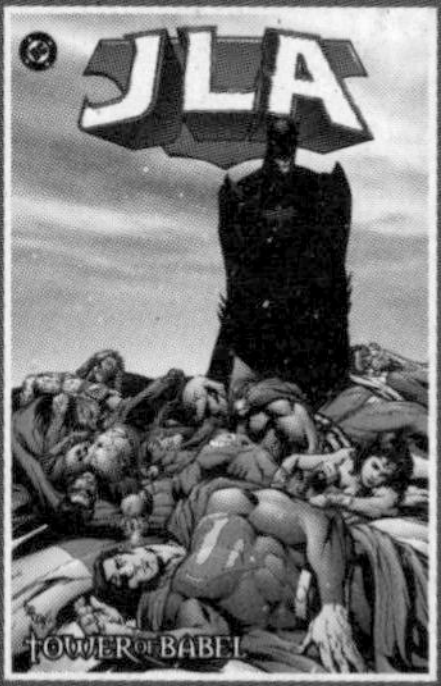
JLA
TOWER OF BABEL

VOLUME 7:
TOWER OF BABEL
Waid/Porter/Dell/various

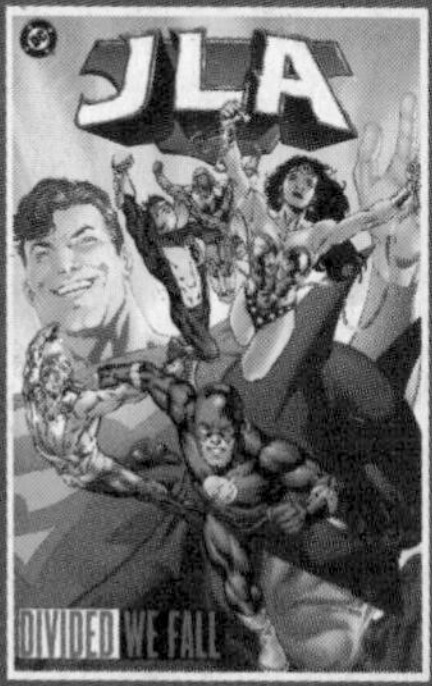
JLA
DIVIDED WE FALL

VOLUME 8:
DIVIDED WE FALL
Waid/Hitch/Neary/various

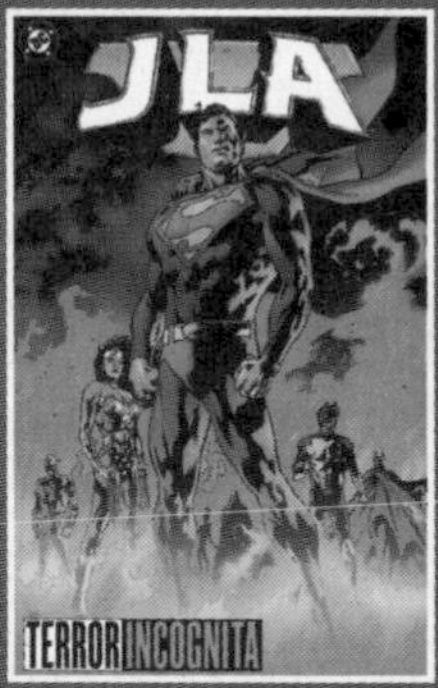
JLA
TERROR INCOGNITA

VOLUME 9:
TERROR INCOGNITA
Waid/Dixon/Beatty/Hitch/various

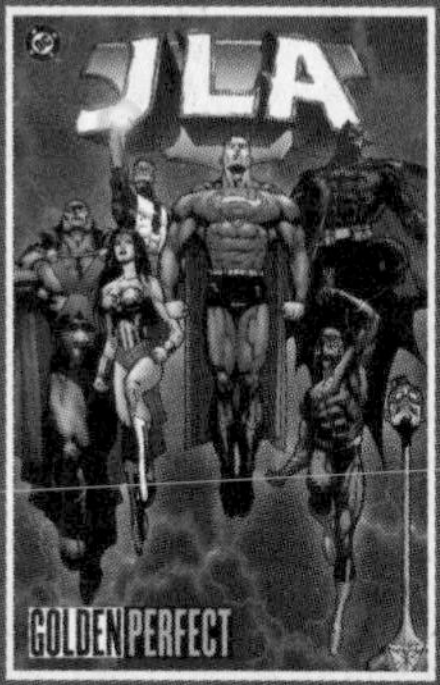
JLA
GOLDEN PERFECT

VOLUME 10:
GOLDEN PERFECT
Kelly/Mahnke/Nguyen

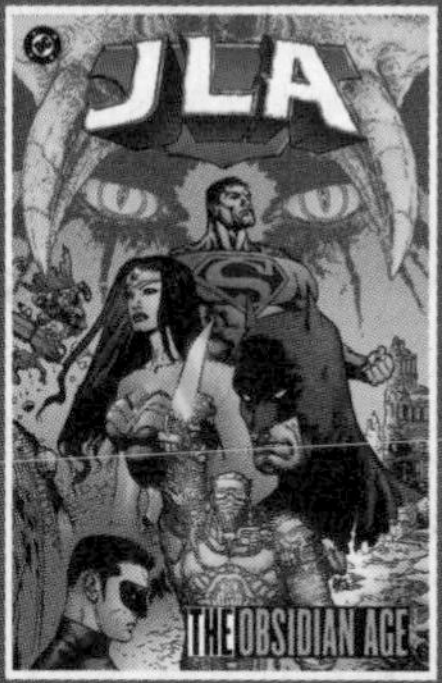
JLA
THE OBSIDIAN AGE

VOLUME 11:
OBSIDIAN AGE BOOK 1
Kelly/Mahnke/Guichet/Nguyen/Propst

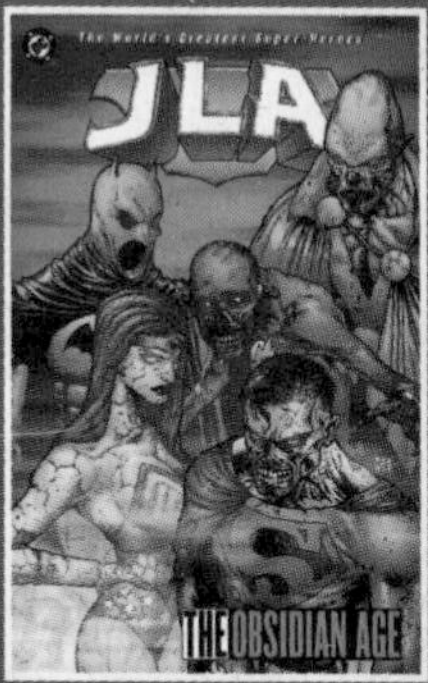
The World's Greatest Super-Heroes
JLA
THE OBSIDIAN AGE

VOLUME 12:
OBSIDIAN AGE BOOK 2
Kelly/Mahnke/Guichet/Larossa/Nguyen/Propst/Milgrom

JLA Volume 13: Rules of Engagement
Kelly/Mahnke/Nguyen/various

JLA Volume 14: Trial by Fire
Kelly/Mahnke/Nguyen

JLA: Earth 2
Morrison/Quitely

JLA: A League of One
Moeller

JLA: One Million
Morrison/Semeiks/various

JLA: Riddle of the Beast
A. Grant/various

JLA: World Without Grown-Ups
Dezago/Ramos/Nauck/various

JLA: Year One
Waid/Augustyn/Kitson/Bair/various

JLA/JSA: Virtue & Vice
Goyer/Johns/Pacheco/Merino

JLA/The Titans: The Technis Imperative
Grayson/Jimenez/Pelletier/various

Justice League: A Midsummer's Nightmare
Waid/Nicieza/various

Justice League of America: The Nail
Davis/Farmer

THE HEROES OF THE JUSTICE LEAGUE CAN ALSO BE FOUND IN THESE BOOKS FROM DC

Across the Universe: The DC Stories of Alan Moore
Alan Moore/Dave Gibbons/various

The Amalgam Age of Comics: The DC Comics Collection
various

Aquaman: Time & Tide
David/Jarvinen/Vancata

Batgirl: Year One
Beatty/Dixon/Martin/Lopez

Batman: Death and the Maidens
Rucka/Janson

Batman: Hush volumes 1 & 2
Loeb/Lee/Williams

Batman: War Drums
various

Bizarro Comics
various

Cosmic Odyssey
Starlin//Mignola/Garzon

Crisis on Infinite Earths
Wolfman/Perez/Giordano/Ordway

Crisis on Multiple Earths
Fox/Sekowsky/Sachs

DC/Marvel Crossover Classics II
various

DC/Marvel Crossover Classics IV
various

A DC Universe Christmas
Various

DC vs. Marvel/Marvel vs. DC
various

The Final Night
Kesel/Marz/Immonen/McKone

Flash & Green Lantern: The Brave and the Bold
Waid & Peyer/Kitson/Grindberg

The Flash: Blood Will Run
Johns/Kolins/Hazlewood

The Flash: Born to Run
Waid/Larocque/Aparo/Mhan/various

The Flash: Dead Heat
Waid/O. Jimenez/Ramos/Faucher

The Flash: Race Against Time
Waid/Augustyn/various

The Flash: The Return of Barry Allen
Waid/Larocque/Richardson

The Flash: Rogues
Johns/Kolins/Hazlewood

The Flash: Crossfire
Johns/Kolins/Hazlewood/various

The Green Arrow by Jack Kirby
various/Kirby

Green Arrow: The Longbow Hunters
Grell

Green Arrow: Quiver
Smith/Hester/Parks

Green Arrow: Sounds of Violence
Smith/Hester/Parks

Green Arrow: The Archer's Quest
Meltzer/Hester/Parks

Green Lantern: Baptism of Fire
Marz/Banks/Pelletier/Tanghal

Green Lantern: Circle of Fire
Vaughan/various

Green Lantern: Emerald Allies
Dixon/Marz/Damaggio/Braithwaite/Banks/various

Green Lantern: Emerald Dawn
Owsley/Giffen/Jones/Bright/Tanghal

Green Lantern: Emerald Dawn II
Giffen/Jones/Bright/Tanghal

Green Lantern: Emerald Knights
Marz/Dixon/Banks/various

Green Lantern: Legacy— The Last Will & Testament of Hal Jordan
Kelly/B. Anderson/Sienkiewicz

Green Lantern: New Journey, Old Path
Winick/Banks/Bright/Eaglesham/various

Green Lantern: Power of Ion
Winick/Eaglesham/various

Green Lantern: Traitor
S. Grant/Zeck/Kane/Kolins/Janson

Green Lantern: Willworld
DeMatteis/Fisher

History of the DC Universe
Wolfman/Perez/K. Kesel

JSA All-Stars
various

The Justice Society Returns
various

Just Imagine...Stan Lee Creating the DC Universe Volumes 1 - 3
Lee/Uslan/Buscema/J. Lee/Kubert/Gibbons

The Kingdom
Waid/various

Kingdom Come
Waid/Ross

Legends: The Collected Edition
Ostrander/Wein/Byrne/K. Kesel

Return to the Amalgam Age of Comics: The DC Comics Collection
various

Super Friends!
various

Super Friends! Truth, Justice & Peace!
various

Superman: The Greatest Stories Ever Told
various

Superman: Godfall
Kelley/Turner/Caldwell/various

Underworld Unleashed
Waid/Peterson/Porter/P. Jimenez/various

Wonder Woman: The Contest
Messner-Loebs/Deodato Jr.

Wonder Woman: Gods of Gotham
Jimenez/DeMatteis/Lanning

Wonder Woman: The Hiketeia
Rucka/J.G. Jones/Von Grawbadger

Wonder Woman: Lifelines
Byrne

Wonder Woman: Paradise Found
Jimenez/various

Wonder Woman: Paradise Lost
Jimenez/various

Wonder Woman: Second Genesis
Byrne

Zero Hour
Jurgens/Ordway/various